EDUCATIONAL DEVELOPMENT OF SCHEDULED CASTES

EDUCATIONAL DEVELOPMENT OF SCHEDULED CASTES
LOOKING AHEAD

S.K. Chatterjee

GYAN PUBLISHING HOUSE

Educational Development of Scheduled Castes: Looking Ahead

ISBN: 81-212-0632-4

Reprinted in 2011 in India by
Gyan Publishing House
23, Main Ansari Road, Daryaganj,
New Delhi - 110002
Phone : 23282060, 23261060
Fax : (011) 23285914
E-mail : books@gyanbooks.com
website: gyanbooks.com

Contents

Dedicated to

Shri Satyakrishna Das Sharma

Preface

In all societies of the world, Education as an instrument of socialization is considered as a powerful catalytic agent for social change. In the Indian context, education has an added importance. It is the most effective change-agent for the improvement of the socio-economic conditions of the Scheduled Castes, removal of their disabilities and acceleration of the integrative process. Realizing the importance of education, the framers of the Constitution included in the Directive Principles of State Policy provisions for free and compulsory education for all children upto the age of 14 years and for promotion and with special care also the educational and economic interests of the weaker sections of the people, and in particular, of the Scheduled Castes and Scheduled Tribes and protection from social injustice and all forms of exploitation. Article 15 (4) enables the State to make special provision for the advancement of any socially and educationally backward class of citizens or for the Scheduled Castes and Scheduled Tribes.

In pursuance of these constitutional provisions a series of measures have been taken both by the Central Government and the State Governments to spread education and literacy among the Scheduled Castes, so that through educational advancement the other two disabilities, social and economic, over may also be remedied. An elaborate programme of pre-matric and post-matric scholarships, reservation of seats in the schools and colleges including technical and professional institutions, establishment of hostels and ashram schools for the children of the Scheduled Castes and other incentives like free midday meals, textbooks, uniforms, etc., are in operation for the last five decades. In quantitative terms, the range of schemes evolved and implemented for the benefit of the Scheduled Castes appear doubtlessly impressive. The financial concessions and other facilities have, however, been availed of by the privileged groups amongst the Scheduled Castes far more than the poorer and more deprived sections as the quantum of assistance has seldom been sufficient enough to induce the really poor to go in for education.

While the literacy rate among the Scheduled Castes has increased from 1.9 per cent in 1931 to 37.41 per cent in 1991 and the enrolment ratio of the Scheduled Caste students in the primary sections has crossed the 100 per cent barrier in 1985 itself, some

Scheduled Caste communities still continue to remain educationally backward and there are some who do not have even a single literate person in their fold.

While the government has been extending the special educational facilities and incentives from one decade to another, it has failed to take congnizance of the castewise and regionwise disparities in the matter of educational facilities and achievements. As a result, the differentials in educational attainment and access to education have also continued to perpetuate.

Disparities among the Scheduled Castes themselves in the matter of literacy, educational development, social position, economic condition and the like existed even before they were grouped together by the Britishers to form the Scheduled Castes in 1935 and these disparities in the same form prevail, even today the only difference is that the disparities have widened in some respects. The lower strata among the Scheduled Castes continue to remain at the bottom while those who enjoy higher literacy, better access to educational facilities and higher social and economic status, have registered better progress during the last fifty years. Thus, a class among the Scheduled Castes has emerged in all the States and Union Territories which has cornered all the educational benefits and privileges, while the needy masses may not even know what they are entitled to.

The present study, perhaps for the first time, has undertaken on an all India basis a castewise analysis of the impact of the various protective measures in the educational sector as reflected in the literacy rates of the Scheduled Castes in each State/UT. The study also compares the educational development trends in the States/UTs at elementary, secondary and other levels of education including professional courses not only within the Scheduled Castes but also between the Scheduled Caste population and the non-Scheduled Caste population.

The different schemes and incentives of the Central Government and the State Governments form an important focus for this study. It also looks at the trend of utilization of these special facilities, examines whether the benefits had accrued equitably to all the communities among them and suggests measures for an allround educational development of the Scheduled Castes.

Non-availability of up-to-date data is a positive impediment to the undertaking of such a study. The First, Second and Third Annual Reports of the National Commission for Scheduled Castes and Scheduled Tribes are not available because these have not yet been placed before the Parliament. Similarly, the University Grants Commission reports on educational development of the Scheduled Castes have not yet been laid on the table of the Parliament and, therefore, the assessment of the UGC on this score is not known to the members of the public. The First Volume of the Sixth All India Educational Survey (1993), was published in 1997 and other volumes are yet to be published. The report of the Working Group on the Welfare of the Scheduled Castes during the Ninth Five Year Plan is yet to be circulated. That is the reason why some of the data in this study, is this stady, are quite old. Even then, utmost efforts have been made to present the latest data to have an idea about the current trends.

It needs to be highlighted that there is hardly any study which has attempted this type of analysis at the all India level. The Commission for Scheduled Castes and Scheduled Tribes, the Ministry of Education and the University Grants Commission were harping on the need for undertaking such a study but they themselves shied away from it. It is hoped that despite limitations, the study would be useful to the policy makers, researchers, students of all shades and those concerned with the uplifit of the Scheduled Castes.

This study may be considered as a companion volume of the project "The Scheduled Castes in India", already published in 4 volumes. In these volumes the origin and growth of the caste system, emergence of the Scheduled Castes during the British regime, different constitutional provisions, genesis and demographic pattern of the Scheduled Castes have been discussed. Now, this instant volume is entirely devoted to the study of educational development of the Scheduled Castes.

I am grateful to Sri B.P. Garg, Managing Director of the Gyan Publishing House for bringing out this book in time.

I am also thankful to my friends and well-wishers who helped me in various ways in completing this project. I refrain from thanking them individually for obvious reasons.

S.K. Chatterjee

List of Tables

1
Constitutional Provisions for Educational Development

Education is the most important element in the development of any community. The role of education as an investment in human resources has been increasingly recognized in all countries. For allround development of the Indian society the importance of educational development of general masses is a well-established fact universally accepted. Social and religious reformers in India realized the importance of education and worked for the educational uplift of the people throughout the ages. Education has special significance, particularly for the weaker sections of the society; for whom, education is an input not only for their economic development but also for instilling in them self-confidence and inner strength, thereby enabling them to face the new and unforseen challenges. The poor progress of the lowest castes, specially those suffering from the disabilities of untouchability, in the traditional Brahminical Sanskrit education in the pre-British days, was partly due to the strong caste prejudices and prevalence of the practice of untouchability. Steeped in ignorance, illiteracy and poverty, they have been target of economic exploitation, harassment, artocities and all forms of social disabilities.

The Britishers brought with them the British liberal education system. Even then, from the records and documents on education it is seen that excepting some singular cases, there was hardly any incidence of education amongst theHarijans", the so-called lower castes before 1813 when the decision of the court of Directors of the East India Company to participate in the promotion of education in India was taken. Thereafter, in the initial stages, participation of the Company was in the form of patronage to the missionary schools only. The educational policy was focused on the expansion of higher education which obviously resulted in the education of the upper castes. But during this phase, every now and then some philanthropic missionaries drew the Company's attention to the illiteracy of the masses and the need for opening elementary schools for the peasantry and other poorer classes. As a result, some Company officials evinced interest in the establishment of vernacular schools on European lines. As and when established, these schools gained popularity over indigenous schools. One of their characteristics was that they were secular institutions and would not mind admitting children irrespective of their caste and creed differences.[1]

In 1854, the Company streamlined its educational policy. In the memorable Woods Despatch, the Company accepted systematic promotion of general education as one of the duties of the State and aimed at transmission and imparting of European knowledge. The Woods Despatch laid down the policy for the British system of education in India. Two of the policy measures were: the constitution of a Department of Public Instruction and introduction of a system of grants-in-aid. It was contemplated that these would foster a spirit of reliance upon local exertions[2] and would, in course, of time render it possible to close or transfer to the management of local bodies, many of the existing institutions. This policy was reaffirmed in 1859 when the administration of the Company was transferred to the Imperial Crown. Due to incentives of grants-in-aid, a number of colleges and schools were opened. Their growth was further augmented by the adoption of the Municipal system, and by some acts passed from 1865 onwards providing for the imposition of local cess for the establishment of schools. As a result, the indigenous institutions got a setback while schools and colleges providing education on the British system flourished.

In fact, it was only a beginning. The Education Commission of 1882 recommended a systematic effort for popularizing education among the lower castes. Policies were laid down and funds were earmarked. But even this reform which ought to have been accepted by all the provincial governments was accepted in different measures. Some provinces took it zealously, while some of the provincial governments did not feel convinced on the need for educating the lower castes. This diverse tendency of covering education for lower castes remained almost a feature with the administration in the provincial governments.

The policy of the British Government to work for the educational development of the lower castes was, however, not without any motive. The confidential note of Sir Sankaran Nair is a pointer to the political motives that might have been instrumental in the formulation of government policies for their education and amelioration;

If English education is imparted to the lower classes, they will be under the influence of not only members of the present type of leaders, which they already are, but also of others as well. These members of the lower classes who have received English education will get into touch with the corresponding English educated members of the other classes who speak a different vernacular. The Hindu lower classes will grow a consciousness of their moral, religious and economic servitude, and will learn that, without the permanence and assistance of the British Government they have little chance of justice at the hands of the superior classes or of their present leaders. Once, the low classes get into touch with one another, they will form a strong body of legal opinion dependent on and in hearty sympathy with the Government. This awakening to a sense of their present service and necessity of cooperation will result from British education. Such education is also essential for the emancipation of the lower classes...It is also necessary that we must enable as many among these classes as possible to avail themselves of higher education. They will realize fully their social and economic degradation due to the hostility of other classes based on religions and there can be little doubt that they will be steadfast in their loyalty to the British Government[3].

Sir Nair's argument was like Lord Macaulay's assumption. But his opinion that one of the advantages of higher education to the lower castes would be uniting them as a distinct minority "dependant on and in heavy sympathy with the Government" came to be true. In India, where the languages of the people differ from one part of the country to another, it is necessary to have one or two common languages for exchange of ideas. At that point of time, such a language could only be English which was also the medium of instruction for higher education.

With the acceptance of the Principle of Diarchy in 1922, education was transferred as a provincial subject to the control of an Indian minister. This created a public enthusiasm for education. The transference policy on education advised the provincial governments to attach more importance to the educational advancement of the Depressed and Backward classes.[4]

After World War I, the attitudes of the British Government towards the policy of universal compulsory education also softened. Vithalbhai Patel took up the unfinished task of Gokhale, and, as a result, the Patel Act (1918) was passed by the Bombay Legislative Council. Other provinces followed suit, and by 1930, 12 Bills, eight of them official, were enacted. Bombay, Bengal, Bihar, Orissa, Punjab, United Provinces, Central Provinces, Madras and Assam, legislated Compulsory Education Acts. But the response to the legislation on compulsory primary education varied from province to province and from area to area. The apathy of the lower castes to compulsory primary education was revealed by the Compulsory Education Committee, set up under the Chairmanship of Sir Narayan G. Chandarvarkar in 1921, by the Bombay Government to review the scope of existing compulsory education both in municipal and rural areas. It was reported by the Committee that communities like *Chambhar*, *Mahar* and *Mang*, were divided among themselves and the majority of them were against compulsion. In Konkan, communities like *Vakkal*, *Kharvi*, *Mocoi* supported compulsion for boys only. One witness from the *Mahar* community said that books and slates should be supplied free. There was appreciable opposition to the system of compulsory education for either or both the sexes from such communities as *Chamar*, *Metri*, *Sunnagar* and others. In Gujarat and Sind also, a large majority of the backward classes opposed compulsion.[5] The question arises is that, at a time when public opinion was strongly in favour of compulsory education, for what reasons did these communities show reluctance to accept the idea? A possible explanation could be their extreme poverty.

The introduction of Provincial Autonomy in 1937 and the assumption of power by the Indian National Congress in seven out of the eleven provinces enlivened the hope that the new leadership would do speedier work for the welfare of lower castes. The scope of developing education among the lower castes also expanded. A study[6] showed that the efforts for the spread of education in the general population also gave a fillip to the lower castes for education, despite the social taboos and economic hardships. The lower castes pupils accounted for 9.46 per cent of the total number of pupils in all educational institutions in the provinces of British India in 1936-37.

Independence ushered in a new era of national development based on the acceptance of a socialistic pattern of society which would secure equitable distribution of wealth and equality of opportunity for all, without any distinction of caste, race, religion, sex or place of birth in education, employment and cultural development. The Directive Principles of State Policy include universal education to all children up to the age of 14 years, promotion, with special care, of the educational and economic interests of the weaker sections of the people, and in particular, of the Scheduled Castes and Scheduled Tribes, and protection from social injustice and all forms of exploitation. The Constitution has also made safeguards to protect the interests of the Scheduled Castes and Scheduled Tribes against any injustice in the matter of establishment of and admission to educational institutions and grants from State funds.

Constitutional Provisions

Articles 15(4), 29, 30, 45-46 and 350-A are the relevant provisions in the Constitution pertaining to educational development of the people. While Article 29 relates to protection of interests of minorities, Article 30 deals with rights of minorities to establish and administer educational institution which also figure under a separate heading 'Cultural and Educational Rights' in the Fundamental Rights chapter of the Constitution. Article 350-A lays down facilities for instruction in the mother tongue at primary stage. Since these three Articles formed the subject matter of a previous study* these provisions are not being discussed again. Moreover, none of these Articles confer any special rights and privileges on the Scheduled Castes. The present study therefore, is confined only to Article 15(4), 45 and 46.

The Constitutional provisions relating to the educational development may be grouped under two categories: provisions

---

* Chapters II and VII of the *Disintegration and Constitution* by the author may be seen.

which are applicable to all the citizens including the Scheduled Castes and Scheduled Tribes, such as Article 45; and Articles which have been specially provided to protect the interest of the Scheduled Castes and Scheduled Tribes, like Articles 15(4) and 46.

Article 15(4) finds place in the Fundamental Rights chapter of the Constitution while Articles 45 and 46 have been included in the chapter on Directive Principles of State Policy.

Article 15(4) provides that, "Nothing in this article or in clause (2) of Article 29 shall prevent the State from making any special provision for the advancement of any socially and educationally backward classes of citizens or for the Scheduled Castes and the Scheduled Tribes."

The object of clause (4) of Article 15, added in 1951 by the Constitution (First Amendment) Act, 1951, is to bring Articles 15 and 29 in line with Articles 16(4), 46 and 340, and to make it Constitutional for the State to reserve seats for backward classes of citizens, Scheduled Castes and Scheduled Tribes in the public educational institutions, as well as to make other special provisions as may be necessary for their advancement. The immediate object of this amendment was to override the decision in *State of Madras V. Champakam (1951) S.C.R. 525*, to the effect that Article 29(2) is un controlled controlled by Article 46 and that the Constitution does not intend to protect the interest of the backward classes in the matter of admission to educational institutions. But though the amendment would validate reservations for the backward classes and the Scheduled Castes and Scheduled Tribes, it would not support the distribution of seats according to communities so as to discriminate between classes who are not backward, *inter se*, in short, the amendment would not sanction any *communal* order.[7]

Clause (4) is an exception to Clause (1) which forbids discrimination on grounds of 'race' or 'caste'. It is also in the nature of an exception to Article 29(2). Being an exception to Clause (1) of Article 15, it cannot be so extended as to in effect destroy the guarantee in Clause (1). Unless the test of backwardness is objectively satisfied, mere good faith of the authorities cannot protect a discriminatory provision under Clause (4).[8]

Article 15(4) is an enabling provision, like Article 16(4), and the reservation, under either provision, should not exceed legitimate limits.[9] It does not create any fundamental right in favour of a member of the classes specified in Article 15. Where, therefore, the Government reserves a percentage of seats for members of backward classes, such reservation will not be applicable if such members already secured the reserved number of seats by competition on their merit; it will be called in aid only to the extent of their deficiency on the merit list.[10]

In making reservations for the backward classes, the State cannot ignore the fundamental rights of the rest of the citizens. A special provision under Article 15(4) must, therefore, strike a reasonable balance between several relevant considerations and proceed objectively.[11]

It follows that in making special provision for the weaker sections for higher education, the State cannot weaken standards of education or lower the efficiency of the scholars to the detriment of national interest.[12]

Article 15(4) speaks of 'classes of citizens' for whom the State can make special provisions to promote, Scholars to the detriment if they are socially and educationally backward. Such provisions may also be made for Scheduled Castes or Scheduled Tribes. The Scheduled Castes, the Scheduled Tribes and other Backward Classes are three different categories whose classification is based on different indices, and the classification of the third-named among them may vary from time to time with reference to the nature of backwardness which is sought to be remedied by the special provisions in respect of it.[13] The Scheduled Castes and the Scheduled Tribes, however, constitute a protected class, apart from any condition of backwardness, as specified in Article 15(4). Hence, the State is entitled to do everything for the uplift of members of these Castes and Tribes, to make reservations for their admission to educational institutions and to impose such conditions as would make the reservation effective.[14] It follows that the Government may relax the rules for admission to such institutions, say, by lowering the minimum qualifying marks or other conditions.[15] Similarly, the State cannot be compelled to make provisions in this regard. It is left to the discretion of the State.[16]

Article 15(4) is, however, wider than Article 16(4) in as much as several kinds of positive action programmes can also be evolved and implemented thereunder, in addition to reservations in educational institutions and other walks of life, to improve the conditions of Socially and Educationally Backward Classes, Scheduled Castes and Scheduled Tribes, whereas Article 16(4) speaks only of one type of remedial measure, namely, reservation of appointments/posts. But even these programmes of positive action under Article 15(4) may sometimes involve a degree of discrimination. For example, if a special residential school is established for Scheduled Castes or Scheduled Tribes at State expense, it is a discrimination against other students, upon whose education a far lesser amount is being spent by the State. It is another matter that such discrimination is not unconstitutional for the reason that it is designed to achieve an important governmental objective.[17]

Except for reserved seats in the Legislatures, the quantum of preferential treatment is unspecified in the Constitution. The Constitution does not explicitly provide any maximum or minimum limitation on the quantum or extent of preferences. The Courts have been unresponsive to claims attempting to establish some minimum quantum of compensatory discrimination; on the other hand in *Balaji v. State of Mysore* the Supreme Court has attempted to supply a constitutional limit to the extent of preference.[18] Proceeding from the notion that Articles 15(4) and 16(4) are provisions of a special and exceptional character, rather than principles that can be given general operation, the Court finds that these provisions should be read as completely excluding or ignoring the fundamental rights of all citizens. It characterized the purpose of these special provisions, not merely as conferring special privileges on the backward classes, but as serving the interests of the whole society by promoting the advancement of the weaker elements. Thus, any scheme for preference can be weighed in terms of the interests of the whole society. In considering reservations in institutions of higher education, it is necessary, then, to balance the policy of advancing the backward against the national interest in the full utilization of talent. Lowering of the quality of graduates, says the Court, is the "inevitable consequences of reservation."[19] But the need for technical, scientific and academic personnel "is so great that it would cause grave prejudice to national interest if considerations of merit are completely excluded by wholesale reservation of seats in all technical, medical, or engineering colleges or institutions of that kind[20]". Thus, special provisions for the backward must be within "reasonable limits," "the interests of the weaker sections of society which are a first charge on the States and the Centre have to be adjusted with the interests of the community as a whole[21]."

Although recognizing the difficulty of adjusting these competing claims, the Court experiences no difficulty in finding that reservation of "practically all the seats available in all the colleges clearly would be subverting the object of Article 15(4)."[22] While reluctant to set definite limits, the Court indicates that "speaking generally and in a broad way, a special provision should be less than 50%; how much less than 50%, would depend upon the relevant prevailing circumstances in each case[23]". The view expressed in *Balaji case* that reservation in excess of 50 per cent will be plainly inconsistent with Article 15(4) has been upheld in *Jayasree v. State of Kerala A. 1976 S.C. 2381, Devadasan v. Union of India, AIR 1964 SC 179* and in many other cases. As a rule, reservation of seats for the Scheduled Castes, Scheduled Tribes and 'socially and educationally backward classes' in excess of 50 per cent of the available seats would be invalid and unconstitutional, while reservation of less than 50 per cent would be upheld. The recent attempt of the State Governments of Tamil Nadu, Karnataka and others of raising the quota of reservation to considerably more than 50 per cent has been scuttled by the Supreme Court when it again reiterated emphatically that the reservation of seats in excess of 50 per cent would be violative of the spirit of the Constitution.[24]

In the chapter on Directive Principles of State Policy, there is a direction in Article 46 which postulates;

> The State shall promote with special care the educational and economic interests of the weaker sections of the people, and in particular, of the Scheduled Castes and the Scheduled Tribes, and shall protect them from social injustice and all forms of exploitation.

The expression "the State" which occurs in this Article or other Articles in the chapter on Directive Principles of State Policy is defined in Article 12 to include the Government and Parliament of India, the Government and the legislature of each of the States and all local or other authorities within the territory of India or under the control of the Government of India.

Article 46 embodies the concept of 'distributive justice which connotes, *inter alia*, (1) the removal of (a) educational inequalities, and (b) economic inequalities, and (2) protection from (c) social injustice, and (d) all forms of exploitation of (i) the weaker section of the people, and in particular, of (ii) the Scheduled Castes and (iii) the Scheduled Tribes. Though the term 'weaker sections of the people' has been used in this Article, it has not been defined anywhere in the Constitution. As a matter of fact, even the Framers did not know what this term 'weaker sections' actually denoted*. Dr. Ambedker felt that the expression 'weaker section' meant 'backward classes' or such other classes who for the moment could not stand on their own legs ie the Scheduled Castes and the Scheduled Tribes,[25] while Sir B.N. Rau, the Constitutional Adviser, who actually drafted this provision, thought that the emphasis was not so much on the backwardness as on the lack of strength to resist exploitation.[26] It was pointed out at the time of framing of the Constitution that as the 'weaker sections' were not defined anywhere in the Constitution, the apprehension was that the whole attention would be directed to 'Scheduled Castes', and, 'weaker sections' would not mean anything at all.[27] Since the 'weaker sections' have not been defined, this has to be decided by the court in each case as to whether it is a weak section of the body politic requiring discriminative protection against other sections. Since there is no ambiguity so far as the Scheduled Castes and the Scheduled Tribes are concerned, the provision of this Article, as apprehended by Sardar Hukam Singh in the Constituent Assembly, is generally invoked in relation to the Scheduled Castes and the Scheduled Tribes.

It may be noted that two provisions relating to Fundamental Rights, viz., Articles 15 and 29(2), have, however, been amended by the Constitution (First Amendment) Act, 1951, in order to give effect to Article 46, notwithstanding the existence of those two Fundamental Rights, to the contrary. By virtue of this amendment, thus, it is now possible for the State to make a special provision, notwithstanding the bar against discrimination on the ground of caste.[28]

* For a detailed discussion, please see chapters VI and VII of the Second Volume of the *Scheduled Castes of India* by the author.

There is a significant difference between Articles 46 and 15(4). Article 46 enjoins on the State to devote special care for the educational and economic interests of the weaker sections of the people, while Article 15(4) enables the State to make special provision only for the advancement of 'socially and educationally backward classes of citizens'. The backwardness under Article 15(4) must be social and educational. It is not either social or educational. It is both social and educational. Article 46 gives stress on 'economic and educational, weakness, while Article 15(4) lays stress on 'social and educational' backwardness. It is possible that a 'socially and educationally' backward section of people may not be 'economically' weak and vice versa. Further, in an educationally backward class, there may be no economic backwardness in which event, Article 46 may not apply, while Article 15(4) will apply.

The Directive Principle contained in Article 45 of the Constitution enjoins that:

> The State shall endeavour to provide, within a period of ten years from the commencement of this Constitution, for free and compulsory education for all children until they complete the age of fourteen years.

Article 45 declares the objective of the State, and, like other Directives, does not confer any justiciable right. Though the Courts are not competent to compel the Government to carry out the Directive or to make any law for that purpose, for example, to provide for free and compulsory education within the time limited by Article 45,[29] this Article nevertheless casts a duty on the State to follow both in the matter of administration as well as in the matter of laws.

Even though the Directive enshrined in Part IV of the Constitution *per se* cannot be enforced by the Court nor can the Court compel the State to undertake legislation to implement a Directive, the Supreme Court has been issuing various directions to the Government and administrative authorities to take positive action to remove the grievances which have been caused by non-implementation of the Directives. The Directives are thus being enforced, indirectly, by the Court by issuing directions.[30]

It may be noted that this Article does not discriminate between any section of people based on religion, caste, race, sex, or place of birth and directs the States to provide (a) free and (b) compulsory education for all children until they complete the age of (c) fourteen years. The education for all children up to the age of 14 years should not only be free but also compulsory, i.e., the State should take such measures as are considered necessary so as to ensure that all children up to the age of 14 years are put through elementary education. It may be pointed out that there are provisions in the Constitution of countries like Russia, Eire, Myanmar, France, former Czechoslovakia, Germany and Costa Rica that enjoin the State to provide free and compulsory primary education.[31]

Article 23(1) of the United Nations Declaration of Human Rights posits:

'Elementary and Fundamental Education shall be free and compulsory.'[32]

Article 46 of the Indian Constitution, however, does not make any distinction between primary and upper primary education. In other words, the education need not be confined to the primary level only. It may go up to the upper primary stage, so long as the child comes up to the age of 14 years. In that sense, Article 45 is an improvement on the United Nations Declaration of Human Rights. It was pointed out in the Constituent Assembly that what was intended by this Article was compulsory 'primary education', because the State could not undertake to give compulsory education of a secondary character.[33] But Dr. Ambedkar explained that this Article was not restricted to free primary education. Every child should be kept in an educational institution under training until the child was of 14 years. The rationale behind this age limit is that Article 24 forbids any child below the age of 14 years to be employed. "Obviously if the child is not to be employed below the age of 14, the child must be kept occupied in some educational institution. That is the object of Article 45".[34]

Of these three Articles, Articles 15(4) and 46 specially concern the Scheduled Castes, while Article 45 concerns all sections of people, including the Scheduled Castes.

In order to find out how far the objective of Article 45 has been achieved during the last 50 years of independence, we propose to examine first the level of literacy and then the progress in Universal

Elementary Education. Needless to say that had the provisions of Article 45 been implemented in letter and in spirit, illiteracy would have been eradicated completely by this time, because all the children up to the age of 14 years would have had free education up to the upper primary stage. Since Article 45 does not postulate discrimination, it would not have been possible to practise discrimination on the basis of caste, creed, religion, income or the like. That is the reason why, while discussing the levelof literacy and the progress in Universal Elementary Education, we propose to focus particular attention on the Scheduled Caste population *vis-a-vis* the general population. Other measures taken so far in pursuance of the provisions of Article 15(4) and Article 46 for the educational uplift of the Scheduled Castes will be discussed in later chapters.

References

1. Goyal, Bhagat Ram, 1981, *Educating Harijans*. Gurgaon: The Academic Press, pp. 79-80.
2. Government of India Resolutions of the Home Department. Nos, 199-211, dated 11th March, 1904, Para 453.
3. Nair, Sankaran, O., Note on Education in India, Delhi, reference-1916, Education Programmes, August, 1916, No. 51.
4. Report, Education in India Under the New Reforms, Proceedings of Education No, 201. February 23, 1920.
5. Desai, D.M. 1953, *Compulsory Education in India*, p. 144, Bombay: Indian Institute of Education.
6. Goyal, op. cit., pp. 89-92.
7. Basu, D.D., 1988, *Shorter Constitution of India*, p. 67. Tenth Edition, New Delhi : Prentice Hall of India Private Limited.
8. *State of A.P. v. Sagar (1968) 2 S.C.J. 788.*
9. *State of A.P.v. Balaram, A. 1972 S.c. 1972 S.C. 1375(1395); Rajendran v. Union of India, A. 1968 S.C. 507.*
10. *Anil v. Dean, A. 1985 Bom. 153 (para 6).*
11. *State of A.P. v. Balaram,* A. 1972 SC 1375 (1395).
12. *Ibid.*
13. Ramachandran, V.G., 1982, *Fundamental Rights and Constitutional Remedies*, pp. 482-84. Second Edition, Vol. I, Eastern Book Company.
14. *State of M.P. v. Nivedita, A. 1981 S.C. 2045 (para 12).*
15. *Sharma v. Union of India, A. 1981 S.C. 588 (paras 9, 11, 12).*
16. *Chamraja v. State of Mysore, A.I.R., 1967, Mys. 21.*
17. *Indra Sawhney v. Union of India, AIR 1993 SC 477 (para 116, SC 578-79).*
18. *Galanter*, Marc 1984, *Competing Equalities*, p. 400. Oxford University Press.

19. *M.R. Balaji v. State of Mysore, AIR 1963 S.C. 649 (P. 662).*
20. *Ibid.*
21. *Ibid.*
22. *Ibid.*
23. *Ibid.*
24. *The Statesman*, September 10, 1994 and November 12, 1994.
25. *Parliamentary Debates*, Vol. XII, 1951, Col. 9097.
26. Rao, Shiva B., 1968, *The Framing of india's Constitution*, p. 55, Vol. IV, The Indian Institute of Public Administration.
27. Singh, Sardar, Hukam *Constituent Assembly Debates* (henceforth *CAD*), Vol. VII, dated 23-11-48, pp. 552-53.
28. Basu, D.D., op. cit., p. 276.
29. *Keshavananda v. State of Kerala (1973), 4 SCC 225 (paras 134, 139, 1714)* and Reference on the *Kerala Education Bill, 1957, A1958, SC. 956.*
30. Basu, op. cit., p. 270.
31. Ramachandran, op. cit., Vol. II, Second Edition, pp. 978-79.
32. *Ibid.*, p. 979.
33. Ahmed, Naziruddin *CAD*, Vol. VII, dated 23-11-48, p. 539.
34. Ambedkar, B.R., *Ibid.*, p. 540.

2
Literacy

Literacy is considered throughout the world as an indicator of the spread of education in society. The literacy status of an individual, caste or community helps in measuring its educational backwardness. It is one of the prime tasks of the Census Operations to give an idea of the rate at which literacy has spread in different areas and among different castes, communities and tribes and also to indicate to what extent the goal of making our entire school-going population literate, has been achieved. The Census data serve as a base in policy formulations for removal of regional and gender disparities by giving added momentum to the spread of literacy in particular areas or among communities which have lagged behind in matters of literacy. The literacy rate of the castes was used as one of the variables in the preparation of the list of 'Scheduled Castes' by the British Government in the 1930s. In independent India also, the literacy status of a community was practically the only parameter for finding the 'educational backwardness' of that community, though school enrolment tests were also sometimes applied.[1] That is the reason why literacy of a community has increasingly assumed such an important role in Indian polity.

The definition of a literate followed during the 1961, 1971 and 1981 Censuses was as follows:

> A person who can both read and write with understanding in any language is to be taken as literate. A person who can merely read but cannot write, is not literate. It is not necessary that a person who is literate should have received any formal education or should have passed any minimum educational standard.

The test that was applied for reading was the ability to read any portion of the printed matter in the enumerator's instruction booklet and the test for writing was the ability to write a simple letter. Children below the age of five years were treated as illiterates even if they were going to a school and might have picked up reading and writing a few odd words. The literacy rate was worked out by dividing the number of literates by the total population, including population below five years of age which by definition was treated as illiterate.[2]

Two important departures were made in the 1991 Census. The literacy status of each individual was ascertained by applying the yardstick of whether one could read and write with understanding in any of the languages. A person who could read but not write was not treated as literate. Recognizing the fact that, ability to read and write with understanding, is not ordinarily achieved until one had some schooling or had at least some time to develop these skills, it was felt by the Ministry of Human Resource Development and the Planning Commission that the population aged seven years and above should be classified as literate or illiterate. A significant departure was thus made in the 1991 Census by canvassing the question on literacy only for the population aged seven years and above unlike the practice followed till 1981 of canvassing the question for population aged five years and above.

Again, while working out the literacy rates, the younger population which by definition is treated as illiterate was not included in the total population as 'their inclusion in the denominator distorts the rates'. So the effective literacy rates have been worked out by dividing literates by the population excluding population below seven years of age which by definition is treated as illiterates.[3]

Of the 838.58 million people counted during the 1991 Census in India, excluding Jammu and Kashmir where the 1991 Census was not held, 688.16 million were aged seven years and above. Of these 688.16 million people, 359.28 million were literates, and 328.88 million were illiterates. This fixes the 1991 Census literacy rate at 52.21 per cent. The male literacy rate is 64.13 per cent and female literacy rate is 39.29 per cent. In the 1981 Census the population of India excluding Assam was 665 million. The 1981 literacy rate was 36.23 per cent. The male literacy rate was 46.89 per cent and the female literacy rate was 24.82 per cent.

The decennial Census of 1991 augurs well on many counts. For the first time, in the history of Census being taken in India, the number of literates has surpassed the number of illiterates. In the case of females, however, the trend of more illiterates than literates continued. Moreover, female literacy increased at a faster pace (ten per cent) than male literacy (eight per cent). Overall, the literacy rate has recorded an increase from about 19 per cent of the population aged five and above in 1951 to 52 per cent of the population aged seven and above in 1991. The rate of female literacy also rose noticeably from nine per cent of the population aged five and above in 1951 to 39 per cent of the population aged seven and above in 1991.[4]

The 1991 Census was not held in Jammu and Kashmir and the 1981 Census was not held in Assam. In order to study the trend of growth of the literates and illiterates during the decade 1981-91, Jammu and Kashmir data for the 1981 all-India figures and the 1991 Census data for Assam have been excluded in Table 2.1 which gives the 1981 and 1991 Census total population; population aged seven years and above and literates and illiterates aged seven years and above for the country, excluding Assam and Jammu and Kashmir. It also gives the literacy rates for males and females by rural-urban residence.

The population of the country, excluding Assam and Jammu and Kashmir, grew by 23.79 per cent during the decade 1981-91 and the population aged seven years and above increased by 24.98 per cent. The growth of literates during the same period was 49.37 per cent where as illiterates increased by only 6.07 per cent during the same period.

Significant sex differentials exist in the literacy rates but these have narrowed down during 1981-91, as the male literates increased by 42.41 per cent while the female literates increased by 63.57 per cent and the male-female differential declined from 26.25 percentage points in 1981 to 25.01 points in 1991. The index of gender equality, i.e., the proportion of:

$$\frac{\text{Ratio of female literates to total literates}}{\text{Ratio of female population to total population}}$$

which should ideally be 100, improved from 69 in 1981 to 76 in 1991.

TABLE 2.1

TOTAL POPULATION,* POPULATION AGED 7 YEARS AND ABOVE, LITERATES, ILLITERATES, AND LITERACY RATE BY SEX AND RURAL-URBAN RESIDENCE, INDIA ** 1981-91.

Population	*Total Rural Urban*	*1981* Persons	Males	Females	*1991* Persons	Males	Females
Total Population	Total	659.30	340.76	318.54	816.17	423.56	392.61
	Rural	502.88	257.56	245.32	602.89	310.98	291.91
	Urban	156.42	83.20	73.22	213.28	112.58	100.70
Population aged 7 years & above	Total	536.21	278.04	258.17	670.17	348.47	321.70
	Rural	406.19	208.31	197.88	490.13	253.07	237.06
	Urban	130.02	69.73	60.29	180.04	95.40	84.64
Literates aged 7 years & above	Total	234.15	157.08	77.07	349.76	223.70	126.06
	Rural	146.60	103.51	43.09	218.32	146.38	71.94
	Urban	87.55	53.57	33.98	131.44	77.32	54.12
Illiterates aged 7 years & above	Total	302.06	120.96	181.10	320.41	124.77	195.64
	Rural	259.59	104.80	154.79	271.81	106.69	165.12
	Urban	42.47	16.16	26.31	48.60	18.08	30.52
Literacy rate among population aged 7 years & above	Total	43.67	56.50	29.85	52.19	64.20	39.19
	Rural	36.09	49.69	21.77	44.54	57.84	30.35
	Urban	67.34	76.83	56.37	73.01	81.05	63.94

* in million

** excludes Assam and Jammu & Kashmir

Source : *Census of India, 1991*, Series 1, Paper 2 of 1992, p. 51

There was a large urban-rural differential in literacy rates. Between 1981 and 1991, literacy increased substantially in both rural and urban areas, but by 1991 the urban literacy rate at 73.01 per cent was quite high, compared to the rural literacy rate of 44.54 per cent. (Table 2.1). The sex ratio among literates, in 1991, was 491 in rural areas and 700 in urban areas, indicating that the sex differential in literacy tends to diminish with urbanization. It is, however, a matter of concern that the urban-rural difference in female literacy has increased. Female literacy varies from eight per cent in Barmer district of Rajasthan to 94 per cent in Kottayam district of Kerala.

These literates are, however, not spread evenly among States and Union Territories. Further, the progress in the spread of literacy has also not been uniform among the States and Union Territories during the 1981-91 decade. In some cases the progress is quite impressive while in some areas it is not so.[5]

Illiteracy

When one looks at the percentage of literacy in India over the years, one finds a steady increase from 16.67 per cent literacy in 1951 to 52.21 per cent in 1991. Yet, in terms of absolute figures the number of illiterates in the country has increased to 3289 lakh in 1991, which is a marginal increase from 3053 lakh in 1981[6] essentially because the rate of increase in literacy was out spaced by the unchecked enormous growth in population in the country. The figure of illiterates in 1991 would have been much more but for the change in the system of calculation of figures of literates and illiterates introduced from the 1991 Census when the population below seven years of age was not counted for arriving at the figures of literates and illiterates. The problem that vexes the minds of the educational thinkers and workers in the field of adult education is, 'how long will it take this country, with the present rate of growth of population and the low rate of increase in literacy, to attain a substantially high level of literacy'.

It is really shocking to note that according to a World Bank estimate, there will be 954 million illiterates in the world by AD 2000 and about 500 million of them will be Indians. Of the total illiterates in the 15-19 age group by AD 2000, 54.3 per cent will belong to India.[7]

The problem of liquidating illiteracy in India, therefore, assumes great significance and has to be attacked on two fronts, namely, expansion of primary education and a much bigger programme of adult literacy [8]. Recent increase in literacy percentage in the country is mostly due to the expansion of primary education. The eradication of illiteracy among adults in India can become a manageable task only if universal and compulsory education of children in the age group 6-14 is assured and the inflow of illiterate persons in the age group 15-35 is prevented by an adequate effort in the field of adult education.

Following the new National Policy of Education (NPE) enunciated in 1986 the National Literacy Mission (NLM) was launched as a societal and technology mission on 5th May, 1988 with the objective of imparting functional literacy to 80 million illiterate adults in the 15-35 age group by 1995.[9] In addition, post-literacy and continuing education programmes have also been launched for drop-outs from adult education centres and neo-literates in order to retain the utility of regular adult education programmes. Appropriate arrangements of postliteracy and continuing education programmes have also been provided in practically every village covered by Total Literacy Campaigns (TLC) through modified type of Jana Shikshan Nilayam (People's Education Centre), Youth Clubs-cum-Library Units or other modes.[10] Specialized programmes like : Integrated Child Development Service (ICDS), Early Childhood Care (ECC) through Mahila Samakhya Programmes such as Functional Literacy of Women (FLOW); Integrated Rural Development Programme (IRDP); National Rural Employment Programme (NREP) benefiting targeted groups, are also being implemented.

It is very clear that, despite all the flowery statements and highflown advertisement campaigns, the efforts made till today will not help eradicate illiteracy by the turn of the century, particularly because of the steady growth of population in India and existing constraints on public expenditure on child and adult education. The recent NCERT publication confirms that at present the coverage of illiterate adults across the country in adult literacy programmes ranges between 10 to 15 per cent of the eligible adults. The expenditure on adult education in any year has never exceeded two per cent of the total expenditure on education in India. At this rate, it is difficult even to imagine a probable date by which illiteracy will be eradicated in India.[11] It is, however, good that universalization of elementary education, eradication of illiteracy in the 15-35 age group and strengthening of vocational education so as to relate it to the emerging needs in the urban and rural settings were the major thrust areas of the Eighth Plan in the education sector. Utilization of formal, non-formal and open channels of learning was the strategy for this purpose.[12]

Scheduled Castes

Since Scheduled Castes are viewed as the most deprived, disadvantaged and suffering sections of the Indian population, it is incumbent to find out the progress made by them so far in the field of literacy.

Comparable statistics relating to the Scheduled Caste population for the 1991 Census are furnished in Table 2.2. As the figures of SC population aged 7 years and above, SC literates and illiterates aged 7 years and above are not availble from the census data, those for the 1981 Census could not be given in Table 2.2.

The decadal growth rate of the Scheduled Caste population was 30.99 per cent as against the growth rate of 23.79 per cent of the total population. Though the number of literates has surpassed the number of illiterates for the total population in the 1991 Census the same is untrue for the Scheduled Caste population. While the number of Scheduled Caste literates has exceeded the number of illiterates in urban areas, the number of illiterates in rural areas is more than double the number of Scheduled Caste literates. Again, the number of literates and the number of illiterates are almost

TABLE 2.2.

TOTAL SC POPULATION, POPULATION AGED 7 AND ABOVE, LITERATES, ILLITERATES, AND LITERACY RATE BY SEX AND RURAL-URBAN RESIDENCE, INDIA,* 1991

Scheduled Caste Population	*Total Rural Urban*	*1991* Total	Males	Females
1	2	3	4	5
Total Population	Total	138,223,277	71,928,960	66,294,317
	Rural	112,343,797	58,342,419	54,001,378
	Urban	25,879,480	13,586,541	12,292,939
Population aged 7 years & above **	Total	111,096,535	57,991,830	53,104,705
	Rural	89,968,731	46,850,882	43,117,849
	Urban	21,127,804	11,140,948	9,986,856
Literates aged 7 years & above	Total	41,562,427	28,946,547	12,615,880
	Rural	29,918,798	21,526,535	8,392,263
	Urban	11,643,629	7,420,012	4,223,617
Illiterates aged 7 years & above**	Total	69,534,108	29,045,289	40,488,825
	Rural	60,049,933	25,324,347	34,725,586
	Urban	9,484,175	3,720,936	5,763,239
Literacy rate among population aged 7 years & above	Total	37.41	49.91	23.76
	Rural	33.25	45.95	19.46*
	Urban	55.11	66.60	42.29**

* excludes Jammu and Kashmir

** calculated from the figures given at pp. 18-19 of Paper 1 of 1993 of *Census of India*, 1991, Series 1.

Source : *Census of India*, 1991, Series 1, Paper 1 of 1993, pp. 14, 18-19.

equally distributed among SC males. But the number of SC female literates constitutes less than one-third of SC female illiterates.

The index of gender equality in case of the total population was 76 in 1991, but it was 64 in case of SC population. This shows that the gender equality is more pronounced among SC population.

The rural-urban differential in literacy rates is slightly more among the SC literates. The rural-urban equality was 85.36 among total population but it was 88.90 among the Scheduled Caste population.

Literacy Gap

The literacy rate among the Scheduled Castes has increased from 1.9 per cent in 1931 to 21.38 per cent in 1981 and to 37.41 per cent in 1991; correspondingly the literacy rate among the Scheduled Tribes has increased from 8.53 per cent in 1961 to 16.35 per cent in 1981 and to 29.60 per cent in 1991. In spite of these increases, not only the levels of literacy among Scheduled Castes and Scheduled Tribes are distinctly lower than those of the people as a whole (52.21 per cent), the but the literacy gaps between SC/ST and the rest of population have rather been widening in successive censuses, as may be seen from Table 2.3 below.

TABLE 2.3
LITERACY RATES

Year	*General*	*SC*	*ST*	*Rest of Population*	*Gap SC*	*Gap ST.*	*Source*
1	*2*	*3*	*4*	*5*	*6*	*7*	*8*
1931	9.5	1.9					a
1961	24.00	10.27	8.53	27.86	17.59	19.33	b
1971	29.40	14.67	11.30	33.80	19.13	22.50	b
1981	36.17	21.38	16.35	41.22	19.84.	24.87	b
1991	52.21	37.41	29.60	57.69	20.28	28.09	c

Sources: (a) Report of the Working Group on the Development of Scheduled Castes duing the Seventh Five-Year Plan, 1985-90, 1985, p.30.

(b) Report of the Working Group on the Development and Welfare of Scheduled Castes during Eighth Five-Year Plan, 1990-95 1990, p.42.

(c) Computed from pp. 211-12 of Paper 2 of 1992 and pp. 18-19 and pp. 44-45 of Paper 1 of 1993, *Census of India, 1991*, Series 1.

The literacy rates among the Scheduled Castes and the Scheduled Tribes recorded an increase of 45.9 per cent and 44.7 per cent respectively during the decade 1971-81 and of 75 per cent and 81 per cent respectively during the decade 1981-91, while the non-SC/ST population registered an increase of 21.9 per cent and 40 per cent respectively during the corresponding period. As Table 2.3 indicates, the literacy gap between the SC and non-SC/ST population and between the ST and non-SC/ST population, instead of narrowing, is increasing in the successive Censuses during the period 1961-91 and in the case of Scheduled Tribes, it is widening very sharply in every Census operation since 1961. This yawning gap in literacy rates is, no doubt, a sad reflection on our ability to achieve the constitutional goal of universal elementary education (UEE) even within fifty years of Independence. That apart, the higher decadal growth rate of SC/ST population and a relatively higher population of children in the age group 0-6 than the total population also contributed to their low literacy status. During the last decade (1981-91), the decadal growth rate of the Scheduled Caste population was 30.99 per cent and that of the total population was 23.79 per cent.[13] The decadal growth rate of Scheduled Tribe population at 25.67 per cent[14] was, however, only slightly higher than that of the total population of the country. But, the Scheduled Tribe population had a relatively higher child population than the total population as well as the Scheduled Caste population. The children in the age-group 0-6 constituted 20.18 per cent of the Scheduled Tribe population in India as against 19.63 per cent of the Scheduled Caste population and 17.94 per cent of the total population.[15]

If we examine the educational development of the Scheduled Castes region-wise and caste-wise, the situation is far from satisfactory. The gap between the literacy rates of Scheduled Caste and others is wider when we compare these figures in respect of rural and urban areas. Similarly, there are intra-caste variations at various levels. The condition of education among Scheduled Caste women is even more unsatisfactory.

Scheduled Caste Literacy Rate by Sex and Rural-Urban Residence

Table 2.4 shows the variations in the percentage of literacy among the Scheduled Castes vis-a-vis all other communities excluding SC/ST in the rural and urban areas and also among the males and females during the 1981 and 1991 Censuses.

Sex differentials in literacy rates narrowed down considerably during the decade 1981-91. The literacy rate of SC females in 1981 (10.93 per cent) was about one-third of their male counterparts (31.12 per cent). The position improved appreciably in 1991 when the SC female literacy rate (23.76 per cent) was nearly half of their counterparts (49.91 per cent). The literacy rate of Scheduled Caste males has registered an increase of 60.38 per cent (from 31.12 per cent in 1981 to 49.91 per cent in 1991) during the decade 1981-91 as against an increase of 117.98 per cent (from 10.93 per cent in 1981 to 23.76 per cent in 1991) in Scheduled Caste female literacy rate during the same period. The rate of increase of female literacy among the Scheduled Castes has thus been much higher over the last decade than the male literacy rate. This is in tune with the trends noticed among the general population .

TABLE 2.4
ALL INDIA LITERACY

	Scheduled Castes				*All communities excluding SC/ST*			
	Total	*Rural*	*Urban*	*Source*	*Total*	*Rural*	*Urban*	*Source*
				1981				
All persons	21.38	18.48	36.60		41.52	34.52	61.11	
Male	31.12	27.91	47.54		52.35	46.14	68.46	
Female	10.93	8.45	24.34	a	29.43	21.68	51.19	
				1991				
All persons	37.41	33.25	55.11		57.69	49.87	75.93	
Male	49.91	45.95	66.60		69.53	63.42	83.40	
Female	23.76	19.46	42.29	b	44.82	35.38	67.48	c

Sources : a Report of the Working Group on Development of Scheduled Castes during the Seventh Five Year Plan, 1985-90, 1985, p.30.

b *Census of India, 1991,* Series 1, Paper 1 of 1993, pp. 18-19.

c *Census of India, 1991,* Series 1, Paper 2 of 1992, p. 51 and Paper 1 of 1993, pp. 18-19, 44-45.

It would be seen from Table 2.4 that literacy rate of Scheduled Castes in rural areas was just half (18.48 per cent) of their counterparts in urban areas (36.60 per cent) and of female Scheduled Castes, the literacy rate in rural areas (8.45 per cent) was almost one-third of the Scheduled Caste females in urban areas (24.34 per cent) in 1981. Though there was a significant improvement during the decade 1981-91, the literacy rate of Scheduled Castes in rural areas was more than half (33.25 per cent) of their counterparts in urban areas (55.11 per cent) and of female Scheduled Castes, the literacy rate in rural areas (19.46 per cent) was a little less than half (42.29 per cent) of the Scheduled Caste females in urban areas in 1991.On comparing these figures for both 1981 and 1991 with non-SC/ST communities, it would be seen that literacy lags amongst them in urban and rural areas were less pronounced.

Inter-state Variations

The literacy trends of States and Union Territories present quite a diversified pattern. Annexure Table 1 shows the literacy rates in the States/Union Territories for both the general population and the Scheduled Caste population, males and females separately, in the 1991 census. This table makes a very interesting reading in regard to the rate of literacy both in relation to the general population and the Scheduled Caste population in the 1991 census.

General Population

(*a*) The rate of literacy is below the All-India average of 52.21 per cent in nine States/UTs in the following order:

(1) Bihar (38.48 per cent); (2) Rajasthan (38.55 per cent); (3) Dadra and Nagar Haveli (40.71 per cent); (4) Arunachal Pradesh (41.59 per cent); (5) Uttar Pradesh (41.60 per cent); (6) Andhra Pradesh (44.09 per cent); (7) Madhya Pradesh (44.20 per cent); (8) Orissa (49.09 per cent); and (9) Meghalaya (49.10 per cent).

The five major States of India, namely, Bihar, Rajasthan, UP, MP and Andhra Pradesh have literacy rates of less than 45 per cent and they together account for almost half (49.28 per cent to be exact of the country's population (excluding Assam and Jammu & Kashmir)).

(b) Seven States have crossed the All-India literacy rate of 52.21 per cent but their literacy rate is below 60 per cent and in six States the literacy rate is between 60 per cent and 70 per cent :

(1) Assam (52.89 per cent); (2) Haryana (55.85 per cent); (3) Karnataka (56.04 per cent); (4) Sikkim (56.94 per cent); (5) West Bengal (57.70 per cent); (6) Punjab (58.51 per cent); (7) Manipur (59.59 per cent); (8) Tripura (60.44 per cent);

(9) Gujarat (61.29 per cent); (10) Nagaland (61.65 per cent); (11) Tamil Nadu (62.66 per cent); (12) Himachal Pradesh (63.86 per cent); and (13) Maharashtra (64.87 per cent).

(*c*) The remaining nine States/UTs may be considered as educationally advanced because their literacy rate is above 70 per cent:

(1) Daman and Diu (71.20 per cent); (2) Andaman and Nicobar Islands (73.02 per cent); (3) Pondicherry (74.74 per cent); (4) Delhi (75.29 per cent); (5) Goa (75.51 per cent); (6) Chandigarh (77.81 per cent); (7) Lakshadweep (81.78 per cent); (8) Mizoram (82.27 per cent); and (9) Kerala (89.81 per cent).

Scheduled Caste Population

(*a*) Six States registered a literacy rate below the All-India SC literacy rate of 37.41 per cent :

(1) Bihar (19.49 per cent); (2) Rajasthan (26.29 per cent); (3) Uttar Pradesh (26.85 per cent); (4) Andhra Pradesh (31.59 per cent); (5) Madhya Pradesh (35.08 per cent); and (6) Orissa (36.78 per cent).

These six States are also below the overall All-India literacy rate of 52.21 per cent in the same order and, they together account for 54.79 per cent of the country's total Scheduled Caste population.

(*b*) In seven States, the rate of literacy is above the All-India SC literacy rate of 37.41 per cent but below the All-India literacy rate of 52.21 per cent:

(1) Karnataka (38.06 per cent), (2) Haryana (39.22 per cent); (3) Punjab (41.09 per cent); (4) West Bengal (42.21 per cent); (5) Meghalaya (44.27 per cent); (6) Tamil Nadu (46.74 per cent); and (7) Sikkim (51.03 per cent).

(*c*) Nine States/UTs recorded the literacy rate between the All-India literacy rate of 52.21 per cent and the All-India non-SC/ST literacy rate of 57.69 per cent:

(1) Himachal Pradesh (53.20 per cent); (2) Assam (53.94 per cent); (3) Chandigarh (55.44 per cent); (4) Pondicherry (56.26 per cent); (5) Manipur (56.44 per cent); (6) Maharashtra (56.46 per cent); (7) Tripura (56.66 per cent); (8) Arunachal Pradesh (57.27 per cent); and (9) Delhi (57.60 per cent).

(*d*) The remaining six States/UTs crossed the All-India non-SC/ST literacy rate of 57.60 per cent:

> (1) Goa (58.73 per cent); (2) Gujarat (61.07 per cent); (3) Dadra and Nagar Haveli (77.64 per cent); (4) Mizoram (77.92 per cent), (5) Daman and Diu (79.18 per cent); and (6) Kerala (79.66 per cent).

It is observed that if the general literacy rate is high in any State/UT, the SC literacy rate is also correspondingly high in that State/UT, and if the general literacy rate is low, the SC literacy rate is also low in that unit. For instance, all the six States which could not attain the All-India SC literacy rate of 37.41 per cent are also the States which could not attain the All-India general literacy rate of 52.21 per cent. Similarly, the literacy rate among the Scheduled Castes has crossed the 70 per cent mark in the States/UTs of Dadra & Nagar Haveli (77.64 per cent), Mizoram (77.92 per cent), Daman & Diu (79.18 per cent) and Kerala (79.66 per cent). All these States/UTs except Dadra & Nagar Haveli are educationally advanced having the general literacy rate of more than 70 per cent. Only Dadra & Nagar Haveli is educationally backward having registered a general literacy rate of 40.71 per cent. This anomalous position cropped up because the literacy rate of the Scheduled Tribes in this Union Territory is a mere 28.21 per cent. There are a few exceptions also. For instance, the literacy rate among the Scheduled Castes has exceeded the general literacy rate in the States of Arunachal Pradesh and Assam, and in the Union Territories of Dadra and Nagar Haveli and Daman & Diu. The SC literacy rates in these States/UTs are (57.27 per cent Assam); (53.94 per cent, Dadra & Nagar Haveli); (77.64 per cent) and (79.18 per cent); as against the general literacy rate of (41.59 per cent, 52.89); per cent, (40.71 per cent); and (71.20 per cent) respectively.

There are also some States where the general literacy rate and the SC literacy rate compares favourably, like Gujarat (61.29 per cent general literacy rate : 61.07 per cent SC literacy rate, Manipur (59.89 per cent: 56.44 per cent), Tripura (60.44 per cent: 56.66 per cent), and Mizoram (82.27 per cent: 77 92 per cent).

Sex Differentials in SC Literacy Rates

There are tremendous inter-state disparities in the spread of literacy among SC males and SC females. Some States have achieved a higher level of literacy status for both SC males and females while others are lagging far behind. The progress made in the spread of literacy is not uniform among SC females and SC males. How they behaved in this respect during the last decade is reflected in Annexure Table I which gives the SC male and SC female literacy rates for 1991 for each State and U.T. The case of SC males is taken up first.

SC Males

(*a*) Among the Scheduled Caste males, the literacy rate was less than the All-India SC male litercay rate of 49.91 per cent in the following six States in that order :

(1) Bihar (30.64 per cent); (2) Uttar Pradesh. (40.80 per cent); (3) Andhra Pradesh (41.88 per cent); (4) Rajasthan (42.38 per cent); (5) Karnataka (49.69 per cent), and (6) Punjab (49.82 per cent).

Though the number of States remained the same in this category, two States, viz., Madhya Pradesh and Orissa interchanged their position with Karnataka and Punjab. Madhya Pradesh and Orissa whose SC literacy rate was less than the All-India SC literacy rate have improved their position so far as the literacy among the SC males was concerned, while it has deteriorated in the States of Karnatak a and Punjab.

(*b*) Eight States registered a literacy rate between the All-India SC male literacy rate of 49.91 per cent and the All-India male literacy rate of 64.13 per cent.

(1) Madhya Pradesh (50.51 per cent); (2) Haryana (52.06 per cent); (3) Orissa (52.42 per cent); (4) West Bengal (54.55 per cent); (5) Meghalaya (54.56 per cent); (6) Tamil Nadu (58.36 per cent); (7) Sikkim (58.69 per cent); and (8) Assam (63.88 per cent).

There is not much change in this category. As mentioned earlier, two States, viz., Madhya Pradesh and Orissa have elevated themselves to this category whereas another State, Assam, could not retain its position in the next higher category.

*See Annexure I at the end of the book.

(*c*) Seven States/UTs recorded a literacy rate between the All-India male literacy rate of 64.13 per cent and the All-India non-SC/ST male literacy rate of 69.53 per cent.

(1) Chandigarh (64.74 per cent); (2) Himachal Pradesh (64.98 per cent); (3) Manipur (65.28 per cent); (4) Pondicherry (66.10 per cent); (5) Andhra Pradesh (66.25 per cent); (6) Tripura (67.25 per cent); and (7) Delhi (68.77 per cent).

There is no significant change in this category. Only Assam was reduced to a lower category because of poor performance and Maharashtra elevated to the next higher category for better performance.

(*d*) Seven States/UTs accounted for a literacy rate above the All-India non-SC/ST male literacy rate of 69.53 per cent :

(1) Goa (69.55 per cent); (2) Maharashtra (70.45 per cent); (3) Gujarat (75.47 per cent); (4) Mizoram (77.54 per cent); (5) Kerala (85.22 per cent); (6) Dadra and Nagar Haveli (88.03 per cent); and (7) Daman and Diu (91.85 per cent).

Thus, the performance of the States of Madhya Pradesh, Orissa and Maharashtra in the field of SC male literacy was better as compared to SC literacy while the performance of the States of Karnataka, Punjab and Assam deteriorated in this arena.

Scheduled Caste Females

The overall picture of Scheduled Caste female literacy is quite encouraging. The increase in their literacy rate during the decade 1981-91 was a whooping 117.98 per cent as against the increase of 52.5 per cent in the case of non-SC/ST females and of 60.38 per cent in the case of Scheduled Caste males.

(*a*) The same six States which registered a literacy rate of less than the All-India SC literacy rate, also recorded a literacy rate less than the All-India SC female literacy rate of 23.76 per cent :

(1) Bihar (7.07 per cent); (2) Rajasthan (8.31 per cent); (3) Uttar Pradesh (10.69 per cent); (4) Madhya Pradesh (18.11 per cent); (5) Orissa (20.74 per cent); and (6) Andhra Pradesh (20.92 per cent).

Only Andhra Pradesh performed better in SC female literacy

because it enjoyed fourth position from the bottom in SC literacy but in SC female literacy its position was sixth from the bottom.

(*b*) Another six States accounted for a literacy rate between the All-India SC female literacy rate of 23.76 per cent and the All-India female literacy rate of 39.29 per cent :

(1) Haryana (24.15 per cent); (2) Karnataka (25.95 per cent); (3) West Bengal (28.87 per cent); (4) Punjab (31.03 per cent); (5) Meghalaya (31.19 per cent); and (6) Tamil Nadu (34.89 per cent).

It may be noted that all these six States and another state Sikkim, registered a literacy rate between the All-India SC literacy rate and the All-India literacy rate. Only Sikkim improved its position in SC female literacy.

(*c*) The number of States returning a literacy rate between the All-India female literacy rate of 39.29 per cent and the All-India non-SC/ST female literacy rate of 44.62 per cent dwindled to seven:

(1) Himachal Pradesh (41.02 per cent); (2) Arunachal Pradesh (41.42 per cent); (3) Maharashtra (41.59 per cent); (4) Sikkim (42.77 per cent); (5) Assam (42.99 per cent); (6) Chandigarh (43.54 per cent); and (7) Delhi (43.82 per cent).

(*d*) Now as many as nine States/UTs recorded a literacy rate of more than 44.82 per cent, *i.e.*, the All-India non-SC/ST female literacy rate, as follows :

(1) Tripura (45.45 per cent); (2) Gujarat (45.54 per cent); (3) Pondicherry (46.28 per cent); (4) Manipur (47.41 per cent); (5) Goa (47.51 per cent); (6) Dadra and Nagar Haveli (66.61 per cent); (7) Daman & Diu (67.62 per cent); (8) Kerala (74.31 per cent); and (9) Mizoram (81.25 per cent).

While the literacy among the Scheduled Caste females has improved in many States/UTs and in one State, *i.e.*, Mizoram, the SC female literacy rate has even surpassed the SC male literacy rate, the position in the States of Bihar (7.07 per cent), Rajasthan (8.31 per cent), and Uttar Pradesh (10.69 per cent) is abysmally poor. The position in three other States, *viz.*, Madhya Pradesh (18.11 per cent), Orissa (20.74 per cent) and Andhra Pradesh (20.92 per cent), though similarly poor, have however, a somewhat better male female literacy ratio as the Table 2.5 illustrates.

From the 1991 Census literacy data, nine different All-India literacy rates have been computed. They are: (1) All-India literacy rate of 52.21 per cent, (2) All-India male literacy rate of 64.13 per cent; (3) All-India female literacy rate of 39.29 per cent; (4) All-India SC literacy rate of 37.41 per cent; (5) All-India SC male literacy rate of 49.91 per cent, (6) All-India SC female literacy rate of 23.76 per cent (7) All-India non-SC/ST literacy rate of 57.69 per cent, (8) All-India male non-SC/ST literacy rate of 69.53 per cent and (a) All-India female non-SC/ST literacy rate of 44.82 per cent.

TABLE 2.5

MALE-FEMALE LITERACY RATIO

Name of States	*Male*	*Female*
Rajasthan	100	19.60
Bihar	100	23.00
U.P.	100	23.00
Madhya Pradesh	100	35.80
Orissa	100	39.60
Andhra Pradesh	100	50.00

The highest All-India literacy rate is that of non-SC/ST male literacy rate at 69.53 per cent and the lowest is that of SC female literacy rate at 23.76 per cent.

The wide regional variations and disparities in the level of literacy of different categories of people, *viz.*, total population, SC population, SC male population, SC female population have been elaborately discussed in the foregoing paragraphs. This has been put in a tabular form in Table 2.6.

Thus, at least six States/UTs have crossed even the All-India non-SC/ST literacy rate (7 in respect of SC male literacy and 9 in respect of SC female literacy). This is, no doubt, a very commendable performance on the part of Goa, Gujarat, Kerala, Mizoram, Dadra and Nagar Haveli and Daman & Diu. The performance of Maharashtra in SC male literacy and of Manipur, Tripura and Pondicherry in SC female literacy is also worth mentioning.

Six States are educationally backward in respect of SC and SC female literacy-Bihar, Rajasthan, U.P., Madhya Pradesh, Andhra Pradesh and Orissa, while four of them (except Madhya Pradesh and Orissa) as also Karnataka and Punjab are educationally backward in respect of SC male literacy. The number of States in this category does not exceed eight in any case.

Rural-Urban Literacy Rates

The question arises: Do the same trends prevail in rural literacy rates as in the case of the two sexes? Do the same States/UTs figure in the high literacy and low literacy category for the rural and urban areas? Is there any variation?

TABLE 2.6

ALL INDIA LITERACY RATES IN DIFFERENT CATEGORIES OF POPULATION

Different Categories of Population	*Below Respective All-India Literacy Rate*	*Above Respective All-India Literacy Rate but Below Respective All-India General Literacy Rate*	*Above Respective General All-India Literacy Rate but Below respective All-India non-SC/ST Literacy Rate*	*Above Respective All-India non-SC/ST Literacy Rate but Below 70 per cent*	*Above 70 per cent*	*Total*
1	2	3	4	5	6	7
Total population	9		5*	8**	9	31*
SC population	6	7	9	2 6	4	28
SC male population	6	8	7	1 7	6	28
SC female population	6	6	7	7 9	2	28

* Includes one State having no SC population
** Includes two UTs having no SC population
*** Includes three State/UTs having no SC population

Annexure Table II gives the literacy rates of SC population, SC male population and SC Female population for rural and urban areas separately in all the State and Union Territories in the 1991 Census. It appears from this Annexure Table that literacy has not spread evenly in rural as well as in urban areas. The number of

States/UTs in the lower literacy category is more in the urban areas than in rural areas and the number of States/UTs in the high literacy category is more in rural areas than in urban areas. This is true for all the three types of populations : SC, SC male and SC female with some minor variations. This can be seen from the Table. 2.7.

TABLE 2.7
ALL-INDIA LITERACY RATES IN DIFFERENT CATEGORIES OF SCHEDULED CASTES POPULATION

Categories of Population	*Below Respective All-India Literacy Rate*	*Above Respective All-India Literacy Rate but below Respective All-India General Literacy Rate*	*Above Respective All-India General Literacy Rate but below Respective All-India non-SC/ST Literacy Rate*	*Above Respective All-India non-SC/ST Literacy Rate*	*Total*
1	2	3	4	5	6
SC population					
Rural	6	6	2	14	28
Urban	10	13	1	4	28
SC male					
Rural	6	8	2	12	28
Urban	11	11	2	4	28
SC female					
Rural	7	5	1	15	28
Urban	8	16	1	3	28

The other question is: Which are the States/UTs figuring in low literacy and high literacy categories? Do the same State/UT figure in all the three types of populations for both the rural and urban literacy?

Rural Literacy

The six States of India, namely, Bihar, Uttar Pradesh, Rajasthan, Madhya Pradesh, Andhra Pradesh and Karnataka are in the low literacy category in respect of rural literacy for all the three types of population. In the case of SC female, Orissa also figures.

* **See Annexure II at the end of the book.**

There is thus a distinct variation in the educationally backward category of States in respect of rural literacy. While Orissa is found to be educationally backward in respect of SC and SC female literacy, it is not so in respect of rural SC literacy. Punjab is educationally backward in respect of SC male literacy but not so in respect of rural SC male literacy. But Karnataka which is educationally backward in respect of SC male literacy only, is also educationally backward in respect of rural literacy for the three types of population.

Thus, Orissa in respect of rural SC literacy and Punjab in respect of rural SC male literacy have improved their position in the matter of educational backwardness, while Karnataka has suffered a setback in respect of rural SC and rural SC female literacy.

In the high literacy category in respect of rural literacy, the number of States/UTs ranges between 15 and 12. Eleven States/UTs (Arunachal Pradesh, Goa, Gujarat, Kerala, Himachal Pradesh, Manipur, Mizoram, Tripura, Delhi, Dadra and Nagar Haveli, and Daman and Diu) are common to all the three types of population. In addition, Maharashtra in respect of rural SC and rural SC male literacy, Assam and Pondicherry in respect of rural SC and rural SC female literacy, and Sikkim and Chandigarh in respect of rural SC female literacy have also crossed the respective All-India non-SC/ST literacy rates.

Of the educationally advanced States/UTs, four (Kerala, Mizoram, Dadra and Nagar Haveli and Daman and Diu) have attained a literacy rate of 70 per cent and above in respect of rural SC literacy. All these four States plus Gujarat have attained the same percentage in respect of rural SC male literacy also and one less (Daman and Diu) in respect of SC female literacy.

The total number of States/UTs which are educationally advanced in rural literacy either in one or more than one type of population is 16, as against 10 which are found educationally advanced in literacy either in one or both the sexes.

Compared to the educationally advanced States/UTs in respect of male-female literacy, the States/UTs which have performed better in respect of rural literacy and, therefore, counted as educationally advanced are: Arunachal Pradesh, Himachal Pradesh and Delhi in respect of rural literacy for all the three types of population,

Manipur and Tripura in respect of SC and SC male literacy, Assam in respect of SC and SC female literacy, Maharashtra and Pondicherry in respect of SC literacy and Sikkim and Chandigarh in respect of SC female literacy.

Thus, the improvement achieved in the matter of rural literacy is worth mentioning as evidenced by the fact that a lesser number of States/UTs are found to be educationally advanced in relation to States/UTs identified as such in respect of male-female literacy.

Urban literacy

A completely different picture, however, emerges in the matter of urban literacy. There is preponderance of States/UTs in low and middle literacy categories whereas only a few find place in high literacy category. This is true for all the three types of population, though there are variations both in respect of number and the States /UTs actually figuring in different categories.

The number of States/UTs in low literacy category varies between eight and eleven. Of these States/UTs Seven (Bihar, Rajasthan, U.P, Orissa, Punjab, Haryana and Meghalaya) are common to all the three types of population. While Madhya Pradesh figures in urban SC and urban SC female population and Andhra Pradesh and West Bengal only in urban SC and urban SC male population, Chandigarh and Manipur figure in urban SC male population. Compared to rural literacy, not only has the number of educationally backward States/UTs increased in respect of urban literacy, but there is a wide difference in regard to the States/UTs included in this category. While Karnataka has improved its position in respect of all the three types of population, Madhya Pradesh and Andhra Pradesh have done so in urban SC male literacy and SC female literacy respectively. The States of Haryana, Punjab and Meghalaya have suffered deterioration in respect of all the three types of population, but the States of Orissa and West Bengal have undergone such deterioration in urban SC and urban SC male population, and the State of Manipur and the Union Territory of Chandigarh only in urban SC male population.

Thus, the three States of Karnataka, Madhya Pradesh and Andhra Pradesh have improved their performance in the field of urban literacy while the seven States/UTs of Haryana, Punjab,

Meghalaya, Manipur, Orissa, West Bengal and Chandigarh have been categorized as educationally backward due to deterioration, either in one or more types of population. The overall position of these seven States/UTs in SC literacy is that all of them, except Orissa, are above the All-India SC literacy rate and Manipur and Chandigarh have even registered a literacy rate above the All-India general literacy rate. Their poor performance in the field of urban literacy calls for a deeper probe.

Only five States/UTs come under the category of educationally advanced. These are Sikkim and Kerala for advancement in all the three types of population, Mizoram for SC and SC female population, Dadra and Nagar Haveli for SC and SC male population and Daman and Diu for SC male population. Considering the high literacy rate to be achieved for coming to this category, the number is not too bad. The high level of urban literacy is responsible for huge accumulation of States/UTs in the middle level, i.e., below the respective All India general literacy rate.

Caste-wise Analysis

The population and literacy rate of each caste as revealed in the 1991 Census has not yet been published. In the absence of the 1991 data, the trend as revealed in the 1981 Census may be looked into.

There were some castes in which not even a single literate was reported in respect of males as well as females in rural and urban areas. Though the population was very small, yet of the 1075 castes, as many as 18 were such where not even a single male in rural areas and 27 in urban areas, was literate. In case of females, as many as 61 castes in rural areas and 50 in urban areas were such that they did not have even a single literate female. In case of rural males the population of these 18 castes varied between 260 and one, while in the case of urban males the population of these 27 castes varied between 81 and one. Similarly, in case of rural females the population of these 61 castes varied between 252 and one, while in case of the 50 castes in urban areas their numerical strength varied between 70 and one. Annexure Table III lists all these castes, separately for males and females by rural and urban areas.

The literacy rates among the Scheduled Caste females were

very low. There were districts in the country where the literacy rate among the Scheduled Caste females was less than one per cent. Table 2.8 explains the position as follows:

TABLE 2.8
DISTRICTS/STATES WHERE LITERACY RATE IS LESS THAN ONE PER CENT

State/District	*Districts Having SC Female Literacy Rate Below 1%*	*Comparative Literacy Rate of non-SC/ST Communities*
Bihar	2.51 State SC female	16.40
District Sitamarhi	0.89%	10.97%
Madhya Pradesh	6.86 State SC female	22.01
District Sidhi	0.58%	7.93%
Uttar Pradesh	3.89 State SC female	16.80
Districts Gonda	0.84%	6.32%
Bahraich	0.77%	6.20%
Rajasthan	2.69 State SC female	15.31
Districts Churu	0.91%	11.99%
Nagaur	0.74%	8.62%
Jaisalmer	0.61%	6.41%
Jalor	0.50%	5.75%
Barmer	0.48%	4.57%

Source: Report of the Working Group on Welfare of the Scheduled Castes during the Seventh Five Year Plan (1985-90), 1985, p. 31.

As per Table 2.8 there were five districts in Rajasthan and one each in Bihar and Madhya Pradesh and two in Uttar Pradesh where the literacy rate of the Scheduled Caste females was less than even one per cent. The Barmer District in Rajasthan had the lowest literacy rate (0.48 per cent) among the Scheduled Caste females in the whole country; but even in this district, the literacy rate of non-SC/ST females was 4.57 per cent which was almost double the Scheduled Caste female literacy rate of 2.69 per cent. Table 2.8 clearly indicated a very high literacy lag between the Schedules Caste females and the non-SC/ST females. The literacy rates of the Scheduled Caste females as indicated in the Table were only fractional but the literacy rates of the non-SC/ST females were in absolute numbers. For instance, the literacy rate of the Scheduled Caste females in Churu district of Rajasthan was only 0.91 per cent, but the non-SC/ST female counterparts in the same district had a literacy rate of 11.99 per cent. There were another 39 districts in the country which had a literacy rate varying between one per cent and two per cent amongst the Scheduled Caste females.[16]

Main Table

The Main Table at the end of Annexure Tables indicates the literacy rate of total population, male population and female populations of each scheduled castes in the States/Union Territories during the 1961, 1971 and 1981 censuses.

From the statistics we see the following trends:

1. The literacy rate of each Scheduled Caste recorded a sharp improvement in successive Census operations since 1961.
2. A few Scheduled Castes, however, registered a low literacy rate in the 1971 Census compared to the 1961 Census and a similar rate in the 1981 Census compared to the 1971 Census.
3. Even in the educationally advanced States/UTs of Kerala, Mizoram, Dadra and Nagar Haveli and Daman and Diu, there were some castes which recorded a very low literacy rate.
4. The difference between the male literacy rate and the female literacy rate was more pronounced in the educationally backward States of Rajasthan (9 times), Bihar (7 times), Haryana (6 times), Uttar Pradesh (6 times), Madhya Pradesh (4 ½ times) and Orissa (3 ½ times).
5. In a few States/ UTs some Scheduled Castes had not even a single literate amongst its female population in the 1981 Census. These were Chandigarh (5 castes), Mizoram (3 castes), Arunachal Pradesh (3 castes), Tamil Nadu (3 castes), Karnataka (2 castes), Himachal Pradesh (1 caste), Meghalaya (1 caste) and Pondicherry (1 caste).
6. Not only were the inter-state variations in literacy rates of the Scheduled Castes very striking, there were also big gaps in the literacy rates amongst the different Scheduled Castes within the same State/UT.

Gap in the Literacy Rate Within the Same State/UT

Though there are educationally backward States and educationally advanced States in the matter of level of literacy of the Scheduled Caste population, it does not necessarily mean that all the Scheduled Caste in the educationally advanced States have recorded a high literacy rate and all the Scheduled Castes in the educationally backward States have registered a low literacy rate. In all the States/UTs, irrespective of their levels of literacy, some castes achieved a high literacy rate while many Scheduled Castes accounted for a low literacy rate. The gap in the literacy rates within the same State/UT will be best understood if the Scheduled Castes having maximum literacy rate and minimum literacy rate in each unit are identified. Table 2.9 gives the names of the Scheduled Castes having maximum literacy rate and minimum literacy rate in each State/UT. The maximum literacy rate varied between 100 per cent in Mizoram and Himachal Pradesh and 27 per cent in Bihar. Among the Scheduled Castes accounting for the lowest literacy it ranged between 'nil' in Himachal Pradesh, Chandigarh and Pondicherry and 40.42 per cent in Dadra and Nagar Haveli. This only goes to show that the inter-state variations in the level of literacy were very sharp.

In each State/UT there are some castes which have much higher literacy rate than the state average for the SC population as a whole. Although the overall SC literacy rate may be low but certain caste groups either because of their rank in the caste hierarchy or due to their small numerical strength or otherwise have attained a unique position as far as educational attainment is concerned. For example, *Gandhila* in Himachal Pradesh and *Brittial Bania* in Mizoram have attained 100 per cent literacy; *Kora* in Tripura have attained 85.7 per cent literacy rate; *Perna* in Chandigarh and *Mahar* in Daman & Diu attained 83.3 per cent while *Bharatar* in Kerala and *Panan* in Tamil Nadu have registered 79.8 per cent and 77.9 per cent literacy rate respectively. These are by no means small achievements.

However, when it comes to deprivation and illiteracy, the position in respect of many castes is very depressing. The gap in literacy rate of different caste groups, even within the SCs is extremely high—ranging from almost total illiteracy to that of almost universal literacy. For example, in Bihar, *Musahara* with a population of 1.4 million have been reeling under total illiteracy, the literacy in their case was only 2.1. per cent. The two extremes are also visible in Himachal Pradesh — *Gandhila* registering 100 per cent literacy and *Sirkiband* showing total illiteracy with not even a single literate person. These extremes exist even at a time when both the castes have equal opportunities and access to educational facilities.

TABLE 2.9

SCHEDULED CASTES HAVING MAXIMUM AND MINIMUM LITERACY RATE IN ALL STATES AND UTs.

Sl. No.	*Name of State/UT*	*Name of Scheduled Caste having* *Maximum Literacy*	*Minimum Literacy*
1.	Andhra Pradesh	Mala Dasu (63.8)	Byagara (7.6)
2.	Arunachal Pradesh	Patni (63.6)	Dugla, Dholi (14.3)
3.	Bihar	Pan, Sawasi (27.0)	Musahar (2.1)
4.	Goa	Chambhar (58.0)	Mahar (25.5)
5.	Gujarat	Lingader (57.4)	Mang Garudi (10.9)
6.	Haryana	Pasi (33.4)	Deha, Dhaya, Dhea(2.3)
7.	Himachal Pradesh	Gandhila, Gandil Gandola (100.0)	Sirkiband (nil)
8.	Jammu & Kashmir	Basith (29.1)	Watal (5.7)
9.	Karnataka	Anamuk (68.3)	Sapari (4.8)
10.	Kerala	Bharatar (79.8)	Domban (16.9)
11.	Madhya Pradesh	Pasi (42.7)	Kotwal (3.8)
12.	Maharashtra	Mahyavanshi, Dhed, Vankar, Maru Vankar (69.8)	Sedma, Ravat (15.6) Shenva, Chenva,
13.	Manipur	Dhupi, Dhobi (58.1)	Yaithibi (21.2)
14.	Meghalaya	Hira (66.7)	Bansphor (7.1)
15.	Mizoram	Brittial Bania, Bania (100.0)	Lalbegi (33.3)
16.	Orissa	Musahar (58.6)	Mundapotta (3.9)
17.	Punjab	Dagi (61.1)	Deha, Dhaya, Dhea (2.5)
18.	Rajasthan	Jingar (37.9)	Kalbelia, Sapera (2.5)
19.	Sikkim	Damai (Nepali)(31.0)	Sarki (Nepali) (16.6)
20.	Tamil Nadu	Panan (77.9)	Jambuvulu (6.9)
21.	Tripura	Kora (85.7)	Musahar (4.2)
22.	Uttar Pradesh	Bhanti (48.8)	Musahar (2.1)
23.	West Bengal	Sunri (54.9)	Musahar (5.3)
24.	Chandigarh	Perna (83.3)	Bagi (nil)
25.	Dadra and Nagar. Haveli	Mahyavanshi, Dhed (61.1)	Chamar (40.4)
26.	Daman and Diu.	Mahar (83.3)	Chambhar (18.2)
27.	Delhi	Adi Dharmi (62.2)	Singiwala, Kalbelia (3.1)
28.	Pondicherry	Madiga (61.5)	Mala, Mala Masti (nil)

In as many as 13 States/Uts, there are caste groups which have recorded literacy rate of less than 5 per cent, thus showing the extreme conditions of educational deprivation under which some caste groups live. It may be mentioned that *Deha* group of castes figure in the two States of Punjab and Haryana and *Musahars* in the three States of Tripura, West Bengal and Uttar Pradesh. Incidentlly, *Musaharas* recorded the highest literacy rate in the State of Orissa.

Scheduled Castes above the Average Scheduled Caste Literacy Rate

Since some Scheduled Castes in each State/UT have registered a higher literacy rate, it is incumbent to find out who they are and what is the level of their achievement. Annexure Table IV gives the average literacy rate of the Scheduled Castes and the Non-SC/ST Communities in each State/UT and also furnishes the names of the Scheduled Castes whose level of literacy has reached that level in the 1981 census. It will be seen from Annexure Table IV that in all the States/UTs, a number of Scheduled Castes have achieved a literacy level not only much above the SC literacy rate but above the non-SC/ST literacy rate also. It will be seen from Table 2.10 that there were as many as 100 Scheduled Castes which had crossed even the literacy rate of non-SC/ST communities. And if we count the Scheduled Castes whose level of literacy had exceeded the SC literacy rate, then the total number would be 533, that is about 50 per cent of the castes listed in the Schedules of the States/UTs had crossed the average SC literacy rate in 1981. Since the level of literacy among the Scheduled Castes has registered a phenomenal improvement in the 1981-91 decade, it is quite likely that the number of the Scheduled Castes crossing these two standards would be much more in 1991. The exact position would, however, be known only when the caste-wise data is at all published by the Census authority. In any case, even in 1981, around 50 per cent of the Scheduled Castes had achieved a level of literacy which was above the average SC literacy rate and of these, about 18 per cent, 100 castes to be precise, had crossed the level achieved by the non-SC/ST communities, that is, their performance even was much better than the non-SC/ST communities, This indicates the educational achievement of certain castes listed as the Scheduled Castes.

*For a detailed discussion please See Chapter IV of the Third Part of the *Scheduled Castes of India* by the author.

TABLE 2.10

LITERACY RATES AMONG SC AND NON-SC/ST COMMUNITIES

Sl. No	Name of of State/UT	No. of the Scheduled Castes having a literacy above the literacy rate of non-SC/ST and SC communities		No. of Total SC in the List
1	2	3	4	5
1.	Andhra Pradesh	7	28	59
2.	Arunachal Pradesh	Nil	8	16
3.	Assam		Not Available	
4.	Bihar	Nil	13	23
5.	Goa	1	2	5
6.	Gujarat	3	7	30
7.	Haryana	Nil	13	37
8.	Himachal Pradesh	7	21	56
9.	Jammu & Kashmir	2	2	13
10.	Karnataka	10	49	101
11.	Kerala	6	24	68
12.	Madhya Pradesh	1	19	47
13.	Maharashtra	11	29	59
14.	Manipur	2	2	7
15.	Meghalaya	5	4	16
16.	Mizoram	4	8	16
17.	Orissa	2	43	93
18.	Punjab	6	10	37
19.	Rajasthan	5	30	59
20.	Sikkim	Nil	1	4
21.	Tamil Nadu	20	25	76
22.	Tripura	1	10	32
23.	Uttar Pradesh	2	28	66
24.	West Bengal	1	23	59
25.	Chandigarh	3	15	36
26.	Dadra & Nagar Haveli	Nil	1	4
27.	Daman & Diu	Nil	2	15
28.	Delhi	Nil	13	36
29.	Pondicherry	1	3	15
	Total	100	433	1075

Population of the Scheduled Castes above the Average SC Literacy Rate

Though the number of castes which had crossed the SC literacy rate in 1981 was roughly 50 per cent of the total number of castes listed in the Schedules, it, however, did not mean that these castes together would account for 50 per cent of the total SC population of the country. It entirely depended on the population size of the individual castes. There were many castes which returned a very insignificant population, even less than .001 per cent of the total SC population while there were many castes or groups of castes which alone accounted for more than 20 per cent or even 50 per cent of the unit's SC population. For the purpose of convenience and getting a close view of the situation, the different castes or groups of castes may be categorized according to their population sizes.

Those communities with a population of 10 per cent or more of the total SC population of the State/UT may be categorized as "very large", those with a population between 10 per cent and 1 per cent of the unit's SC population as "large; while those returning a population between 1 per cent and 1 per cent may be termed as "small". "very small" communities are those having a population ranging between .1 per cent and .01 per cent. The communities accounting for a population between .01 per cent and .001 per cent may be classified as "negligible" and those less than .001 per cent may be categorized as "most negligible". Therefore, the percentage of SC population covered by a caste would entirely depend on the category to which that caste belongs. If it falls under "most negligible" category, the population represented by it would be insignificant, while the population would be sizeable if the caste comes under "very large" category. A study shows that the total number of castes coming under "very large" and "large" categories was 258 in number accounting for 90.78 per cent of the country's SC population in the 1981 Census. Therefore, to find out the population represented by these five hundred and odd communities, it is better to go through Annexure Table V which gives not only the population of each of the communities as per the 1981 censuses but also the category to which they belong. Asynopsis of the information is given in Table 2.11.

TABLE 2.11

STATEWISE POPULATION OF SCs HAVING LITERACY RATE GREATER THAN NON-SC/ST COMMUNITIES

Sl. No.	*Name of State/ UT*	*Population of the Scheduled Castes having a Literacy Rate above the Literacy Rate of*			
		Non-SC/ST Communities		*SC Communities*	
1	2	3		4	
1.	Andhra Pradesh	(7)	55,585 (0.70%)	(28)	3,941,253 (49.5%)
2.	Arunachal Pradesh		nil	(8)	1,614 (55.29%)
3.	Assam			NA	
4.	Bihar		nil	(13)	7,042,657 (69.44)
5.	Goa	(1)	6,438 (31.22%)	(2)	474 (2.30%)
6.	Gujarat	(3)	52,735 (2.16%)	(7)	1,727,271 (70.84%)
7.	Haryana		nil	(13)	1,416,148 (57.47%)
8.	Himachal Pradesh	(7)	13,997 (1.33%)	(21)	582,712 (55.29%)
9.	Jammu & Kashmir	(2)	132,254 (26.59%)	(2)	199,613 (40.13%)
10.	Karnataka	(10)	44,666 (0.80%)	(49)	996,648 (17.81%)
11.	Kerala	(6)	148,168 (5.81%)	(24)	1,532,078 (60.10%)
12.	Madhya Pradesh	(1)	30,310 (0.41%)	(19)	1,886,539 (25.64%)
13.	Maharashtra	(11)	157,066 (3.51%)	(29)	2,879,664 (64.28%)
14.	Manipur	(2)	379 (2.13%)	(2)	5,216 (29.38%)
15.	Meghalaya	(5)	438 (7.98%)	(4)	1,836 (33.43%)
16.	Mizoram	(4)	17 (12.59%)	(8)	76 (55.56%)
17.	Orissa	(2)	336 (0.0087%)	(43)	2,199,998 (56.91%)
18.	Punjab	(6)	747,643 (16.57%)	(10)	-1,449,398 (32.12%)
19.	Rajasthan	(5)	18,941 (0.32%)	(30)	3,995,284 (68.43%)
20.	Sikkim		nil	(1)	5,980 (32.71%)
21.	Tamil Nadu	(20)	79,149 (1.07%)	(25)	5,805,377 (78.16%)
22.	Tripura	(1)	14 (0.0045%)	(10)	173,671 (55.95%)
23.	Uttar Pradesh	(2)	11,194 (0.048)	(28)	17,494,964 (74.59%)
24.	West Bengal	(1)	252,331 (2.10%)	(23)	6,534,577 (54.45%)
25.	Chandigarh	(3)	51 (0.08%)	(15)	26,536 (41.71%)
26.	Dadra & Negar. Haveli		nil	(1)	943 (46.20%)
27.	Daman & Diu		nil	(2)	1,765 (62.74%)
28.	Delhi		nil	(13)	552,544 (49.26%)
29.	Pondicherry	(1)	39 (0.04%)	(3)	6,489 (6.71%)
	Total	(100)	1,751,751 (1.67%)	(433)	60,461,414 (57.72%

Figures in the brackets indicate the number of castes and the percentage of total SC population of the State/UT in 1981.

It will appear from Table 2.11 that the 533 castes which had crossed the average level of literacy of SC population, accounted for 59.39 per cent of the country's total SC population and about 1.67 per cent of the total SC population, represented by 100 castes/

groups of castes, had even performed better than the non-SC/ST communities.

The All-India average of 59 per cent was, however, not attained by each and every State/UT. Some States/UTs gave a better account of themselves while some were lagging far behind. Among the States/UTs whose performance was much below the standard, mention may be made of Pondicherry, Karnataka and Madhya Pradesh, where only seven per cent, 18.6 per cent and 26 per cent respectively of the SC population could cross the respective State's average SC literacy rate. The other States/UTs whose achievement was far from satisfactory were, Manipur (31 per cent); Goa (33 per cent); Sikkim (33 per cent); Meghalaya (41 per cent); and Chandigarh (42 per cent). The poor performance of these States/UTs was largely offset by the improved performance of Tamil Nadu, Uttar Pradesh, Bihar, Rajasthan, Maharashtra, Jammu & Kashmir and Kerala where the castes/groups of castes which had crossed the SC literacy rate accounted for 79 per cent, 75 per cent, 69 per cent, 69 per cent, 68 per cent, 67 per cent and 66 per cent respectively, of the State SC population. In these States the 'very large' and 'large' categories of castes/groups of castes had a higher literacy rate compared to the States/UTs whose performance was much below the standard. Another fact which needs to be mentioned is that these States together accounted for 53.30 per cent of the country's total SC population whereas the States/UTs identified for poor performance had only 13.54 per cent of the country's SC population.

Annexure Table V shows the trend of advancement of different categories of castes/groups of castes in the matter of literacy. The point is how many of the 533 castes belong to very 'large' and 'large' categories and how many to other categories gives the composition of categories of these 533 castes/groups of castes. It may be seen from this Table that 41 'very large' and 100 'large' categories of castes/groups of castes had crossed the SC literacy rate. These 141 castes constituted 26.46 per cent of the 533 castes. If we remember the fact that the share of 'very large' and 'large' categories of castes to the total number of Scheduled Castes was 24.20 per cent, then it can be said that these categories of castes had showed a marginal improvement in the matter of literacy. Because of this, the share of the population covered by these 533 castes was a little more than their share in the total number of castes (59 per cent population as against 50 per cent of the castes).

TABLE 2.12
CASTES HAVING LITERACY RATE ABOVE THE NON -SC/ST AND SC LITERACY RATES

Sl. Name of State/UT	Categories of castes attaining a literacy rate above the non-SC/St literacy rate							SC literacy rate					
	Very large	Large	Small	Very small	Negli-gible	Most negli-gible	Total	Very large	Large	Small	Very small	Negli-gible	Most negli-gible
	1	2	3	4	5	6		1	2	3	4	5	6
1. Andhra Pradesh		3	3	1		7	1	3	6	10	7	1	
2. Arunachal Pradesh							2	3	3				
3. Assam			Not Available										
4. Bihar								2	4	2	4	1	
5. Goa	1						1		1	1			
6. Gujarat		1			2		3	2		1	3	1	
7. Haryana								1	3	2	4	2	1
8. Himachal Pradesh	1	1	2	1	2	7	2	4	6	4	5		
9. Jammu & Kashmir	1	1				2	1			1			
10. Karnataka			2	5	3		10		3	9	22	11	4
11. Kerala	3	1	1	1		6	1	6	6	8	2	1	
12. Madhya Pradesh		1			1		7	9	2	1			
13. Maharashtra	1	5	1	4		11	2	3	5	10	7	2	
14. Manipur		2				2	2						
15. Meghalaya	2	3			5	1	3						
16. Mizoram	4				4	2	5	1					

17. Orissa			1	1	2	2	6	11	12	10	2	
18. Punjab	1	1	1		3		6	1	3	3		3
19. Rajasthan		1	4		5	1	9	8	9	9	3	
20. Sikkim							1					
							3					
21. Tamil Nadu		1	7	6	6	20	20		5	4	10	3
22. Tripura			1		1	3	2	1	2	2		
23. Uttar Pradesh		2		2	1	5	2	11	9			
24. West Bengal		1			1	3	3	7	9	1		
25. Chandigarh		3			3	1	4	4	6			
26. Dadra & N. Haveli					1							
27. Daman & Diu						1		1				
28. Delhi							1	2	5	4		
29. Pondicherry			1		1		3					
Total	3	17	19	29	9	100	38	83	98	125	75	14

It will also appear from this Table that there was preponderance of 'small', 'very small', 'negligible' and 'very negligible' categories of castes in Karnataka (56 out of 59, i.e., 94.91 per cent) and there was not even a single caste from the 'very large' category. The 'very large' category of castes constituted 55.61 per cent of the total SC population of the State. This fact can give an idea of the dismal showing in the level of literacy of this State in terms of population coverage, especially when the number of castes attaining this standard was unusually high, 58.42 per cent (59 out of 101). In Madhya Pradesh, not only did the group of castes in the 'very large' category (i.e., the Chamar group of castes) accounting for 52.25 per cent of the total SC population of the State, not attain this level of literacy, but also the number of castes attaining this standard was very low, only 42.55 per cent (20 out of 47). In that sense, Madhya Pradesh may be regarded as the most backward amongst the educationally backward States.

Only 100 castes/groups of castes covering 1.67 per cent of the country's SC population had crossed the non-SC/ST literacy rate. While many of the States could not achieve this standard, some States made significant progress in terms of population coverage. These were, Goa (31.22 per cent); Jammu & Kashmir (26.59 per cent); Punjab (16.57 per cent); Mizoram (12.59 per cent); Meghalaya (7.98 per cent); and Kerala (5.81 per cent). The performance of Maharashtra (3.51 per cent); Gujarat (2.16 per cent); Manipur (2.13 per cent); and West Bengal (2.10 per cent) was also good. It is observed that another 29 castes/groups of castes, listed in Table 2.13, were within five per cent range of the level achieved by the non-SC/ST communities. Considering this and also the high level of literacy achieved by these Communities, their acheivement, is simply spectacular and praiseworthy.

The level of literacy of many of the communities listed as the Scheduled Castes could have been judged in a more realisitc and pragmatic manner, had the castes/sub-castes not been grouped together under one serial. If the literacy rate of each of the castes and sub-castes was tabulated separately, it could have given a correct picture of the level of literacy of each of them. Grouping together so many castes, sometimes even 20 or 30, under one caste-group, has stood in the way of making a correct assessment of the situation.

TABLE 2.13
LIST OF 29 CASTES/GROUPS OF CASTES WHICH WERE WITHIN 5 PER CENT RANGE OF THE NON-SC/ST LITERACY RATE IN 1981.

Sl. No.	*Castes*	*Location*
1.	Madari Kuruva, Madasi Kuruva	in Andhra Pradesh
2.	Ager	
3.	Halsar, Haslar, Hulasvar, Halasvar,	
4.	Turi	all in Gujarat
5.	Balmiki, Bhangi, Chuhra, Chura, Chuhre	in Himachal Pradesh
6.	Jolaha	in Jammu & Kashmir
7.	Kudumban	
8.	Tirgar, Tirbanda	both in Karnataka
9.	Kakkalan	
10.	Semman	
11.	Vannan	all in Kerala
12.	Khatik	in Madhya Pradesh
13.	Bahna, Bahana	
14.	Dhor, Kakkayya, Kankayya, Dohor	
15.	Tirgar, Tirbanda	
16.	Halsar, Haslar, Hulasvar, Halasvar	all in Maharashtra
17.	Patni	in Manipur
18.	Bhuinmali	in Meghalaya
19.	Bhanjra	in Punjab
20.	Chandal	in Rajasthan
21.	Cheruman	
22.	Maila	
23.	Mundala.	
24.	Thandan	
25.	Tiruvalluvar	
26.	Vathiriyan	all in Tamil Nadu
27.	Kanugh	in Tripura
28.	Sanaurhiya	in Uttar Pradesh
29.	Sanhai	in Chandigarh

Position of Some Selected Scheduled Castes

This gives us an opportunity of examining the position of some selected Scheduled Castes who were retained in the list of the Scheduled Castes in spite of their objection in 1933 or who unsuccessfully pleaded for according them a higher social status during the census operations in the 30s.*

Table 2.14 lists out these selected Scheduled Castes in the four States namely West Bengal, Uttar Pradesh., Bihar and Madhya

Pradesh. Their literacy rates as recorded in the Censuses of 1961, 1971 and 1981 as also the average SC literacy rate in these States in 1961, 1971 and 1981 will facilitate a meaningful comparison of their relative achievements during these periods.

It would be seen from Table 2.14 that of the ten Scheduled Castes of West Bengal who represented against their inclusion in the list of Scheduled Castes in 1933 but failed in their mission, the level of literacy of seven of them was all along higher than the State's SC literacy rate. One of them (Tiyar) had a literacy rate below the State's SC literacy rate in 1961, but achieved a higher literacy rate from 1971 onwards. Only Bagdi and Bhuimali communities had a level of literacy below the State's SC literacy rate. The Scheduled Castes whose literacy rate was above the State's SC literacy rate accounted for 54.55 per cent of the State's SC population in 1981.

Of the six castes of Uttar Pradesh which claimed a higher social status in the 30s, the literacy rate of only two of them—Chamar and Dhobi—was all along higher than the State's SC literacy rate, and that of Kori had exceeded the State's SC literacy rate only in 1981 while the other three are yet to reach that level. The two castes which maintained a higher literacy rate all through accounted for 61.13 per cent of the State's total SC population in 1981.

Dusadh of Bihar also had a higher literacy rate than the State's SC literacy rate all along. It accounted for 26.19 per cent of the State's SC population in 1981.

The three castes of Madhya Pradesh which demanded a higher social status in the 30s but ultimately found themselves in the list of the Scheduled Castes, also maintained a much higher literacy rate than the State's SC literacy rate during the last three census operations. These three castes together represented 10.46 per cent of the State's SC population in 1981.

These castes which vehemently protested at being enlisted with a group of castes of supposed lower social status many decades earlier had maintained a uniform higher literacy rate during the last three decades and would, in all probability, maintain the same trend in the 1991 Census as well. The data regarding their level of literacy in the earlier two decades are unavailable because castewise

TABLE 2.14

POSITION OF SOME SELECTED SCHEDULED CASTES WHO PLEADED ACCORDING FOR HIGHER SOCIAL STATUS

Name of Scheduled Castes in States	*Literacy rate in* 1961	1971	1981	*Population as per 1981 Census*
1	2	3	4	5
A. West Bengal				
1. Bagdi	8.74	10.79	13.96	
2. Bhuimali	11.32	17.41	21.22	
3. Dhoba, Dhobi	18.93	24.27	38.79	251,737
4. Jalia Kaibartta	17.95	20.46	30.16	318,344
5. Jhalo Malo, Malo	14.41	19.18	25.51	154,557
6. Namasudra	21.03	26.86	35.87	1,692,233
7. Pod, Poundra	21.68	27.31	36.48	1,536,197
8. Rajbanshi	14.75	17.56	24.65	2,258,760
9. Sunri	28.58	22.41	54.95	252,331
10. Tiyar	8.06	20.40	25.33	82,108
All Scheduled Castes	13.58	17.80	24.37	6,546,267 (54.55%)
B. Uttar Pradesh				
1. Bawaria	10.33	7.85	13.69	
2. Beldar	4.70	6.55	9.94	
3. Chamar, etc.	7.41	10.49	15.98	12,914,218
4. Dhobi	7.20	10.88	15.76	1,423,574
5. Kanjar	5.85	8.67	7.05	
6. Kori	6.50	9.94	15..24	
All Scheduled Castes	7.14	10.20	14.96	14,337,792 (61.13%)
C. Bihar				
1. Dusadh, etc.	7.0	7.9	12.4	2,655,832 (26.19%)
All Scheduled Castes	5.9	6.5	10.4	
D. Madhya Pradesh				
1. Katia	13.31	18.99	29.54	95,647
2. Khangar	17.02	23.43	20.25	96,529
3. Mahar, etc	15.00	25.32	31.67	577,240.
All Scheduled Castes	7.89	12.49	18.97	769,416 (10.4%)

Please see Chapter 25 of Third Part of the *Scheduled Castes of India* by the author for a detailed discussion.

data was not computed in the 1941 and 1951 Censuses. Had it been tabulated, it could have given us an opportunity of assessing their level of literacy since their enumeration as the Scheduled Castes *vis-a-vis* other Scheduled Castes of these States. In any case, the trend as revealed in the last three censuses may lead one to conclude that this level of literacy would have been achieved by these Castes irrespective of the fact whether they were included in the lists of the Scheduled castes or not. Their level of literacy was consistently higher all along *vis-a-vis* the other Scheduled Castes.

Apart from these selected Scheduled Castes, there were many Scheduled Castes which had maintained a higher literacy rate than the State's SC literacy rate throughout these three censuses. Out of the 533 castes/groups of castes which had crossed the respective unit's SC literacy rate in 1981, as many as 341 castes had registered a literacy rate above the SC literacy rate in all the three Censuses conducted in 1961, 1971 and 1981. Their details are given in AnnexureTable VI. The unit-wise number of these castes/groups of castes, as also the number of castes/groups of castes which had crossed the SC literacy rate in 1981 is given in Table 2.15.

TABLE 2.15

NUMBER OF THE SCHEDULED CASTES HAVING A LITERACY RATE HIGHER THAN THE SC LITERACY RATE IN THREE SUCCESSIVE CENSUSES, 1961-81

Sl. Name of No.State/UT	No of castes having higher Literacy Rate in the Successive censuses	Population in in the 1981 censuses and percentage of SC population in the state	NO of Castes Above SC Literacy Rate only in 1981	.Col3 as Percentage of of col.5
1	2	3	4	5 6
1. Andhra Pradesh	23	3,782,629 (47.51%)	35	66
2. Arunachal Pradesh	7	850 (29.12%)	8	87
3. Assam		Not Available		
4. Bihar	10	6,933,314 (68.36%)	13	77
5. Goa	3	6,912 (33.52%)	3	100
6. Gujarat	4	1,115,325 (45.74%)	10	40

7. Haryana		9.1,414,702 (57.41%)	13	69
8. Himachal Pradesh	22	596,378 (56.58%)	28	79
9. Jammu & Kashmir	3	321,905 (64.72%)	4	75
10. Karnataka	31	947,503 (16.93%)	59	53
11. Kerala	23	1,661,980 (65.19%)	30	77
12. Madhya Pradesh	15	1,825,974(24.81%)	20	75
13. Maharashtra	20	1,336,916 (29.84%)	40	50
14. Manipur	3	3,172 (17.87%)	4	75
15. Meghalaya	5	1,090 (19.85%)	9	56
16. Mizoram	4	14 (10.37%	12	33
17. Orissa	22	1,976,846 (51.14%)	45	49
18. Punjab	15	2,196,721 (48.69%)	16	94
19. Rajasthan	27	1,582,058 (27.10%)	35	77
20. Sikkim		nil	nil	
21. Tamil Nadu	31	5,852,253 (78.79%)	45	69
22. Tripura	4	169,280 (54.54%)	11	36
23. Uttar Pradesh	17	15,815,041 (67.43%)	30	57
24. West Bengal	15	4,395,924 (36.63%)	24	62
25. Chandigarh	15	25,350 (39.85%)	18	83
26. Dadra & Nagar. Haveli	1	943 (46.20%)	1	100
27. Daman and Diu	2	1,765 (62.74%)	2	100
28. Delhi	8	487,807 (43.49%)	13	62
29. Pondicherry	2	4,931 (5.10%)	4	50
Total	341	52,457,523 (50.8%)	533	69

It would appear from Annexure Table VI that these 341 castes/groups of castes, which constituted 64 per cent of the castes/groups of castes crossing the SC literacy rate in 1981, had maintained this standard throughout the 30-year long period. If the literacy rates of these castes for the 1951 Census were available, that would have, in all likelihood, revealed the same trend. So many castes/groups of castes, about 32 per cent of the total SC castes/groups of castes, giving such a good account of themselves only shows that in the matter of literacy they were all along above the other castes. A clearer picture would have emerged if the literacy rate of each caste/sub-caste/sub-sub-caste had been tabulated in all the censuses, instead of showing the literacy rate of the group of castes. Grouping of castes together had no doubt, stood in the way of making a realistic appraisal of the entire situation.

The States whose performance was below the All-India average of 64 per cent were Mizoram, Tripura, Gujarat, Orissa, Pondicherry, Maharashtra, Karnataka, Meghalaya, Uttar Pradesh, West Bengal and Delhi. While the three educationally backward States of Uttar Pradesh, Orissa and Karnataka have recorded a performance below the All-India average; the other three educationally backward States of Bihar, Madhya Pradesh and Rajasthan, however, followed the All-India trend. In these States, around 75 per cent of the castes/ groups of castes whose level of literacy was more than the 1981 SC literacy rate, had maintained a higher level of literacy throughout the last three Censuses. This lends credence to the fact that even in the educationally backward States, the same castes/groups of castes attained a higher rate of literacy throughout, while others lagged behind.

In regard to population covered by these 341 castes/groups of castes, it is observed that they account for 50.08 per cent of the country's SC population. In case of the castes registering a literacy rate above the SC literacy rate in 1981, the ratio between the percentage of castes and the percentage of population was 50:59 but in case of castes maintaining a higher literacy throughout, the ratio was 32:50. The higher percentage of population covered by the 32 per cent of castes was effected because of the fact that most of the 'very large' and 'large' categories of castes had maintained this uniform standard. As a matter of fact, 77 per cent of the 'very large' category and 80 per cent of the 'large' category of castes, whose literacy rate was higher than the SC literacy rate in 1981, had recorded higher literacy all through.

A study* has revealed that the Chamar group of castes figures in the 'very large' category in 17 States/UTs and in the 'large' category in five States/UTs. It is seen that the Chamar group of castes has registered a uniform level of higher literacy in ten States where it is in 'very large' category and in two States where it is in 'large category', i.e., in more than 50 per cent of the States/UTs this group of castes has maintained a higher literacy rate all through. These States/UTs are : Bihar, Goa, Haryana, Himachal Pradesh, Jammu & Kashmir, Maharashtra, Manipur, Orissa, Punjab, Uttar Pradesh, Chandigarh and Delhi. Among the major States where this, group of castes failed to show this, feat, mention may be made of Madhya Pradesh, Rajasthan, Gujarat, Karnataka and West Bengal.

---

*Please see Chapter 25 of the Third volume of The Scheduled Castes in India by the author for a detailed discussion.

Comparatively, the record of the Bhangi group of castes was unimpressive. In five States it figures in 'very large' category and in 11 States/UTs in 'large' category. Out of these States/UTs, the Bhangi group of castes could maintain a uniformly higher level of literacy in six States where it is placed in 'large' category, i.e., in 2/5th of the States/UTs they had this unique record. These States are Bihar, Goa, Himachal Pradesh, Madhya Pradesh and Rajasthan. In ten States/UTs it could not achieve this level. Among them the major States are Gujarat, Haryana, Punjab and West Bengal.

Thus, both the Chamar and Bhangi groups of castes could not achieve a higher literacy rate all through in the States of Gujarat and West Bengal.

Higher Literacy Rate and Elementary Education

Since an increase of 75 per cent in the literacy rate of Scheduled Castes during the decade 1981-91 was registered on an All-India basis, it is expected that this increase will be reflected in the matter of considerably narrowing down the existing hiatus between the rural and urban areas, between males and females and above all, between the individual castes among the Scheduled Castes.

But the rate of literacy does not necessarily indicate the level of educational attainment. In modern times, there are two aspects of human education. One is literacy, the other is the quality of literacy. Literacy is related to the success or failure of the State in ensuring that the population inhabiting it acquires the ability to read and write. After achieving a certain level of literacy the modern State engages in improving the quality of literacy by educating its people in terms of quality of life and existence, which is attained by learning the arts, the crafts, science and technology to manage, develop and improve the quality of life. The founding fathers of the Indian Constitution were very much alive to the values of literacy and education, which is why they provided free and compulsory education for all children up to the age of 14 years under Article 45 of the Constitution. If this constitutional provision was implemented in its true spirit, not only would illiteracy have long been eradicated from our society, but the quality of life also would have improved a lot.

References

1. Galanter, Op. cit. p. 225.
2. Sharma, O.P., 1990, *Scheduled Castes Population and Literates,* p.3. New Delhi: Kar kripa Publishers.
3. *Census of India, 1991Series 1, Paper 2 of 1992,* p. 49.
4. *Education for All, The Indian Scene,* Department of Education, Ministry of Human Resource Development, Government of India, 1993, pp. 29-30.
5. *Ibid.,* p. 30.
   Census of India, 1991, Series 1, Paper 2 of 1992, pp. 50-52.
6. *India, A Reference Manual,* 1993, p. 101.
7. Samyak, V.K., 1993, *India Beyond Today and Tomorrow,* p.101. Allied Publishers.
8. Rege, K.B., 1973 *Magnitude of Illiteracy in India, 1961-81* NCERT.
9. *Programme of Action* (henceforth *POA*), 1992, Government of India Ministry of Human Resource Development, Department of Education 1993, p. 20.
10. *Report of the CABE Committee on Policy,* Government of India, Ministry of Human Resource Development, Department of Education, January 1992, p. 37.
11. Samyak op. cit., p. 104.
12. *India, A Reference Manual,* 1993, p. 84.
13. *Census of India, 1991, Series 1, Paper 1 of 1993,* p. 3.
14. *Ibid.,* p. 6
15. *Ibid.,* p. 8.
16. *Report of the Working Group on the Welfare of Scheduled Castes* (henceforth *RWGSC*) during the Seventh Five Year Plan (1985-90), 1985, p. 31.

3
Universal Elementary Education

Under Article 45 of the Constitution of India there is a Directive on the State to provide free and compulsory education to all children up to the age of 14. This constitutional obligation of the country envisages universal provision of educational facilities for both primary and upper primary stages. The provision of Article 45 presupposes that the goal of achieving universalisation of elementary education should have been realized by 1960, i.e., within ten years of the commencement of the Constitution. This target date was first revised to 1970, then to 1976, 1988 and 1990.[1] The National Policy on Education (NPE), 1986 fixed revised time targets for achieving universal and free education up to the age of 11 by 1990 and up to the age of 14 by 1995.[2] The revised NPE 1992, however, contemplates providing free and compulsory education of satisfactory quality to all children up to 14 years of age before AD 2000.[3] The new thrust in elementary education emphasizes three aspects: (1) universal access and enrolment; (2) universal retention of children up to 14 years of age, and (3) a substantial improvement in the quality of education to enable children to achieve essential level of learning.[4]

The task of universal education in the age group 6-14 is obviously stupendous and has to be attempted in three phases, to be pursued simultaneously.[5]

(1) The first phase is universal provision of schools. Primary and middle schools will have to be established within easy accessible distance from the home of every child.

(2) The second phase is that of universal enrolment. Although the total enrolment in elementary education in the country has increased from 223 lakh in classes I-VIII in 1950-51 to around 905 lakh in 1979-80,[6] 1360.3 lakh in 1991-92,[7] and 1570.5 lakh in 1995-96,[8] the achievement has been largely offset by population growth on the one hand and by the problem of drop-outs and stagnation on the other. The proportion of enrolment of SC/ST

children continues to be much less than their population, proportion except in case of primary education where the enrolment ratios are comparable to the general enrolment.[9] Again, the number of non-attending children is not equitably distributed between the different States and Union Territories. This is the least in the educationally advanced States like Kerala, Tamil Nadu, Maharashtra and Gujarat. But it forms a very large proportion of the total number of non-attending children in the educationally less advanced States like Uttar Pradesh, Madhya Pradesh, Rajasthan and Orissa.

(3) The third phase is that of universal retention. The drop-outs are still high. According to the Ministry of Human Resource Development estimates in 1995-96, 61 out of 100 children enrolled in Grade I in primary schools seem to reach Grade V and 42 reach Grade VIII.[10] There appears to have been some improvement in the level of retention because according to an estimate made in 1986, of every 100 children that entered Class I, only 49 reached Class V and only 31 reached Class VIII, the corresponding figures for the Scheduled Caste children being 44 and 26 respectively.[11] The drop-out rates will have to be reduced or eliminated so that every child enrolled in Class I remains in school till he or she completes the Upper Primary School or reached the age of 14. That is the reason why the Revised NPE, 1992, has given the highest priority to solving the problem of children dropping out of schools and to ensuring children's retention at schools. This effort will be fully coordinated with the network of non-formal education.[12]

The following paragraphs have been devoted to the study on: (1) Existing schooling facilities - the number of Primary and Upper Primary Schools and the Primary and Upper Primary Schools within various distance slabs, both in general habitations and in predominantly Scheduled Caste habitations; (2) Enrolment of children in primary sections and upper primary sections and the hiatus between the rural and urban areas, between the boys and girls in relation to the general students vis-a-vis the Scheduled Caste students; (3) Drop-outs and stagnation in the primary sections and upper primary sections for the general students as well as the Scheduled Caste students; and lastly, (4) Resources for elementary education, in order to have a comprehensive idea about the position of Scheduled Caste students in the matter of Universal Elementary Education (UEE) in relation to the general students.

Educational Facilities at Different School Stages

In order to achieve the objective of UEE, the most important prerequisite is that schools, both primary and upper primary, are made available in all places for all children, rural and urban, throughout the country. Annexure Table VII shows the educational facilities and enrolment at different school stages in various plan periods, from 1946-47 to 1995-96.

Primary Schools

It would be seen from Annexure Table VII that whereas the number of primary schools almost trebled in the first twenty years of independence (from 1.35 lakh in 1946-47 to 3.87 lakh in 1965-66), the pace of progress considerably slackened during the next thirty years, when it increased by 50 per cent only, the overall increase during these 50 years being four times (from 1.35 lakh in 1946-47 to 5.90 lakh in 1995). The number of primary schools registered an increase of 321 per cent during the period 1950-51 to 1995-96 (from 1.84 lakh to 5.90 lakh). If we consider the fact that the population increased from 36.1 crore to 93.42 crore[13] during the same period, i.e., an increase of 262 per cent, then the increase in the number of primary schools does not appear to be at all impressive. Again, many of these schools have no infrastructural and teaching facilities. The Fifth All-India Survey revealed that in 1986, 0.4 per cent of the primary schools had no teacher, 28.90 per cent had only a single teacher and another 31.86 per cent had only two teachers (the corresponding figures for the rural areas being 0.46 per cent, 31.45 per cent and 34.07 per cent respectively),[14] and 7.52 per cent of the primary schools were functioning in open spaces, 0.49 per cent in tents, 5.53 per cent in thatched huts and 13.92 per cent in *kachcha* buildings and the remaining 72.54 per cent in *pucca*/ partly *pucca* buildings, including one-room ones.[15]

If we take into account the fact that only 26.18 per cent of the primary schools had library facilities, 55.41 per cent had adequate supply of chalks and 71.84 per cent had adequate supply of dusters, 16.74 per cent had both almirahs and trunks/boxes, 15.78 per cent only almirahs and another 36.14 per cent had only trunks/boxes, while 31.34 per cent had neither almirahs nor boxes/trunks for keeping records, 54.50 per cent did not have any mats/furniture for students, 41.75 per cent had no playground facilities and 38.17

per cent schools could not provide either a chair or a table for the teachers,[16] the standard and facilities of teaching in these schools could very well be imagined. A study, initiated in 1989 and conducted in 23 States covering over 60,000 pupils by the National Council of Educational Research and Training (NCERT), the findings of which were released in 1995, has expressed concern over the declining levels in primary schools. It has found the achievements in arithmetic and language in Class V to be lower than Class IV. The study revealed that differences between the aggregate achievement of boys and girls did not have the same direction. Differences in favour of boys were noted in Rajasthan, Tripura, Uttar Pradesh and West Bengal, while the reverse was true in Meghalaya, Punjab, Sikkim and Delhi. No differences were noted in Kerala, Tamil Nadu and Jammu & Kashmir. "The evidence of deterioration in achievement as children move up is disturbing and demands serious attention of administrators and teachers", it said and stressed the need for an intensive study of the problem. Inadequate knowledge of the teachers about their teaching subjects was another finding. About their educational qualifications, the study showed that more than four per cent of the teachers were non-Matriculates, while 17 per cent were graduates, the rest having obtained schooling between Classes X and XII.[17] Another, study conducted jointly by the Indian Statistical Institute (ISI) and the State Council of Educational Research and Training (SCERT) in 1991-93 in 882 Government and non-Government primary schools covering 11,406 students studying in Class IV in 17 districts of West Bengal revealed the dismal standard of learning. 16 per cent of the students could not read at all, while 56 per cent could with difficulty read from the textbooks. Only 20 per cent of the students could achieve the minimum standard fixed at 48 marks for Bengali and 50 for Arithmetic.[18] Looking at how the progress of primary education works, an analyst rightly wonders whether the expansion of educational facilities was meant for educating children or for providing teaching jobs to educated young people.[19]

At present, the whole atmosphere of the schools, particularly those in rural areas — such as the quality of teachers, furniture and educational equipment — is so depressing and unattractive that it does not have the power to hold the children in such schools. It is a mistaken belief that by opening any kind of schools the constitutional obligation of the State for providing free and compulsory elementary education is'discharged. Social justice demands that all the schools, including those in rural areas, should be compatiable to, if not better than, the best schools in the country, so that the children are not deprived of proper educational facilities in these schools. As it stands, not much care had been taken in that direction, especially in the last three decades. Now there is the unique situation of primary schools, even in urban areas, being closed down for dearth of students and at the same time a long queue of students seeking admission in well-run Government schools, not to mention the 'elite' non-Government ones, where only a fortunate few have any chance for admission, may be through the device of 'lottery'. Hence, the plight not only of the children who are denied the opportunity of proper schooling facilities in a 'standard' school, but also of their parents can well be imagined. It has been suggested that the Government should declare all poorly equipped schools as 'Educationally Priority Areas' and bring them to the level of best schools in the country. This is, no doubt, a stupendous task, but as pointed out by Dr K.L. Srimali, himself a former Union Minister for Education, the Government cannot ignore this responsibility, if equality of opportunity to all the children of this country, irrespective of caste, creed, sex, religion or social background, is to be assured.[20] It is good that this point has been taken note of by the revised NPE, 1992, which pledges to give due emphasis on substantial improvement in the quality of education to enable all children to achieve essential levels of learning.[21]

Upper Primary Stage

There is a direct correlation between the number of Upper Primary Schools and the number of Primary Schools, because the number of Upper Primary Schools should be such that each and every child after completing his schooling in the primary section can get a chance to continue his education in the Upper Primary School so as to meet the constitutional obligation of the State to provide free and compulsory upper primary education as well. Though there has been a 21-fold increase in the number of Upper Primary Schools in the 50 years since Independence (from 8,294 in 1946-47 to 171,216 in 1995-96), as Annexure Table VII indicates, and a 14-fold increase during the period 1950-51 to 1995-96, the number of Upper Primary Schools is inadequate enough to meet the demands of children, even after taking into account the fact that only one out of every two children enrolled in Class I in the primary section goes for education in the Upper Primary School. The inadequate number of Upper Primary Schools, is also directly responsible for the heavy drop-out rates and thus, a vicious chain reaction sets in.

It is now envisaged that the infrastructure at the Upper Primary stage will be expanded in order to increase enrolment at that stage. The existing norm of providing an upper primary school within three km walking distance is generally inconvenient for girls. This norm has been relaxed and the new ratio between primary and upper primary school is 2:1. It has been decided to upgrade every second primary school to the upper primary level during the Eighth Plan period. It is, however, primarily the responsibility of the State Governments to observe this norm of school-mapping.[22]

Before 1976, education was largely the responsibility of States, the Central Government being only concerned with certain areas like coordination and determination of standards in technical and higher education, etc. In 1976, through a constitutional amendment, education became the joint responsibility of the Centre and the State. Various centrally sponsored schemes in the elementary education sector have been initiated to supplement the efforts of States for achieving the target of UEE. Operation Blackboard was started in 1987-88 to provide every primary schools in the country with an acceptable level of physical facilities and basic amenities and a second teacher in single-teacher schools. This programme has been expanded to cover upper primary schools and to provide three teachers in every primary school. Provision had been made in the budget for 1994-95 to provide under Operation Blackboard a third teacher in primary schools with enrolment of more than 100 children.[23]

The POA, 1992 calculated that in order to achieve UEE, the school system will have to cater to about 18 crore children by AD 2000, as against about 13.6 crore in 1991-92. The increase in student population would require an additional 11 lakh classrooms to be built in the next seven years. This also calls for increasing the number of teachers from the present 27 lakh to 45 lakh, based on the teacher-pupil ratio of 1:40.[24] This is an uphill task and can only be implemented if there is an political will.

Primary Schools and Upper Primary Schools within Various Distance Slabs

In order to achieve the objectives of UEE, an enjoined in the Constitution, an important prerequisite is that a primary school/ upper primary school be provided within a convenient walking distance from the homes of every child.

Primary Schools

Annexure Table VIII gives the habitatoin and population, of both general and Scheduled Caste, in rural areas according to primary schooling facilities available within various distance slabs as revealed by the All-India Educational Surveys conducted by the NCERT during the period 1957-93.

All Habitations: The first Survey (31 March, 1957) revealed that 59.75 per cent of the rural population had primary sections within habitations of residence, while 83.09 per cent had primary sections either in their habitations or at a walking distance of one mile (1.6 km). It was estimated that 99.03 per cent of the rural population could be served with schooling facilities at the primary stage within the habitations of their residence or 'nearby' by the then existing primary sections and the proposed new schools.

According to the Second Survey (31 March, 1965), out of the 982,251 rural habitations identified, 373,086 (37.98 per cent) accounting for 71.48 per cent of the rural population had primary sections within their own habitations and 856,816 (87.23 per cent) habitations were served by primary sections either within them or within a walking distance of one mile meeting the needs of 94.96 per cent of the rural population.

The Third Survey (31 December, 1973) revealed that out of 953,734 rural habitations identified, 422,766 (44.33 per cent) habitations had primary sections within them, while 720,809 (75.59 per cent) enjoyed the facilities either within the habitations themselves or within a walking distance of one km. These met the needs of 76.12 per cent and 90.34 per cent of the rural population respectively. However, 9.90 per cent of the habitations covering a population of 3.42 per cent was not served even up to two km.

During the Fourth Survey (30 September, 1978) a total number of 964,664 rural habitations were identified among which 451,457 (46.80 per cent) had primary sections within them, while a total of 773,998 (80.24 per cent) habitations were served either through primary sections within them or within a walking distance of one km. In terms of population, 78.53 per cent rural population was served by primary sections in the habitations of residence, while 92.82 per cent of the rural population had these facilities either within their own habitations or within a distance of one km. But, 6.84 per cent of the habitations covering a population of 2.15 per cent was not served even up to two kms.

The Fifth Survey (30 September, 1986) identified a total number of 981,864 rural habitations in the country with a population of 593,560,310. Out of these habitations, 502,343 (51.16 per cent) had primary sections within them, while 320,834 (32.68 per cent) had this facility outside them up to a distance of one km. Thus, as many as 823,177 (83.84 per cent) habitations could be considered to be served according to the above criteria. The remaining habitations were served by the facilities for primary schooling at greater distances. The survey revealed that there were still 52,543 (5.35 per cent) habitations that did not have primary sections even up to a distance of two km.

So far as the rural population was concerned, 80.38 per cent was served by primary sections in the habitation of their residence. Besides, 14.07 per cent of the rural population which did not have a primary section within their own habitations, had this facility at varying distances up to one km. Thus, on the basis of the defined criteria, 94.45 per cent of the rural population had a primary section either within their own habitation or within a walking distance of one km. A small fraction (1.49 per cent) of the rural population was not served even up to a distance of two km.

The Sixth Survey (30 September, 1993) revealed that out of 1,060,612 rural habitations identified, 528,051 (49.79 per cent) habitations had primary sections within them, while 884,089 (83.36 per cent) enjoyed the facilities either within the habitations themselves, or within a walking distance of one km. These met the needs of 77.81 per cent and 93.76 per cent of the rural population respectively. However, 5.92 per cent of the habitations covering a population of 2.00 per cent was not served even up to two km.

So, 87.23 per cent, 75.59 per cent, 80.24 per cent, 83.84 per cent and 83.36 per cent respectively of the habitations in the rural areas had primary sections either within the habitations or within a walking distance of one km (1.6 km in the case of the Second Survey) at the time of the Second, Third, Fourth, Fifth and Sixth, All-India Educational Surveys, covering 94.96 per cent, 90.34 per cent, 92.82 per cent, 94.45 per cent and 93.76 per cent of the rural population respectively. In terms of distance, a sizeable number of habitations were having primary sections at a distance of more than one km and 5.92 per cent of them covering 2.00 per cent of the population were having primary sections not even within a distance of two kms at the time of the Sixth All-India Educational Survey in 1993.

Predominantly Scheduled Caste Habitations: Since one of the inhibiting factors that prevented children belonging to the Scheduled Caste communities from attending schools was non-availability of the schooling facilities in the habitation of residence. Data on availability of the schooling facilities in habitations predominantly populated by Scheduled Castes (i.e., the habitations in which the Scheduled Caste population constitutes 50 per cent or more) were collected for the first time during the Fourth All-India Educational Survey.[25] It was found that out of 964,664 rural habitations, 69,038 (7.1 per cent) were predominantly populated by the Scheduled Castes with a population of 23,219,446. It was also revealed that more than 80 per cent (80.91 per cent to be exact) of these habitations were concentrated in population slabs below 500 and, in fact, 49.69 per cent of such habitations were in the population slabs below 200.[26] Of these habitations, 21,799 (31.58 per cent) habitations had primary sections in them and 53,823 (77.96 per cent) were served by primary sections either in the habitation of residence or within a walking distance of one km. Again, 4,311 (6.24 per cent) habitations did not have primary sections up to a distance of two kms. In terms of population, 62.40 per cent population in these habitations was served by primary sections in the habitation of residence and 88.94 per cent was served either in the habitation of residence or within a distance of one km 2.74 per cent of the population was not served up to two km.

The Fifth Survey revealed that there were 77,780 habitations predominantly populated by the Scheduled Castes with a population of 31,785,596. Of them, 29,297 habitations (37.67 per cent) had primary sections within the habitation of residence while another 34,166 habitations (43.92 per cent) had primary sections within a walking distance of one km, covering a population of 66.31 per cent and 24.83 per cent respectively. There were still 4,230 (5.44 per cent) habitations covering a population of 723,415 (2.28 per cent) that did not have primary sections even up to a distance of two kms.

During the Sixth Survey (30 September, 1993) a total number of 120,517 habitations were identified as predominantly populated by the Scheduled Castes with a population of 53,993,578. Of them, 44,629 (37.03 per cent) habitations had primary sections within the habitations, while another 54.559 (45.27 per cent) habitations had primary sections within a walking distance of one km covering a population of 64.27 per cent and 27.05 per cent respectively. There were still 6638 habitations (5.51 per cent) covering a population of 13,30,644 (2.46 per cent) that did not have primary sections even up to a distance of two km.

A comparative chart of statistics relating to the Sixth Survey, as in Annexure Table VIII, shows that in respect of availability of primary sections within the habitation or at a distance between one km and two km, the Scheduled Caste habitations are comparatively worse than the other habitations, but, for the category 'between 0.1 to 1.0 km', the Scheduled Caste habitations are in a better position, while a near-parity situation exists in respect of the category 'beyond 2 km'. In regard to population served by the primary sections within a certain distance, the Scheduled Caste population is comparatively worse than the other population in both the categories 'up to 1.0 km' and 'beyond 2 km', but is comparatively better placed in 'between 0.1 to 1.0 km' and 'between 1.0 km and 2.0 km' categories.

Upper Primary Schools

Table 3.1 gives the growth of schooling facilities at the upper primary stage since the First Survey, both in regard to other habitations and predominantly Scheduled Caste habitations. When the First and Second All-India Educational Surveys were conducted in the years 1957 and 1965 respectively, a distance of three miles or five km. (approximately) was considered to be a convenient walking distance for children in Classes VI to VIII, i.e., upper primary stage. This distance limit was later brought down to three kms ever since the Third All-India Educational Survey in 1973.

TABLE 3.1
SCHOOLING FACILITIES AT UPPER PRIMARY STAGE IN RURAL HABITATIONS WITHIN VARIOUS DISTANCE SLABS

		%age of Habitation Served within			*%age of Population served within*			*Source*
All-India Survey	*Year in which conducted*	*The Habitation*	*Distance 3 km*	*5 km*	*The Habitation*	*Distance 3 km*	*5 km*	
1	*2*	*3*	*4*	*5*	*6*	*7*	*8*	*9*
				(a) General Population				
First	1957	3.13		50.34				a
Second	1965	7.07		72.39	25.45		82.20	b
Third	1973	8.69	58.26	78.43	28.86	71.97	86.91	c
Fourth	1978	10.74	66.86	85.52	33.47	78.83	92.09	d
Fifth	1986	13.13	74.00	89.84	36.85	83.98		e
Sixth	1993	13.87	76.15	90.28	37.02	85.00	94.70	f
				(b) Scheduled Caste Population				
Fourth	1978	3.59		88.4	12.92	74.14	91.28	g
Fifth	1986	,	74.43			79.38		h
Sixth	1993	6.5	77.64	91.77	18.50	82.54	94.06	i

Sources: a — p. 41 of Fifth All-India Educational Survey, 1986, Vol. I.
b — p. 53 of Fourth All-India Educational Survey, 1978.
c — p. 33 of Third All-India Educational Survey,1973.
d — p. 54 of Fourth All-India Educational Survey, 1978.
e — p. 41 of Fifth All-India Educational Survey, 1986, Vol. I.
f — p. 41 of Sixth All-India Educational Survey, 1993, Vol. I.
g — pp. 63-64 and p. 197 of Fourth All-India Educational Survey, 1978.
h — p. 44 of Fifth All-India Educational Survey, 1986, Vol. I.
i — p. 42 of Sixth All-India Educational Survey, 1993, Vol. I.

General Habitations : All the six All-India Educational Surveys conducted so far reveal that the percentage of habitations served by an upper primary school or section within the walking distance of five kms increased from 50.34 in 1957 to 90.28 in 1993. However, when viewed from the revised distance criterion of three km, the percentage dropped to 76.15 in 1993. This percentage at the time of the Third Survey in 1973 was 58.26. Though the recorded growth could be considered encouraging, it reveals how distant is the goal of providing upper primary schooling facilities within a distance of three km.

There is a similar growth of percentage of the population served by a school at the upper primary stage within a walking distance of three km. From 71.97 per cent in 1973, it has moved up to 85.00 per cent in 1993. This increase in the availability of the facility in 17.89 per cent of the habitations and to 13.03 per cent of the population in 20 years does not apparently look to be spectacular. However, if we consider the difficult geographical conditions in hilly and desert regions in some States, and the existence of a very large number of extremely small habitations, it is no mean achievement.

Predominantly Scheduled Caste Habitations: Table 3.1 reveals that of the habitations predominantly inhabited by the Scheduled Castes during the Fourth Survey, only 3.59 per cent (2,479) habitations were served by middle sections in them catering to 12.92 per cent of population of these habitations. Only 8011 (11.6 per cent) habitations accounting for 8.72 per cent of the population were not served by a middle section within five kms. It is heartening to note that about three-fourths (74.14 per cent) of the population was served within a distance of three kms and 91.28 per cent of the population within a distance of five kms, which compared favourably with the 92.09 per cent in case of the general population.

During the Sixth Survey, 77.64 per cent of the total number of habitations predominantly populated by those belonging to the Scheduled Castes had a school at the upper primary stage within a walking distance of three kms. It is a matter of satisfaction that this percentage was slightly more than the corresponding one for the general population, which was 76.15 per cent. However, the percentage of the population served with an upper primary section in case of the Scheduled Caste habitations was 82.54 as against 85.00 for the general habitations. This difference was due to the fact that the habitations predominantly populated by those belonging to the Scheduled Castes were smaller in size than those of the general population.

Enrolment

Primary Section

Table 3.2 gives the enrolment of children in primary sections (Classes I-V) since 1946-47 along with the corresponding figure of enrolment of the Scheduled Caste children as also their growth percentage.

General Population: The enrolment of children in the primary section has increased manifold since 1946-47. In the first 20 years it increased five times whereas in the next 30 years it more than doubled itself, the overall increase being eleven times during the period 1946-47 to 1995-96 (from 96 lakh to 1097 lakh). Though the enrolment in the primary sections has considerably overtaken the increase of 262 per cent in population during the period 1951-95, all children could not be put through the primary schooling, even within 50 years of Independence.

With the increase in the overall enrolment of children, the enrolment of girls has also increased. Girls constituted 36.20 per cent of the total enrolment in 1965, 37.67 per cent in 1973, 38.27 per cent in 1978 and 40.81 per cent in 1986, as shown in Table 3.3.

The Report of the Sixth Survey (1993) has not been published till now. The Annual Report of the Department of Education, Ministry of Human Resource Development for the year 1996-97, however, indicates that in 1995-96, girls constituted 43.17 per cent of the total enrolment in primary sections (473 lakh out of 1097 lakh).[27] Thus, the girls' enrolment showed a steady rise throughout this 30-year period. In 1965, girls constituted a little over one-third of the total enrolment and in 1995, they constituted more than two-fifths of the total enrolment. Though the percentage of girls' enrolment has increased, it has not yet touched 50 per cent. According to the Ministry of Human Resource Development Report.[28], the States/UTs of Sikkim (48.63 per cent), Kerala (48.68 per cent), Pondicherry (48.58 per cent), Goa (47.97 per cent), Nagaland (47.89 per cent), Daman & Diu (47.82 per cent), Andaman

TABLE 3.2

ENROLMENT OF CHILDREN IN PRIMARY SECTIONS, 1946-95.

Period	*Enrolment of all Children*	*Growth Percentage*	*Source*	*Enrolment of SC Children*	*Growth Percentage of SC Children*	*SC Enrolment as % of Total Enrolment*	*Source*
1	*2*	*3*	*4*	*5*	*6*	*7*	*8*
1946-47	9,647,317		a				
1951-52	16,288,960	68.84	a				
1956-57	23,922,567	46.86	a				
1961-62	29,474,377	23.21	a				
1965	48,834,588	65.68	a				
1973	61,255,290	25.43	a	8,077,567	-	13.19	b
1978	68,602,224	11.99	a	10,106,897	25.12	14.73	c
1986	85,913,478	25.23	a	14,704,908	45.49	17.12	d
1995	109,734,292	27.73	e	18,537,423	26.06	16.89	f

Sources: a — Annexure Table VII.
b — p.30 of Third All-India Educational Survey, 1973.
c — p.51 of Fourth All-India Educational Survey, 1978.
d — p.39 of Fifth All-India Educational Survey, 1986, Vol. I.
e — P.261 of Annual Report, 1996-97, PART-1, Department of Education, Ministry of Human Resource Development.
f — p.263, *Ibid.*

& Nicobar Islands (47.80 per cent), Meghalaya (47.75 per cent), West Bengal (47.59 per cent), Mizoram (47.35 per cent), Maharashtra (47.30 per cent), Punjab (47.28 per cent) and Manipur (47.00 per cent) were slowly approaching the target of 50 per cent of girls' enrolment.

TABLE 3.3

ENROLMENT OF GIRLS IN PRIMARY SECTION

Survey	*Period*	*Rural*	*Urban*	*Total*	*Source*
Second	1965	34.26	43.20	36.20	a
Third	1973	35.79	44.05	37.67	b
Fourth	1978	36.18	44.75	38.27	c
Fifth	1986	39.48	45.16	40.81	d

Sources : a — pp. 3-4 of Second All-India Educational Survey, 1965.
b — p. 28 of Third All-India Educational Survey, 1973.
c — pp. 46-47 of Fourth All-India Educational Survey, 1978.
d — p. 36 of Fifth All-India Educational Survey, 1986, Vol. I.

Though the percentage of girls' enrolment in the rural areas has steadily increased since 1965, from 34.26 per cent in 1965 to 39.48 per cent in 1986 as against an increase from 43.20 per cent to 45.16 per cent in the urban areas during the same period, as Table 3.3 indicates, the percentage of girls' enrolment was comparatively lower in rural areas (39.48 per cent) than in urban areas (45.16 per cent) even in 1986. A better position is expected to be revealed by the Sixth Survey (1993).

Scheduled Castes : As Table 3.2 reveals, the overall enrolment in Classes I to V increased from 612.55 lakh to 686.02 lakh between 1973 and 1987, registering an increase of 11.99 per cent, whereas ,during the same period, the Scheduled Caste enrolment increased from 80.77 lakh to 101.06 lakh accounting for an increase of 25.12 per cent. The overall enrolment in Classes I to V increased from 686.02 lakh to 859.13 lakh between 1978 and 1986, registering an increase of 25.23 per cent, the corresponding increase in case of the Scheduled Caste children being 45.49 per cent. The overall enrolment in Classes I to V increased from 859.13 lakh to 1097.34 lakh between 1986 and 1995 accounting for an increase of 27.73 per cent, the corresponding increase in case of the Scheduled Castes being 26.06 per cent. The increase in enrolment of the Scheduled Caste children during the 22-year period (1973-95) was 119.49 per cent as against a corresponding increase of 79.21 per cent in the total enrolment. This increased enrolment of the Scheduled Caste children in the primary sections has been reflected in the Scheduled Caste literacy rate, which increased by 75 per cent during the decade 1981-91.

In all, there were 18,537,423 Scheduled Caste students in Classes I-V and they constituted 16.89 per cent of the total enrolment in these classes during the year 1995, which was marginally higher than their share in the total population of 16.73 per cent in the 1991 census. The corresponding percentages at the time of the Fifth Survey (1986), Fourth Survey (1978) and Third Survey (1973) were 17.12, 14.73 and 13.19 respectively.

The increase in the Scheduled Caste enrolment, however, did not follow the general trend of an increase in enrolment in rural areas. Rather, it was just the opposite. In their case, the percentage of enrolment in rural areas declined in 1986 compared to 1978. While the percentage of the Scheduled Caste boys' enrolment not only in rural areas but in urban as well decreased, the percentage of the Scheduled Caste girls' enrolment showed an improvement in both rural and urban areas in 1986 compared to 1978, as would be evident from the Table 3.4.

TABLE 3.4
GENERAL VS SCHEDULED CASTE ENROLMENT IN PRIMARY SCHOOLS OF GIRLS AND BOY

	General enrolment				*Scheduled Caste enrolment*			
	Boys	Girls	Total	Source	Boys	Girls	Total	Source
				Fourth Survey (1978)				
Rural	63.82	36.18	75.70		67.31	32.69	79.70	
Urban	55.25	44.75	24.30		59.07	40.93	20.30	
Total	61.73	38.27		a	65.64	34.36		b
				Fifth Survey (1986)				
Rural	60.52	39.48	76.59		62.81	37.19	78.76	
Urban	54.84	45.16	23.41		56.40	43.60	21.24	
Total	59.19	48.81		c	61.45	38.55		d

Sources: a — pp. 46-47 of the Fourth All-India Educational Survey, 1978.
b — p. 51, *Ibid.*
c — p. 36 of the Fifth All-India Educational Survey, 1986, Vol. I.
d — p. 39 *ibid.*

In 1978, the proportion of boys attending schools was more than the girls. Of the total Scheduled Caste enrolment, 65.64 per cent were boys and 34.36 per cent were girls. For the rural areas, the corresponding percentages for boys and girls were 67.31 and 32.69. In the urban areas, girls constituted 40.93 per cent of the Scheduled Caste enrolment.

In 1986, the gap between the boys and girls appeared to have narrowed down. Of the total enrolment of children belonging to the Scheduled Caste in 1986, 61.45 per cent were boys and 38.55 per cent were girls. Girls' enrolment in rural areas (37.19 per cent) was lower than that in urban areas (43.60 per cent).

In 1995, out of the total SC enrolment of 18,537,423, 7,601,593 (41 per cent)[29] were girls whereas it was 43.17 per cent for the general girl students, i.e., a difference of 2.17 percentage point. In 1986, it was 2.26 percentage points (40.81 per cent and 38.55 per cent) and in 1978, it was 3.91 percentage points (38.27 per cent and 34.36 per cent). Thus, the gap was not only between SC boys and SC girls but also between SC girls and General girls has considerably narrowed down over the years. This is a welcome development.

Upper Primary Stage

The enrolment of children in upper primary sections since 1946-47 along with the corresponding figure of enrolment of Scheduled Caste children, as also their growth percentage is given in Table 3.5.

General Population : The enrolment of children in Classes VI to VIII has increased 36 times during the first 50 years of Independence (from 11.30 lakh in 1946-47 to 410.14 lakh in 1995). In the first 20 years it increased two and a half times. When viewed against a nine-fold increase in the enrolment of children in the primary sections during the same period, the progress in the enrolment of children in the upper primary sections after Independence may appear to be satisfactory, but the recent surveys have revealed that we are still far from achieving the target of compulsory free education to all children up to the age of 14. At the time of the Second Survey (1965), only 30.15 per cent of children of the age group 11-13 were in Classes VI-VIII, which marginally improved to 33.15 per cent during the Third Survey (1973), and to 36.92 per cent during the Fourth Survey (1978).[30] In 1985-86, 56.63 per cent

TABLE 3.5

ENROLMENT OF CHILDREN IN UPPER PRIMARY SECTIONS, 1946-47

Period	*Enrolment of all Children*	*Growth Percentage*	*Source*	*Enrolment of SC Children*	*Growth Percentage of SC Children*	*SC Enrolment as Percentage of Total Enrolment*	*Source*
1	2	3	4	5	6	7	8
1946-47	1,129,955		a				
1951-52	1,880,726	67.69	a				
1956-57	4,392,223	133.42	a				
1961-62	12,136,018	176.31	a				
1965-66	10,244,621	-15.59	a				
1973-74	14,387,748	40.44	a	1,218,728		8.74	b
1978-79	17,958,477	24.82	a	2,012,412	65.12	11.21	b
1986	27,272,336	51.69	a	4,006,855	99.11	14.69	b
1995	41,014,136	50.39	c	5,853,823	46.10	14.27	d

Sources: a — Annexure Table VII.
b — pp. 50-51 of the Fifth All-India Educational Survey, 1986, Vol. I.
c — p. 261, Annual Report, 1996-97, Ministry of Human Resource Development, Department of Education.
d — p. 263, *Ibid.*

children of the age group 11-14 were in Classes VI-VIII, which increased to 67.6 per cent in 1995-96.[31]

The overall annual increase in enrolment at the upper primary stage between the Third and the Fourth Surveys was found to be 4.96 per cent, while that was 6.48 per cent between the Fourth and the Fifth Surveys. An encouraging feature of it is that in both the periods, the rate of increase in enrolment has been more in rural areas than in urban areas. For example, the increase in rural areas was 6.0 per cent per annum as against 5.4 per cent in urban areas during the period between the Third and Fourth Surveys. Similarly, the annual increase during the period between the Fourth and the Fifth Surveys was 7.72 per cent in rural areas as against 4.55 per cent in urban areas. Yet, it will be seen from Table 3.6 that rural areas are still lagging behind the urban areas in the matter of achievement of enrolment at the upper primary stage.

TABLE 3.6

ENROLMENT OF GIRLS AND BOYS AT UPPER PRIMARY STAGE IN RURAL AND URBAN AREAS

		Enrolment in Classes VI-VIII					
Survey	*Area*	*Boys*	*Percentage to Total*	*Girls*	*Percentage To total*	*Total*	
1	2	3	4	5	6	7	
	R	6517388	73.36	2366171	26.64	8883559	(60.5)
Third	U	3319758	60.31	2184431	39.69	5504189	(39.5)
(1973)	T	9837146	68.37	4550602	31.63	14387748	
	R	7910325	72.18	3049879	27.82	10960204	(61.0)
Fourth	U	4175944	59.67	2822329	40.33	6998273	(39.0)
(1978)	T	12086269	67.30	5872208	32.70	17958477	
	R	12089291	68.19	5640427	31.81	17729718	(65.0)
Fifth	U	5551065	58.17	3991553	41.83	9542618	(35.0)
(1986)	T	17640356	64.70	9631980	35.30	27272336	

Source: p. 49 of the Fifth All-India Educational Survey, 1986, Vol. I.
R — Rural
U — Urban

According to the Fifth Survey, the total enrolment at the upper primary stage was 27,272,336 out of which 65.0 per cent belonged to rural areas. At the time of the Third Survey, it was 60.5 per cent and at the time of Fourth Survey, it was 61.0 per cent. However, when compared to the child population, the enrolment was considerably lower in rural areas.

A crucial aspect of education in the implementation of Universal Elementary Education which has been neglected in the past is the 'girls' education". The Fifth Survey, like the earlier Surveys, revealed a huge gap in the enrolment between boys and girls at the upper primary stage. This is particularly so in rural areas in many States. According to the Fifth Survey, the percentage of girls at the upper primary stage was 35.30. Though it has slightly increased from 32.70 in the Fourth Survey and 31.63 in the Third Survey, the overall position of girls' enrolment has not changed much in rural areas. In rural areas, the percentage of girls' enrolment has increased from 26.64 in the Third Survey to 31.81 in the Fifth Survey.

The position as revealed in the Sixth Survey (1993) has not yet been made known. But the Department of Education, Ministry of Human Resource Development, Annual Report for the year 1996-97 indicates that in 1995, out of the total enrolment of 4,10,14,136 students, 1,60,42,890 (39.12 per cent) were girls.[32] During the 22-year period (1973-95), the enrolment of girls in the primary sections increased by 8.50 (from 37.67 per cent to 43.17 per cent) percentage points, whereas it increased by 7.49 (from 31.63 per cent to 39.12 per cent) percentage points in the upper primary sections. So, it can be said that the increase in the enrolment of girls students in the upper primary sections was commensurate with that of the primary sections.

Scheduled Castes: The enrolment of children belonging to the Scheduled Caste population at the upper primary stage was 5,853,823 in 1995. The Third Survey (1973) reported an enrolment of 1,218,728 students. Therefore an increase of 380.32 per cent was registered during the period 1973-95 as against a corresponding increase of 185.06 in general enrolment. This shows a tremendous increase in the Scheduled Caste enrolment — an average increase of 17.27 per cent per annum between the period 1973 and 1995. This rate of growth is much higher than that for the general population (4.09 per cent). In spite of this excellent growth in their enrolment, the Scheduled Caste students constituted only 14 27 per cent of the total enrolment in Classes VI-VIII during 1995, which was much below their share in the total population.

Table 3.7 presents the actual enrolment of both boys and girls belonging to the Scheduled Caste population in Classes VI-VIII in rural and urban areas.

TABLE 3.7
ENROLMENT OF THE SCHEDULED CASTE STUDENTS AT UPPER PRIMARY STAGE IN RURAL AND URBAN AREAS

Survey	*Rural*	*Urban*	*Total*	*Boys*	*Girls*	*Total*
1	2	3	4	5	6	7
Third (1973)	796,115 (65.32)	422,613 (34.68)	1,12,8728	923,623 (75.79)	295,105 (24.21)	1,218,728
Fourth (1978)	1,327,159 (65.95)	685,253 (34.05)	2,012,412	1,492,745 (74.18)	519,667 (25.82)	2,012,412
Fifth (1986)	2,732,141 (68.19)	1,274,714 (31.81)	4,006,855	2,759,724 (68.88)	1,247,131 (31.12)	4,006,855

Source : pp. 50-51 of the Fifth All-India Educational Survey, 1986, Vol. I.

At the time of the Fifth Survey, 68.2 per cent enrolment belonging to the Scheduled Caste students was found in rural areas, while the Fourth and Third Surveys reported 65.9 per cent and 65.3 per cent respectively.

As regards the enrolment of girls belonging to the Scheduled Caste population, the Fifth Survey found 31.12 per cent girls in Classes VI-VIII. In the Fourth Survey the percentage of the girls was 25.82 and in the Third Survey 24.21. Though the overall increase in enrolment of girls between the Third and Fifth Surveys (1973-86) was considerably more than the increase in enrolment of the Scheduled Caste students during the same period — 412.29 per cent as against 328.77 per cent — it was still lower than the enrolment of the general girls. The gap between these two categories had, however, narrowed down during this period.

In 1995, out of the total SC enrolment of 58,53,823 students in the middle sections, 21,52,901 (36.78 per cent) were girls.[33] This indicates that the gap between the enrolment of boys and girls had narrowed down over the years — from 24.21 per cent in 1973 to 36.78 per cent in 1995, which is, however, much less than their enrolment in the primary sections which was 41 per cent in 1995. The main reason for the low rate of increase in Scheduled Caste girls' education is the disappointing performance in the State of Rajasthan, Uttar Pradesh, Bihar and Madhya Pradesh, wherein the percentage of girls was the lowest during the year 1995, viz., 20.20, 20.82, 25.25 and 28.91 respectively. The States where the percentage of enrolment of girls belonging to the Scheduled Caste was the highest were Pondicherry (50.19 per cent), Tripura (49.76 per cent), Kerala (48.58 per cent), West Bengal (47.96 per cent) and Manipur (47.18 per cent).[34]

Enrolment Ratio

We can look at this problem from another angle, i.e., the enrolment ratios of students belonging to all communities vis-a-vis the Scheduled Castes. The enrolment ratio is calculated as follows:

$$\frac{\text{Enrolment of SC students on roll}}{\text{Population of SC in the corresponding age group}} \times 100$$

The enrolment ratio of the Scheduled Caste students at Primary Stage increased from 82.2 per cent 1980-81 to 84.8 per cent in 1986-87, 102.2 per cent in 1990-91 and 111.91 per cent in 1995-96. Similarly, the corresponding enrolment at Middle Stage increased from 29.1 per cent in 1980-81 to 40.0 in 1986-87, 47.7 per cent in 1990-91 and 61.33 per cent in 1995-96. The details of the increase in gross enrolment ratios are given in Table 3.8.

The enrolment ratio of Scheduled Caste students at the Primary Stage increased at a greater speed during the decade 1986-95. It even overtook the enrolment ratio for the total enrolment. However, the enrolment ratio of Scheduled Caste students was much lower than the corresponding enrolment ratio for students belonging to all communities at the Upper Primary Stage.

The state-wise enrolment ratios of general students and SC students at primary stage and upper primary stage in 1995-96 are given in Tables 3.9 and 3.10 respectively so that an idea could be had about the inter-state variations in the enrolment ratios of SC students and that of SC girls in relation to general students and general girls.

TABLE 3.8
ENROLMENT RATIO OF SCHEDULED CASTE AND TOTAL ENROLMENT RATIO DURING 1980-96

Class		*1980-81*	*1986-87*	*1990-91*	*1995-96*
		(a) Total Enrolment			
Classes I-V	Girls	69.9	79.21	85.97	93.3
	Total	84.6	95.96	101.03	104.3
Classes VI-VIII	Girls	31.1	38.95	46.13	54.9
	Total	44.2	53.14	60.11	67.6
		(b) Scheduled Caste Enrolment			
Classes I-V	Girls	57.8	64.8	80.6	95.12
	Total	82.2	84.8	102.2	111.91
Classes VI-VIII	Girls	16.2	26.5	33.3	46.77
	Total	29.1	40.0	47.7	61.33
Source		a	b	b	c

* relates to non-SC/ST students.

Sources: a — State-wise Information on Education of Scheduled Castes and Scheduled Tribes, Ministry of Education, 1985, p. 4.
b — Programme of Action, 1992, Ministry of Human Resource Development of Education, p. 35.
c — Annual Report, 1996-97, Ministry of Human Resource Development, Department of Education, pp. 262 and p.264.

TABLE 3.9
ENROLMENT RATIO OF GENERAL STUDENTS AND SCHEDULED CASTE STUDENTS IN CLASSES I-V IN 1995-96

Sl. No.	*States/UTs*	*General*			*Scheduled Caste*		
		Boys	*Girls*	*Total*	*Boys*	*Girls*	*Total*
1	2	3	4	5	6	7	8
1.	Andhra Pradesh	99.6	89.9	94.9	140.68	121.73	131.4
2.	Arunachal Pradesh	115.5	103.9	110.0	25.33	27.50	26.2
3.	Assam	133.4	124.0	128.8	257.62	239.07	248.5
4.	Bihar	93.0	55.4	75.1	102.04	51.39	77.8
5.	Goa	90.6	100.5	95.1	105.31	116.77	110.4
6.	Gujarat	158.3	106.8	131.41	213.43	155.06	182.9
7.	Haryana	86.4	84.8	85.6	108.12	105.84	107
8.	Himachal Pradesh	108.4	113.7	110.8	115.15	115.75	115.4
9.	Jammu & Kashmir	88.6	72.2	81.2	96.14	83.43	90.6
10.	Karnataka	131.1	123.5	127.4	158.59	137.96	148.5

(Continued on next page)

(*Table 3.9 Contd...*)

1	2	3	4	5	6	7	8
11.	Kerala	98.4	95.4	96.9	107.64	102.45	105
12.	Madhya Pradesh	112.9	88.9	101.4	129.68	93.68	112.2
13.	Maharashtra	125.5	120.2	122.9	268.31	257.96	263.3
14.	Manipur	93.1	100.3	96.4	153.65	179.19	165
15.	Meghalaya	105.3	125.4	114.4	...	...	...
16.	Mizoram	112.6	124.8	118.1	...	...	...
17.	Nagaland	120.6	135.5	127.3	...	...	...
18.	Orissa	113.4	78.2	95.6	152.85	95.29	123.7
19.	Punjab	92.4	90.7	91.5	134.77	129.98	132.4
20.	Rajasthan	129.3	75.3	103.4	121.53	48.62	86.5
21.	Sikkim	104.2	118.4	110.6	103.75	114.00	108.4
22.	Tamil Nadu	159.3	145.6	152.6	176.76	154.02	165.6
23.	Tripura	122.7	124.4	123.5	147.05	144.14	145.7
24.	Uttar Pradesh	104.3	72.0	89.1	88.94	42.05	68.8
25.	West Bengal	128.6	122.3	125.5	129.79	116.93	123.5
26.	A & N Islands	76.6	69.2	72.9	...	...	...
27.	Chandigarh	36.4	40.4	38.2	82.85	92.93	87.3
28.	D & N Haveli	121.0	102.7	112.7	74.67	87.00	79.6
29.	Daman & Diu	93.0	88.6	90.8	...	...	...
30.	Delhi	67.7	77.8	72.1	83.49	91.76	87
31.	Lakshadweep	125.3	125.3	125.3	...	...	...
32.	Pondicherry	117.2	133.3	124.5	141.29	170.18	154.4
	India	114.5	93.3	104.3	127.56	95.12	111.91

Source: Annual Report, 1996-97, Ministry of Human Resource Development, Department of Education, pp. 262 and 264.

TABLE 3.10
ENROLMENT RATIO OF GENERAL STUDENTS AND SCHEDULED CASTE STUDENTS IN CLASSES VI-VIII IN 1995-96

Sl. No.	*States/UTs*	*General*			*Scheduled Caste*		
		Boys	*Girls*	*Total*	*Boys*	*Girls*	*Total*
1	2	3	4	5	6	7	8
1.	Andhra Pradesh	57.3	41.8	49.7	67.03	42.63	55.082
2.	Arunachal Pradesh	61.3	45.2	53.3	21	13	17
3.	Assam	91.6	65.9	79.1	190.13	161.51	176.16
4.	Bihar	47.5	21.9	35.3	38.2	14.03	26.62
5.	Goa	95.1	84.1	89.6	69.5	55.33	62.79
6.	Gujarat	81.1	61.5	71.6	117.32	76	97.32
7.	Haryana	70.9	56.7	64.2	65.81	47.85	57.36
8.	Himachal Pradesh	112.7	90.5	101.8	90.14	63.06	76.80

(Continued on next page)

(Table 3.10 Contd...)

1	2	3	4	5	6	7	8
9.	Jammu & Kashmir	73.3	46.8	60.5	80.24	59.68	70.34
10.	Karnataka	78.1	66.8	72.6	81.78	57.60	70.04
11.	Kerala	105.1	101.5	103.3	118.31	114.56	116.46
12.	Madhya Pradesh	91.6	43.3	68.4	80.98	35.62	59.19
13.	Maharashtra	92.4	77.2	85.0	180.15	137.47	159.53
14.	Manipur	69.4	63.2	66.4	93.64	92	92.86
15.	Meghalaya	51.6	45.5	48.6	...	...	...
16.	Mizoram	67.3	67.7	67.5	...	...	...
17.	Nagaland	52.5	51.2	51.9	...	...	...
18.	Orissa	73.0	39.8	56.2	71.82	43.17	57.29
19.	Punjab	74.0	65.0	69.7	79.75	64.83	72.65
20.	Rajasthan	79.9	32.0	56.9	78.13	21.44	50.93
21.	Sikkim	50.5	50.8	50.7	50.83	43.17	47.00
22.	Tamil Nadu	118.2	99.5	109.1	111.26	84.74	98.34
23.	Tripura	66.8	57.0	62.0	63.43	66.69	65.01
24.	Uttar Pradesh	72.3	34.9	54.7	53.34	15.82	35.70
25.	West Bengal	102.8	91.5	97.2	72.03	69.00	70.59
26.	A & N Islands	73.5	68.6	71.1	...	...	...
27.	Chandigarh	36.4	34.9	35.6	68.33	59.02	68.83
28.	D & N Haveli	59.2	40.8	50.6	99	93	96.00
29.	Daman & Diu	92.5	84.7	83.7	...	...	...
30.	Delhi	71.1	67.3	69.3	72.66	68.66	70.83
31.	Lakshadweep	112.0	81.2	96.6	...	...	...
32.	Pondicherry	113.0	109.6	111.3	147.36	154.87	151.03
	India	79.5	54.9	67.6	74.88	46.77	61.33

Source: Annual Report, 1996-97, Ministry of Human Resource Development, Department of Education, pp. 262 and 264.

Primary Stage

Though the enrolment ratio of the Scheduled Caste students has crossed the enrolment ratio of total enrolment in 1990-91 as well as in 1995-96, the enrolment ratio of SC girls has also been higher than that of the total enrolment for girls in 1995-96. Whereas there was sexwise variation in the level of enrolment ratio achieved, there was much variation between different States. It woud appear from Table 3.9 that the enrolment ratios of total SC students and of SC boys and SC girls exceeded that of general total students and of general boys and girls in 19 States/UTs — Andhra Pradesh, Assam, Goa, Gujarat, Haryana, Himachal Pradesh, Jammu & Kashmir, Karnataka, Kerala, Madhya Pradesh, Maharashtra, Manipur, Orissa, Punjab, Tamil Nadu, Tripura, Chandigarh, Delhi and Pondicherry. The enrolment ratios were lower than that of general students on all the three counts in six States/UTs — Arunachal Pradesh, Rajasthan, Sikkim, Uttar Pradesh., Dadra and Nagar Haveli, and West Bengal (except boys). In the State of Bihar, though the enrolment ratios of total SC students and of SC boys were higher than that of the general students, it was lower in respect of girls.

Another feature which merits special mention is that the enrolment ratios not only of SC boys but also of SC girls were 100 per cent or more in many States. It has even crossed 200 per cent in the three States (Assam, Gujarat and Maharashtra) in relation to SC boys and in two States (Assam and Maharashtra) in relation to girls. But for the poor performance of Rajasthan and Uttar Pradesh, the two populous States, the All-India enrolment ratio of SC children would have been even higher.

Upper Primary Stage

In contrast to the primary stage, the enrolment ratio of SC student at the upper primary stage was much lower than the corresponding enrolment ratio for students belonging to all communities. In case of SC girls, though the enrolment ratio has nearly trebled during the period 1980-95, it was much lower than the corresponding enrolment ratio for girls belonging to all communities. In spite of this dismal picture, it does not necessarily mean that the enrolment ratio of the Scheduled Caste students was lower than that of the general students in all the States. As would be evident from Table 3.10, in 11 States/UTs, the enrolment ratio of SC students was higher than that of the general students in respect of all the three categories. These are: Andhra Pradesh, Assam, Gujarat, Jammu & Kashmir, Kerala, Maharashtra, Manipur, Chandigarh, Dadra & Nagar Haveli, Delhi and Pondicherry. The enrolment ratio of SC children was higher than that of the general students in respect of total enrolment and either of boys/girls in three States - Orissa (except boys), Punjab (except girls), and Tripura (except boys). So many States/UTs — 14- registering an increase in enrolment ratio in the middle section is really an achievement. If the educationally backward States of Bihar, Rajasthan, Madhya Pradesh and Uttar Pradesh had given better attention to the progress in education, specially of the Scheduled Caste children, then the overall position not only of SC children but also of general students would have been much better.

Wastage - Drop-outs and Stagnation

Universalisation of Elementary Education in its totality is still an elusive goal and will continue to be so if universal retention of children in schools cannot be ensured. The ideal situation in the field of education will be achieved when a child enrolled in Class I leaves the school only after completing his or her education in Class VIII within the stipulated period. As the 'Programme of Action, 1986' put it crisply, "enrolment by itself is of no importance if children do not continue beyond one year, many of them not seeing the school for more than a few days."[35] Even in 1986, drop-out rates continued to be significant, retention of children in schools was low and wastage considerable.[36] In one word, wastage in Indian school education has set at naught the efforts directed at Universal Elementary Education.

The term 'wastage' covers the phenomena 'drop-outs' and 'repetition'. Whereas 'drop-out' refers to the premature withdrawal of pupils from the educational cycle at a particular stage of instruction, 'repetition', 'retardation' or 'stagnation' refers to the continuance of pupils in the same grade for more than one academic year on account of unsatisfactory progress. While drop-outs directly constitute wastage, repetition adds to it by lengthening the effective duration of the course.[37]

Drop-out and stagnation are higher among the Scheduled Caste students than among the students of other communities on account of varied reasons. Parental attitudes have not been very much encouraging and supportive towards education of their children who are either detained at home to look after the younger ones or to assist their parents in their occupation so as to supplement their earnings. When a student drops out in the middle of his or her educational career, the entire investment on education goes waste. The educational development of the students is also impaired on account of frequent failure leading to stagnation. As a significant measure for combating the stagnation problem, the Ministry of Education had suggested to the States "to introduce the ungraded system and 'non-detention' policy so that every child shall complete one class in each year and will be promoted to the next higher grade till he or she completes class VIII, but with adequate safeguards by way of periodic assessment and evaluation on a continuing basis".[38] This policy of non-detention at the primary stage is retained in the Revised National Policy on Education, 1992 as well,[39] making evaluation as disaggregated as feasible. Since no-detention policy is envisaged at the primary stage, the main function of evaluation will be diagnostic in nature so as to provide remedial help to the pupils. A flexible scheme of Continuous Comprehensive Evaluation (CCE) at the elementary stage has been evolved so as to make the evaluation process an integral part of teaching and learning at this stage. These evaluations will be reported in the form of grades on a comprehensive proforma.[40] This policy of discontinuance of the system of 'promotion' from one class to the higher one on the basis of results in the annual examination has solved the problem of 'stagnation' at the primary stage.

The staggering proportions of drop-outs render the task of fulfilling the constitutional objective of universal elementary education rather impossible and make the system of school education counter-productive. One can get an idea of the wastage from the decline in the number of children enrolled in different classes from I-V and VI-VIII.

Primary Stage

The distribution of enrolment in Classes I-V as revealed in the Educational Survey is given in Table 3.11.

Though the retention rates have consistently shown signs of improvement during the period 1965-86, it is still far away from achieving the optimum level when retention rate could be brought to 100 per cent or near it in Class V.

As was expected, the retention rate of the Scheduled Caste children was much less compared to the general children, which has, however, improved quite appreciably during the period 1973-86. It is, however, expected that the retention rates of both the general students and the Scheduled Caste students would improve further during the Sixth Survey (1993).

Upper Primary Stage

The retention rates at the upper primary stage are, however, comparatively better as Table 3.12 will indicate.

TABLE 3.11

DISTRIBUTION OF ENROLMENT FROM CLASSES I TO V

Class	*Second Survey*	*Third Survey*		*Fourth Survey*		*Fifth Survey*	
	General	*General*	*SC*	*General*	*SC*	*General*	*SC*
1	2	3	4	5	6	7	8
Class I	37.77	34.93	39.79	31.42	34.91	28.97	29.91
Class II	20.89	22.67	23.17	22.91	23.33	21.25	21.84
Class III	16.80	17.73	16.70	18.55	18.10	19.07	19.22
Class IV	13.67	13.72	11.80	14.87	13.48	16.40	15.90
Class V	10.87	10.95	8.54	12.25	10.18	14.31	13.13
Source	a	b	c	d	e	f	g
Retention rate in class V	28.78	31.35	21.46	39.00	29.16	49.40	43.90

Sources : a — p. 31 of the Second All-India Educational Survey, 1965.
b — p. 29 of the Third All-India Educational Survey, 1973.
c — p. 30, *Ibid.*
d — p. 40 of the Fourth All-India Educational Survey, 1978.
e — p. 51, *Ibid.*
f — p. 38 of the Fifth All-India Educational Survey, 1986.
g — p. 39 of *Ibid.*

TABLE 3.12
RETENTION RATES AT THE UPPER PRIMARY STAGE

Class	Second Survey General	Third Survey General	Third Survey SC	Fourth Survey General	Fourth Survey SC	Fifth Survey General	Fifth Survey SC
1	2	3	4	5	6	7	8
Class VI	39.93	40.12	40.54	39.40	40.48	38.51	38.67
Class VII	32.59	32.77	32.54	32.92	32.94	32.70	32.94
Class VIII	27.48	27.11	26.92	27.68	26.58	28.79	28.39
Source	a	b	c	d	e	f	g
Retention rate in Class VIII	68.82	67.57	66.40	70.25	65.66	74.77	73.42

Sources : a — p. 47 of the Second All-India Educational Survey, 1965.
b — p. 44 of the Third All-India Educational Survey, 1973.
c — pp. 328-33, *Ibid.*
d — p. 71 of the Fourth All-India Educational Survey, 1978.
e — pp. 884-87, *Ibid.*
f — p. 48 of the Fifth All-India Educational Survey, 1986, Vol. I.
g — pp. 1072-73, *Ibid.*

The improvement in retention rates was, however, less spectacular when compared with that at the primary stage; the increase was only 8.65 per cent during the period 1965-86. An important trend at upper primary stage is that the retention rates of both the general students and the Scheduled Caste students have reached near parity by 1986. The same trend is likely to be maintained in the Sixth Survey (1993) as well.

Drop-outs

One can get a better idea of the wastage from the drop-out rates in different classes from Table 3.13.

TABLE 3.13
DROP-OUT RATES IN 1988-89

Classes	*Scheduled Caste*			*General*		
	Male	*Female*	*Total*	*Male*	*Female*	*Total*
I-V	47.24	53.39	49.62	46.74	49.69	47.93
I-VIII	64.37	73.60	67.78	59.38	68.31	65.40
I-X	76.52	85.62	79.88	72.68	79.46	75.36

Source : Educational for All, The Indian Scene, Ministry of HRD, p. 119.

Drop-out rate is calculated as follows:

Drop-out rate from Classes I to V for the year 1988-89=

$$\frac{\text{No. of students enrolled in Class V in 1988-89}}{\text{No. of students enrolled in Class I in 1984-85}} \quad 100$$

Drop-out rate from Classes I to VIII for the year 1988-89=

$$\frac{\text{No. of students enrolled in Class VIII in 1988-89}}{\text{No. of students enrolled in Class I in 1981-82}} \quad 100$$

The ratio does not take into account repeaters and children who enter the system after Class I.

The drop-out rates at all the three stages of education in 1988-89 are higher among the SC students than the general students and it is still higher among the SC girl students when compared with that of the general girl students and the SC boy students.

The yearwise break-up-of drop-out rates among all communities and the Scheduled Castes for both the primary stage and the upper primary stage for the years 1980-81 to 1988-89 is given in Table 3.14 shows that the drop-out rates among the students belonging to all communities in the primary section as well as in the upper primary section declined over the years during this 8-year period, though an upward swing was noticed in 1986-87 in the primary section and in 1983-84 in the upper primary section.

As regards the SC students, the declining trend in drop-out rates was arrested in the primary section in two years — 1982-83 and 1987-88 — and in the upper primary section only in 1985-86. The overall improvement in the drop-out rates in both the primary section and the upper primary section was, however, higher than that of the students belonging to all communities. An improvement of 11.13 percentage points in the primary section and that of 9.06 percentage points in the upper primary section was registered as against 10.54 percentage points and 8.63 percentage points respectively, in regard to students belonging to all communities during this 8-year period.

TABLE 3.14

DROP-OUT RATES : 1980-81 TO 1988-89

Period	*Scheduled Caste*		*All Communities*	
	Primary	*Upper Primary*	*Primary*	*Upper primary*
1980-81	60.16	76.84	75.66	86.71
1981-82	59.21	74.76	74.00	84.99
1982-83	60.27	72.44	72.44	83.35
1983-84	57.84	72.36	70.63	83.74
1984-85	55.40	72.16	69.40	82.86
1985-86	52.53	72.50	65.56	81.86
1986-87	50.79	69.15	66.12	80.19
1987-88	51.38	68.81	65.21	80.01
1988-89	49.62	67.78	64.53	78.08

Source: Education for All, The Indian Scene, Ministry of Human Resource Development, Department of Education, 1993, p. 117.

The latest information regarding drop-out rates is available for the categories of students only during the year 1995-96. These were 39.37 at primary stage and 57.77 for Classes I-VIII.[41] Though no separate figures for the Scheduled Caste students are available, it is quite likely that the drop-out rates have declined in their case as well. The latest information for the Scheduled Castes is available for the year 1989-90, which indicates that the drop-out rates have decreased marginally to 49.03 at primary stage and to 67.62 at upper primary stage. The Statewise break-up is given in Table 3.15.

TABLE 3.15

STATE-WISE BREAK UP OF DROP-OUT RATES OF SCHEDULED CASTES-1989-90

Sl. No.	State/UT	*Primary Stage*			*Middle Stage*		
		Boys	Girls	Total	Boys	Girls	Total
1.	Andhra Pradesh*	60.53	65.83	62.80	77.41	85.44	80.85
2.	Arunachal Pradesh	-	-	-	-	-	-
3.	Assam	46.88	55.89	50.80	64.91	63.47	64.30
4.	Bihar	67.69	73.50	69.33	83.37	89.79	85.04
5.	Goa	39.27	32.06	36.02	55.52	65.68	60.28
6.	Gujarat	24.95	45.55	34.13	50.40	70.34	59.11
7.	Haryana	33.90	43.18	38.00	59.19	75.36	65.71
8.	Himachal Pradesh	36.29	36.50	36.39	32.27	41.88	36.44
9.	Jammu & Kashmir	39.27	30.39	35.84	50.11	52.73	51.10
10	Karnataka	51.05	59.59	54.90	62.11	73.77	67.08
11.	Kerala	0	1.78	0.50	19.04	15.60	17.37
12.	Madhya Pradesh	36.31	52.37	42.41	62.34	79.40	67.78
13.	Maharashtra	38.54	51.58	44.60	52.90	69.77	60.54
14.	Manipur	79.86	82.21	81.03	84.89	86.07	85.48
15.	Meghalaya	33.13	41.88	37.46	27.86	51.85	39.64
16.	Mizoram	-	-	-	-	-	-
17.	Nagaland	-	-	-	-	-	-
18.	Orissa*	55.16	59.22	56.77	75.97	83.19	78.76
19.	Punjab	36.53	41.59	38.79	63.36	70.56	66.52
20.	Rajasthan	60.42	74.37	63.89	69.53	83.53	72.18
21.	Sikkim	70.00	67.85	69.04	84.96	83.67	84.37
22.	Tamil Nadu	22.56	29.68	25.92	51.04	53.14	51.97
23.	Tripura	58.21	63.09	60.47	75.87	81.84	78.60
24.	Uttar Pradesh	32.89	51.69	38.86	57.92	69.52	60.87
25.	West Bengal*	58.54	66.71	61.92	74.18	84.88	79.02
26.	A & N Islands	-	-	-	-	-	-
27.	Chandigarh	0	0	0	0	0	0
28.	D & N Haveli	18.60	36.96	28.09	0	0	0
29.	Daman & Diua	-	-	-	-	-	-
30.	Delhi	33.74	35.74	34.63	47.68	58.61	52.79
31.	Lakshadweep	-	-	-	-	-	-
32.	Pondicherry	0	0	0	0	11.96	5.45
	India	45.93	53.74	49.03	64.29	73.10	67.62

* Relates to 1988-89

@ Included in Goa

Source : Educational Development of Scheduled Castes and Scheduled Tribes, Status and Programmes, Ministry of Human Resources Development, Department of Education, 1995, p. 32.

It would appear from Table 3.15 that the drop-out rates of the Scheduled Caste students varied from State to State. These were less than the All-India drop-out rates at the primary stage in 16 States/UTs, viz., Goa, Gujarat, Haryana, Himachal Pradesh, Jammu and Kashmir, Kerala, Madhya Pradesh, Maharashtra, Meghalaya, Punjab, Tamil Nadu, Uttar Pradesh, Chandigarh, Dadra and Nagar Haveli, Delhi and Pondicherry, while these were higher than the All-India average in the remaining ten States of Andhra Pradesh, Assam, Bihar, Karnataka, Manipur, Orissa, Rajasthan, Sikkim, Tripura, and West Bengal for all the three categories of students — boys, girls and total.

More or less the same picture emerged in the drop-out rates at the Middle stage. These were lower than the All-India average for all the three categories of students in 14 States/UTs, namely, Goa, Gujarat, Himachal Pradesh, Jammu & Kashmir, Kerala, Maharashtra, Meghalaya, Punjab, Tamil Nadu, Uttar Pradesh, Chandigarh, Dadra and Nagar Haveli, Delhi and Pondicherry and were lower for only two categories of students in three States — Assam (except boys), Haryana (except girls) and Karnataka (except girls). All these States/UTs except Assam and Karnataka registered the same trend at the primary stage. In the remaining nine States of Andhra Pradesh, Bihar, Manipur, Orissa, Rajasthan, Sikkim, Tripura, West Bengal and Madhya Pradesh (except boys), the drop-out rates were higher than the All-India average. All these States except Madhya Pradesh showed the same trend at the primary stage. Thus, while Assam and Karnataka had improved their position at the middle stage, Madhya Pradesh could not retain its position.

Another fact which should not be lost sight of is the miserable position of the Eastern and North-Eastern States. Orissa, Bihar, West Bengal, Sikkim, Tripura and Manipur, and partly Assam have failed to tackle the problem of drop-outs among the Scheduled Caste students in an effective manner.

Unless effective ways and means are devised for drastically minimizing the staggering proportions of drop-outs the constitutional objective of imparting free and compulsory elementary education to all children, including those belonging to the Scheduled Castes, up to the age of 14 will remain an unattainable one.

Resources for Education

The egalitarian goals and the practical, development-oriented objectives of Indian society can be realised only by making adequate investments in education for the implementation of such programmes as: the universalisation of elementary education; liquidating illiteracy, equality of access to educational opportunities to all sections throughout the country; enhancing the social relevance, quality and functional effectiveness of educational programmes; generating knowledge and developing technologies in scientific fields crucial to self-sustaining economic development and creating a critical consciousness of the values and imperatives of national survival.[42]

Education is funded largely by the Central and State Governments — the post-Independence contribution of non-governmental sources of func'ing dwindled from about 32 per cent in 1950-51 to 11.2 per cent in 1983-84[43]. Elementary education is funded almost wholly by the Government.

After the inception of planning in 1950-51, spending on education as a proportion of GNP increased steadily from about 1.2 per cent to about 3.9 per cent in 1989-90, while expenditure on elementary education increased from 0.48 per cent of GNP in 1950-51 to 1.72 per cent in 1989-90, as will be eviident from Table 3.16.

TABLE 3.16
PUBLIC EXPENDITURE ON EDUCATION AS A SHARE OF GNP (PERCENTAGE)

Year	*Total*	*Primary*	*Upper Primary*	*Elementary*
1950-51	1.2	0.40	0.08	0.48
1960-61	2.5	0.45	0.31	0.76
1970-71	3.1	0.65	0.47	1.12
1980-81	3.1	0.71	0.48	1.19
1989-90	3.9			1.72*

Source : Education for All, The Indian Scene, Ministry of HRD, p. 77.

While the increase was significant, the availability of resources was inadequate due to financial constraints and competing priorities. As a result, a study by the NCERT found that it was the hard core of the population which had been left out and it might take 50-100 years with the present rate and existing policies to provide universal elementary education to these communities.[44]

It is, indeed, axiomatic that without adequate resources educational reconstruction would remain a mere slogan. The Kothari Commission on Education (1966) had first put forth the view that public expenditure on education should be six per cent of the GNP. This view has been reiterated time and again and has come to acquire the characteristic of a national resolve. The NPE, 1992 had proclaimed that from the Eighth Plan onwards the outlay on education would uniformly exceed six per cent of the National Income.[45] Though all the Five-Year Plans had stressed the importance of education as crucial for national development and survival, in actuality, education has been treated as residual sector in the matter of allocation of resources.[46] The Plan outlay for education which was 7.2 per cent in the First Five-Year Plan, declined to 2.6 per cent in the Sixth Five-Year Plan. This declining trend was arrested in the Seventh outlay.[47] In the Eighth Five-Year Plan 4.9 per cent of the plan-resources were allocated to education.[48] But during the first three years of the plan, education received only 3.5 to 3.9 per cent of the total plan resources. Hence there is a need to significantly step up the plan resources for education. Unless this is done, the national commitment, reiterated by the Prime Minister, of allocating six per cent of national income from the Ninth Plan period onwards would remain an elusive goal for a long time. As a matter of fact, it is now being increasingly felt[49] that 8 to 10 (or higher) per cent of the national income would be needed for the educational system to fulfil the government's stated goal of education for all by AD 2000.

An intra-sectoral analysis of the plan expenditure on education during the different plan periods, given in Table 3.17, brings into sharp focus two distinct periods since planning began in 1950-51, with the plan holiday (1966-69) as the transition period. In the first phase, expansion of higher and technical education received a higher *inter se* priority. Two things happened by the end of the first phase, one , there was a realisation that the network of higher and technical institutions was sufficient to meet the anticipated manpower needs. Secondly, elementary education came to be perceived as a minimum need.[50]

TABLE 3.17

PLAN EXPENDITURE ON DIFFERENT SECTORS OF EDUCATION (PERCENTAGE)

Sector	*Ist Plan Expdt. 1951-56*	*2nd Plan Expdt. 1956-61*	*3rd Plan Expdt. 1961-66*	*Plan Holiday Expdt. 1966-69*	*4th Plan Expdt. 1969-74*	*5th Plan Expdt. 1974-79*	*6th Plan Expdt. 1980-85*	*7th Plan Expdt. 1985-90*	*Annual Plan Outlay 1990-92*	*8th Plan Outlay 1992-97*
Elementary education	56	35	34	24	30	35	33	37	37	47
	(850)	(950)	(2010)	(750)	(2390)	(3170)	(8360)	(28490)	(17290)	(92010)
Secondary education	13	19	18	16	18	17	21	24	22	18
	(200)	(510)	(1030)	(530)	(1400)	(1560)	(5300)	(18320)	(10530)	(34980)
Adult education						9	6	9	9	
							(2240)	(4700)	(4160)	(18480)
Higher education	9	18	15	24	25	22	22	16	12	8
	(140)	(480)	(870)	(770)	(1950)	(2050)	(5590)	(12010)	(5880)	(15160)
Others	9	10	12	11	14	4	4	3	2	4
	(140)	(300)	(730)	(370)	(1060)	(1060)	(1080)	(1980)	(1180)	(7510)
Technical education	13	18	21	25	13	12	11	14	17	14
	(200)	(490)	(1250)	(810)	(1060)	(1070)	(2730)	(10830)	(8230)	(27860)
Total	100	100	100	100	100	100	100	100	100	100
	(1530)	(2730)	(5890)	(3230)	(7860)	(9120)	(25300)	(76330)	(47270)	(196000)

Note: Figures in parenthesis in millions of rupees

Source : *Education for All, The Indian Scene*, MHRD, 1993, p. 121.

Many educationists also questioned the policy of laying greater stress on the expansion of higher education at the cost of elementary education, even though the rates of social return from secondary and general higher education are considerably less than those from primary and middle school education.[51] Studies have also been made in the United States which establish beyond doubt that the rate of return from college education is lower than that from elementary and secondary education.[52] So there was a plea for allocation of funds for the improvement of the quality of primary education,[53] which calls for a total change in the strategy of educational planning.

Perhaps, realising the importance of spending on elementary education, there was a marked jump upward in public expenditure on elementary education, as would be evident from Table 3.18.

It would be seen that during the 1980s alone, the public expenditure on elementary education increased by 4.5 times, from Rs 15,373 million at the beginning of the decade to Rs 68,883 million in 1989-90. Elementary education began to receive a higher proportion of plan allocation on education. This trend which received appreciable boost after NPE, 1986 has become still more pronounced during the Eighth Plan. While the expenditure on education accounted for 4.2 per cent of the GNP in 1992-93[54], the share of elementary education in total public expenditure on education is about 45 to 46 per cent.[55]

In the past, elementary education in India was funded largely by the State Governments. The National Policy on Education, 1886 gave an operational definition to the concurrency of education enshrined in the Constitution by the Constitution (Forty-Second Amendment) Act, 1976. With the launching of centrally sponsored schemes to promote non-formal education and improve the quality of elementary education, the Central Government's share in plan expenditure on elementary education has increased considerably. From a mere 9.7 per cent of the total plan expenditure on elementary education in 1984-85, it increased almost four-fold to 37.1 per cent in 1987-88, but again decreased to 28 per cent in 1991-92.[56]

An upswing in Central financial support for universalisation of elementary education satisfied a long-felt need. As early as 1986, the Indian Education Commission had articulated the need for according priority to elementary education. Again, in 1929, the Hartog Committee, after making an indepth study of primary education, observed that the Government of India should serve as a centre of educational information for the whole of India and should be constitutionally enabled to make good such financial deficiencies in the interests of India as a whole.[57]

TABLE 3.18

PLAN AND NON-PLAN EXPENDITURE ON ELEMENTARY EDUCATION IN INDIA

(Rs. in.10 million at current prices)

Year	*Plan*	*Expenditure Non-Plan*	*Total*	*Share in Total Expenditure on Education*
1980-81	91.0	1446.3	1537.3	45.6
	(5.9)	(94.1)	(100)	
1981-82	103.4	1557.3	1660.7	43.8
	(6.2)	(93.8)	(100)	
1982-83	158.9	2013.2	2172.1	45.6
	(7.3)	(92.7)	(100)	
1983-84	218.8	2256.5	2475.3	45.4
	(8.8)	(91.2)	(100)	
1984-85	263.5	2591.4	2854.9	44.9
	(9.2)	(90.8)	(100)	
1985-86	266.7	3181.6	3448.3	46.2
	(7.7)	(92.3)	(100)	
1986-87	346.2	3535.5	3881.7	45.9
	(8.9)	(91.1)	(100)	
1987-88	572.9	4283.8	4856.7	46.6
	(11.8)	(88.2)	(100)	
1988-89	714.0	4825.8	5539.8	44.6
	(12.9)	(87.1)	(100)	
1989-90	966.1	5922.2	6888.3	45.8
(14.0)	(86.0)	(100)		
1990-91(R)	907.4	6917.2	7824.6	45.2
	(11.6)	(88.4)	(100)	
1991-92(B)	963.3	7050.9	8014.2	43.8
	(12.0)	(88.0)	(100)	
Rate of growth	23.92%	15.49%	16.12%	

Source : *Education for All, The Indian Scene*, MHRD, 1993, p. 122.

The expenditure on elementary education received a boost, ironically not under the nation's own constitutional obligation, but under the pressure of International Bodies. The World Conference on Education for All, held in Jomtien (Thailand) in March 1990, is a landmark in that it unfolded the possibility of donor assistance for basic education on terms which do not compromise national autonomy in policy and programme formulation and implementation.[58] A number of foreign-aided programmes have been designed to address certain facets of universal elementary education, like the *Mahila Samakhya* (a Dutch assisted Programme in the States of Gujarat, Karnataka, Andhra Pradesh and U.P.); Andhra Pradesh Primary Education Project (fully supported by the Overseas Development Administration); *Siksha Marmi Project Lok Jumbish* in Rajasthan (supported by the Swedish International Development Authority); Bihar Education Project (supported by the UNICEF); U.P. Basic Education Project (funded by World Bank) and District Primary Education Programme (DPEP) supported by a multitude of international organizations in a number of States. A large part of the expenditure of these projects is fully reimbursed by external aid organizations and the remaining part is met by the States. According to an estimate,[59] the expected flow of external funding for elementary education during the Eighth Five-Year Plan (1992-97) for all these projects would be Rs. 24,517.9 million out of the total outlay of Rs. 29,262.9 million. This leads many to caution that the growth in public expenditure on elementary education is largely a 'borrowed growth'.[60] There may be a setback in the inflow of foreign funds due to the economic sanctions imposed by the US, Japan and Germany in the wake of the Pokhran explosion.

Challenge Ahead

Whatever it might be, it cannot be denied that over the years there has been a very impressive increase in the number and spread of institutions as well as enrolment in the elementary sector of education. Universal provision of institutions has been substantially achieved at the primary stage (Classes I-V). According to the Sixth All-India Educational Survey (1993), 93.76 per cent of the rural population had primary schools within a walking distance of one km; 85.00 per cent of the rural population was served with the upper primary sections within a walking distance of three km. For the pre-dominantly Scheduled Caste habitations in rural areas, the corresponding figures were 91.32 per cent and 82.54 per cent respectively. The number of primary schools increased from 1.84 lakh in 1951-52 to 5.90 lakh in 1995-96. Similarly, the number of upper primary schools went up to 1.71 lakh in 1995-96 as compared to 12,124 in 1951-52. The gross enrolment of 6-11 age group increased from 42.6 per cent in 1950-51 to 104.3 per cent in 1995-96. Likewise, the gross enrolment of 11-14 age group increased from 12.7 per cent in 1950-51 to 67.6 per cent in 1995-96. For the Scheduled Caste children the enrolment ratio in primary stage was 111.91 per cent and in upper primary stage 61.33 per cent in 1995-96. Though the participation of the Scheduled Castes is now more or less in proportion to their share in population at the primary stage, the sex disparity still persists. Much ground is yet to be covered to achieve parity in the matter of education at the upper primary stage.

The drop-out rates, however, continued to be very high. It was 47.93 per cent in Classes I-V and 65.40 per cent in Classes I-VIII in 1988-89 compared to 49.62 per cent and 67.78 per cent respectively for the Scheduled Caste students. The main causes of wastage in education among the SC students have been identified as social disability, persistent poverty, poor nutritional standards, poor home conditions with unhealthy environments and inadequate accommodation, apprehensions of rejection on account of perpetual exploitation and failures, internalised feelings of disappointing experiences in life and as a consequence the overall apathy towards education, especially when children in their families are treated as economic assets, who start contributing to the family income by their work at an early age. Highlighting the fact that children from these communities are generally first generation learners, the Working Group on Development and Welfare of Scheduled Castes during the Eighth Five-Year Plan commented that it is to be recognized and accepted that economic development of the Scheduled Castes in isolation is not a solution to their problems and educational development as an integrated part of their comprehensive development package has to be properly monitored.[61]

The National Policy on Education, 1986 and its Programme of Action gave unqualified priority to Universal Elementary Education and introduced many innovations. The emphasis was shifted from enrolment *per se* to enrolment as well as retention. The NPE 1986 was unambiguous about removal of disparities and attainment of equalisation of educational opportunities for the Scheduled Castes, Scheduled Tribes and other backward sections, specially girls. The

POA detailed a number of strategies aimed at accelerating their rate of enrolment and retention. The need for concerted efforts for bringing about equality of educational opportunity and achievement for the Scheduled Castes, Scheduled Tribes, and other backward sections of the society was reiterated time and again. In 1992, some modifications were undertaken to the NPE, 1986. This revised NPE, like the previous one, placed greater stress on the education of the Scheduled Castes, Scheduled Tribes, other educationally backward sections and areas, minorities and physically and mentally handicapped. The central focus in the Scheduled Castes' educational development in this revised NPE, 1992, is their equalisation with non-SC population at all stages and levels of education — rural male, rural female, urban male and urban female.[62] The Programme of Action (POA) on the new NPE, 1992, was formulated after taking into account the experience gained in the implementation of NPE, 1986 and its POA. The 1992 POA, like the previous one, also contains a separate section on the education of the Scheduled Castes. Some of the important programmes of action, apart from reservations and specific incentives, which have a bearing on Universal Elementary Education of the Scheduled Castes, are as follows:

(1) In opening primary and upper primary schools priority would be given to the needs of the Scheduled Caste habitations and hamlets. As far as possible, pre-primary section will be an integral part of such schools.

(2) For the Scheduled Caste children access and enrolment will be assured primarily in the formal school. Where the Scheduled Caste children are unable to attend the formal school, provision for non-formal and distance education centres will be made to ensure universal access and enrolment.

(3) It will be the responsibility of the teachers to organize drives at the beginning of every academic session to enrol all school-age children, specially girls, belonging to the Scheduled Castes, Scheduled Tribes and other backward sections. For this purpose, active assistance of voluntary agencies and local communities shall be taken. Traditional and folk media can be very effective in reaching parents and children in remote areas to motivate them.

(4) Adequate incentives will be provided for the children of the Scheduled Castes, Scheduled Tribes and other backward sections in the form of scholarships, uniforms, textbooks, stationery and mid-day meals.

(5) Operation Blackboard shall cover within a period of two years all schools in tribal areas and *'Harijan Bastis'* irrespective of the date on which the school was set up.

(6) The indigent families among the Scheduled Castes/ Scheduled Tribes will be given incentives to send their children, particularly girls, to schools.

(7) It will be ensured that Minimum Level of Learning (MLL) already set-up for primary schools will be achieved and that the necessary standards of three rupees are acquired by all children in the Scheduled Caste/Scheduled Tribe communities. Effective methodologies for measurement of MLL will be implemented.

(8) Where teachers are unavailable in schools located in the Scheduled Caste/Scheduled Tribe localities, crash programmes for giving suitable training to eligible persons from Scheduled Castes/Scheduled Tribes will be started. The eligible amongst them will be appointed as teachers in the schools.

(9) A chain of pace-setting institutions from primary to higher secondary will be established in areas of the Scheduled Caste/Scheduled Tribe concentration for providing quality education to talented learners as well as for upgrading ther achievement levels of comparatively slow learners in these communities.[63]

It is, no doubt, a fact that along with the other segments of population the SC population have also enjoyed the fruits of Universal Elementary Education and there is no dearth of governmental efforts in ensuring that the SC population should also register progress as much as, if not more than, the general population. It would, however, not be proper to assume that all the Scheduled Castes in a State/UT have attained the same standard in elementary education or that all the regions in a State have progressed uniformly in Universal Elementary Education. The various reports including survey reports of the Government, discussed above, have not projected the castewise disparities in the matter of educational facilities or achievements among the Scheduled Castes in elementary education. We have seen in Chapter II that there was considerable hiatus between one Scheduled Caste community and another and between one region and another in the matter of literacy. Some Scheduled Caste communities have progressed, while others have not. It is quite likely that similar disparities exist between one Scheduled Caste community and another, and between one region and another in the matter of UEE as well. Though the POA, 1992 talks of 'participative planning' to formulate familywise and childwise design of action to ensure that every child attends school[64] , and completes the elementary education until the age of 14 years, sadly enough, not much study on this aspect of the problem in the matter of realization of UEE has been conducted. The urgent need of the day is to identify the Scheduled Caste communities as also the areas which have been denied the fruits of UEE so that, corrective and remedial measures can be taken to rectify the imbalances and the disparities, so as to improve their prospects for further education. Unless this is done, some Scheduled Caste communities will continue to remain educationally backward as they are now, and the UEE in its totality will remain an elusive goal.

References

1. *RWGSC* during the Seventh Five Year Plan (1985-90), 1985, p. 33.
2. *Report of the Fifth All-India Educational Survey,* 1986, Vol. I, National Council of Educational Research and Training, p. 13.
3. *National Policy on Education* (henceforth *NPE*), 1986 with modifications undertaken in 1992, Ministry of Human Resource Development, Department of Education, New Delhi, para 5.12, p. 20.
4. *Ibid.,* para 5.5, p. 18.
5. *Education in the Fifth Five Year Plan,* 1974-79, Ministry of Education, 1972, p. 14.
6. *Fourth Report of the Commission for Scheduled Castes and Scheduled Tribes (1981-82),* p. 61.
7. *Education for All, The Indian Scene,* Department of Education, Ministry of Human Resource Development, December 1993, p. 112.
8. *Annual Report, 1996-97,* Department of Education, Ministry of Human Resource Development, p. 261.
9. *Programme of Action* (Henceforth *POA*), 1992, p. 35.

10. *Annual Report, 1996-97*, Department of Education, Ministry of Human Resource Development, pp. 267-68.
11. *Report of the Fifth All-India Educational Survey*, 1986, Vol. I, *op.cit.*, pp. 1012-13 and 1018-19.
12. *NPE*, 1992, para 5.12, p. 20.
13. *Selected Educational Statistics*, 1996-97, Ministry of Human Resource Development, Department of Education, p.v.
14. *Report of the Fifth All-India Educational Survey*, op. cit., Vol. II, pp. 888-89.
15. *Ibid.*, Vol. I, p. 116.
16. *Ibid.*, Vol. II, pp. 135-75.
17. *The Statesman*, February 2, 1995, p. 6.
18. *Ananda Bazar Patrika*, March 26, 1995, p. 5.
19. Acharya, Paramesh, *Education: Politics and Social Structure*, In *Education and the Progress of Change*, ed. Ratna Ghosh and Mathew Zachariah, Sage Publications, 1987, p. 71.
20. Srimali, K.L., Planning for Equality of Educational Opportunity, In *School Education in India*, pp. 91-96 ed. P.L. Malhotra, B.S. Parakh and C.H.K. Misra, National Council of Educational Research and Training.
21. *NPE*, 1992, p. 18.
22. *POA*, 1992, para 7.5.4., p. 38
23. Para 40 of the Budget Speech, 1995, *The Statesman*, March 16, 1995, p. 10.
24. *POA*, 1992, para 7.5.5., p. 38.
25. *Report of the Fourth All-India Educational Survey*, 1978, p.21.
26. *Ibid.*, pp. 13-14.
27. *Annual Report, 1996-97*, Department of Education, Ministry of Human Resource Development, p. 261.
28. *Ibid.*
29. *Ibid.*, p. 263.
30. *Report of the Fourth All-India Educational Survey*, 1978, p. 53.
31. *Annual Report, 1996-97*, Department of Education, Ministry of Human Resource Development, p. 28.
32. *Ibid.*, p. 261.
33. *Ibid.*, p. 263.
34. *Ibid.*
35. *POA*, 1992, p. 34.
36. *Ibid.*
37. *IAMR Occasional Paper No. 1/1972*, Institute of Applied Manpower Research, New Delhi, p. 1.
38. *RWGSC* during the Seventh Five Year Plan, 1985, p. 32.
39. *NPE*, 1992, p. 18.
40. *POA*, 1992, p. 107.
41. *Annual Report*, 1996-97, Ministry of Human Resource Development, Department of Education, pp. 267-68.

42. *NPE*, 1992, pp. 48-49.
43. *Education for All, The Indian Scene*, op. cit., p. 76.
44. Nautiyal, K.C. and Sharma, Y.D., 1979, *Equalisation of Educational Opportunities for Scheduled Castes and Scheduled Tribes*, p. 27, NCERT.
45. *NPE*, 1992, para 11.4, pp. 49-50.
46. *Report of the CABE Committee on Policy*, Ministry of Human Resource Development, Department of Education, January, 1992, p. 74.
47. *NPE, 1986, Implementation Report*, p. 22, Ministry of Human Resource Development, Department of Education, September 1987.
48. Tilak, Jandhyala, B.G. 1995, Budget for Education, *The Hindu*, April 14.
49. *Ibid.*
50. *Education for All, The Indian Scene*, op. cit., p. 80.
51. Blaug Mark, *An Introduction to the Economics of Education*, pp. 240-41, London, Allen Lane, The Penguine Press, 1970.
52. Walter L. Garms and Others, School Finance, *The Economics and Politics of Public Education*, Prentice Hall Inc. 1978, pp. 56-58, quoted by K.L. Srimali, Planning for Equality of Educational Opportunity, In *School Education in India*, p.93. Ed. P.L. Malhotra, et al, *op cit.*
53. Shrimali, K.L., *Ibid.*, pp. 93-4.
54. Tilak, Jandhyala, B.G., *The Hindu*, April 14, 1995, p. 8.
55. *Education for All, The Indian Scene*, op. cit., p. 82.
56. *Ibid.*
57. *Interim Report of the Indian Statutory Commission (Hartog Committee)* 1929, p. 346.
58. *Education for All, The Indian Scene*, op. cit., p. 88.
59. *Ibid.*, p. 124.
60. Tilak, Jandhyala B.G., *The Hindu*, April 14, 1995, p. 8.
61. *RWGSC* during the Eighth Five Year Plan (1990-95), 1990, p. 42.
62. *NPE*, 1992, p. 11.
63. *POA*, 1992, pp. 5-7.
64. *Ibid.*, p. 34.

4

Special Facilities for Educational Advancement of the Scheduled Castes

Articles 15(4) and 46 of the Constitution of India provide special safeguards for the educational development of the Scheduled Castes and the Scheduled Tribes and enable the State to make special provisions for their educational advancement. The directives enshrined in the Constitution have been reflected in various Five - Year Plans which have sought to raise the level of education among the Scheduled Castes and the Scheduled Tribes. In the First and Second Five-year Plans, the educational schemes for the Scheduled Castes and the Scheduled Tribes were the following:

1. Scholarships (pre-matric and post-matric);
2. Opening ot Schools in Tribal Areas;
3. Grants of books, hostel fees;
4. Opening of Residential Schools, Balwadis Community Centres, etc.

Gradually the scope of programmes for educational development in the various five-year plan periods broadened. A mid-term appraisal of the Fourth Plan showed that nearly half of the Backward Classes Sector allocation (48 per cent) was mainly spent on educational programme alone.[1] The pattern of educational programmes for the Scheduled Castes of the Government of India and of the State Governments is given below:

Central and Centrally Sponsored Programmes

A number of Centrally Sponsored Schemes are being continued for the Scheduled Castes, the Scheduled Tribes and other backward classes. These are:

(i) Post-matric scholarships;

(ii) Pre-matric scholarships for children of those engaged in unclean occupations;
(iii) Boys' and Girls' Hostels;
(iv) Book Banks;
(v) Upgradation of merit of SC/ST students;
(vi) Coaching and allied schemes;
(vii) National Overseas Scholarship and passage grants for higher studies abroad; and
(viii) Grants-in-aid to voluntary organizations.

In addition to these, two schemes in the central sector have also been approved, viz.,

(ix) Educational complex in low literacy pockets for development of women's literacy in tribal areas, and
(x) Special educational development programmes for Scheduled Caste girls belonging to very low literacy levels.

These programmes are in addition to the special thrust given to the weaker sections in the general programmes for educational development like opening of schools, running of Non-Formal Education (NFE) Centres and Adult Education Centres, schemes of Operation Blackboard, upgradation of merit of the SC/ST students, etc.[2] Except the National Overseas Scholarship Scheme, all others are of the type of 50:50 sharing basis between the Centre and the States.[3]

State Sector Schemes (selected ones)

1. Scholarships and stipends at various levels;
2. Supply of textbooks, stationery, equipment, uniform, sports material;
3. (*a*) Administration of Balwadis, Primary Schools, Middle Schools, Higher Secondary Schools;
(*b*) Attendance prize to students;
4. Residential Schools;
5. Amenities to boarders in private hostels and financial assistance for sharing rental accommodation;
6. Hostels (and reservation of seats in general hostels);
7. Merit Scholarships;
8. Expenses of those reading in public schools;
9. Reimbursement of examination fees and tuition fees at various levels of education;

10. Excursions;
11. Mid-day meals;
12. Loans to students for pursuing education;
13. Vocational craft classes;
14. Introduction of modern trades and training centres for self-employment;
15. Coaching and study centres;
16. Awards to teachers;
17. Houses for teachers.[4]

In addition, the Ministries of Education, Labour and Agriculture and the University Grants Commission have also been providing various other facilities to the Scheduled Caste/ Scheduled Tribe students, namely,

(i) Reservation of seats in educational institutions including Engineering and Medical colleges, Technical Institutions, Sainik schools and Navodaya vidyalayas Kendriya vidyalayas;
(ii) Relaxation in age and marks for admission;
(iii) Research scholarships and fellowships.

There is no separate scheme for award of scholarships/stipends to the SC/ST students under the Ministry of Education. However, reservations have been made for the SC/ST students at pre-matric level under the two following schemes of the Ministry (now Ministry of Human Resource Development):

Pre-matric Scholarships

Rural Talent Scholarships Scheme : The objective of this scheme is to achieve greater equalization of educational opportunities by providing a fillip to the development of potential talents from rural areas by educating them in good schools. Under this scheme, scholosarships are granted to talented students from rural areas from classes VIII to XII. The total number of scholarships available under this scheme at present is 43,000 per year. Out of this, 13, 000 scholarships are reserved for the SC/ST students. The rates of scholarship vary from Rs 30/ to Rs 100/ per month in accordance with the stage at which the student is enrolled and whether he or she is a hosteller or non-hosteller.[5] The selection of students under this scheme is done at two stages. At the first stage, selection is made through an examination conducted at block level. The selected candidates have to appear in a test conducted at district level at the second stage. Final selection is made with Community Development Block as a unit and the top students in the order of merit are awarded scholarships blockwise.

Post-matric Scholarships/Fellowships Offered by the University Grants Commission

(i) Junior Research Fellowships: The University Grants Commission conducts a national level test for recruitment to the post of Lecturers and for the award of Junior Research Fellowship (JRF) to ensure minimum standards of the entrants in the teaching profession and research. SC/ST candidates are provided relaxation up to 10 per cent cut-off marks for the JRF test and all the Scheduled Caste and Scheduled Tribe candidates qualifying for the JRF are awarded Fellowship. In case no vacancy is available, UGC provides Supernunerary positions of JRF to the universities. The JRF is available for five years.

50 JRFs are awarded every year in Science and Humanities including Social Sciences to SC/ST candidates who appear in National Eligibility Test (NET) and qualify the eligibility test for lecturership.[6]

(ii) Research Associateships : The UGC awards Associateships to undertake research in the field of Science, Humanities, Social Sciences, Engineering and Technology and Gandhian Studies. The Associateship is tenable initially for a period of three years and extendable for another term not exceeding two years.

The total number of awards under the scheme is 260 every year, out of which 40 positions are reserved for the Scheduled Caste/ Scheduled Tribe candidates. The Associateships are awarded in different slabs ranging between Rs. 2800-Rs. 3300- to Rs 4325- Rs. 5000, per month. The award also covers a contingency grant of Rs. 7, 500 p.a. and Rs. 10000 p.a. for Humanities and Science subjects respectively.[7]

(iii) Research Fellowship in Engineering and Technology : The UGC awards 60 research fellowships every year in Engineering and Technology including Agricultural Technology, to undertake advanced study and research leading to Ph.D. The age limit for the

award is 40 years, relaxable by five years for SC/ST candidates.[8]

(*iv*) *Teacher Fellowship :* The UGC provides short-term teacher fellowship of one year duration to enable teachers in affiliated colleges to do M.Phil or Ph.D. Teachers are paid a living expense allowance of Rs 750 per month, and a travelling allowance to and from the research centre. A contingency grant of Rs 5000 per annum for teachers in Humanities and Social Sciences, and Rs 7500/ per annum for teachers in Science subjects is also available under the Scheme.[9]

Fifty Teacher Fellowships (20 for Ph.D. and 30 for M.Phil are awarded to teachers belonging to SC/ST categories.[10]

Scholarships under the National Council of Educational Research and Training (NCERT)

(*i*) *National Talent Search Scheme (NTS):* The NCERT is operating a scheme of National Talent Scholarships aimed at identifying and nurturing talent at the post-secondary stage. Under this scheme, 750 scholarships are offered every year to talented students of which 70 scholorships have been reserved for the SC/ST candidates. These are available from class XI onwards up to post-graduation level.[11]

(*ii*) *Scholarships in Regional Colleges of Education:*Scholarships are awarded to the SC/ST students admitted to the four regional colleges of education run under the NCERT. The rates of scholarships vary depending on the level of the course.[12]

(*iii*) *Educational and Vocational Guidance Course:* All the Scheduled Caste/Scheduled Tribe students admitted to the course of educational and vocational guidance are awarded scholarships.[13]

Scholarships Offered by the Ministry of Labour

(*i*) ITI Scholarships: A stipend is awarded to the SC/ST trainees admitted to ITIs. To supplement the Government of India stipend, some State Governments like Andhra Pradesh, Himachal Pradesh, Madhya Pradesh, Maharashtra, Orissa, Tamil Nadu, Uttar Pradesh Delhi and Pondicherry have their own schemes for award of scholarships/stipends to the SC students pursuing studies in ITIs. The rates of stipends, however, vary from State to State.[14]

(*ii*) *Apprentice Training:* All apprentices recruited under the Apprenticeship Act, 1961 are paid stipends at the rate prescribed under Rule 7 of the Apprenticeship Rules, 1962. These vary from Rs 400 to Rs 700 per month. The Boards of Apprenticeship Training make special efforts to provide training facilities to all the applicants belonging to the Scheduled Castes/Scheduled Tribes even in excess of the quota earmarked for these communities. The candidates under the Apprenticeship Training Scheme are selected by the industrial organisations/establishments, and necessary instructions are given to them to ensure selection of all the SC/St candidates who apply for training under the scheme.[15]

(*i*) *For study in Agriculture and Veterinary Sciences:* No less than 240 scholarships @ Rs 300 per mouth with a contingent grant of Rs 750 per annum are provided exclusively to the SC/ST students for study at graduate level in Agricultural and Veterinary Sciences.

(*ii*) *Fellowships awarded by ICAR:* Twenty per cent of scholarships are reserved for the SC/ST students in Junior Fellowship, Senior Fellowship and Post-Doctoral Fellowship awarded by the Indian Council of Agricultural Research. These are for Masters, Ph.D, and Post-doctoral courses respectively.[16]

Note : It is quite likely that the rates under the various schemes, mentioned in the foregoing paragraphs, have been revised by this time.

Centrally Sponsored Schemes

Post-matric Scholarships Scheme

One of the most important Centrally Sponsored programmes under the Backward Classes Sector is the scheme to award post-matric scholarships to the SC/ST students pursuing their studies in recognized educational institutions in India. The Elyperumal Committee on Untouchability, Economic and Educational Development of the Scheduled Castes considered the post-matric scholarships Scheme "as the most extensive in coverage and far-reaching in significance in the educational advancement of Scheduled Castes."[17] The objective of this scheme is to provide financial assistance to the SC/ST students studying at post-matriculation/post-secondary level so as to enable them to complete their higher education in College/Univirsity as well as through

Correspondence Courses including distance and continuing dostamce and centinuing education. This is an open ended scheme under which the number of beneficiaries is not determined by the plan outlay and all the eligible SC/ST students are awarded scholarships. The level of expenditure reached at the end of each plan period becomes committed and is taken over by the States. Only the outlays, over and above that level, whether due to an increase in the number of scholarships or due to an increase in their rates, or both, are met by the Central Government. Started during 1944, the scheme was meant only for the Scheduled Castes and its implementation restricted to the then British Indian Provinces only. The scope of the scheme was extended in 1948-49 to benefit the Scheduled Tribes. During the first year of its implementation 114 Scheduled Caste students got the scholarships and in 1948-49, the number of the Scheduled Castes and the Scheduled Tribes beneficiaries was 647 and 84 respectively. Till 1958-59, the scheme was implemented by the Ministry of Education, but with the increasing number of scholarships and for quick disbursement of scholarships, the Post-matric Scholarships Scheme is implemented through the State Governments/Union Territory Administrations, according to the regulations framed by the Government of India. The scheme was transferred from the ministry of Education to the Department of Social Welfare in January 1968 and later to the Ministry of Home Affairs and it is now being administered by the Ministry of Social Justice and Empowerment, which releases funds to the States/UTs for the operation of the Scheme.

The Post-matric Scholarships Scheme covers maintenance allowance, reader charges for blind students, reimbursement of compulsory non-refundable fees, expenses on approved study tours and preparation of thesis/dissertation papers, and book allowance for students pursuing correspondence courses etc. As per the Government of India regulations governing the Post-Matric Scholarships Scheme, the Scheduled Castes (Hindus, Sikhs and neo-Buddhists) and the Scheduled Tribes are eli[5]gible for award of such scholarships irrespective of their place of study. Those pursuing their post-matric studies outside their home State/UT are also sanctioned scholarships by their respective State/UT to which they belong. The Scheduled Castes converted to Christianity are not eligible for Government of India post-matric scholarships. Those in full-time employment but continuing their post-matric studies are not given maintenance allowance under the scheme. The means test adopted for the Scheduled Caste students is also now applicable for the Scheduled Tribe students and those whose parents' annual income exceeds Rs 44,500 are not considered eligible for award of this scholarship. The scheme also benefits only the first two children of the parents and the third and subsequent children are denied benefits of such scholarships. This restriction has been relaxed in case of girls with effect from October 1, 1995.

Prior to 1974-75, the rate of post-matric scholarships was fixed at Rs 27 per month for day scholars and Rs 40 per month for boarders in undergraduate classes. The rate for students pursuing professional courses was Rs 60 per month for day scholars and Rs 75 for boarders. The rates were revised during 1974 which varied from Rs 50 to Rs 100 per month in case of day scholars, and Rs 75 to Rs 125 for hostellers depending on the course of their study.[18]

The scheme has been modified w.e.f. 1-10-95, thereby revising the maintenance allowance rates, income ceilings for eligibility and study courses. It has been decided to revise income ceiling once in two years and to link it with the Consumer Price Index for Industrial Workers.

The present rates[19] of maintenance allowance under the scheme of Post-matric Scholarships for the SC/ST students are as in Table 4.1 :

TABLE 4.1
MAINTENANCE ALLOWANCE RATES UNDER THE POST-MATRIC SCHOLARSHIP SCHEME GROUPS COURSES IN BRIEF

		Rate of Scholarship	
		Day Scholar	*Hosteller*
1	2	3	4
A	Degree and Post Graduation level Courses in Medical (including B.A. M.& S. etc.), Engineering, Agriculture, Veterinary Science, Fisheries, etc.	Rs 190	Rs 425
B	Diploma level courses in Medical, Engineering etc., Commercial Pilot License course, Degree and post		

(*Continued to next page*)

	Graduation Courses in Business Administration, Nursing/Pharmacy, etc., Post graduate courses in Science subjects. Other diploma courses in Professional and technical subjects.	Rs 190	Rs 290
C.	Certificate courses in Engineering/ Technology, etc., Diploma courses in Agriculture, Pharmacy, Veterinary Science, Fisheries, Dairy Development, Degree/Post-graduate and Diploma courses in Teacher's Training, Library Science, Physical Education etc. Post-graduate courses in Arts and Commerce subjects.	Rs 190	Rs 290
D	General Courses up to graduate Level (2nd year and onwards).	Rs 120	Rs 230
E	Classes XI and XII in 10+2 system, Intermediate courses and first year of general courses up to graduate level.	Rs 90	Rs 150

Students pursuing correspondence courses including distance and continuing education are now eligible to get book allowance of Rs 500 p.a. in addition to reimbursement of compulsory course fees[20].

The scheme also provides for study tour charges up to Rs 500 per annum[21] thesis typing/printing charges up to Rs 600, and a reader allowance for blind scholars of Rs 100, Rs 75 and Rs 50 per month for courses in Groups A, B, C, D and E respectively.[22]

To supplement the Government of India scholarship amount, the Government of Andhra Pradesh has sanctioned full mess charges to the SC/ST hostellers. Under this scheme, the entire boarding and lodging charges, which are more than the rates prescribed by the Government of India, are sanctioned by the State Government, and the expenditure over and above the Government of India rates is met from the State funds. The SC/ST students of postgraduate and professional courses residing in College/University attached hostels, are also given full mess charges and pocket money of Rs 25 per month per boarder over and above the Government of India maintenance allowances. The additional amount paid by the State Government to the students of intermediate and postgraduate courses is Rs 25 and Rs 55 respectively, and is meant for hostellers. In addition to the above, the State Government also sanctions book grants and stipends for the students doing their research.

The Government of Tamil Nadu is supplementing the Government of India post-matric scholarship amount. The amount of State post-matric scholarship being more than the amount sanctioned by the Government of India, the difference in the amount is met by the State Government.

The rates of Post-matric scholarships prescribed by the Government of Uttar Pradesh for different courses of studies are also more than the Government of India rates and the difference of the scholarship amount incurred over and above the rates fixed by the Government of India is met from the State funds.[23]

The Government of Karnataka sanctions extra boarding and lodging charges up to Rs 150 per month, if the Government of India post-matric scholarship holders reside in recognized hostels.

In Kerala, students who are awarded Government of India post-matric scholarships are also allowed to enjoy the financial assistance from the State Government scheme to the extent the Government of India scholarship falls short of the amount of State scholarship.[24]

The number of Post-matric scholarships awarded to the SC/ST students and the total expenditure incurred every year since the inception of the scheme up to the Sixth Five-Year Plan (1984-85) may be seen in Annexure Table IX. The growth of this scheme over the years can be judged from the fact that in 1944-45, the first year of its introduction, there were only 114 scholarship holders under this scheme. The number of tribal scholarship holders was 84 in 1948-49 when it was introduced for them for the first time. This number rose to 5.06 lakh (4.28 lakh SC and 0.78 lakh ST) at the end of the Fifth Plan period (1979-80) and to 8.86 lakh at the end of the Sixth Plan period (1984-85). The number of scholars was of the order of 12.24 lakh (9,24 lakh SC and 3.00 lakh ST) at the end of the Seventh Plan period (1989-90)[25] and 20.79 lakh estimated at the end of the Eighth Plan Period (1992-1997).[26]

The expenditure incurred for the implementation of this scheme during the Sixth Plan period was 140.94 crore,[27] and an allocation of Rs 114.57 crore was made for the Seventh Plan.[28] During the Eighth Plan period (up to December 31, 1996) a total of Rs 511.64 crore have been released to the States/UTs.[29] The annual committed liability of the State Governments on this account during the Eighth Plan period was Rs 142.37 crore[30], which is likely to increase to nearly Rs 300 crores during the Ninth Plan period.

As Annexure Table IX reveals, up to 1984-85 a total of 80,41,768 students including 1,269,550 students belonging to the Scheduled Tribes had been covered under this scheme. Another 169.99 lakh SC/ST scholars including roughly 34 lakh belonging to the Scheduled Tribes have been benefited by this scheme during the period 1985-86 to 1996-97 as shown in Table 4.2.

TABLE 4.2

NUMBER OF SC/ST SCHOLARS BENEFITING FROM THE POST-MATRIC SCHOLARSHIP SCHEME

Year	*Number of Students Covered (in lakh)*	*Source*
1985-86	9.90*	
1986-87	10.89	a
1987-88	11.30*	
1988-89	11.70*	
1989-90	12.24	b
1990-91	14.18	c
1991-92	14.97	d
1992-93	15.31	d
1993-94	14.90	d
1994-95	15.34	d
1995-96	18.47	d
1996-97	20.79**	e

* estimated,

** anticipated

Sources :a- p. 304 of Twenty-eighth Report of the Commissioner for SC/ST.
b- p. 15 of Annual Report of the Ministry of Welfare, 1992-93.
c- p. 13 of Annual Report of the Ministry of Welfare, 1993-94.
d- p. 16 of Annual Report of the Ministry of Welfare, 1995-96.
e.-p. 22 of Annual Report, Ministry of Welfare, 1996-97

So about 2.50 crores of the SC/ST students had been covered by this scheme up to 1996-97. out of which roughly 47 lakhs were STs and the remaining 2.03 crores were SCs. If it is presumed that on an average a student enjoyed this scholarship for a period of four years, then at least 51 lakh Scheduled Caste students had so far been covered by this scheme, the bulk of whom (46 lakhs) belonged to the post 1969-70 period.

Although the value of each scholarship is low and the gap constantly widening with inflation and a similar gap in the matter of the 'Means Test' exists, the scheme is particularly noteworthy because of its open-ended nature, i.e., all eligible SC/ST students are entitled to the scholarships at all levels of post-matric education. Considering the fact that during the last 25 years not less than 46 lakh students have been benefited by this scheme, it is no doubt an impressive achievement. One has, however, every reason to ask who are these 46 lakh recipients, to which caste and sub-caste they belong and what is their contribution to the uplift of their brethren.

Pre-matric Scholarships for the Children of those Engaged in Unclean Occupations Irrespective of Religion

A Centrally Sponsored Scheme of pre-matric scholarships to children of those engaged in unclean occupations like scavenging of dry latrines, tanning and flaying, irrespective of religion was introduced from the academic year 1977 in order to provide good school education to them. It was observed that persons engaged in such occupations were rendering great service to the society but the percentage of school drop-outs among their children was much larger and this resulted in their continued backwardness. Under the scheme, 1,000 scholarships were awarded to those children studying in Classes VI to X in institutions having hostel facilities. These facilities were made available to the children of those parents whose income did not exceed Rs 500 per month. Not more than one child in the family was eligible for the award of this scholarship. The rate of scholarships was Rs 100 per month to meet the expenditure of tuition fees, cost of boarding and lodging, cost of books and other incidental charges. An additional allowance of Rs 45 per month was also given to cover expenditure on uniforms, clothing, towels, toilets, etc. The scholars were not required to render any help to the parents during the course of their studies. This scheme is being financed jointly by the Centre and States on matching grant basis from the year 1979-80.[31] Central assistance is provided to the State Governments on 50:50 basis over and above the committed liability, i.e. the total expenditure incurred on the scheme in the terminal year of the previous Five Year Plan. The scheme is implemented through the State Governments/Union Territory Administrations.

The main objective of this scheme is to provide good quality education to children of those engaged in unclean occupations by keeping them away from the dirty and unhygienic surroundings under which their parents live. There were, however certain inherent defects in the scheme and hence the response of the State Governments towards it was unsatisfactory. The scheme was suitably modified duing 1986-87. The children from the families of sweepers who have traditional links with the job of scavenging have also been included in this scheme from the year 1986-87.[32] The other modifications made in the scheme are mentioned below:

(i) increase of rates of scholarships from Rs 145 to Rs 200 p.m. for Classes VI to VIII and Rs 250 p.m. for Classes IX to XI;
(ii) increase of the income ceiling limit from Rs 500 p.m. to Rs 1000 p.m.;
(iii) provision for renting hostel buildings where hostel facilities are not available;
(iv) provision for appointment of a full-time hostel warden where the number of children is large, otherwise one of the school teachers may be appointed as hostel warden on some extra remuneration.

During 1985-86, the expenditure incurred on this scheme was only Rs 0.25 crore against an allocation of Rs 2.50 crore and the number of students benefited was 9,286. With the modification of the scheme during 1986-87, the coverage of children which had been very slow all along, was expected to improve. But even during the year 1988-89, only 12,820 children were covered under this scheme. Since this scheme covered only hostellers and not day-scholars, the Working Group on development and welfare of the Scheduled Castes during Eighth Five Year Plan (1990-95) suggeste modification of the scheme suitably so as to include day-scholars also with scholarships of Rs 40 p.m. for Classes I to V, Rs 55 p.m. for Classes VI to VIII and Rs 75 p.m. for Classes IX and X; expand the scope of children residing in hostels from Classes III to X and provide an amount of Rs 500 per scholar per annum to all hostellers and enhancing the income ceiling limit from Rs 1,000 to Rs 1,500 per month.[33]

These suggestions of the Working Group were acted upon and from November 1, 1991 the scheme covered day-scholars from Classes I to X, for whom the scholarship rates were Rs 25 p.m. for Classes I to V, Rs 40 p.m. for Classes VI to VIII and Rs 50 p.m. for Classes IX and X. The scheme also covered hostellers from Classes III to X. The scholarship rates for hostellers in Classes III to VIII were Rs 200 p.m. and Rs 250 p.m. for those in Classes IX and X. The scholarship was provided for 10 months in a year. An ad hoc grant of Rs 500 per annum to all hostellers and day-scholars was also provided. The income ceiling limit was enhanced to Rs 1,500 per month.[34]

The scheme has further been modified with effect from 25th February 1994. Now there is no income ceiling and also there is no restriction as to the number of children of the same parents who would be eligible for award of scholarship up to Class VIII, subject to the condition that if a third or subsequent child is born after 1.4.93 a total of only two children in the family would be eligible for such scholarships. In respect of Classes IX and X, only two children of the same parents would be eligible for the award of scholarships. Income ceiling has been removed.[35]

The modified scheme attracted a larger number of students. The coverage under the scheme was 90,912 students in 1991-92,[36] 99,254 in 1992-93, 1,30,715 in 1993-94, 1,76,253 in 1994-95, 2,40,628 in 1995-96 of general courses up to graduate level. Rs 90 Rs 150 and 2,50,000 (provisional) in 1996-97.[37] Though large number of students are being covered under this scheme, the children of those engaged in flaying and tanning have remained virtually excluded from this scheme as systematic surveys have not been conducted to identify eligible children for this scheme. Without more focussed and systematic efforts at identification, the coverage of the scheme will remain limited and its basic objective of providing formal education to all children of these groups, so as to open up other opportunities for them in the future, will remain unfilfilled.

Central assistance released to various State Governments / UTs were 4.00 crores in 1991-92,[38] Rs 6.39 crores in 1992-93, Rs 5.61 crores in 1993-94, Rs 6.25 crore in 1994-95 Rs 8.92 crores in 1995-96

Rs 5.55 crore in 1996-97 (up to 31.12.96)[39]

Until recently, some of the scholarship rates provided under the scheme were more favourable than the rates prescribed for Post-matric Scholarships. However, these also now require immediate revision keeping in view increases based on indexing with All India Consumer Price Index (APCPI) for industrial workers so that its effectiveness is not undermined.

Girls' Hostels

It has been observed that the SC/ST girls have lagged far behind the SC/ST boys in the matter of education. It was with a view to giving impetus to girls' education among these communities that the Centrally Sponsored Scheme of construction of girls' hostels was started during the Third Five-Year Plan (1961-66). The scope of the scheme which initially provided for the construction/extension of hostel buildings was widened during the Fifth Five-Year Plan (1974-79) to include provision for the construction of hostel buildings, award of stipends, maintenance of hostels and facilities for meeting special requirements of the SC/ST girls studying in middle and higher levels of education. The integrated scheme was designed to enable the hostels to develop into multipurpose institutions where the Scheduled Caste/Scheduled Tribe girls may be trained in arts, crafts, skills, games, house-keeping, etc. In one hostel 100 inmates can be accommodated, of which ten per cent of seats may be reserved for non-SC/ST students. The ceiling limit of grants-in-aid for construction of girls' hostel buildings was revised in May 1979,[40] in 1985,[41] and again in 1994-95 when the ceilings on the cost of construction of hostel buildings were removed. Now the cost of construction of a hostel is to be worked out on the basis of State/UT PWD rates. However, if a State/UT is following CPWD rates, the cost shall be worked out on the basis of the rates, whichever is lower. In the case of State/UT following only CPWD rates, the CPWD rate will be applied.[42]

During the Fifth Plan period (1974-79), an expenditure of Rs 1.95 crores was incurred on the scheme in all the States[43] and during the Sixth Plan period, a provision of Rs 13 crores was made under this scheme for hostels for both the Scheduled Caste and the Scheduled Tribe girls. During the Seventh Plan period an allocation of Rs 31.95 crore was made. Outlay for the Eighth Plan for this scheme was Rs 26.00 crore.

Since 1979-80, the expenditure on this scheme is shared by the Centre and the States on matching basis (50:50). Central assistance is also provided through State Governments/UT Administrations to the Voluntary Organizations/Non-Government/ Private Organizations only for the extension of hostels, provided the organization is willing to bear ten per cent of the total expenditure and remaining 90 per cent in such cases is sharable between the Central and State Governments on 50:50 basis.[44]

Up to the end of 1978-79, 916 girls' hostels were constructed in the States/UTs.[45] Since then the number of girls' hostels has increased and by the end of 1989-90, about 1900 hostels had been constructed under this scheme benefiting more than 90,000 girls.[46] The yearwise release of Central assistance, number of hostels sanctioned with capacity of students during the Eighth Plan period are as Shown in Table 4.3.

TABLE 4.3
YEARWISE AND SANCTION OF RELEASE OF CENTRAL ASSISTANCE EACH HOSTEL WITH CAPACITY OF GIRLS

(up to 31-12-96)

Years	*Amount Released*	*No. of Hostels*	*No. of Inmates*
1992-93	5.33 crore	177	9,547[47]
1993-94	6.00 crore	213	19,452[48]
1994-95	6.20 crore	73	7,208[49]
1995-96	5.65 crore	90	7,546[50]
1996-97	4.37 crore[51]		

The impact of the scheme is, however, affected in many places by inadequate planning and construction delays, inappropriate site selection, and poor management and provision facilities by the concerned State Governments. These deficiencies undermine efforts at promoting the education of girls in particular, in view of the special requirements of location, watch and ward, etc., in the case of girls' hostels. In addition to construction costs, central assistance should include a realistic one-time grant for certain basic non-recurring items of expenditure which are essential for improving the quality of life, such as a library, utensils, and cots, at very little additional cost.

The Working Group on development and welfare of the Scheduled Castes during Eighth Five-Year Plan suggested that all the educationally backward districts in the country, particularly in States like Uttar Pradesh and Bihar, should be covered by constructing hostels for the SC girls during the Eighth Five -Year Plan, for which an amount of Rs 200 crore would be required.[52] It is disheartening to note that States like Bihar, Rajasthan and Uttar Pradesh, where literacy rate of the SC women is less than 11 per cent as per the 1991 Census, did not come forward with adequate proposals for raising the capacity of hostels for the SC girls.

Boys' Hostels

One of the most important reasons for the slow progress of the educational development of the Scheduled Castes is the lack of adequate hostel facilities. The Working Group on the development of the Scheduled Castes during the Seventh Five Year Plan (1985-90), therefore, felt the necessity of inclusion of a centrally sponsored scheme for construction of boys' hostels during the Seventh Five-Year Plan on the pattern of the existing centrally sponsored scheme for Girls' hostels so that there could be at least two hostels for boys in each district headquarters in the country.[53] The scheme was introduced in the year 1989-90. It is implemented on the pattern of Girls' hostels.[54] The Working Group on development and welfare of the Scheduled Castes during the Eighth Five-Year Plan has suggested that this scheme should be extended to cover all the educationally backward districts in the country[55]

The outlay for the Eighth Plan under this scheme was Rs 33.00 crores[44] against which an amount of Rs 41.20 crore has been released up to 31.12.96. The year-wise release of Central assistance, number of hostels sanctioned with capacity of students during the Eighth Plan are as shown in Table 4.4.

TABLE 4.4
YEARWISE RELEASE OF CENTRAL ASSISTANCE AND SANCTION OFHOSTELS WITH CAPACITY OF BOYS

Year	*Amount Released (in crore)*	*No. of Hostels*	*No. of Inmates*
1992-93	5.00	200	10,270[56]
1993-94	6.50	101	7,020[57]
1994-95	10.00[58]		
1995-96	6.20	134	11,297[59]

It appears that Andhra Pradesh and Karnataka have shown keen interest in implementing the scheme followed by Gujarat, Bihar, Maharashtra, Tamil Nadu and Uttar Pradesh. It is not understood as to how States like Madhya Pradesh having sizeable SC population with low literacy rate among the SCs has not evinced interest in the scheme of construction of hostels for the SC boys.[61]

Book Banks for the SC/ST Students

The SC/ST students who generally belong to the economically weaker sections of the society, cannot afford to purchase all the costly books of medical and engineering courses. In pursuance of the recommendations of the High Power Committee, the Union Ministry of Home Affairs, therefore, started a centrally sponsored scheme for establishing Book Banks in various medical and engineering colleges in the country from 1978-79 for lending sets of textbooks on medical and engineering degree courses to the SC/ST students.[62]

This scheme having proved to be very useful to the SC/ST students in pursuing medical and engineering courses, the Working Group on the development of the Scheduled Castes, during the Seventh Five-Year Plan, felt that the scope of this scheme might be extended to cover all the professional courses which would help a larger number of the SC students in pursuing professional education. In order to make the scheme more effective and meaningful, the Working Group thought it desirable to give a set of textbooks to each SC/ST student pursuing a professional course and who was eligible for post-matric scholarship.[63] The Working Group on development and welfare of the Scheduled Castes during the Eighth Five-Year

Plan also recommended the expansion of the scope of this scheme for covering other professional courses like Veterinary Science, B.Sc. (Agriculture), Law and Polytechnics, etc., during the Eighth Five-Year Plan and provision of one set of books to each student.[64] The Ninth Plan Working Group felt that the scheme should be extended to cover all post-matric scholarship recipients in categories "A" and "B" courses of that scheme.[65]

At present, under the scheme, Books Banks are established not only in Medical and Engineering Colleges, but also in Veterinary and Agriculture Colleges and Polytechnics. Indian systems of Medicine and Homeopathy are also covered under the scheme. Previously, one set of books was used by four students. Now each set of textbooks is to be shared by two students.[66]

The scheme which is administered through the State Governments/UT Administrations, is being financed jointly by the Centre and the States on a 50:50 basis from 1979-80, subject to the following ceiling on costs per set of textbooks for different courses:[67]

Courses	*Ceiling Cost Per Set (in Rs.)*
Medical (including Indian systems of Medicine/Homeopathy)	7,500
Engineering	7,500
Veterinary	5,000
Agriculture	4,500
Polytechnic	2,400

The life period of one set of books has been fixed as three years; this means that every three years funds will be provided for getting new sets of books. A provision of Rs 3 crores was made for this sucheme during the Sixth Plan but unfortunately the expenditure during the period was only Rs 0.96 crore. For the Seventh Plan, an outlay of Rs 2.25 crore was provided for this scheme. During 1985-86 the number of SC/ST beneficiaries was 16,822[68] rising to 21,000 in 1990.[69] In 1991-92, Rs 56.26 lakh were released as central assistance to benefit 24,245 students.[70] During the Eighth Plan period, an amount of Rs 11.24 crores has been released (up to

December, 1996) benefiting 108,946 students. The yearwise break-up is given in Table 4.5.

TABLE 4.5
YEARWISE BREAK-UP OF AMOUNT RELEASED FOR BOOK BANKS DURING 1992-97

	Amount released (Rs in crore)	*No. Benefited*
1992-93	0.67	11,582[71]
1993-94	3.33	32,120[72]
1994-95	3.50	37,877[73]
1995-96	2.64	27,367[74]
1996-97	1.10[73]	

Centrally Sponsored Scheme of Upgradation of Merit of the SC/ ST Students

Under this scheme, central assistance is provided on 100 per cent basis to State Governments/UT Administrations for providing remedial and special coaching to the SC/ST students. The scheme was started in 1987-88 by the Ministry of Human Resource Development (Department of Education). It was transferred to the Ministry of Welfare in the middle of 1993-94. This is intended to help the SC/ST students studying in Classes IX to XII by providing them extra coaching both remedial and special with a view to removing their social and educational deficiencies and facilitating their admission to professional courses such as Medical and Engineering, etc., where entry is based on competitive examinations. The outlay for the Eighth Plan under the scheme was Rs 2.60 crores. The total grant released during 1993-94 was Rs 0.15 to benefit 334 SC/ST students in only five States.[75] A total amount of Rs 1.00 crore was released in 1994-95 to benefit 2336 SC/ST students in 11 States.[76] In 1995-96, an amount of Rs 22.17 lakhs was released to five States only.[77] The scheme has a great deal of potential provided it is properly utilised by the States/UTs.

Coaching and Allied Schemes for the SC/ST

The Government of India sanctioned the scheme in 1958-59 to improve the intake of the SCs/STs in various government services such as IAS/IP5/Allied Services and services under the Public Sector Undertakings by providing pre-examination training to candidates for examinations held by the Union Public Service Commission, State Public Service Commissions, Banking Service Recruitment Boards and other recruiting bodies.

The Ministry of Welfare has been administering the scheme since the Fourth Plan (1969-74). The Ministry finances (a) Pre-Examination Training Centres (PETCs) set up by the State governments and the universities and (b) private coaching institutions. The State run PETCs are funded by the Centre and the State Governments on a matching basis over and above the committed liability of the State Governments in the terminal year of the privious Five Year Plan. The committed liability is borne by the State Governments from its own resources. The Centres run by the Universities and the Union Territory Administrations are reimbursed the actual expenditure. Private coaching centres are paid on a contractual basis. The coaching is provided to the SC/ST candidates in three broad categories of examinations. These are Central Civil Services, Medical and Engineering Entrance Examinations and other service examinations including the State Civil Services. The Scheme provides for a monthly stipend of Rs. 400 for the hostellers and Rs. 100 per month for the day scholars. The norms for payment of remuneration to the teachers in the training centres have been fixed for some of the examinations. Teachers coaching candidates for civil services examinations are paid an honorarium up to Rs 500 for a lecture of two hours duration.

Benefits of the scheme have accrued to a sizeable number of candidates, approximately 11,000 students each year. At present, 131 PETCs run by 22 States/UTs, 18 universities and four private coaching institutions of Delhi have been receiving assistance under the Scheme.

However, a review of the Scheme as implemented at present shows glaring imbalances both in terms of the geographical spread of these centres as well as in terms of the coverage of examinations/ vocations. For example, in the States of Arunachal Pradesh, Mizoram and Sikkim and the UTs of Andaman & Nicobar Islands, Chandigarh, Dadra and Nagar Haveli, Daman & Diu and Lakshdweep there are no coaching centres. Similarly in large states such as Bihar, West Bengal, Karnataka, Tamil Nadu there are no institutes providing coaching for Medical and Engineering Entrance examinations. The disciplines of management, chartered accoutnancy, cost accountancy which have a great employment potential are also not covered in any of these centres. The PETCs under the aegis of state Government provide coaching largely for the clerical grade and other Group 'C' examinations. However, the need for more centres for Medical and Engineering, Central Civil Services and other professional courses is of great importance as the shortfall in recruitment of the SC/ST candidates in Group 'A' and 'B' posts of Central Government, Public Sector Undertakings and Banks is much higher.

Apart from a few centres such as Guru Nanak Dev University, Amritsar, Punjab University, Patiala and private coaching institutes (Rau's study Circle. S.N. Das Gupta College and Sachdeva New P.T. College_ the results from other centres are poor. Most of the PETCS have been functioning from rented building. The PETCs have also not been able to provide hostels/library facilities to the candidates.

In order to remove the drawbacks identified, the scheme was modified in 1994 to bring within its ambit coaching institutes of repute on the one hand and pre-examination coaching for new disciplines such as management, hotel management, accountancy, armed forces examinations on the other. The States have been requested to recommend names of the reputed private coaching institutes which could be selected for sponsoring candidates under this scheme. A committee under the chairmanship of Secretary, Ministry of Welfare (now Ministry of Social Justice and Empowerment) has been set up to decide on the inclusion of new centres under this scheme.

Norms for Coaching Institutes

The Committee has evolved a set of norms for including institutes under this scheme. These are:

(1) The institute should be a registered trust or society and or recognised by the concerned State/UT's Education and Social Welfare Departments or affiliated to the nearest University.

(2) The institute should have at least three years of successful experience to impart coaching in the courses for which inclusion under the scheme is proposed.

(3) A minimum 15 per cent success rate in the relevant examination in previous three years has been stipulated as the bench mark for inclusion.

(4) The institute should have adequate accommodation, teaching equipment as well as library and hostel facilities.
(5) The institute should have qualified and competent teaching staff.[78]

At the suggestion of the Planning Commission, a Task Force has been set up by the Ministry to review and suggest suitable modifications to the scheme. An All-India meeting with the Heads of State Welfare Departments and Universities was organized by the Welfare Ministry on 29-6-1996 to review the implementation of the scheme. Some of the suggestions made included

(1) Spreading out of the coaching centres where concentration of SC/ST population exists and facilities for coaching do not exist;
(2) Careful selection of students;
(3) Coaching to be made available in relation to the availability of reserved vacancies; and
(4) Constitution of Monitoring Committee at States/District level and award to the best PETC.[79]

During the Eighth Plan Period, central assistance of Rs 8.00 crores was released to the State Governments/universities/private institutions.[80]

National Overseas Scholarships and Passage Grants for Higher Studies Abroad

The Government of India initiated a scheme in 1954-55 for the award of national overseas scholarships to the Scheduled Caste/Tribe, Denotified, Nomadic and Semi-Nomadic Tribes, SC converts to other religions and the children of Landless Agricultural labourers/Traditional Artisans for advanced Degree and Post-Doctoral studies abroad. Preference is given to studies in Engineering, Technology, Medicine, Agriculture and Science. At the Bachelor's and Master's degree levels also specific courses have been approved recently for award of scholarships. Selected candidates are allowed three years after the year of selection within which they are required to obtain admission in foreign institutions, for which assistance is also provided by the Indian Missions abroad. The scholarships are provided to the students by the Indian Missions during their stay abroad, which cover the payment of tuition fees, maintenance and contingency allowances, and travel expenses. The rates of scholarships and other allowances under the scheme are given below:[81]

1. Maintenance Allowance:
   (a) Bachelor's Degree Course — US $ 5940 p.a.
   (b) Postgraduate Course — US $ 6600 p.a.
   (c) Post Doctoral Course — US $ 7700 p.a.
2. Contingency Allowance — US $ 385 p.m.
3. Equipment Allowance — Rs. 1100/-
4. Poll Tax — US $ 150
5. All compulsory fees of the University/Institute, such as Tuition Fee, Admission Fee, etc., and the Health/Medical Insurance premium if any.
6. Cost of economy class air passage both ways up to destination and back by the shortest route.
7. 2nd class rail fare from place of residence to the airport, and back.

The number of scholarships which was six initially, was increased to 12 in 1955-56 and to 21 in 1972-73. 25 in 1990,[82] and to 30 in 1991.[83] These awards are offered to candidates belonging to the Scheduled Castes (17 awards), the Scheduled Tribes (9 awards), the Scheduled Caste converts to other religions or their dependants (2 awards), Denotified, Nomadic and Semi-nomadic Tribes (1 award) and Children of landless agricultural labourers and traditional artisans of communities other than above (1 award). Since the inception of the scheme in 1954-55, a total of 732 candidates have been awarded the scholarships and 525 candidates had availed of it.[84]

In addition to 30 National Overseas Scholarships, Passage Grants are also provided to students who are in receipt of a merit scholarship from a foreign Government or Institute, in case such scholarship does not include the costs of passage. Passage Grants are available each year to the Scheduled Castes (4 awards), the Scheduled Tribes (4 awards) and Denotified and Semi-Nomadic Tribes (1 award).[85]

Special Educational Development Programme for Scheduled Caste Girls Belonging to Very Low Literacy Level

The scheme is in operation from 1996-97 providing a package of educational inputs through residential schools for Scheduled Caste girls in areas of very low Scheduled Caste Female Literacy where traditions and environment are not conducive to learning. The schools would supplement existing measures to impart and consolidate literacy and promote quality education among Scheduled Caste Girls of first generation learners in areas of low literacy. The scheme is implemented by the Zila Parishad of the concerned District.

The schools will function in suitable hired premises. Such premises should be sufficient to accommodate Classrooms, Hostels, Kitchen and Staff Quarters and should preferably allow for expansion of school, if subsequently required. All-inclusive, grants-in-aid will be provided under the scheme to the Zila Parishad @Rs 11,340 per annum per student in Class 1 split in two components (Rs. 4900/for direct facilities to students and Rs 6440) for infra-structural and other running cost, including staff). No fees, charges or contributions will be levied from the students. Each school will have 25 girls in Class 1. The intake will be from among girls who are first generation learners from families identified for the prupose of the Integrated Rural Development Programme, as being below the poverty line. Priority in intake should be given to the particularly disadvantaged amongst the Scheduled Castes such as the children of scavengers, flayers, and tanners.

The 1981 Census identified 48 districts situated in Bihar, Madhya Pradesh, Rajasthan and Uttar Pradesh where the literacy of Scheduled Caste Girls was less than two per cent. The scheme accordingly covers only these Districts.

As against the target of 21 residential schools for the year 1996-97, 14 residential schools have so far been sanctioned in eight Zila Parishads of Madhya Pradesh and three residential Shools in three Zila Parishads of Uttar Pradesh. The total expenditure incurred up to 31-12-96 under the scheme was Rs 19.84 lakh.[86]

This is a good scheme, if properly implemented. This scheme may be extended subsequently to other States as well, to cover those Scheduled Castes whose literacy rate is much below the State average.

Aid to Voluntary Organizations

The main purpose of giving grants-in-aid to Voluntary Organizations of All-India character engaged in the welfare of the SC/ST and Other Backward Classes, is to improve the educational and socio-economic conditions of these communities through voluntary efforts of the non-official agencies. Under this scheme started by the Government of India in 1953-54, only those voluntary agencies which have been registered for a year and have given some evidence of voluntary involvement in adult education and social upliftment are eligible for financial assistance. Grants-in-aid to the extent of 90 per cent of approved costs on various schemes are provided to the eligible voluntary organizations. Programmes for social upliftment of the SCs are also considered for financial assistance under the scheme. To ensure active participation of these organizations, they are expected to contribute ten per cent of the grant. It is also desirable to have SC members in the managing committee in adequate number and capacity. The Government of India has also issued detailed guidelines on Aid to Voluntary Organizations.

The various schemes for which grants-in-aid are given to the voluntary organizations include residential schools, day schools, hostels, child welfare centres, etc., and training in various disciplines like typewriting and stenography, computer application, tailoring and embroidery, motor driving, electronics and various industrial trades. Nearly 400 organizations are being funded under this scheme.[87]

To ensure that the grantee complies with the terms and conditions of the grants and that the welfare schemes are run on proper lines, the officers of the Ministry of Welfare, Directors of the Scheduled Castes and the Scheduled Tribes and the National Commission for the SCs and STs inspect the aided schemes and give their suggestions and send their inspection reports to the Ministry of Welfare. Measures to improve the working and effectivenes of this scheme of voluntary organizations have to be worked out in consultation with the representations of voluntary organizations reputed for their sincerity integrity and effectiveness.[88]

State Schemes

Apart from these and other Centrally Sponsored Schemes, the State Governments/Union Territory Administrations have a number of Schemes like scholarships including pre-matric scholarships, merit scholarships, special scholarships for very backward communities, attendance scholarships for girls, freeships, hostel facilities, residential schools (Ashram Schools), remedial and special coaching schemes and other incentives like free mid-day meals, textbooks, uniforms, etc., for boys and girls belonging to the SC/ST communities not only for primary section but for higher education as well. There are also provisions for reservation of seats in educational institutions including professional and technical education for the SC/ST students and relaxation in norms for admission in terms of minimum marks for selection, age limit, fees for admission/examination, etc. The domain of their activities, however, varies form State to State.

Details of the facilities/schemes as on 1983-84[89] are noted below. It is quite likely that the rates of stipends and other facilities have undergone a revision by this time and even the percentages of seats reserved for the SC/ST fixed on the basis of their population proportion in the State have been refixed in many States/UTs. Lack of up-to-date, data however, stands in the way of furnishing the latest information.

Reservation of Seats in Educational Institutions

Insertion of Clause (4) of Article 15 by the First Constitutional Amendment Act, 1951 enables the State to make special provision for the advancement of (1) any socially and educationally backward classes of citizens, or for (2) the Scheduled Castes, and (3) the Scheduled Tribes. Since education, general as well as technical, is a potent factor in the uplift of these communities, the Government of India considered it desirable that all possible facilities should be afforded and efforts made to enable the students belonging to the SC/ST communities to gain admission in educational institutions including technical institutions.

The Ministry of Education, vide its letter dated November 23, 1954, addressed to the Chief Secretaries of all State Governments has suggested that 20 per cent seats should be reserved for the

SC/ST students in educational institutions and where admissions are restricted to candidates who obtain certain minimum percentage of marks and not merely the passing of a certain examination, there may be a five per cent reduction for such candidates provided that the lower percentage does not fall below the minimum required to pass the qualifying examination.

Further, on April 15, 1964, the Ministry of Education addressed another communication to all the State Governments and the universities suggesting that 20 per cent of seats in all technical institutions should be reserved for the SC/ST candidates with a distinct share of 15 per cent for the SC and 5 per cent for the ST (since increased to 7.5 per cent from August 1982) and that this reservation is interchangeable between them. Five per cent reduction of marks to pass the qualifying examination should also be allowed to them. If there is a maximum age limit, it may be raised by three years for the SC/ST students.

Similarly, the Ministry of Health and Family Welfare, vide its letter dated December 12, 1972 addressed to the Vice-Chancellors of the universities having Medical Faculties, had requested that the universities might consider the feasibility of reserving 20 per cent of seats in Postgraduate Medical and Dental Colleges, i.e., 15 per cent for the SCs and 5 per cent for the STs. It was also suggested in that letter that these candidates should also be given a concession of 5 per cent marks in the minimum percentage of marks required for admission to such courses and that in case 20 per cent seats earmarked for them remain vacant, a further relaxation in the marks should be given to them in order of merit among themselves so that all the reserved seats are filled by candidates belonging to these communities. The Ministry of Health and Family Welfare, having observed that the State Governments/Universities/Medical Colleges, etc., were not giving due concessions in the matter of admission to post-graduate Medical and Dental courses to students of SC/ST, had again requested the concerned State Governments/universities to extend the above concession to the students belonging to the enlisted communities.

The UGC on its part as a follow up, invited the attention of the universities to the guidelines issued by the Ministry of Education and Social Welfare regarding reservation of seats for the SC/ ST students in the universities/colleges. It was mentioned that according to the recent arrangements, 20 per cent of the seats were reserved for the SC/ST candidates who were also given a concession of five per cent marks in the minimum percentage of marks required for admission in any course. It was later observed that even with these concessions, some of the seats in the reserved quota remained vacant as adequate number of SC/ST candidates with requisite marks were not available. Accordingly, it was suggested that in case the 20 per cent seats earmarked for them remain vacant, a further relaxation in the marks may be given to them in order of merit amongst themselves, so that all the reserved seats can be filled by candidates belonging to these categories.[90]

Guidelines to Kendriya Vidyalayas : Till 1976-77, no reservation of seats for the SC/ST students was made for admission to Kendriya Vidyalayas. The Kendriya Vidyalaya Sangathan, however, decided to reserve 15 per cent and 7.5 per cent seats for the SC and the ST candidates respectively, in respect of new admissions to Kendriya Vidyalayas from the academic year 1976-77. The reservation quota was to apply to the total number of children given fresh admission in a Kendriya Vidyalaya at the beginning of a session and not to the fresh admissions made in each class. The Kendriya Vidyalaya Sangathan issued another instruction to all the Kendriya Vidyalayas in August 1978 to ensure that the quota reserved for the SC/ST students was utilized to the maximum extent possible and for that purpose, issued the following guidelines:

(*i*) The conditions of transferability of parents may be relaxed and children of even non-transferable SC/ST employees may be admitted, where necessary;

(*ii*) If any examination is held for admission to Kendriya Vidyalayas, candidates belonging to the SC/ST may be allowed a concession of five per cent marks in the standard fixed for other candidates from the academic session 1979-91.[77]

Keeping in view the guidelines of the Central Government, almost all the State Governments/Union Territory Administrations have formulated their own schemes for reservation of seats for the Scheduled Caste students in colleges providing general and professional education and in technical institutions. In States/UTs like Orissa, Tripura, Andhra Pradesh, Karnataka, Tamil Nadu, Uttar Pradesh., West Bengal and Pondicherry, seats have been reserved at school level as well. In States/UTs like Arunachal Pradesh, Mizoram, Nagaland, Sikkim, Lakshadweep and Dadra and Nagar Haveli, having predominantly Scheduled Tribe population and negligible or no population of the Scheduled Castes, seats have not been specifically reserved for the SC/ST students. The percentage of seats reserved varies from State to State, the highest being 20 in Haryana and the lowest is two in Manipur in relation of the Scheduled Caste students. This wide variation is explained by the fact that different States/UTs have different percentage of SC population. In Central government institutions, the percentage is, however, fixed and there is no variation.

Apart from the reservation of seats in the educational institutions, many States/UTs have also relaxed the eligibility criterion. In most States/UTs a relaxation of five per cent marks is given. The actual position in regard to reservation of seats in the educational institutions as also the relaxation in marks in eligibility criterion for admission in each State/UT, as in 1983-84, is indicated in Annexure Table X.

Pre-matric Stipends

Elementary education up to class VIII is free in all the States/UTs. Opening of educational institutions is sufficient to attract students from the general mass, but mere provision of schools and free education may not have the same impact on the SC/ST students on the educational front. To attract greater number of the SC/ST students to join their studies, apart from providing special incentives like supply of free uniform, books, mid-day meals, the scheme for providing stipend to the SC/ST students at pre-matric classes is in vogue in many States/UTs. Available information regarding the rates of these stipends to the SC/ST day scholars are furnished in Annexure Table XI.

It would be evident from Annexure Table XI that all the States/UTs, excepting Tamil Nadu and Arunachal Pradesh, have introduced this scheme of granting stipends at pre-matric level.

The rate of stipend, however, is not uniform and in some States the scheme is meant for the SC girls only. An income criteria has also been fixed in some States/UTs. Some States like Madhya Pradesh, Punjab and Rajasthan claim that these stipends are awarded by them to all the eligible SC students.[92] As a large number of States/UTs are still far away from the target of universal coverage, the Commissioner for the SC/ST recommended in his 27th report (1979-81) that this scheme of pre-matric stipends should be made an open-ended one like the post-matric scholarships and all the eligible SC/ST students should be awarded scholarships.[93] The Working Group on development of the Scheduled Castes during the Seventh Five-Year Plan (1985-90) also recommended that there should be provision of scholarship/stipend to all children belonging to the Scheduled Castes with 100 per cent coverage at all levels. They also recommended that the amount of scholarship should not be less than Rs 40 per month.[94] The Working Group on development and welfare of the Scheduled Castes during the Eighth-Five-Year Plan (1990-95) also reiterated that all the Scheduled Caste children studying in pre-matric classes should be given scholarships.[95] It also proposed to give Rs 60 per month for ten months in a year to indigent SC/ST families as an incentive for sending their girls to the primary schools. The total cost for covering 51.41 lakh children would be Rs 308.47 crore annually. The total requirement of funds under the scheme during the Eighth Five-Year Plan was estimated by the Working Group to be Rs 1542.37 crore or Rs 1550.00 crore.[96]

Post-matric Scholarships

In Arunachal Pradesh, scholarships are given to pre-university students of Rs 100 p.m. for 10½ months in a year and Rs 175 p.m. for degree courses. The parental income ceiling is fixed at Rs 1000 p.m.

In Karnataka, the State Government provides scholarships varying from Rs 40 to Rs 75 p.m. to students whose parental income is less than Rs 10,000 p.a. This scholarship is admissible to those who are not eligible for the Government of India Post-matric scholarship.

In Kerala, under the Post-matric scholarship scheme of the State Government, the SC/ST students are given a lump sum grant varying from Rs 80 to Rs 750, depending upon the course of study, plus a monthly stipend of Rs 130 for those residing within eight

Kms and Rs 150 for those residing beyond eight kms from the educational institutions. There is no income ceiling under this scheme. In case of hostellers, instead of stipend, actual boarding and lodging charges are paid under this scheme.

In Maharashtra, financial assistance of Rs 1000 p.a. is given to backward class students studying in medical and engineering courses. A maintenance allowance of Rs 1200 p.a. is given to backward class students residing in hostels attached to professional colleges.

Under the Post-matric scholarship scheme of the Sikkim Government, scholarships of Rs 300 p.m. are awarded to students whose parental income is less than Rs 1000 p.m. This is also a general scholarship in which 15 per cent of the scholarships are reserved for the SCs and 15 per cent for the STs.

Merit Scholarships to SC Students

In Andhra Pradesh, merit scholarships are given to top ten students for post-matric studies up to postgraduate level, on the basis of marks secured in the annual examinations since S.S.C. Rates vary from Rs 2000 p.a. to Rs 6,000 p.a. for boys and Rs 2500 p.a. to Rs 7000 p.a. for girls.

In Arunachal Pradesh, merit scholarships of Rs 50 p.m. are given in Classes IX and X to those who have secured first 30 positions in Class VIII; Rs 75 p.m. in Classes XI and XII to those who have secured first 20 positions in Class X and Rs 100 p.m. for two years after Class XII for pursuing higher studies to those who have secured first ten positions in Class XII/ P.U.C. The parental income ceiling for this scholarship is Rs 1250 p.m.

In Haryana, merit scholarships are given at the rate of Rs 40 p.m., Rs 50 p.m. and Rs 60 p.m. in Classes IX, X and XI respectively to the SC girls.

In Karnataka, the students who secure 60 per cent marks and above are provided additional scholarships of Rs 75 p.a. in Classes V to VII and Rs 100 p.a. in classes VIII to X. Students who secure 50 per cent marks and above and less than 60 per cent marks are provided additional scholarships of Rs 50 p.a in Classes V to VII and Rs 75 p.a. in Classes VIII to X.

In Orissa, merit prizes are awarded to the SC/ST students on the basis of matriculation examination results. A grant of Rs 350 p.a. is given to Arts and Commerce students and Rs 450 p.a. for Science students and students studying in diploma and degree courses in Engineering.

In Rajasthan, merit scholarships are awarded to one boy and one girl student from each Panchayat Samiti in the tribal sub-plan areas. Scholarship is awarded on the basis of marks obtained in class VIII examination. An amount of Rs 1000 for the whole season is given to students admitted in selected schools and Rs 500 to students in other schools. Scholarships in special subjects (Mathematics and Science) are also given to students in schools located in the tribal sub-plan areas. The rates of scholarships are Rs 40 p.m. in class IX, Rs 50 p.m. in class X and Rs 60 p.m. in class XI.

In West Bengal, special merit scholarship of Rs 400 p.m. and Rs 500 p.m. is given to the day-scholars and hostellers studying in Classes IX to XII respectively.

Scholarships to the SC Students in Convent and Residential Schools

In Andhra Pradesh, scholarships to the SC students studying in Convent/Residential schools are paid at the following rates: classes I to V @ Rs 20 p.a., classes VI to VIII @ Rs 25 p.a. and classes IX to XII @ Rs 30 p.a. The income ceiling is Rs 12,000 p.a.

In Orissa, students admitted to public schools are provided scholarships of Rs 200 p.m. for ten months in a year.

In Sikkim, there is a general scholarship scheme for students in classes I to X in which four out of every ten scholarships are earmarked for the SC/ST students. The rate of scholarship is Rs. 200 p.m. For the award of this scholarship there is an income ceiling of Rs 1000 p.m.

Scholarships to Postgraduate Students and to Research Scholars

In Andhra Pradesh, scholarships of Rs 100 p.m. are paid over and above the stipend paid by universities or Government of India to students in Postgraduate courses like MD, MS, etc. Students pursuing M.Phil, Ph.D., etc, but not in receipt of any other scholarship, are given scholarship of Rs 400 p.m. under this scheme.

In Gujarat, Bhangi students studying in Medical, BDS and Ayurvedic courses and whose parents' income is up to Rs 15,000 p.a., are granted full scholarship from State Funds at the rates of the Government of India.

In Mizoram, Ph.D. students who have completed M.Phil are awarded fellowships of Rs 700 p.m. with Rs 3000 p.a. as contingency grant. Those who have taken Ph.D. course directly and those taking M.Phil course are awarded Rs 600 p.m. as Research Fellowship and Rs 3000 p.a. as contingency grant.

Attendance Scholarship for Girls

That the enrolment of girls in schools is much lower than that of boys was revealed in all the All-India Educational Surveys, including the Sixth Survey (1993). Some State Governments have instituted scholarships for girls as an incentive for them to attend school. These scholarships are meant to bring the girls of school-going age to school and to retain them there. In 1986, only 47,111 (6.40 per cent) schools out of the total number of 7,35,771 schools in the country were providing attendance scholarships to girls.

At all stages of school education 3,75,979 girls were being benefited by this incentive scheme. Of these beneficiaries, 70.44 per cent were studying in rural schools. Further, 57.70 per cent of the beneficiaries belonged to the Scheduled Castes and 16.05 per cent to the Scheduled Tribes, which together accounted for 73.75 per cent of the beneficiaries. The break-up of the beneficiaries at different stages of school education can be seen in Table 4.6.

Interest Free Loans

In Himachal Pradesh interest free loans up to Rs 2000 are granted to those students whose parental annual income does not exceed Rs 2000. The loan is recoverable in 20 instalments after four years from the date of disbursement of the loan.

In Tamil Nadu, loan scholarship is given only to hostellers for pursuing their degree/postgraduate degree courses. An annual grant varying from Rs 500 to Rs 970 is given under this scheme.

In Tamil Nadu, a lump sum grant of Rs 300 is given to all SC/ST students who secure an aggregate of 60 per cent marks in SSLC/Matric examination for continuing their study in recognized institutions. Bright Students Award is given to two boys and two girls each from the SC (Hindu), STs, and SCs converted to Christianity in each district selected on the basis of the marks secured in SSLC examination. Scholarship is given at the rate of Rs 80 p.m. tll the completion of Post-matric studies subject to a maximum of six years. Gandhi Memorial Award is given to one boy and one girl from the SC (Hindu) from each district on the basis of Higher Secondary marks. The rate of scholarship is Rs 15000 for first year and Rs 1000 per year for the remaining periods, subject to a maximum period of 6 years for pursuing post-matric studies

TABLE 4.6

BREAK-UP OF ATTENDANCE SCHOLARSHIPS FOR GIRLS ACCORDING TO SCHOOLS AND BENEFICIARIES

Type of Schools	*No. of Schools*	*No. of Beneficiaries*			*Total*
		Scheduled Castes	*Scheduled Tribes*	*Other*	
1	2	3	4	5	6
Primary	24,563 (4.65%)	97,071 (64.45%)	23,987 (15.92%)	29,562 (19.63%)	150,620
Upper Primary	15,053 (10.83%)	80,533 (54.20%)	25,241 (16.99%)	42,816 (28.81%)	148,590
Secondary	5,599 (10.65%)	25,228 (50.78 %)	7,078 (14.25%)	17,372 (34.97%)	49,678
Higher Secondary	1,896 (12.26%)	14,107 (52.07%)	4,021 (14.84%)	8,963 (33.09%)	27,091

Source : pp. 185-88 of Fifth All-India Educational Survey, 1986.

In Dadra and Nagar Haveli, cash award for the top three students in annual examinations is given to the SC/ST students from classes V to VIII. The rates are: Rs 70 p.a. for 1st prize, Rs 60 p.a. for 2nd prize and Rs 50 p.a. for 3rd prize.

In Delhi, merit scholarships are given at the following rates : Rs 10 p.m. for class VI, Rs 15 p.m. for class VII and Rs 20 p.m. for class VIII for all students securing 60 per cent marks or more, and Rs 20 p.m. for class IX, Rs 25 p.m. for class X, Rs 30 p.m. for class XI and Rs 35 p.m. for class XII for all students securing 55 per cent marks or more. There is another Open Merit Scholarship scheme under which some scholarships are reserved for the SC/ST students. The selected students get scholarships at the rate of Rs 50 p.m. for ten months in a year from classes VI to VIII.

In Pondicherry, all SC students who secure more than 65 per cent marks in Xth standard examination are given a merit prize of Rs 300. Dr. Ambedkar Memorial Award is given to one SC student from each region of Pondicherry on the basis of XII class examination. A lump sum of Rs 1000 is paid to the selected student provided the student has secured at least 55 per cent marks.

Freeships

The Scheduled Caste students are provided free education up to certain level in almost all the States/UTs. Up to Class VIII in two States/UTs (Punjab and Chandigarh) education is free up to class X; in five States/UTs (Assam, Meghalaya, Nagaland, UP. and Goa., Daman and Diu); up to class XII; in nine States, UTs (Gujarat, Himachal Pradesh, Sikkim, Tamil Nadu, West Bengal, Arunachal Pradesh, Andaman and Nicober Islands, Dadra and Nagar Haveli and Delhi); up to matriculation in one State (Orissa), up to intermediate in one state (Andhra Pradesh), up to degree in one UT (Pondicherry); up to postgraduate in one State (Jammu and Kashmir) and up to all levels in nine States/UTs (Bihar, Haryana, Karnataka, Kerala, Madhya Pradesh, Maharashtra, Rajasthan, Tripura and Lakshadweep). Information is lacking in respect of two States (Manipur and Mizoram).

In addition to freeships, as many as 21 States/UTs have also exempted the SCs from payment of examination fees as follows:

up to class X in three UTs states (Chandigarh Daman and Diu and Goa),

up to class XII in six States/UTs (Gujarat, Madhya Pradesh, Sikkim, Tamil Nadu, West Bengal and A & N Islands),

up to matriculation in one State (Orissa).

up to all levels in seven States/UTs (Bihar, Himachal Pradesh, Kerala, Karnataka, Punjab, Tripura and Lakshadweep),

Public examination in one State (Haryana), and

Board examinations in four States/UTs (Jammu and Kashmir, Arunachal Pradesh, Delhi and Dadra and Nagar Haveli).

The details of these facilities may be seen in Annexure Table XII.

Ashram Schools

Ashram schools are opened in tribal areas providing free education, boarding and lodging facilities to the tribal children who inhabit inaccessible hills and forests without proper communication facilities. Besides general education, the Ashram schools also impart training in agriculture and crafts like blacksmithy, carpentry and weaving for boys and tailoring for girls. In Orissa, the residential schools for girls are called Kanyashrams, while the Ashram schools are meant for boys. Such schools are run by State Governments as well as by non-official organizations. The programme for the establishment and maintenance of Ashram schools is also included in the tribal sub-plan of the States in which such sub-plans have been formulated. In some States, Ashram schools have also been opened to cater to the educational needs of the Scheduled Castes.

The number of Ashram schools in various States/UTs catering to the needs of both the SC and ST students is shown in Table 4.7.

Considering the inadequate number of Ashram schools for the Scheduled Caste students, the Working Group on development and welfare of the Scheduled Castes during the Eighth Five-Year Plan recommended that in educationally backward regions, i.e., where the literacy rate among the Scheduled Castes is very low, there should be Ashram Schools for the Scheduled Caste boys and girls at the primary level.[97]

Backward Classes Hostels

It has been observed that generally the SC/ST students do not have necessary facilities at home for studies, while the general

TABLE 1.7
NUMBER OF ASHRAM SCHOOLS IN VARIOUS STATES/UTs, 1983-84

Sl. No.	*States/UTs*	*Level of Schooling*	*No. of Ashram Schools for*		
			SC	*ST*	*Total*
1.	Andhra Pradesh	Primary lèvel	9	436	445
		Middle level	46	7	53
2.	Assam	for SC/ST			5
3.	Bihar		39	56	95
4.	Gujarat	Primary level	38	205	243
		Middle level	–	40	40
5.	Himachal Pradesh	Primary level for SC/ST			3
		Middle level for SC/ST			1
6.	Karnataka		63	62	125
7.	Kerala	Primary level	-	9	9
8.	Madhya Pradesh	up to middle level	31	221	252
9.	Mahara-shtra	up to class VIII	–	325	325
		up to class X	–	91	91
10.	Manipur	Primary level	–	2	2
		Middle level	–	1	1
		Secondary level	–	1	1
11.	Rajasthan	Primary level	1	7	8
		middle/secondary level	–	22	22
12.	Tamil Nadu		–	160	160
13.	Orissa	Residential Sevashrams (Classes I to V)	2	41	43
		Middle education standard (Ashram schools Kanyashrams for classes IV to VII)	3	52	55
		Residential High Schools (Classes IV to X)	3	100	103
		Residential Sevashrams (primary school)	90	1059	1149
14.	Tripura	Classes I to VIII	–	1	1
		Classes I to X	–	1	1
15.	Uttar Pradesh	for SC/ST			33
16.	West Bengal	Classes V to VIII for SC/ST			12
		Classes I to XII		1	1
17.	Arunachal Pradesh	Primary level	–	134	134

		Middle level	–	124	124
		Secondary level		40	40
		Higher secondary level	–	17	17
18.	Dadra & Nagar Haveli	Classes I to X	-	1	1
19.	Goa, Daman & Diu	Classes I to VIII	-	2	2

Source : pp. 12-65 of Educational Facilities to SC/ST, Ministry of Education, 1985.

students are far better placed in this regard. Most of the SC/ST students being first generation learners, also do not have the facility of proper guidance by their parents. Hostels, which provide atmosphere for studies as well as facilities for coaching and guidance, therefore, play a very important role in the promotion of education among the SC/ST students. In this connection, a study was conducted by the Government of Karnataka on the performance of hostellers in S.S.L.C. Examination held during April 1978, which revealed that the performance of the SC/ST hostellers in the examination was far better as compared to those who had no hostel facilities. In case of the SCs, while among day scholars, only 35 per cent of students who appeared for the above mentioned examination could pass, among the hostellers the pass percentage was as high as 53.5. Similarly, among the STs only 37.2 per cent of the students who appeared in the examination could pass, but the corresponding percentage among the ST hostellers was 68.00. According to the findings of the study, facilities in hostels like free boarding, lodging, supply of textbooks and stationery, special coaching, etc., were mainly responsible for the better performance of the SC/ST hostellers as compared to the day-scholars.[98]

Hostels for the SC/ST boys and girls are constructed under the Backward Classes Sector of the State Plans and Tribal Sub-plan. Non-Official organizations running hostels for the SC/ST students also receive grants-in-aid from State Governments/Union Territory Administrations and also from the Government of India. A consolidated list indicating the number of Government Welfare Hostels for the SC/ST, prepared on the basis of available data, is given in Annexure Table XIII. This information pertains to the period 1983-84. Hence, it is quite likely that the number of hostels has increased substantially by this time.

The number of Government hostels for the SCs/STs is inadequate in many States. In his 27th Report (1979-81) the Commissioner for the SC/ST observed that the number of backward class hostels continued to be inadequate in Bihar, Rajasthan, Himachal Pradesh, Kerala and Uttar Pradesh and reiterated that the Governments of the States with large SC/ST population, in which the number of Backward Class Hostels was inadequate, should take urgent steps to increase the number thereof adequately.[99] The Commission for the SC/ST also recommended in 1980 that all the State Governments/Union Territory Administrations should take immediate steps in providing hostel facilities for the SC/ST students in both pre-matric and post-matric classes.[100]

The Third All-India Educational Survey on Hostel Facilities for the Scheduled Castes conducted by the National Council of Educational Research and Training (NCERT) during December, 1973 also throws light on this problem. From the statistics received from 13 States (Andhra Pradesh, Bihar, Gujarat, Haryana, Karnataka, Kerala, Madhya Pradesh, Maharashtra, Rajasthan, Tamil Nadu, Tripura, Uttar Pradesh and West Bengal) and two Union Territories (Dadra and Nagar Haveli and Pondicherry), the report has highlighted the inadequacy of hostel facilities in different States. According to the survey, Uttar Pradesh with the highgest Scheduled Caste population did not have the required percentage of hostels. With only 3.2 per cent of the total number of hostels, Uttar Pradesh ranked only eighth in the country in numerical strength of hostels, while Maharashtra having the lowest percentage of the Scheduled Caste population (6 per cent) had the second highest number of hostels among all the States/UTs. Andhra Pradesh, with 14.51 per cent Scheduled Caste population had the maximum number of hostels, i.e., 1036 hostels constituting 26.46 per cent of the total hostels. Surprisingly enough, Haryana having as high as 18.88 per cent of the Scheduled Caste population had only two hostels in the State for the Scheduled Castes.[101] The position remained almost the same even after a decade. Andhra Pradesh had the maximum number of hostels followed by Maharashtra. Uttar Pradesh continued to be in a bad shape, so also did Punjab, Himachal Pradesh and Haryana.

The shortage of hostel facilities is sought to be met by construction of new hostels, expansion of the existing hostel buildings, opening of new hostels in rented buildings and providing alternate accommodation facilities to the SC/ST students to run their own mess. It is, however, the common experience that indiscriminate opening of hostels does not help in proper utilization of the hostel facilities. In some places, the hostels are overcrowded to accommodate boarders over and above the sanctioned strength, while in other cases many of the seats continue to be vacant due to dearth of the SC/ST candidates. A number of studies were conducted by the field offices of the Commission for the SC/ST in 1976-79 on the working of welfare hostels in Karnataka, Orissa, Rajasthan and Chandigarh. In Karnataka, out of 27 hostels visited during 1978, full strength was achieved only in eight hostels and in one hostel the strength exceeded the sanctioned strength. Shortfall in attaining the full strength was noticed in 18 hostels accounting for 66.7 per cent of the total sample. In Orissa, it was revealed during 1977-78 that hostels were opened indiscriminately without keeping in view the local demands, and such hostel buildings were utilized for the purposes other than that for which those were constructed. These were being used either as classrooms, teachers' quarters, office rooms and for other purposes. In one hostel in Jaipur in Rajasthan, it was found in 1978-79 that only one-third of the sanctioned strength of the hostel could be achieved and the rest of the seats were lying vacant due to non-availability of suitable candidates. In Chandigarh, it was found in 1976-77 that all the three hostels run by the S.G.G.S. Khalsa College, Mohilpur, Guru Ravi Dass Sabha, Ludhiana and Guru Nanak National College for Women were lying vacant due to non-availability of suitable candidates.[102] The findings of the above studies indicated that due care was not taken to assess the local requirements before the new hostels were constructed. The Commission for the SC/ST, therefore, recommended that district authorities should annually review the capacity of seats in the hostels for the SC/ST and rationalize the facilities according to the demand at block/tahsil levels. As regards girls' hostels, it was suggested that care should be taken to ensure that hostel buildings were not used for purposes other than girls' hostels. These hostels should have compound walls as well as attached wardens' quarters. As far as possible, location of girls' hostels should not be in forlorn and isolated places.[103]

Reservation of Seats in Hostels

It is often argued that setting up of hostels exclusively for the SC/ST students leads to isolation of the weaker sections who are not given opportunity to mingle with the students of other castes from the beginning of their career-making. The Study Team on Social Welfare and Welfare of Backward Classes (Renuka Ray Study Team) in their Report presented in July 1959, recommended that there should be no separate institutions, hostels and colonies exclusively for the Scheduled Castes and that in all general hostels, controlled and assisted by the Government, at least ten per cent seats should be reserved for the Scheduled Castes.[104]

The Department of Social Welfare of the Government of India was in agreement with this recommendation.[105] As a matter of policy, some States have taken steps in this direction for intermingling of the SC/ST students with those belonging to other castes in hostels. With a view to avoiding segregation on community basis and to promoting social integration of students of different communities, all the denominational hostels run by the Social Welfare Department, Karnataka, have been converted to non-denominational ones and 25 per cent of the seats in Welfare hostels have been reserved for admission of non-SC/ST students. In case, sufficient number of students belonging to other castes are unavailable, the vacant seats are filled up by the SC/ST students. In Tamil Nadu, twenty per cent of the seats in Welfare hostels are reserved for the students of Backward Classes and five per cent for the Forward Class students. Similarly, in Kerala, in all the hostels run by the Directorate of Harijan Welfare and Tribal Welfare, ten per cent of the seats are reserved for admitting the students other than SC/ST.[106] In Bihar, in the SC hostels, 85 per cent seats are reserved for SCs and 15 per cent for others. In Rajasthan, in the hostels established for the SCs, STs, etc. 60 per cent of the seats are reserved for the backward classes, for whom the hostel is meant and ten per cent for the other backward classes excepting the TAD hostels which are meant exclusively for the STs. In Pondicherry, in the hostels meant exclusively for the SC/ST students, 20 per cent of the seats are reserved for students from other communities.[107]

The Basumatari Committee on the Welfare of the SC and ST in their 17th Report presented on December 16,1970 opined that Government's administrative machinery should be geared up to ensure that benefits of hostels constructed and maintained at State expenditure for the SC/ST students were utilized primarily by students belonging to such communities. The Committee also recommended that Government should also ensure that all general hostels constructed with funds provided by the Governments at the Central and State levels or maintained by non-official agencies with grants given by the Government make suitable provision for the SC/ST students and that efforts were made to attract them in larger numbers.[108]

In view of these recommendations, the Government of India in the Ministry of Education and Youth Services under Memo No. F. 19-6/71. T. 5 dated February 5,1971 asked all the State Governments-all Engineering Colleges and Polytechnic Institutions to ensure that the existing hostel facilities are made available to the SC/ST students as recommended by the Parliamentary Committee on the Welfare of the SC/ST and efforts made to attract them in larger number to these hostels.[109] The Ministry of Education and Youth services in its Memo No. F. 16-6/70-U.I. dated February 27,1971 addressed to all State Governments/UTs/all Universities/and the University Grants Commission asked them to implement the recommendation of the Parliamentary Committee that all general hostels constructed with funds provided by the Government at the Central and State levels or maintained by non-official agencies with grants given by the Government make suitable provision for the SC/ST students and that efforts are made to attract them in larger numbers.[110]

With a view to avoiding segregation and instilling a sense of social equality amongst the SC/ST students by increasing their intake in general hostels, it was recommended in the 21st report (1971-73) of the Commissioner for the SC/ST that 25 per cent seats should be reserved for the SC/ST students in all general hostels.[111] The matter also came up for discussion in the eighth meeting of the High Power Committee on October 20,1978 in which it was recommended that necessary steps should be taken to ensure that the facility of admission to hostels was not denied to the SC/ST students and it was suggested that there should be reservation for the SC/ST in respect of allotment of seats in these hostels. In pursuance of this recommendation, the Union Ministry of Home Affairs issued instructions in January 1979 to all States/UTs, that necessary steps should be taken to reserve accommodation for the SC/ST students in all general hostels run by them or, by Voluntary Organizations receiving grants-in-aid, in proportion to the population of these communities in the respective States, UTs and also to give them weightage over and above this proportion, keeping in view their educational and economic backwardness.[112] The University Grants Commission has also issued necessary instructions to all the institutions assisted by it to reserve 20 per cent of the seats in such hostels for students belonging to the SC/ST. The University Grants Commission has also decided that its assistance for construction of hostels in backward areas would be at the rate of 75 per cent of the total expenditure as against 50 per cent available for other areas.[113] The response of the State Governments/Union Territory Administrations in this regard is encouraging. A good number of the State Governments/Union Territory Administrations have taken steps on the lines of instructions issued by the Ministry of Home Affairs.

Some State Governments/Union Territory Administrations have fixed a definite percentage of reservation in general hostels for the SC/ST students and the same is indicated in Table 4.8.

Students living in hostels run or subsidized by the State Governments are supposed to be provided with furniture, bedding and linen, textbooks, stationery, library books, newspapers, indoor and outdoor games, haircuts, fares or passes for commuting to their schools and colleges, clothes to wear and washing soap, etc. These are free of cost, in addition to free lodging and boarding with food as per nutritional standards specifically spelt out and defined. The actual provision of facilities, however, varies from State to State. Available information on rates of stipends and other facilities in welfare hostels have been indicated at Table XIV.

In spite of these impressive investments in the hostel scheme, only a few of the hostellers seem to be satisfied with the facilities provided. According to a study, only 23 per cent of the school hostellers and 11 per cent of the college hostellers say that they are "fully satisfied" with the hostel facilities provided. As many as 35 per cent of the school hostellers and 31 per cent of college hostellers are only "partly satisfied," and 38 per cent of the school hostellers and 54 per cent of the college hostellers say that they are "dissatisfied" with the facilities.[114]

TABLE 4.8
PERCENTAGE OF SEATS RESERVED IN GENERAL HOSTELS FOR THE SC/ST STUDENTS

Sl. No.	*State/UT*	*Percentage of Reservation for*		*Remarks*	*Source*
		Scheduled Castes	*Scheduled Tribes*		
1	2	3	4	5	6
1.	Andhra Pradesh	20	5		a
2.	Assam	6.5	8.5 in plains 4.5 in hills	7% seats are reserved for SCs and 10% for STs in Plains and Hills, respectively, in the hostels run by voluntary organizations.	a
3.	Delhi	10		for both SCs and STs	a
4.	Gujarat	15	5		a
5.	Karnataka	25		for both SCs and STs	a
6.	Madhya Pradesh	15	20		a
7.	Manipur	50 for SCs and STs in Central Valley district		More than 90% pre-matric and post-matric students district in Govt. as well as in aided hostels in the Hills district are SCs and STs	
8.	Orissa	10 for both SCs and STs			a
9.	Pondicherry			It is reported that adequate accommodation facilities are available for SC hostellers	
10.	Tamil Nadu	18 for both SCs and STs			a
11.	Uttar Pradesh	18	nil		a
12.	West Bengal	15	5		a
13.	Himachal Pradesh	15	7		b
14.	Kerala		25	3	c
15.	Tripura	29	15	In hostels attached to colleges	d
16.	Goa, Daman & Diu			All SC/ST students are provided hostel accommodation	e

Sources : a–p. 199 of 27th report of the Commissioner for SC/ST.
b–p. 24 of Educational Facilities to SC/ST, Ministry of Education, 1985.
c–p. 28, *Ibid.*
d–p. 51, *Ibid.*
e–p. 62, *Ibid.*

In order to find out the source of their dissatisfaction, one is tempted to refer to the report submitted by the Basumatari Committee in December, 1970 to the Fourth Lok Sabha and to recall the several shortcomings in the functioning of hostels that were recorded therein.

The Committee recorded that some of the hostels were housed in totally unsuitable buildings and surroundings, and that the living conditions of the inmates were far from satisfactory. It complained about lack of interest and concern on the part of the people running these hostels. Apart from describing the paucity of facilities in the hostels, the Committee brought out the fact the the Scheduled Caste students were not always in sound financial position to reach out to hostel facilities. They are so poor that they did not even have the fare to reach the hostel for seeking admission.[115]

But the position has not shown any sign of improvement since the submission of the Basumatari Committee's report, rather it has declined further as indicated by newspaper reports. The State Minister for Backward Class Welfare of Andhra Pradesh after visiting four Government-run hostels for backward classes and Scheduled Castes in Khammam district said on February 11, 1991 that the children lived in sub-human conditions. The children had no plates or trays and food was served on floor. He saw many children eating in plastic glasses or rejected polythene sachets while keeping the pigs and dogs at bay. Similarly, most of the children he saw did not have a shirt and the half-pants they were wearing were often in tatters. He said at least 50 children he met were suffering from various skin ailments and other diseases. About two dozen children had ugly patches of scabies on the faces and bodies. The children told him that no doctor had visited them for months. They made petitions to the hostel warden several times but nothing happened. The Minister said that he was afraid that many children might be suffering from serious diseases but could not be sure unless a medical check-up was done. He said the latrines were overflowing and a foul smell pervaded the entire atmosphere. What was worse, he did not find any trace of studies, which was the main purpose of keeping the children in hostels. Since the wardens absconded for months, the children never bothered about studies.[116]

If this is the condition prevalent in hostels in Andhra Pradesh which boasts of having established the largest number of hostels for backward classes in the entire country, the conditions of hostels in other States/UTs can very well be imagined.

Special Coaching Schemes

In order to remove difficulties at the earlier stages of education and improve the performance of the SC children in schools and colleges as also in medical, engineering and other professional courses, the scheme of providing preparatory training, remedial teaching and special coaching to SC/ST students have been in operation in many States/UTs. Some State Governments also provide coaching for State/Central Services competitive examinations. The details of the Schemes in vogue in various States/UTs are noted below.

Remedial Coaching Scheme at School Level : In Andhra Pradesh, coaching is provided to students in classes VIII and X to prepare them for Board Examinations. The scheme is being operated in 23 districts with 15 centres per destirct for class VIII and ten centres per district for class X.

In Assam, grants of Rs 1000 p.a. per school are given for coaching the SC/ST students at high school level. During 1984-85, 400 schools were given grants for this purpose.

In Gujarat, additional coaching is provided in subjects like science, English and Mathematics to backward class students studying in classes VIII to X and residing in grants-in-aid hostels. Three part-time teachers having specialization in these subjects are engaged in each centre and are paid an honorarium of Rs 50 p.m. for coaching the students. Three classes are held in each week. Each centre is paid Rs 1650.

In Haryana, remedial coaching is provided at selected centres for students in classes IX, X and XI.

In Jammu and Kashmir, there are seven coaching centres providing special coaching for preparing students for examinations at pre-matric level.

In Karnataka, remedial coaching is given to all SC/ST students who have failed in SSLC examination.

In Kerala, remedial coaching is provided to students appearing in SSLC and college examinations.

In Maharashtra, the directorate of Tribal Development has a scheme of conducting coaching classes to teach students who are weak in english, mathematics and science at school level.

In Manipur, remedial coaching is provided to the SC/ST students in mathematics and science from classes VI to X.

In Orissa, remedial coaching is given to students of Class X studying in Harijan and Tribal Welfare Department High Schools.

In Rajasthan, remedial coaching facilities in subjects of science and Mathematics are available at the SC/ST hostels at school level.

In Sikkim, remedial pre-examination coaching is provided to students appearing in classes X and XII examinations.

In Tamil Nadu a scheme of remedial coaching in English, Mathematics and Science for about one and a half hours a day after the school hours was introduced for the benefit of SC/ST students in classes VIII to X in selected High/Higher Secondary Schools, numbering 500 in the year 1981-82. This scheme has been extended to classes XI and XII from 1982-83 in about 300 schools where special coaching is given in English, mathematics, physics, chemistry, zoology, botany, commerce and accountancy. The heads of the institutions and teachers involved in the programmes are paid an honorarium of Rs 50 p.m.

In Tripura, remedial coaching is provided for the inmates of hostels in english and mathematics for Middle/Secondary/ Higher Secondary examinations.

In Uttar Pradesh, remedial coaching is provided to students of classes X and XII in Science, English and Mathematics for the preparation of Board examinations. This scheme is in operation in 28 districts. Pre-entance examination for medical and engineering is also provided to the SC/ST students.

In West Bengal, there are 385 schools with 1785 coaching units with the maximum intake capacity of ten SC/ST students per unit which provides remedial coaching to students studying in classes V to X.

In Arunachal Pradesh, special coaching is organized for students appearing in the Board examinations.

In Chandigarh, remedial coaching is given to the SC children for Classes I to V.

In Pondicherry, tutorial facilities are provided to the SC students in middle and secondary level classes by appointment of suitable part-time teachers for a strength of not less than 50 SC students in a particular stage.

Remedial Coaching Scheme at College Level : In Andhra Pradesh, remedial coaching was given to degree and intermediate students in. 519 degree and junior colleges during 1984-85. Special coaching in spoken English is also provided to students coming from non-English medium schools.

In Gujarat, remedial coaching is provided in Medical and Engineering courses for the SC/ST students. The lecturers are paid an honorarium of Rs 25 per lecture. Three lectures are given in a week.

In Karnataka, in all Government colleges remedial coaching is given to the SC/ST students. In the engineering and Polytechnic courses, the SC/ST students are provided special coaching for the first six months to bring them at par with the rest of the students.

In Madhya Pradesh, remedial courses have been started in 15 colleges situated in tribal areas. In Engineering colleges and Polytechnics also, remedial coaching is provided to the SC/ST students. Pre-examination coaching is given in hostels attached to higher secondary schools for appearing in Medical and Engineering courses.

In Tamil Nadu, remedial coaching is provided to the SC/ST students studying in degree courses in all Government and Aided Arts Colleges numbering about 190. For covering all the courses at degree level, these coaching classes are held for a period of not less than two months. A lump sum grant of Rs 1000 is given to each college for this purpose. Remedial coaching is also given to the SC/ST students in egineering colleges.

In Delhi, remedial coaching is given in Engineering, IIT and Polytechnic courses.

Coaching for State/Central Services Competitive Examinations : In Andhra Pradesh, the coaching centre at Osmania University provides coaching for IAS and Allied Services. It is proposed to extend this facility for providing coaching for Staff Selection Commission, Andhra Pradesh Public Service Commission Examinations, Medical and Engineering Entrance Examinations, etc.

The Assam Administrative College provides coaching for competitive examinations to the SC/ST students.

In Bihar, the University of Ranchi runs a coaching centre for preparing the SC/ST students for the All-India competitive examinations.

In Gujarat, in pre-examination coaching, the SC/ST candidates are provided training for examinations conducted by the UPSC, Gujarat Public Service Commission, Gujarat Panchayat Services, Banks, etc. A stipend of Rs 85 p.m. is given to day-scholars and Rs 125 p.m. to those residing in hostels. The lecturers are paid an honorarium of Rs 20 per lecture. These training courses are conducted for a period of two to three months.

In Haryana, there are three centres in the State which provide coaching for various competitive examinations.

In Himachal Pradesh, coaching is provided to the SC/ST students at the H.P. Institute of Public Administration for HAS/ IAS/ pre-medical competitive examinations.

In Karnataka, there are five pre-examination coaching centres preparing students for various competitive examinations.

In Kerala, three centres are running pre-examination coaching for the SC/ST students.

In Manipur, the pre-examination training centres at Imphal provides free coaching to all candidates including SC/ST for All-India Civil Service Examinations.

In Meghalaya, pre-examination coaching for competitive examinations (IAS/ Central Services) is given at North-eastern Hill University for the SC/ST students.

In Punjab, training is imparted for Central /State Services Examinations in the Training Centre at Patiala. Training is imparted in stenography to both unemployed and employed SCs. A stipend of Rs 100 p.m is given to those who are unemployed.

In Rajasthan, the State Government is running a pre-examination training centre for the SC/ST candidates for All-India Civil Services Examinations. The intake capacity is 40. Free accommodation and coaching facilities are provided during the four months of training. A stipend of Rs 150 p.m is also provided to the trainees.

In Channai, coaching classes are conducted for the SC/ST candidates appearing for Group IV Services Examinations conducted by the Tamil Nadu Public Service commission. 17 centres have been set up for this purpose. Pre-examination coaching for National Defecnce Academy/Indian Military Academy Examination is given to the SC/ST candidates in the Special Training Institute, Channai.

In Uttar Pradesh, coaching is provided for higher level competitive examinations like Civil Services Examinations/ Provincial Civil Services Examinations.

In Pondicherry, pre-examination training is given to the SC students for appearing in various competitive examinations.

In West Bengal, the Scheduled Castes and Tribes Welfare Directorate runs courses for preparing candidates belonging to the SC/ST communities intending to appear at competitive examinations for jobs. For the West Bengal Civil Services Examination the Directorate is running two Pre-Examination Training Centres (PETC) located at Maulana Azad College, Calcutta and A.C. College, Jalpaiguri. It also runs a PETC for Miscellaneous Services and Clerkship Examinations at Bikash Bhavan, Salt Lake. At Suffee Commercial College, Calcutta, the Directorate runs courses for typing and stenography.

Free Textbooks

The distribution of free textbooks and even stationery to students is one of those incentives which are given by the State Governments/ Union Territory Administrations to attract children to school and to retain them there. In 1984-85, all States/UTs except Kerala, Manipur, Uttar Pradesh and Delhi had some scheme of providing free textbooks, stationery, etc., to the students including the SC/ST students at different levels of school education. It is revealed by the Fifth All India Educational Survey (1986) that 416,730 (56.54 per cent) schools covering all stages of school education have the provision of free textbooks to students. According to this Survey, 33,524,152 students of all stages of school education are being benefited by this incentive scheme. Of these beneficiaries, 77.16 per cent are studying in rural schools and the remaining 22.84 per cent in urban schools. Among the beneficiaries, 41.27 per cent are girls. Further, 24.82 per cent of the beneficiaries belong to the Scheduled Castes and 11.71 per cent to the Scheduled Tribes, which together accounts for 36.53 per cent of the total number of beneficiaries.[117]

The position is indicated in Table 4.9.

TABLE 4.9

NUMBER OF BENEFICIARIES OF FREE TEXTBOOKS IN 1986

Type of School	*No. of Schools*	*Number of beneficiaries*			
		SC	*ST*	*Others*	*Total*
1	*2*	*3*	*4*	*5*	*6*
Primary	315,213 (59.62%)	5,159,161 (26.50%)	2,585,073 (13.28%)	11,722,537 (60.22%)	19,466,771
Upper Primary	70,872 (50.98%)	1,888,652 (18.59%)	1,021,312 (10.05%)	7,249,287 (71.36%)	10,159,251
Secondary	23,529 (44.77%)	932,323 (34.55%)	236,421 (8.76%)	1,529,556 (56.69%)	2,698,200
Higher Secondary	7,116 (46.01%)	341,121 (28.43%)	81,590 (6.80%)	777,219 (64.77%)	1,199,930
Total	416,730	8,321,157 (24.82%)	3,924,396 (11.71%)	21,278,599 (63.47%)	33,524,152

Source : pp. 183-85 of Fifth All India Educational Survey, 1986.

The scheme varies from State to State. In West Bengal, there is no income limit for the SC/ST students for availing of the Book Grant. The rates are as follows :

Class V	Rs 20.00
Class VI	Rs 50.00
Classes VII to VIII	Rs 150.00
Class IX	Rs 200.00
Class X	Rs 100.00

Free Uniform

It is a fact that the children from weaker sections of the society often do not go to schools mainly owing to economic reasons. One of the reasons is the lack of suitable clothing for going to school. Though it is an Uneasy task to provide a school uniform to every student, all States/UTs except Kerala, Manipur, Mizoram, Nagaland, Punjab, Sikkim, Uttar Pradesh and Lakshadweep have tried to provide free uniform at least in a limited number of schools.

The Fifth All India Educational Survey (1986) shows that out of 735,771 schools in the country, 308,201 (41.89%) covering all the stages of education have some scheme or the other for providing the incentive of free uniform to students. As revealed during the Fifth Survey, 16,067,242 students are being benefited by this incentive scheme at all stages of school education. Of these beneficiaries, 77.44 per cent are studying in rural schools and 22.56 per cent in urban schools. Among these beneficiaries, 33.04 per cent belong to the Scheduled Castes and 11.60 per cent to the Scheduled Tribes. Further, among the beneficiaries, 49.98 per cent are girls.[118]

The number of beneficiaries in different stages of school education is indicated in Table 4.10.

TABLE 4.10

NUMBER OF BENEFICIARIES OF FREE UNIFORM IN 1986.

Type of School	No. of Schools	Number of Beneficiaries SC	ST	Others	Total
1	2	3	4	5	6
Primary	247,588 (46.83%)	3,774,269 (36.06%)	1,255,614 (12.00%)	5,435,633 (51.94%)	10,465,516
Upper Primary	48,050 (34.56%)	1,068,706 (25.62%)	523,396 (12.55%)	2,578,648 (61.83%)	4,170,750
Secondary	9,548 (18.17%)	294,152 (33.87%)	69,565 (8.01%)	504,835 (58.12%)	868,552
Higher Secondary	3,015 (19.50%)	172,799 (30.40%)	15,851 (2.79%)	373,774 (66.81%)	562,424
Total	308,021	5,309,926 (33.04%)	1,864,426 (11.60%)	8,892,890 (55.36%)	16,067,242

Source : pp. 180-183 of Fifth All-Indiua Educational Survey, 1986.

Mid-day Meals

Schemes to provide mid-day meals for school children have a beneficial impact not only on nutrition of the child but also on school attendance. Introduced in 1982 by the M.G. Ramachandran regime, the Tamil Nadu Government's pioneering programme on nutrition of the child in socially disadvantaged communities in rural and urban areas has not only won the acclaim of international agencies like the UNICEF and World Bank, but also inspired other States to launch similar programmes to attract children to schools and to retain them there. All State Governments except Bihar, Gujarat, Jammu & Kashmir, Kerala, Maharashtra, Manipur, Mizoram, Nagaland and Uttar Pradesh have been operating mid-day meals scheme in schools for the students including the SC/ST students. The Fifth All India Educational Survey (1986) reveals that out of 735,771 schools in the country, 187,016 (25.42 per cent) covering all the stages of school education have the provision of mid-day meals for children. As revealed by the Survey, of the 22,553,505 beneficiaries, 78.41 per cent are studying in rural schools.

Among the beneficiaries, 59.02 per cent are boys and 40.98 per cent are girls. 20.05 per cent of the beneficiaries belong to the Scheduled Castes and 12.81 per cent to the Scheduled Tribes, which together account for 32.86 per cent of the beneficiaries.[119]

The number of beneficiaries in different stages of school education is given in Table 4.11.

The Working Group on Development and Welfare of the Scheduled Castes during the Eighth Five-Year Plan suggested that mid-day meals should become an integral part of the school education system to ensure full enrolment and continued attendance of the SC children, particularly of girls from the community.[120] As primary education is highly emphasized, the Government of India has decided to extend this scheme by phases from the financial year 1995-96[121] to improve enrolment, attendance and retention of school children in primary schools. The first Centrally Sponsored mid-day meal programme was launched on August 15,1995 in a Government school near Delhi under the National Programme of Nutritional Support to Primary Education (NPNSPE) as part of the Centre's ambitious social welfare programme. The programme, projected to cost Rs 610 crore in 1995-96, Rs 1474 crores in 1996-97 and Rs 2226 crores in 1997-98, it will cover in the first phase, 30 million children in all government, local body and private aided primary schools (class I-V) in 2500 Blocks in some of the most backward regions in the country and another 120 million children when it is extended to the entire country.[122]

TABLE 4.11

NUMBER OF BENEFICIARIES IN DIFFERENT STAGES OF SCHOOL AND EDUCATION

Type of School	*No. of Schools*	*Number of Beneficiaries* *SC*	*ST*	*Others*	*Total*
1	*2*	*3*	*4*	*5*	*6*
Primary	147,647 (27.92%)	2,997,849 (21.93%)	2,277,196 (16.66%)	8,394,675 (61.41%)	13,669,720
Upper Primary	33,757 (24.84%)	1,077,902 (15.24%)	547,371 (7.74%)	5,448,007 (77.02%)	7,073,280
Secondary	3,784 (7.20%)	237,101 (23.84%)	48,927 (4.92%)	708,563 (71.24%)	994,591
Higher Secondary	1,824 (11.82%)	208,347 (25.54%)	14,846 (1.82%)	592,721 (72.64%)	815,914
Total	187,016	4,521,199 (20.05%)	2,888,340 (12.81%)	15,143,966 (67.14%)	22,553,505

Source : pp. 178-80 of Fifth All-India Educational Survey, 1986, Vol. I.

The various Central and Centrally Sponsored Schemes and the Schemes in the State Sector, detailed above, primarily aim at creating a congenial atmosphere for promotion and development of education for such weaker sections of population known as Scheduled Castes and Scheduled Tribes so that they do not remain in a disadvantageous position as compared to other sections in the matter of availing educational opportunities. So far, governments have evidently given a marked stress upon granting financial and material assistance to the Scheduled Castes for inducing them towards education. In quantitative terms, the range of schemes evolved and implemented for the benefit of the Scheduled Castes appear doubtlessly impressive. But, considering the magnitude of the problem of bringing these entire communities within the fold of education, these measures have touched only a fringe of the problem. There are several shortcomings in the nature and modus operandi of these schemes, like inadequacy of financial or material assistance, i.e. scholarships, stipends, book grants, uniform or mid-day meals, delay in grants of stipends/scholarships, book grants or books, stationery and equipments, etc., cumbersome and bureaucratic procedures followed in granting financial assistance, poor hostel facilities, lack of awareness of the facilities, etc.

Theoretically speaking, any Scheduled Caste child, if he or she wishes to pursue higher studies, can do so without any let or hindrance. Seats are reserved for him or her at all levels of education including technical and professional education. A specific number of fellowships/overseas scholarships are also earmarked for him. There are about 5000 hostels for backward class and another 3500 SC girls'/boys' hostels for their free boarding and lodging, apart from other ancillary facilities including free food, and if one wants, one can get accommodation in any general hostel where seats are reserved. There are provisions for stipends and for free special coaching in specific subjects for preparing them for competitive services examinations. A set of books for Medical/Engineering/Agriculture/Polytechnic courses is provided to each SC student of such courses. Apart from freeships in educational institutions, the post-matric scholarships scheme covers almost all the SC students in post-matric stage of education. About 12.6 lakh SC students were covered by the post-matric scholarships scheme in 1992-93 and the projected beneficiaries in 1996-97 are expected to be more than 15 lakh.

Compared to the importance given to the post-matric education of the SC children, the pre-matric education did not receive equal importance and attention from the Planners and Administrators. Though almost all the States/UTs grant pre-matric scholarships to the SC children under various schemes and there are special schemes for children of those engaged in unclean occupations and for girls of indigent SC families in pre-matric stage, get the quantum of financial assistance in pre-matric stage of education is grossly insufficient and hence the coverage is highly inadequate. As in the case of post-matric scholarships scheme sometimes the instalment may not be received even till the middle of the session and in some cases at the fag end of the session. consequently, only those who can afford or get some support from the voluntary organizations can continue their education. While those who do not have such a benefit have to go without education even though they are eligible. The policy of attaching higher weightage to post-matric education than pre-matric educaiton has been anomalous and similar to the act of drawing a cart by putting it before the horse. It is here that the major loophole lies and is responsible for bulk of the students belonging to the Scheduled Castes not being able to move up the education ladder. As this creates a situation in which those students who have been able to cross the initial hurdle at the primary and secondary level are able to move up with ease but those who are unable to cross the first hurdle are doomed for the life. The porposal to include all the children of 6-11 year age group in the scheme should be given a serious thought, as it is at this crucial age that incentives are required to compensate the opportunity costs and to attract the students to school.[123] One, however, feels that if the constitutional obligation of providing free compulsory elementary education to all children up to the age of 14 was scrupulously and meticulously followed, not only would illiteracy have been completely eradicated by this time but other concomitant advantages like, fall in the rate of growth in population, better living conditions, etc., would have ensued, making the country richer.

It is generally alleged that the schemes of financial assistance have failed to come up to the expectations of helping the poorer sections of the Scheduled Castes. The financial concessions and other facilities have been availed of, more by the privileged groups amongst the Scheduled Caste communities, than the poorer and more deprived sections as the quantum of assistance has seldom been sufficient enough to induce the 'really poor' to go in for education. It is held that "free tuition does not mean free education to the majority of SC" as the opportunity cost of education for poorer sections is much higher than the well-to-do groups. It has been rightly observed that "equal access for unequal groups is not true equality."[124]

There has been a large scale expansion of access to schooling but the quality of inputs and management of rural schools leaves much to be desired. This has led to rural-urban differentials which is manifested in regional inequalities. All steps need be taken to ensure that the quality of rural schooling is the same as that of urban schools and those who are enrolled are able to complete the required cycle of education without frequent repetitions.

It will not be proper to assume that the mere provision of educational facilities, financial and other incentives would automatically ensure utilization of these benefits. Several studies indicate that such facilities are availed of only by the 'elite' section of the Scheduled Caste population and these benefits have failed to trickle down to the needy masses who do not even know what they are entitled to. The real problem is how to bring this vast deprived group within the fold of education and ensure that they are equally benefited, if not more, by the existing educational opportunities actually meant for them.

References

1. *Fourth Report of the Commission for Scheduled Castes and Scheduled Tribes (1981-82)*, p. 60.
2. *POA, 1992*, pp. 8-9.
3. *RWGSC* during the Eighth Five-Year Plan (1990-95), p. 43.
4. *Fourth Report of the Commission for SC/ST (1981-82)*, pp. 60-61.
5. *Educational Development of Scheduled Castes/Scheduled Tribes*, status and Programme Ministry of Education, 1995, p. 15
6.. *Ibid.*, p. 11.
7. *Annual Report*, University Grants Commission, 1995-96, pp. 126-27
8. *Ibid.*, p. 126.
9. *Ibid.*, p. 120.
10. *Educational Development of SCs/STs, Status and Programmes*, op. cit., p. 11.
11. *Ibid.*, p. 17.
12. *Education Facilities to Scheduled Castes/Scheduled Tribes*, Ministry of Education, 1985, pp. 5-8.
13. *Ibid.*
14. *Ibid.* p. 11.
15. *Educational Development of SC/STs, Status and Programmes*, op. cit., p. 13.
16. *Educational Facilities to SCs/STs*. op. cit., p. 11.
17. *Report of the Committee on Untouchability, Economic and Educational Development of the Scheduled Castes and other Connected Documents*, 1969, p. 196.
18. *Second Report of the Commission for Scheduled Castes and Scheduled Tribes (1979-80)*, p. 166.
19. *Annual Report*, 1996-97, Ministry of Welfare, p. 94.
20. *Ibid.*, p. 23.
21. *Ibid.*
22. *Ibid.*, 1994-95, p. 18.

23. *Second Report of the Commission for SC/ST (1979-80)*, p. 166.
24. Educational Facilities to SCs/STs, op. cit., p.26, p.28.
25. *Annual Report*, Ministry of Welfare, 1992-93, p. 15.
26. *Ibid.*, 1996-97, p. 22.
27. *Twenty-eighth Report of the Commissioner for Scheduled Castes and Scheduled Tribes* (henceforth *RCSCST*) (*1986-87*), p. 304.
28. *Ibid.*
29. *Annual Report*, Ministry of Welfare, 1996-97, p. 22.
30. *Ibid*, 1994-95, p.18.
31. *RCSCST*, 27th (1979-81), p. 202.
32. *RCSCST*, 28th (1986-87), pp. 307-8.
33. *RWGSC*, during the Eighth Five-Year Plan, 1990, p. 45.
34. *Annual Report*, Ministry of Welfare, 1992-93, p. 15.
35. *Ibid.*, 1996-97, p. 23.
36. *Ibid.*, 1995-96, p. 17.
37. *Ibid.*, 1996-97, p. 24.
38. *Ibid.*, 1995-96, p. 17.
39. *Ibid.*, 1996-97, p. 24.
40. *RCSCST*, 27th (1979-81), p. 197.
41. *RCSCST*, 28th (1986-87), p. 306.
42. *Annual Report*, Ministry of Welfare, 1996-97, p. 24.
43. *RCSCST*, 27th (1979-81), p. 198.
44. *Annual Report*, Ministry of Welfare, 1996-97, p. 24.
45. *RCSCST*, 27th (1979-81), p. 198.
46. RWGSC during the Eighth-Five Year Plan, 1990, p. 45.
47. *Annual Report*, Ministry of Welfare, 1993-94, p. 14.
48. *Ibid.*, 1994-95, p. 22.
49. *Ibid*, p. 20.
50. *Ibid*, 1996-97, p. 97.
51. *Ibid.*, p. 24.
52. *RWGSC* during the Eighth Five-Year Plan , 1990, p. 45.
53. *RWGSC* during the Seventh Five-year Plan, 1985, p. 35.
54. *Annual Report*, Ministry of Welfare, 1992-93, p. 15.
55. *RWGSC* during the Eighth Five-Year Plan, 1990, p. 45.
56. *Annual Report*, Ministry of Welfare, 1994-95, p. 22.
57. *Ibid.*, p.144.
58. *Ibid.*, 1995-96, p.21.
59. *Ibid.*, p.94.
60. *Ibid.*, 1996-97, p.25.
61. *Ibid.*, 1994-95, p.22.
62. *RCSCST*, 26th (1978-79), p. 174.
63. *RWGSC* during the Seventh Five -Year Plan, 1985, p. 35.
64. *RWGSC* during the Eighth Five -Year Plan, 1990, p. 47.
65. *RWGSC* during the Ninth Five -Year Plan, (interim), 1996, p. A. 3.

66. *Annual Report*, Ministry of Welfare, 1992-93, p. 17.
67. *Ibid.*, 1996-97, p. 25.
68. *RCSCST*, 28th (1986-87), p. 307.
69. *RWGSC* during the Eighth five-Year Plan, 1990, p. 43.
70. *Annual Report*, Ministry of Welfare, 1992-93, p. 16.
71. *Ibid.*, 1993-94, p. 14.
72. *Ibid.*, 1994-95, p. 19.
73. *Ibid.*, 1996-97, p. 25.
74. *Ibid.*, p.99.
75. *Ibid.*, 1994-95, p. 20.
76. *Ibid.*, 1995-96, p. 19.
77. *Ibid.*, 1996-97, p. 99.
78. *Ibid.*, 1994-95, pp. 20-21.
79. *Ibid.*, 1996-97, p. 26.
80. *Ibid.*, 1993-94, p. 15.
    Ibid., 1994-95. p. 21
    Ibid., p. 1996-97. p. 26
81. *Ibid.*, p. 102.
82. *RWGSC* during the Eighth Five-Year Plan, 1990, p. 43.
83. *Annual Report*, Ministry of Welfare, 1992-93, p. 16.
84. *Ibid.*, 1996-97, p. 27.
85. *Ibid.*, 1995-96, p. 18.
86. *Ibid.*, 1996-97, p. 26.
87. *Ibid.*, 1994-95, p. 22.
88. *Ibid.*, p.150.
89. *Educational Facilities to SCs/STs, op.cit.*, pp. 12-66.
90. *Second Report of the Commission for SC/ST* (1979-80), p. 170.
91. *RCSCST*, 27th (1979-81), p. 167.
92. *Ibid.*, p. 201.
93. *Ibid.*
94. *RWGSC* during the Seventh Five -Year Plan, 1985, p.43.
95. *RWGSC* during the Eighth Five -Year Plan, 1990, p.46.
96. *Ibid.*, p. 44.
97. *Ibid.*, p. 46.
98. *RCSCST*, 27th (1979-81). pp. 195-96.
99. *Ibid.*, p. 197.
100. *Second Report of the Commission for SC/ST* (1979-80). p. 155.
101. *Ibid.*,
102. *Ibid.*, pp. 156-57.
103. *Ibid.*, p. 156.
104. *Seventeenth Report of the Parliamentary Committee on the Welfare of Scheduled Castes and Scheduled Tribes*, Fourth Lok Sabha, SCTC 30. December, 1970, para 3.1. p. 26
105. *Ibid.*, para 3.2, p. 26.

106. *Second Report of the Commission for SC/ST* (1979-80), p. 158.
107. *Educational Facilities to SC/ST,* op. cit., p. 17, 44, 65.
108. *Seventeenth Report of the Parliamentary Committee on the Welfare of SC/ST, op.cit.,* para 3.13, p. 30.
109. *Third Report of the Parliamentary Committee on the Welfare of SC/ST, 5th Lok Sabha,* SCTC 31, pp. 20-21.
110. *Ibid.,* p.22.
111. *RCSCST,* 21st (1971-73), p. 61.
112. *RCSCST,* 27th (1979-81), p. 199.
113. *Second Report of the Commission for SC/ST* (1979-80), p. 158.
114. Chitnis, Suma, 1981, *A Long Way to Go... Report on a survey of SC High School and College students in fifteen States of India,* p. 115, Allied Publishers.
115. *Seventeenth Report of the Parliamentary Committee on the welfare of SC/ST,* 4th Lok Sabha, SCTC 30, op. cit., pp. 47-53.
116. *The Hindustan Times,* February 12, 1991.
117. *Report of the fifth All-India Educational Survey,* 1986, vol. I, pp. 183-85.
118. *Ibid.,* pp. 180-83.
119. *Ibid.,* pp. 178-80.
120. *RWGSC* during Eighth Five-Year Plan, 1990, p. 43
121. Para 23 of the Budget Speech of the Union Finance Minister, *The Statesman,* March 16, 1995, p. 15
122. *The Statesman,* August 20, 1995, p. 15.
The Hindu, August 23, 1995, p. 12.
123. Aggarwal, Yash and Sibou, Sarika, 1994 *Educating Scheduled Castes* p. 397, National Institute of Educational Planning and Administration.
124. Premi, Kusum K. 1977 *Privileges Given to the Scheduled Castes in Eduction A Critical Analysis,* Paper presented at Workshop on Alternative Educational features (Novemebr 16, 21-1997) Policy Planning and Education Unit, NCERT, 1977, (Memeographed), p. 4., quoted by Nautiyal and Sharma, op. cit., p. 30

5

Advancement in Higher Education

Recognizing the role of education as an effective instrument for bringing about change in the attitudes and aspirations of people, the Central and State Governments have invested resources to strengthen the educational programmes and make these accessible to the deprived and backward sections of the Indian society, namely, the Scheduled Castes and the Scheduled Tribes. An elaborate programme of pre-matric and post-matric scholarships, reservation of seats in the schools and colleges, establishment of hostels and ashram schools for the children of the Scheduled Castes/Scheduled Tribes and other benefits mentioned in the preceding chapter, are in operation for the last 50 years. While scholarships and freeships have been instituted to enable the Scheduled Caste students to overcome their economic handicaps and hostels have been established to enable them to overcome the handicaps of living away from school and college facilities, the provision of reservation aims at helping them overcome restriction to their admission to educational institutions regardless of whether these restrictions are rooted in caste discrimination or in their inability to measure up to the performance level of more advantaged students. It is of considerable interest to find out how these facilities have been made use of by them and what is the level of their progress in the field of education.

The progress in education up to the elementary level, i.e., class VIII of the general students as well as the Scheduled Caste students has been discussed in Chapter III. The Constitution imposed an obligation on the State to provide free and compulsory elementary education to all children up to the age of 14 years, irrespective of caste, creed, sex or religion, within ten years of the commencement of the Constitution, i.e., by 1960. Sadly enough, the State could not fulfil its constitutional obligation even within 48 years of the Constitution and, in all likelihood, will not be able to accomplish by the end of the twentieth century The lackadaisical manner in which this Directive of the Constitution has been implemented, raises doubt whether the State is really serious to provide education to all up to a certain standard. It is true that children belonging to the Scheduled Castes enjoy certain facilities, but, considering the magnitude of the problem, these are not enough for finding an easy and quick solution to it. Moreover, unless the machinery employed to implement the various plans and programmes for the educational development of the Scheduled Castes are enthused to work with a missionary zeal, all efforts will, in effect, come to nought.

So far as the educational facilities in the Secondary Section, Higher Secondary Section, Colleges including Professional Institutions and Universities are concerned, the State provides certain facilities to a section of the population, broadly categorised as the Scheduled Castes, solely on the basis of their birth in certain castes. Inclusion of a community in the Schedule entitles their members to certain benefits and facilities which others are not entitled to, no matter whether they are educationally, culturally, economically and socially at the same level. It is, therefore, worth finding out the effect of these facilities, discussed in Chapter IV, on the educational attainments of the Scheduled Castes in higher education, i.e., above the level of elementary education, which is, in any case, universal.

The importance of Secondary stage of education and more so of Higher Secondary stage of education as a terminal stage for a large number of student population and also as a feeder stage to their professional education cannot be underscored. In both the situations, these stages are very significant as they basically form the foundation for the future of an individual. In fact, the grades obtained at these stages become, more often than not, the crucial deciding factor about whether an individual is going to continue his studies in future or enter the world of work. An assessment of facilities both at the secondary and the higher secondary stage of education made in the Sixth All-India Educational Survey (1993) for the general as well as the Scheduled Caste population is indicated in Table 5.1.

Table 5.1 reveals that 2.48 per cent of the total number of habitations predominantly populated by those belonging to the Scheduled Castes had schooling facilities at secondary stage within

TABLE 5.1

SECONDARY /HIGHER SECONDARY/EDUCATION FACILITIES AVAILABLE AMONG SCHEDULED CASTES/ GENERAL POPULATION

	General		*Scheduled Castes*	
	Habitations Having Secondary Sections	*Population Served by Secondary Sections*	*Habitations Having Secondary Sections*	*Population Served Secondary by sections*
Within habitation	53,505 (5.04%)	18.29%	2,990 (2.48%)	8.50%
WIthin 2 km	306,614 (28.91%)	27.16%	39,868 (33.08%)	34.24%
WIthin 5 km	739,529 (69.73%)	77.91%	87,989 (73.01%)	78.03%
Within 8 km	899,582 (84.82%)	90.06%	105,491 (87.53%)	90.34%
Beyond 8 km	161,030 (15.18%)	9.94%	15,026 (12.47%)	9.66%

Source : pp. 59-60 of Sixth All India Educational Survey, 1993.

HIGHER SECONDARY EDUCATION

	General		*Scheduled Castes*	
	Habitations Having Higher Secondary Sections	*Population served by Higher Secondary Sections*	*Habitations Having Higher Secondary Sections*	*Population Served by Higher Secondary Sections*
Within habitation	11,728 (1.11%)	5.36%	620 (0.51%)	2.30%
Within 2 km	151,252 (14.26%)	15.24%	18,971 (15,74%)	18.00%
Within 6 km	464,248 (43.77%)	46.08%	58,280 (48.36%)	52.25%
Within 8 km	604, 161(56.96%)	63.60%	73,938 (61.35%)	67.03%
Beyod 8 km	456,451 (43.04%)	36.40%	46,579 (38.65%)	32.97%

Source : pp. 74-75 of Sixth All India Educational Survey, 1993.

their own habitations covering 8.50 per cent of the Scheduled Caste population in rural areas. The corresponding figures for the general population were 5.04 per cent and 18.29 per cent respectively. This difference was due to the fact that habitations predominantly populated by the Scheduled Castes were smaller in size than those of the general population. However, 33.08 per cent of the habitations predominantly populated by the Scheduled Castes had these facilities within a distance of two km, 73.01 per cent had these facilities within a distance of five km and 87.53 per cent had these facilities within a distance of eight km as against 28.91 per cent, 69.73 per cent and 84.82 per cent of the general habitations respectively. In terms of population, 34.24 per cent of the Scheduled Caste population in rural areas were served within a distance of two km, 78.03 per cent within a distance of five km and 90.34 per cent within a distance of eight km as against 27.16 per cent, 77.91 per cent and 90.06 per cent of the general population respectively. Thus, both in terms of habitations within the various distance slabs and the number of population served by the secondary schools, the Scheduled Caste population were better placed than the general population.

In regard to schooling facilities at the Higher Secondary stage within a distance of two km, six km and eight km, the habitations predominantly populated by the Scheduled Castes were in a much better position compared to the general population in terms of habitations and population coverage. As many as 15.74 per cent of the habitations predominantly populated by the Scheduled Castes had schooling facilities within a distance of two km, 48.36 per cent within a distance of six km and 61.35 per cent within a distance of eight km as against 14.26 per cent, 43.77 per cent and 56.96 per cent of the general habitations respectively. In terms of population coverage, 18 per cent of the Scheduled Caste population in rural areas were served within a distance of two km, 52.25 per cent within a distance of six km and 67.03 per cent within a distance of eight km, the corresponding figures for the general population being 15.24 per cent, 46.08 per cent and 63.60 per cent.

Enrolment — Secondary Stage

In 1946-47, there were 3,659 secondary schools in the country with a total enrolment of 1,571,397 students.[1] In 1996-97, there were

73,127 secondary schools with a student population of 17,861,774.[2] So, during this 50 year period, there was a 20 fold increase in the number of schools, while the studentship increased 11 fold.

During the period between 1978 and 1996-97, there was an increase of 99 per cent (from 36,675 to 73,127) in the total number of schools, as against an increase of 101 per cent in the total enrolment (from 8,872,141 to 17,861,774). The Scheduled Caste enrolment, though much lower than their share in the total population , witnessed a higher rate of increase at 222 per cent (from 697,601 to 2,245,317[3]) during the same period.

The enrolment of general students and the Scheduled Caste students in classes IX and X in 1986, as revealed in the Fifth All-India Educational Survey and in 1996-97 has been shown in Table 5.2.

TABLE 5.2

ENROLMENT IN CLASSES IX AND X

General Students					*Scheduled Caste Students*				
Boys	*Girls*	*Total*	*% of Girls*	*Source*	*Boys*	*Girls*	*Total*	*% of Girls*	*Source*
				1986					
7866884	3653112	11519996	31.71	a	1109172	404399	1513571	26.72	b
				1996-97					
11234324	6627450	17861774	37.10	c	1513428	731889	2245317	32.60	d

Sources : a — Statement 6. 18, p. 68 of Fifth All-India Educational Survey, 1986.
b — Statement 6. 20, p. 69, *Ibid.*
c — p. 31 of Selected Educational Statistics, Ministry of Human Resource Development, Department of Education, 1996-97.
d — p. 56, *Ibid.*

In 1996-97, the total number of students enrolled in classes IX and X was 17,861,774. Of them, 37.10 per cent (6,627,450) were girls. At the time of the Fifth Survey (1986), the total enrolment in these classes was 11,519,996 of which 3,653,112 (31.71 per cent) was that of girls. Thus, the period between 1986 and 1996 witnessed an increase of 55.05 per cent in the total enrolment. The corresponding increase in the enrolment of boys and girls was 42.80 per cent and 81.42 per cent respectively. Although the proportion of girls in the total enrolment has increased marginally from 31.71 per cent in 1986 to 37.10 per cent in 1996, it is encouraging to note that increase in the exclusive enrolment of girls has been very substantial to the tune of 81.42 per cent during this period.

Among all the States and Union Territories, Delhi (52.58 per cent) had the largest percentage of girls in the total enrolment. Next in order came Kerala with 51.68 per cent, followed by Punjab (50.70 per cent) and Mizoram (50.14 per cent). Besides these four States/UTs, there were ten other States and Union Territories — Goa, Manipur, Meghalaya, Nagaland, Sikkim, A and N Islands, Chandigarh, Daman and Diu, Lakshadweep and Pondicherry in which the percentage was more than 45. On the other hand, the percentage of girls was found to be below the All-India level in case of Bihar (26.13 per cent), Jammu and Kashmir (36.45 per cent), Madhya Pradesh (30.17 per cent), Orissa (35.63 per cent), Rajasthan (24.73 per cent), Uttar Pradesh (23.11 per cent) and Dadra & Nagar Haveli (24.30 per cent).[4] Amongst these States/UTs, the position of Bihar, Madhya Pradesh, Rajasthan, Uttar Pradesh and Dadra and Nagar Haveli was evidently dismal.

Scheduled Caste Enrolment

There were 2,245,317 Scheduled Caste students enrolled in classes IX and X in 1996-97. The enrolment of the Scheduled Caste students in these classes was found to be 12.57 per cent of the total enrolment whereas the Scheduled Castes constituted 16.48 per cent of the country's population in 1991. The corresponding percentage at the time of Fifth Survey (1986), however, was slightly higher at 13.14. Although the proportion of girls in the total enrolment has increased substantially from 26.72 per cent in 1986 to 32.60 per cent in 1996, the male-female disparities continues to be more pronounced among the Scheduled Castes. It is, however, heartening to note that the increase in the exclusive enrolment of the Scheduled Caste girl in the period 1986-96 has been 80.98 per cent, which compares favourably with that of 81.42 per cent registered by the general girl students.

Another welcoming trend is that in as many as eight States/UTs, the percentage of enrolment of SC girls was higher than that of general girls. For instance in Chandigarh it was 67.43 per cent for the SC girls as against 49.92 per cent for the general girls; followed by Delhi (56.22 per cent : 52.88 per cent); Kerala (52.54

per cent : 51.68 per cent); Assam (46.29 per cent : 44.67 per cent); Himachal Pradesh (44.40 per cent : 43.21 per cent); Dadra and Nagar Haveli (40.90 per cent . 24.90 per cent); Jammu and Kashmir (37.90 per cent : 36.42 per cent) and Madhya Pradesh (30.84 per cent : 30.17 per cent). At the same time, in some States the percentage of enrolment of the Scheduled Caste girls was abysmally low. It was 10.68 per cent in Rajasthan, followed by 14.12 per cent in Uttar Pradesh, 22.00 per cent in Bihar and 27.71 per cent in Orissa.[5] Unless the enrolment of SC children, particularly of SC girls registers a sharp increase, the overall position is not likely to improve.

Higher Secondary Education

The Third Survey had revealed that there were 9,505 higher secondary schools in the country in 1973. The number rose to 10,429 at the time of the Fourth Survey (1978), registering an increase of 9.72 per cent. At the time of the Fifth Survey(1986), this number stood increased to 15,465, which was 48.29 per cent more than the number of schools in 1978. The reason for this abnormal increase might be that the States had tried to uniformly adopt 10+2 pattern of education as recommended by the Education Commission (1964-66). In the process, in a large number of schools, classes XI-XII might have been introduced, thus increasing the number of higher secondary schools much more between 1978 and 1986 than between 1973 and 1978.[6] In 1996, the number of higher secondary schools increased to 25,045[7], registering an increase of 61.95 per cent during this period.

The enrolment of boys and girls, both of general population and Scheduled Caste population, as recorded in the Fifth Survey (1986) as well as in 1996 is given in Table 5.3.

As many as 6,412,716 students were studying in classes XI and XII in 1996 as against the corresponding number of 3,509,571 in 1986, registering a phenomenal increase of over 82 per cent between 1986 and 1996. Girls constituted 30.77 per cent of the total enrolment in 1986 and 35.33 per cent in 1996. The increasing trend of enrolment of girls at the secondary stage continued at the higher secondary stage as well. The girl students accounted for an increase of 109.76 per cent in enrolment during the period 1986-96.

TABLE 5.3

ENROLMENT IN CLASSES XI AND XII

General				Scheduled Castes			
Boys	Girls	Total	Source	Boys	Girls	Total	Source
			1986				
2,429,508 (69.23%)	1080,063 (30.77%)	3,509,571	a	299231 (76.52%)	91841 (23.48%)	391072	b
			1996				
4,147,170 (64.67%)	2265546 (35.33%)	6,412,716	c	490,883 (70.68%)	203618 (29.32%)	694,501	d

Sources: a-p. 84 of Fifth All-India Educational Survey, 1986, Vol. I.
b- p. 1085 of Fifth All India Educational Survey, 1986, Vol. II.
c- p. 30 of Selected Educational Statistics, 1996-97.
d- p. 55, *Ibid*.

There were 694, 501 students belonging to the Scheduled Castes in the higher secondary sections in 1996, as against 391,072 in 1986, thereby registering an increase of 77.89 per cent. These 694,501 SC students were 10.83 per cent of the total enrolment, as against 11.14 per cent recorded in 1986. As the enrolment of the Scheduled Caste students could not keep pace with the increase in the total enrolment during period 1986-96, their share in the total enrolment fail marginally in 1996 as compared to 1986. It is a point for consideration as to why the Scheduled Caste students are not interested in joining the higher secondary courses.

The SC girls constituted 23.48 per cent of the total SC enrolment in 1986 and 29.32 per cent in 1996. The increase in the exclusive enrolment of the SC girls during the period 1986-87 was 121.71 per cent, which was marginally higher than the corresponding increase in the enrolment of the general girls.

Statewise percentage of enrolment among the Scheduled Caste students in classes IX-X and XI-XII in 1996 is given in Table 5.4.

TABLE 5.4
SCHEDULED CASTE ENROLMENT AT VARIOUS STAGES OF SCHOOL EDUCATION, 1996

Sl. No.	Name of State UT	% of SC in Total Population in in 1991 Census	Percentage of SC in Total Enrolment in Classes I-V	Classes VI-VIII	Calasses IX-X	Classes XI-XII
	1	2	3	4	5	6
1.	Andhra Pradesh	15.92	20.92	16.74	15.43	9.19
2.	Arunachal Pradesh	0.47	0.16	0.23	0.31	0.39
3.	Assam	7.40	11.76	8.47	14.13	11.83
4.	Bihar	14.55	15.08	10.68	8.25	9.11
5.	Goa	2.08	2.24	1.53	1.17	1.11
6.	Gujarat	7.41	9.00	9.61	9.92	8.70
7.	Haryana	19.75	26.09	17.86	12.09	9.61
8.	Himachal Pradesh	25.34	25.64	23.06	15.84	11.99
9.	Jammu & Kashmir	8.31	9.61	8.39	7.60	6.10
10	Karnataka	16.38	16.57	16.28	13.63	10.71
11.	Kerala	9.92	10.74	11.01	10.23	5.88
12.	Madhya Pradesh	14.55	16.72	14.25	13.72	10.44
13.	Maharashtra	11.09	12.71	14.03	13.41	13.41
14.	Manipur	2.02	2.58	2.76	2.62	3.43
15.	Meghalaya	0.51	0.58	1.94	2.08	3.39
16.	Mizoram	0.10	0.012			
17.	Orissa	16.20	18.94	15.23	9.58	15.19
18.	Punjab	28.31	39.80	28.80	22.83	14.86
19.	Rajasthan	17.29	14.48	16.54	15.09	8.4
20.	Sikkim	5.93	5.72	5.36	5.38	5.11
21.	Tamil Nadu	19.18	19.86	16.15	15.18	13.69
22.	Tripura	16.36	17.80	15.34	15.46	12.78
23.	Uttar Pradesh	21.04	15.86	13.79	14.30	12.48
24.	West Bengal	23.62	21.63	15.95	9.99	8.17
25.	Chandigarh	16.51	25.57	18.61	14.78	7.61
26.	Dadra & Nagar Haveli	1.97	1.91	3.64	5.85	3.57
27.	Daman & Diu	3.83	4.39	4.89	6.02	4.49
28.	Delhi	19.05	19.49	20.05	5.47	6.37
29.	Pondicherry	16.25	20.11	21.72	17.17	14.13
	All-India	16.48	16.63	14.50	12.57	10.83
	Co-efficient of Equality		100.91	87.99	76.27	65.72

Source: pp. 30-32 and 55-58 of Selected Educational Statistics, 1996-97.

For the sake of meaningful comparison, the enrolment position in classes I-V and VI-VIII during the same period as also the percentage of SC population to total population of the State/UT, according to the 1991 Census, is indicated in this Table as well.

It will be evident from this Table that the percentage of enrolment of Scheduled Caste students to total students has exceeded the respective State/UT's Scheduled Caste population strength at the Secondary stage in Assam, Gujarat, Kerala, Maharashtra, Manipur, Meghalaya, Dadra and Nagar Haveli, Daman & Diu and Pondicherry and at the Higher Secondary stage in the States/UTs of Assam, Gujarat, Maharashtra, Manipur, Meghalaya, Dadra & Nagar Haveli and Daman & Diu.

While these States/UTs had also registered a higher enrolment ratio in classes I-V and VI-VIII (except Dadra & Nagar Haveli in classes VI-VIII), some States like Andhra Pradesh, Jammu & Kashmir, Punjab, Chandigarh and Delhi which had a better enrolment ratio both in classes I-V and VI-VIII, could not keep the same standard either at the Secondary stage or at the Higher Secondary stage. There were States like Bihar, Goa, Haryana, Karnataka, Madhya Pradesh, Orissa, Tamil Nadu and Tripura which could not even maintain their record of higher enrolment ratio in classes I-V in upper primary sections and in other higher classes.

One more point which emerges from this Table is that there is a sharp reduction in the All-India enrolment ratio as one moves up in the education ladder. For instance, while the coefficient of Equality (CE) in enrolment ratio in casses I-V was 100.91, it came down to 87.99 in Classes VI-VIII, 76.27 in classes IX-X and to 65.72 in Classes XI-XII, i.e., almost a 35 per cent reduction at the Higher Secondary stage. It may be noted that the CE had deteriorated since 1986, as would be evident from Table 5.5, which gives the comparative figures in 1986.

The rates of wastage and stagnation among the Scheduled Caste students are still considerably higher than those among the non-SC/ST students. What is, however, more agonising is the fact that in spite of the incentives/educational facilities being made available to the members of this community, they not only lag much behind the rest of the population in their educational attainment, specially at the Secondary and Higher Secondary stages, but the gap is widening further in many States.

TABLE 5.5
SCHEDULED CASTE ENROLMENT AT VARIOUS STAGES OF SCHOOL EDUCATION, 1986.

Sl. No.	*Name of State/ UT*	*% of SC in Total Population in 1991 Census*	*Percentage of SCin total enrolment in*			
			Classes I-V	*Classes VI-VIII*	*Classes IX-X*	*Classes XI-XII*
1	2	3	4	5	6	7
1.	Andhra Pradesh	14.87	18.94	15.96	14.67	12.09
2.	Arunachal Pradesh	0.46	0.80	0.47	0.27	0.31
3.	Assam	6.24	10.57	9.40	9.29	6.11
4.	Bihar	14.51	12.16	9.42	7.79	9.75
5.	Goa	2.05	2.47	1.37	0.87	0.50
6.	Gujarat	7.15	9.34	9.61	10.05	9.94
7.	Haryana	19.07	21.15	14.38	11.26	7.26
8.	Himachal Pradesh	24.62	24.58	19.65	15.03	8.01
9.	Jammu & Kashmir	8.31	8.69	8.39	7.18	3.82
10.	Karnataka	15.07	15.81	12.80	12.37	13.53
11.	Kerala	10.02	11.26	13.10	12.51	16.22
12.	Madhya Pradesh	14.10	18.44	17.31	15.76	14.12
13.	Maharashtra	7.14	13.86	13.36	13.17	6.57
14.	Manipur	1.25	1.62	1.39	1.50	2.67
15.	Meghalaya	0.41	1.08	1.31	1.64	2.03
16.	Mizoram	0.03	0.00	0.00	0.00	0.00
17.	Orissa	14.66	17.26	12.01	10.91	8.77
18.	Punjab	26.87	32.43	22.82	18.25	12.98
19.	Rajasthan	17.04	16.74	13.39	12.02	9.89
20.	Sikkim	5.78	6.43	4.53	3.45	3.06
21.	Tamil Nadu	18.35	20.18	18.69	15.36	15.60
22.	Tripura	15.12	17.70	15.39	13.20	10.31
23.	Uttar Pradesh	21.16	20.08	16.77	15.31	13.25
24.	West Bengal	21.99	24.80	18.82	16.27	12.90
25.	Chandigarh	14.09	20.61	14.77	6.49	3.36
26.	Dadra & Nagar Haveli	1.97	4.29	7.93	8.56	7.74
27.	Daman & Diu	3.56	3.69	4.23	3.71	2.81
28.	Delhi	18.03	21.20	16.40	12.37	8.05
29.	Pondicherry	15.99	17.43	14.99	11.31	8.88
	All-India	15.75	17.12	14.69	13.14	11.14
	Co-efficient of Equality		108.70	93.27	83.43	70.73

Source: pp. 1206-07 of Fifth All-India Educational Survey, Vol. II, 1986.

The two States having the highest number of Scheduled Caste population, namely, Uttar Pradesh and West Bengal, have given a very poor account of themselves in all these four stages of enrolment in 1996. As a matter of fact, a distinct downward trend is noticeable in their case since 1986. In 1986, the percentage of SC enrolment to total enrolment was much higher in all these four stages. It was 20.08 per cent, 16.77 per cent, 15.31 per cent and 13.25 per cent in 1986 as against 15.86 per cent, 13.79 per cent, 14.30 per cent and 12.48 per cent in 1996 in Uttar Pradesh. In West Bengal, it was 24.80 per cent, 18.82 per cent, 16.27 per cent, 12.90 per cent in 1986 as against 21.63 per cent, 15.95 per cent, 9.99 per cent and 8.17 per cent respectively in 1996. The miserable performance of these two States has been reflected in the CE in 1996.

Enrolment at College Stage

According to the guidelines issued by the Union Ministry of Education (since renamed as Human Resource Development) from time to time to all the State Governments/Union Territory Administrations as well as the Universities, 22.5 per cent of the seats in all educational and technical institutions should be reserved for the Scheduled Castes and the Scheduled Tribes at a distinct rate of 15 per cent and 7.5 per cent (effective from August 23, 1982), respectively. This reservation is interchangeable, i.e., if sufficient number of candidates are unavailable to fill up the seats reserved for the Scheduled Tribes, these can be filled by suitable candidates from the Scheduled Castes and vice versa. Where admissions are restricted to candidates who obtain a certain minimum percentage of marks and not merely by passing of certain examinations, five per cent reduction for the Scheduled Castes/Scheduled Tribes was recommended, provided that the lower percentage prescribed did not fall below the minimum required to pass the qualifying examination. The Ministry had also suggested that, in case the 22.5 per cent seats earmarked for the Scheduled Castes/Scheduled Tribes, remained unfilled, a further relaxation in marks could be given to them, in order of merit inter se among them so that all the reserved seats were filled by candidates belonging to these categories.[8]

It may also be pointed out that different State Governments/ Union Territory Administrations have different percentages of the Scheduled Caste/Scheduled Tribe populations. Reservation of a uniform percentage of seats for these communities in educational institutions in different States/UTs does not, therefore, appear to be logical. So, while the guidelines issued by Union Ministry of Education is applicable to all Central Universities/Institutions, revised guidelines have been issued by most of the States/UTs to reserve seats for the Scheduled Caste/Scheduled Tribe students in proportion to their population in the respective States/UTs, as mentioned in Chapter IV.

In pursuance of the recommendations of the Committee on welfare the Scheduled Castes and Scheduled Tribes (42nd Report), the UGC issued guidelines to all Universities/Institutions deemed to be Universities under letter No. F.1-26/76 (CP) dated May 4, 1976 for setting up special cells in the Universities to ensure implementation of orders regarding reservation for the SC/ST students in admissions and recruitment as per guidelines issued by the Government of India from time to time. The UGC also informed that it would provide financial assistance to the universities for the creation of the special cells.[9]

AnSCT Cell was also set up by the UGC in January 1979, inter alia, with a view to vigorously watching the effective implementation of reservation orders in favour of the Scheduled Castes/Scheduled Tribes, relating to their access to higher education. It is the responsibility of this Cell to circulate the decisions of the Government of India and University Grants Commission among Universities and Colleges. The UGC's revised guidelines for full implementation of reservation in admission for the SC/ST students in all courses and faculties/departments in all Universities and Colleges from academic year 1989-90 onwards circulated under D.O.No.F.I-6/89(SCT) dated July 30, 1989 of the Additional Secretary, UGC is given in Appendix I. According to these guidelines, the Scheduled Caste/Scheduled Tribe candidates who have marks above the level by which general category students are admitted, should not be counted towards reserved quota at all and should be included in the general merit list of admissions. Seats should be reserved for the SC/ST students in every course and in every faculty/department and should be filled only with the SC/ST candidates and not with others. In order to ensure admissions up to the reserved percentages, it is irrational to apply to them the criteria like minimum eligibility marks and cut off point marks.

Entrance tests should be utilised for the purpose of arranging the SC/ST candidates in the inter se merit list. As the head of the university family, the Vice Chancellor will have to take full responsibility by ensuring that the reservation for the SCs/STs, according to these guidelines, is fulfilled in letter and spirit without any distortion and deviation.

It also devolves on this cell to collect regularly an annual factual position regarding coursewise admissions by reservation to candidates belonging to the SC/ST for different courses by a stipulated date and to take follow-up action, wherever required. Such information about the actual position was collected from 1977-78 onwards and analysed. In October 1982, the UGC published a document captioned "Facilities to Scheduled Castes and Scheduled tribes in Universities and Colleges". It contained an analysis on the position of actual admission and employment of the SCs/STs in universities and colleges for 1977-78. A similar document containing an analysis on the position of actual admission and employment of the SCs/STs in universities and colleges during 1978-79 was published in January 1985 by the UGC.

Information regarding the actual admissions of the SC students to the undergraduate and postgraduate courses, separately grouped into ten areas of learning, during 1977-78 and 1978-79, is given in Table 5.6. In addition, similar information in respect of these courses grouped as professional and non-professional is given at the bottom of the Table.

It would be seen that in the undergraduate courses, the Scheduled Castes had been able to get less than ten per cent seats in all areas except Arts courses ,that too in 1977-78. In Medicine, Agriculture and Veterinary Science courses, they obtained a marginally larger percentage of seats in 1978-79 compared to 1977-78.

In all the professional courses clubbed together, the Scheduled Caste students had been able to secure only 7.45 per cent seats in 1978-79, which was a little higher than 6.8 per cent seats secured in 1977-78. In non-professional courses, they had been able to get only 7.30 per cent seats in 1978-79, which was less than what they could secure in 1977-78. In postgraduate courses, the position of the Scheduled Caste students was worse. Except in Arts courses in which they could secure 10.5 per cent seats in 1977-78 and 10.54 per cent in 1978-79, the percentage of seats secured by them was less than five per cent in all the areas of learning except Commerce in both the years. Compared to 1977-78, the position, however, improved marginally in both the professional and non-professional courses in 1978-79.

TABLE 5.6
PERCENTAGE OF SC ENROLMENT TO TOTAL ENROLMENT IN TEN AREAS OF UNDERGRADUATE AND POSTGRADUATE COURSES DURING 1977-79

	Group	*Percentage of SC Enrolment to Total Enrolment in*			
		1977-78		*1978-79*	
		U.G.Course	*P.G.Course*	*U.G.Course*	*P.G.Course*
1	2	3	4	5	6
1.	Arts	10.4	10.5	9.85	10.54
2.	Science	4.4	3.6	4.44	2.93
3.	Commerce	4.7	5.2	4.76	5.42
4.	Education	6.1	3.6	6.24	3.42
5.	Engineering & Technology	6.1	2.9	6.16	1.92
6.	Medicine	8.5	4.3	9.98	3.69
7.	Agriculture	6.0	2.8	8.39	4.48
8.	Veterinary Science	5.6	1.5	7.02	1.37
9.	Law	6.8	1.8	7.47	3.97
10.	Others	13.5	1.7	5.93	3.56
	Professional	6.8	3.2	7.45	3.48
	non-Professional	7.7	8.1	7.30	8.17
	Source	a	a	b	b

Sources: a- p. 172, para 6.49 of 27th Report of the Commissioner for SC/ST.
b- p. 309, para 33 of 28th Report, *Ibid.*
p.-11, Facilities to SCs/STs in Universities and Colleges, UGC, 1985.

What is latest position in this respect? The UGC has refrained from publishing any document so far. In the absence of the UGC publications, the information as collected from the data released by the Department of Education, Ministry of Human Resource Development for the years 1995-96 and 1996-97 is given in Table 5.7.

TABLE 5.7
PERCENTAGE OF SC ENROLMENT TO TOTAL ENROLMENT IN SIX AREAS OF UNDERGRADUATE AND P.G., COURSES1995

	Group	*Percentage of SC Enrolment to Total Enrolment in*			
		1995-96		*1996-97*	
		U.G,.Course	*P.G. Course*	*U.G. Course*	*P.G. Course*
	1	2	3	4	5
1.	Arts	11.23	13.48	10.65	13.62
2.	Science	7.19	7.14	6.94	7.35
3.	Commerce	5.35	7.58	4.97	7.09
4.	Education	10.27		11.67	
5.	Engineering & Technology	6.65		7.31	
6.	Medicine	9.02		8.82	
	Source	a	b	c	d

Sources: a — pp. 17-19 pp. and 38-43 of Selected Educational Statisticsl 1995-96.
b — pp.15-16 and 35-37, *Ibid.*
c — pp. 27-29 and 48-53 of Selected Educational Statistics, 1996-97.
d — pp. 25-26 and 45-47, *Ibid.*

It would appear that at the undergraduate level there has been substantial increase in the intake of the SC students in courses like Education (nearly 80 per cent) and Science (nearly 50 per cent), marginal increase in courses like Arts, Commerce and Engineering & Technology and a slight decrease in the course of Medicine.

At the postgraduate level, there has been phenomenal increase in the enrolment of the SC students in Science (more than double), Commerce (nearly 50 per cent) and Arts (30 per cent) courses.

The growth of the Scheduled Caste enrolment at graduate and postgraduate levels based on comparative figures for 1995-96 and 1996-97 may be seen in Table 5.8.

It will be seen from this Table that at the graduate level (excluding professional and technical courses) the percentage of the Scheduled Caste students in the country as a whole decreased from 8.91 in 1995-96 to 8.48 in 1996-97, i.e., a decline of 0.43 per cent point. Of the States/UTs which registered a negative growth, Delhi heads

TABLE 5.8

GROWTH OF SC ENROLMENT AT GRADUATE AND POST-GRADUATE LEVELS DURING THE YEAR 1996-97

Sl. No.	*States/UTs*	*Percentage of SC Enrolment to Total at*					
		Postgraduate Level			*Graduate Level*		
		1995-96	*1996-97*	*growth of enrolment*	*1995-96*	*1996-97*	*growth of enrolment*
1.	Andhra Pradesh	16.73	16.73	0	10.04	10.02	-0.02
2.	Arunachal Pradesh	0	0	0	1.18	0	-1.18
3.	Assam	7.53	7.84	+0.31	9.07	9.12	+0.05
4.	Bihar	2.81	2.84	+0.03	3.38	2.92	-9.46
5.	Goa	1.00	1.32	+0.32	0.24	0.60	+0.36
6.	Gujarat	11.97	11.01	-0.96	8.31	7.28	-1.03
7.	Haryana	9.19	11.15	+1.96	5.52	8.10	+2.58
8.	Himachal Pradesh	13.44	12.65	-0.79	9.78	9.72	–0.06
9.	Jammu & Kashmir	3.44	3.55	+0.11	2.91	2.91	0
10.	Karnataka	14.89	13.80	-1.09	10.20	10.50	+0.30
11.	Kerala	13.13	13.52	+0.39	9.41	9.41	0
12.	Madhya Pradesh	9.15	9.02	-0.13	7.93	7.93	0
13.	Maharashtra	16.07	17.37	+1.30	11.60	11.66	+0.06
14.	Manipur	0.77	3.29	+2.52	7.68	4.46	-3.42
15.	Meghalaya	2.11	2.22	+0.11	3.14	3.26	+0.12
16.	Mizoram	0	0	0	0	0	0
17.	Orissa	5.52	5.86	+0.34	6.84	7.20	+0.36
18.	Punjab	7.28	6.64	-0.64	9.78	10.12	+0.34
19.	Rajasthan	16.60	16.04	-0.56	10.65	10.44	-0.21
20.	Sikkim	0	0	0	3.39	2.70	-0.69
21.	Tamil Nadu	11.02	11.02	0	13.01	12.98	-0.03
22.	Tripura	13.52	15.90	+2.38	13.33	13.08	-0.25
23.	Uttar Pradesh	11.31	11.66	+0.35	9.85	10.36	+0.51
24.	West Bengal	3.90	3.61	-0.29	7.93	7.12	-0.81
25.	Chandigarh	3.38	10.70	+7.32	2.02	84.24	*2.22
26.	Dadra & Nagar Haveli	0	0	0	0	0	0
27.	Daman & Diu	0	0	0	4.97	4.29	-0.68
28.	Delhi	6.12	3.03	-3.09	5.65	2.02	-3.63
29.	Pondicherry	12.78	11.41	-1.37	12.50	12.66	+0.16
	India	11.03	11.09	+.06	8.91	8.48	-0.43
	Source	a	b		c	d	

Sources: a- pp. 15-16 and 35-37 of Selected Educational Statistics, 1995-96.

b- pp. 25-26 and 45-47, *Ibid.*, 1996-97.

c- pp. 17-18 and 38-40, *Ibid.*, 1995-96.

d- pp. 38-40 and 48-50, *Ibid.*, 1996-97.

the list (3.63 per cent point) followed by Manipur (3.42), Arunachal Pradesh (1.18), Gujarat(1.03), West Bengal (0.81), Sikkim (0.69), Daman Diu (0.68), Bihar(0.46), Tripura (0.25), Rajasthan (0.21), Himachal Pradesh (0.06), Tamil Nadu (0.03), and Andhra Pradesh (0.02) in that order.

At the post graduate level (only Arts, Science and Commerce courses), the percentage of the Scheduled Caste students increased marginally from 11.03 in 1995-96 to 11.09 in 1996-97, thereby registering an increase of 0.06 per cent point. The position would have improved further but for the negative performance of Delhi (3.09), Pondicherry (1.37), Karnataka (1.09), Gujarat (0.96), Himachal Pradesh (0.79), Punjab (0.64), Uttar Pradesh (0.35), and West Bengal (0.29).

Admission of the Scheduled Caste Students in Medical and Engineering Colleges

The Scheduled Castes and Scheduled Tribes students are generally poor in Mathematics and Science. So Scheduled their performance in these subjects at the school level is unsatisfactory. With a weak foundation in these subjects they hardly succeed in competing with general students for admission in professional courses like Engineering and Medicine. Due to lack of proper orientation at the family level and suitable guidance in the school, the SC/ST students also do not develop any aptitude for pursuing technical courses of study. This results in dearth of sufficient number of qualified doctors and engineers from among the SC/ST communities.

Engineering Colleges

In pursuance of the recommendations of the All India Council for Technical Education (AICTE) made in December 1963, the Union Ministry of Education issued guidelines to all the State Governments and universities in April 1964 that 20 per cent of seats in all technical institutions should be reserved for the Scheduled Castes and the Scheduled Tribes with a distinct rate of 15 per cent for the former and five per cent (since raised to 7.5 per cent) for the latter. This reservation was inter-changeable, i.e., if a sufficient number of candidates were unavailable to fill up the seats reserved for the Scheduled Tribes, these could be filled up by suitable

TABLE 5.9

PERCENTAGE OF SC ENROLMENT TO TOTAL ENROLMENT IN B.E./B.SC (TECH) /B. ARCH DURING 1995-97 ENROLMENT OF SC STUDENTS IN B.E./B.SC.(TECH)/B.ARCH. DURING THE YEAR

Sl. No.	State/UT	1995-96 Total Student	SC Student	%age of Enrolment	C.E.	1996-97 Total Student	SC Student	%age of Enrolment	C.E.
1	2	3	4	5	6	7	8	9	10
1.	Andhra Pradesh	30476	3980	13.06	82	30476	3980	13.06	82
2.	Arunachal Pradesh	262	13	4.96	1055	291	16	5.50	1170
3.	Assam	3246	417	12.85	174	3323	427	12.85	174
4.	Bihar	6272	287	4.58	31	6381	290	4.54	31
5.	Goa	822	11	1.34	60	831	10	1.20	54
6.	Gujarat	15833	932	5.89	79	17698	1026	5.80	78
7.	Haryana	3139	526	16.76	85	4132	602	14.57	74
8.	Himachal Pradesh	629	89	14.15	56	691	98	14.18	56
9.	Jammu & Kashmir	750	41	5.41	65	795	44	5.53	67
10.	Karnataka	74023	3306.	4.57	28	73385	3522	4.80	29
11.	Kerala	13110	651	4.97	50	13277	667	5.02	51

12. Madhya Pradesh	11320	1174	10.37	71	10598	1269	11.97	82
13. Maharashtra	80380	3378	4.20	38	83454	3725	4.46	40
14. Orissa	2625	241	9.18	57	4981	365	7.33	45
15. Punjab	3161	571	18.06	64	4196	677	16.13	57
16. Rajasthan	4551	-	-	-	4551	-	-	-
17. Tamil Nadu	39017	4308	11.04	58	39017	4308	11.04	58
18. Tripura	479	107	22.34	137	479	114	23.80	145
19. Uttar Pradesh	14229	89	0.63	3	14229	89	0.63	3
20. West Bengal	7687	332	4.52	18	9604	2005	20.88	88
21. Chandigarh	39	3	7.69	47	474	73	15.40	93
22. Delhi	3947	438	11.10	58	4262	375	7.87	41
23. Pondicherry	1137	198	17.41	107	1274	219	17.19	106
India	317134	21084	6.65	40	328399	24001	7.31	44
Source	a	b		c	d			

C.E stands for Coefficient of Equality

Sources: a- p. 18 of Selected Educational Statistics, 1995-96.

b-p. 41, *Ibid.*

c- p. 28 of Selected Educational Statistics, 1996-97.

d- p. 51, *Ibid.*

candidates from the Scheduled Caste and vice versa. A minimum qualifying standard was to be prescribed for admission to any technical institution. Students belonging to the SC/ST were to be eligible for admission to the reserved seats if they attained this minimum, without any reference to the gap between their marks and marks of the last person admitted to the open seats. Where admissions were restricted to candidates who obtained certain minimum percentage of marks and not merely the passing a certain examination, a five per cent reduction could be allowed for the SCs/STs provided that the lower percentage prescribed did not fall below the minimum required to pass the qualifying examination. Almost all the State Governments/Union Territory Administrations have reserved seats for the SC/ST candidates in Engineering Colleges in proportion to the population of these communities in those States/UTs.

Statewise information regarding the enrolment of the SC students in B.E./B.Sc.(Eng)/B.Arch. Courses at graduate level during the years 1995-96 and 1996-97, the percentage of SC enrolment to total enrolment and the Coefficient of Equality for the Scheduled Castes is given in Table 5.9.

It would be seen from Table 5.9 that out of the total enrolment of 317,134 students in these courses at the graduate level in the country in 1995-96, 21,084 students belonged to the Scheduled Castes, thereby constituting 6.65 per cent of the total enrolment. The co-efficient of equality for the Scheduled Caste students in this faculty was 40. Statewise, the enrolment position was far from satisfactory in almost all the States except Arunachal Pradesh (1055), Assam (174), Tripura (137), and Pondicherry (107), where the coefficient of equality exceeded 100. The enrolment position of these communities in these courses was very bad in Uttar Pradesh, West Bengal, Karnataka and Bihar, where the coefficient of equality for the Scheduled Castes was as low as 3, 18, 28 and 31 respectively.

The position improved marginally in 1996-97. Out of the total enrolment of 328,399, 24,001 belonged to the Scheduled Castes. Their co-efficient of equality rose to 44. The coefficient of equality in enrolment was very good in Arunachal Pradesh (1170), Assam (174), Tripura (145) and Pondicherry (106). The enrolment position continued to be bad in Uttar Pradesh (3), Karnataka (29) and Bihar (31).

There, however, appears to be some anomalies in the figures mentioned in Table 5.9. For instance, not a single student belonging to the Scheduled Castes was enrolled in Rajasthan in both these years, which is simply absurd. In Uttar Pradesh only 89 SC students were enrolled in both these years, which again is too small a number compared to the vast number of SC student population in the State. In West Bengal, there were only 332 SC students in 1995-96 and in the next year the number jumped to 2005. Again, 11,265 more students (all categories) were enrolled in 1996-97. It is really doubtful if so many new seats could be created in an year in a faculty like Engineering. However, these figures, in the absence of any other reliable figures, at least indicate the trend in admissions of SC students.

The University Grants Commission prepared a document on facultywise enrolment of Scheduled Caste students in the University Teaching Department/University Colleges for the year 1991-92 on the basis of information obtained from 90 such Institutions. Of these 90, only 25 Institutions in 10 States and one Union Territory did furnish information about the actual position of admission of students in the Engineering Faculty. The information furnished by these colleges is indicated in Table 5.10.

TABLE 5.10

ENROLMENT OF SCHEDULED CASTE STUDENTS IN THE ENGINEERING AND TECHNOLOGY FACULTY IN UNIVERSITY TEACHING DEPARTMENT/UNIVERSITY COLLEGES FOR THE YEAR 1991-92

Sl. No.	*State/University/Instt. Deemed to be University*	*Total No.of Students*	*SC Students*	*%age of SC students*	*Co-efficient of Equality*
1	2	3	4	5	6
Andhra Pradesh					
1.	Andhra Pradesh Agri.	139	20	14.39	97
Delhi					
2.	School of Planning & Architecture.	245	28	11.43	60
Gujarat					
3.	Gujarat Agricultural	70	9	12.86	174
4.	Sardar Patel University	8	-	-	-
5.	South Gujarat	204	16	7.84	106

Haryana				
6. Kurukshetra University	262	30	11.45	58
7. Maharishi Dayanand	22	3	13.64	69
8. National Dairy Research Instt.	74	10	13.51	68
Karnataka				
9. Gulbarga	274	47	17.15	105
Kerala				
10. Calicut	36	2	5.56	56
11. Cochin Univ. of Science & Technolgy.	70	6	8.57	86
Madhya Pradesh				
12. Dr. M.S.Gour	59	-	-	-
13. Guru Ghasidas	2	-	-	-
14. Indira Gandhi Krishi	3	1	33.33	229
Maharashtra				
15. Amravati	94	-	-	
16. Bombay	997	43	4.31	39
17. Dr. Baba Sahib Ambedkar Tech.	33	7	21.21	191
18. G.N.D.T. Women's	1562	79	5.06	46
19. Yashwant Rao Chavan	53	-	-	-
Nagaland				
20. Nagaland	15	3	20.00	-
Punjab				
21. Guru Nanak Dev	84	-	-	-
22. Punjab	64	16	25.00	88
23. Thapar Instt. of Engg. & Tech.	1070	92	8.60	30
Uttar Pradesh				
24. Banaras Hindu	702	2	0.28	1
25. Dayalbagh Educational Instt.	252	42	16.67	79
Total	6394	456	7.1	43

It would be seen from Table 5.10 that six colleges did not furnish any information regarding admission of the SC students and in one college it was negligible. The number of the SC students, admitted exceeded the total reserved seats in six colleges, while it ranged between 75 per cent and 100 per cent in four colleges, between 75 per cent and 50 per cent in five colleges and between 30 per cent and 50 per cent in three colleges.

This Table indicates that in at least 32 per cent of the colleges the enrolment position of the Scheduled Caste students was very

TABLE 5.11

ENROLMENT OF SCHEDULED CASTE STUDENTS IN MEDICAL COLLEGES DURING 1995-96 AND 1996-97

Sl. State/UT	Enrolment of SC Students in Medical Colleges at Graduate Level							
	in 1995-96				in 1996-97			
	Total Students	SC Student	%age of Enrolment	C.E.	Total Student	SC Student	%age of Enrolment	C.E.
1 2	3	4	5	6	7	8	9	10
1. Andhra Pradesh	7833	1086	13.86	87	78.33	1086	13.86	87
2. Assam	2298	164	7.14	96	2356	173	7.34	99
3. Bihar	14112	1290	9.14	63	14265	1328	9.31	64
4. Goa	654	20	3.06	138	666	25	3.75	169
5. Gujarat	1839	67	3.64	49	10600	700	6.60	89
6. Haryana	2209	250	11.32	57	2009	207	10.30	52
7. Himachal Pradesh	649	90	13.87	55	812	108	13.30	52
8. Jammu & Kashmir	1470	92	6.26	75	1559	98	6.29	76
9. Karnataka	7288	-	-	-	5060	201	3.97	24
10. Kerala	3367	268	7.96	80	4691	350	4.46	75
11. Madhya Pradesh	4740	531	11.20	77	4740	531	11.20	77
12. Maharashtra	26415	2667	10.10	91	27779	2759	9.93	90
13. Manipur	408	12	2.94	146	441	17	3.85	191
14. Orissa	2806	294	10.48	65	2851	294	10.31	64
15. Punjab	3364	526	15.64	55	3519	549	15.60	55
16. Rajasthan	4017	-	-	-	4017	-	-	-

17. Tamil Nadu	11316	1470	12.99	68	11316	1470	12.99	68
18. Uttar Pradesh	6910	181	2.62	12	6910	181	2.62	12
19. West Bengal	3770	348	9.23	39	3770	348	9.23	39
20. Chandigarh	-	-	-	-	40	-	-	-
21. Delhi	4098	469	11.44	60	4623	105	2.27	12
22. Pondicherry	887	136	15.36	94	1328	167	12.58	77
India	110450	9961	9.02	55	121185	10697	8.82	54
Source	a	b			c	d		

C.E. stands for Co-efficient of Equality.

Sources: a-p. 19 of Selected Educational Statistics, 1995-96.
b-p. 43, *Ibid.*
c-p. 20 of Selected Educational Statistics, 1996-97.
d-p. 52, *Ibid.*

good and in another 21 per cent of the colleges it was moderately good, while in the remaining 47 per cent of the colleges it was poor/very poor. What is, however, distressing is that even the UGC could not collect information regarding admission of the SC students from all the Engineering colleges of this country, to have a meaningful study of the enrolment position in this Faculty.

Medical Colleges

Graduate Courses

Like the Engineering colleges, admission in the Medical colleges are made either on the basis of entrance tests or on the basis of the candidate's merit in the qualifying examinations. Instructions issued by the Ministry of Health and Family Welfare regarding reservation of seats for the SC/ST candidates are being followed by almost all the Medical colleges in the country.[10] The State Governments, have, however, issued instructions to the Medical colleges/universities to reserve seats for the SC/ST students in under grduate courses in proportion to the population of these communities in the respective States. The Medical Council of India (MCI) has recommended relaxation of the eligibility criteria for admission to the seats reserved for the SC/ST students at undergraduate level in Medical colleges. The council has decided that, in respect of candidates belonging to the SC/ST, the minimum marks required for admission shall be 40 per cent in lieu of 50 per cent for general candidates. Where the seats reserved for the SC/ST students in any State cannot be filled for want of the requisite number of candidates fulfilling the minimum requirements prescribed for that State, then such vacant seats may be filled up on All-India basis with the Scheduled Caste and Scheduled Tribe candidates getting not less than the minimum pass percentage or reverted to the general category. Various State Governments, however, have allowed different percentages of relaxation in marks for admission of the SC/ST candidates to undergraduate Medical courses.[11]

Information regarding Statewise number of total students and the Scheduled Caste students enrolled in undergraduate Medical courses, percentage of SC enrolment to total enrolment and the coefficient of equality of the SC students for the years 1995-96 and 1996-97 are given in Table 5.11.

It would be seen from this Table that, out of the total number of 110,450 students enrolled to these courses in all the States/ UTs in 1995-96, 9,961 students belonged to the Scheduled Castes, constituting 9.02 per cent of the total enrolment. The coefficient of equality of enrolment of the Scheduled Castes for these courses was 55. Statewise, the enrolment position was very good in Manipur, Goa, Assam, Pondicherry and Maharashtra where the coefficient of equality for the Scheduled Castes was 146; 138; 96; 94 and 91 respectively. The enrolment position was very bad in Uttar Pradesh., where the coefficient of equality was only 12. In other States, the coefficient of equality for the Scheduled Castes ranged between 39 and 87.

In 1996-97, the position detericrated marginally. Out of the total enrolment of 121,185 students, only 10,697 belonged to the Scheduled Castes, accounting for 8.82 per cent of the total enrolment. The coefficient of equality (C.E.) was 54. The States of Manipur, Goa and Assam continued to maintain a higher C.E. of 191, 169, and 99 respectively, whereas the position deteriorated slightly in Maharashtra where the C.E. was 90. Uttar Pradesh. registered the lowest C.E. of 12 and so also Delhi.

There appears to be some anomalies in these figures. For instance, there were no SC candidate in Karnataka in 1995-96 but 201 such students were shown in 1996-97. There was not a single SC student in Rajasthan in both these years. In Delhi, the number of SC students declined by 364 in one year which does not appear to be plausible. The total number of students registered an increase by 10,735 in 1996-97, which indicates that there was some mistake somewhere.

In order to increase the enrolment of the SC/ST students in the undergraduate medical courses, the Medical Council of India has recommended that the State Governments and universities should arrange special coaching classes for the SC/ST candidates before the qualifying competitive examination to enable them to come up to the appropriate standard for admission to the medical courses. The Government of Madhya Pradesh introduced a scheme to give special coaching in Science/Mathematics/Biology to selected SC/ ST students at the stage of Higher Secondary/first year of B.Sc. in selected schools and colleges before their admission to professional courses to enable them to improve their educational performance as well as to compete well in the entrance test for admission to Medical and Engineering colleges.[12] Many State Governments/ Union Territory Administrations have taken up similar schemes.

The instructions regarding reservation of seats in educational institutions stipulate that the seats reserved for the SC/ST students are interchangeable, i.e., if a sufficient number of the Scheduled Tribe students are unavailable to fill the seats reserved for the candidates belonging to these communities, the vacant seats may be filled by suitable candidates from the Scheduled Castes and vice versa. It has been observed that, in a number of cases suitable candidates belonging to the Scheduled Tribes are unavailable to fill the seats reserved for them and such seats are filled by suitable Scheduled Caste candidates. Available information[13] indicates that this rule of interchangeability has been availed of by the SC candidates rather than by the ST candidates.

It has been observed that the performance of the SC/ST students admitted to various courses in Medical colleges on relaxed standards against reserved seats is unsatisfactory. In this connection, a study[14] was conducted by a Study Team of the organization of the Commissioner for Scheduled Castes and Scheduled Tribes during September 1979 in Raipur, Madhya Pradesh. It was revealed therefrom that although all the candidates including the SC/ST had to take the entrance tests for admission to Jawaharlal Nehru Medical College, Raipur, the State Pre-Medical Test Board had lowered the minimum percentage of qualifying marks for the SC/ ST candidates to 35. Since very few SC/ST candidates could secure this percentage, it was sometimes lowered to even 15 per cent so that more reserved seats could be filled up. The study team collected information regarding the performance of the SC/ST students in the college from 1964 to 1973, which revealed that their performance was unsatisfactory. Out of 42 Scheduled Caste students admitted during these years, four students took four and a half years to pass the final examination, six students took five to six years, six students took six to seven years, seven students took as along as seven to eight years to pass the examination, while three students were rusticated and two got migration to other colleges. Similarly, out of 23 Scheduled Tribe students admitted during the period, only one passed the examination within four and a half years, five students passed it in five to six years, five students took six to seven years, three students took seven to eight years, while two students took eight to 10 years. 14 Scheduled Caste and four Scheduled Tribe students were also reported to have left their study leading to a lot of wastage. It was reported that in spite of special coaching given to the SC/ST students during the first year of the course, their performance had not improved much.

In another study,[15] reported to have been conducted in the Medical Faculty at Baroda (Gujarat) from April 1976 to October, 1980, it was revealed that, during the four and a half years period, out of 120 candidates belonging to the SC/ST, who appeared for the final M.B.B.S. Examination, only 58 could get through. Of these 58 students, 21 passed in the first attempt, 24 in the second, nine in the third and four in the fourth attempt. Sixty-two candidates could not get through even after the fourth attempt. In 1980, out of the 28 SC/ST students who appeared for the final M.B.B.S. Examination, only 13 could get through. Out of these 13, three passed in the fourth attempt, seven in the second and only three students could pass in the first attempt. It was also revealed that the student who stood first among the reserved category, secured 186 marks less than the first meritorious candidates in the open competitive list and 36 marks less that the last meritorious candidate. The findings of the study are disquieting. In this connection, the UGC has made provisions for remedial courses for the weaker students to come up to the required level. For this purpose, the UGC gives 100 per cent assistance to the universities/colleges. However, it is learnt that the response from the universities/colleges to this scheme has not been encouraging. The UGC has also suggested to the universities/colleges to start preparatory courses for the students belonging to the SC/ST communities during holidays and vacations, to make up their deficiencies and to improve their communication skills.[16] Remedial courses and coaching classes for weak SC/ST candidates in Medical colleges will enable them to pull on well in their studies along with the general students.

Post graduate Courses

According to the instructions issued by the Government of India in the then Ministry of Health and Family Welfare in 1972 to the Vice-Chancellors of the Universities having Medical Faculties and all the State Governments/Union Territory Administrations, 20 per cent of the seats in Postgraduate Medical and Dental Colleges should be reserved — 15 per cent for the Scheduled Castes and five per cent for the Scheduled Tribes, without seriously affecting the standards of medical education. It was also suggested by the Ministry that these candidates should be given a concession of five per cent in the minimum percentage of marks required for admission to any of these courses. It was further suggested that in case earmarked seats for these communities remained vacant, a further relaxation in marks could be given to them in order of merit, inter se among themselves, so that all the seats were filled by candidates belonging to these categories. These instructions were also sent to the All India Institute of Medical Sciences (AIIMS), New Delhi and the Post-Graduate Institute of Medical Sciences, Chandigarh in October 1974.[17] According to available information, most of the States/UTs have made reservation a Practice for SC/ST candidates in the matter of admission to Postgraduate medical courses.

The Medical Council of India has not provided for any relaxation in the minimum standard for the admission of the SC/ST candidates to Postgraduate medical courses. However, as mentioned in the above para, the Union Ministry of Health had issued guidelines to all the State Governments and the universities concerned to give a concession of five per cent in the minimum percentage of marks required for admission of candidates belonging to these categories in these courses. So far as the Medical Institutions controlled by the Central Government, viz., AIIMS, New Delhi, PGIMER Chandigarh, and JIPMER, Pondicherry, are concerned, no relaxation is allowed to the SC/ST candidates for admission to Postgraduate courses in these institutions. Available information in respect of relaxation in minimum marks allowed to the SC/ST candidates for admission to these courses indicate that a number of State Governments as well as Medical Institutes controlled by the Central Government have not made any provision for relaxation in minimum marks prescribed for admission of the SC/ST candidates to these courses.[18]

Professional Courses

Apart from the Engineering and Medical faculties, there are many other professional courses like Agriculture, Veterinary, Law but separate data for each of them are unavailable. The UGC collected information from the universities including Deemed and Central Universities regarding representation of the SCs/STs in teaching/non-teaching jobs, admission to first year professional as well as non-professional courses, etc, during the year 1995-96. Only 90 State Universities, 21 Deemed Universities and seven Central Universities responded. Of them 41 universities (31 States, seven Deemed and three Central) did not run professional courses and the remaining 77 universities furnished information about

TABLE 5.12

ADMISSION OF SC STUDENTS TO 1ST YEAR PROFESSIONAL COURSES IN 71 UNIVERSITIES DURING THE YEAR 1995-96

Sl. No.	*State/UT*	*No. of Universities*	*No. of Total Students*	*No. of SC Students*	*%age of SC Students*	*C.E.*
1	2	3	4	5	6	7
1.	Andhra Pradesh	8	7035	1046	14.87	93
2.	Assam	2	435	27	6.21	84
3.	Bihar	4	6380	376	5.89	40
4.	Gujarat	3	4675	580	12.41	167
5.	Haryana	3	999	158	15.82	80
6.	Himachal Pradesh	1	133	17	12.78	50
7.	Jammu & Kashmir	1	648	42	6.48	78
8.	Karnataka	6	7290	800	10.97	67
9.	Kerala	2	790	64	8.10	82
10.	Madhya Pradesh	4	932	165	17.70	122
11.	Maharashtra	9	3161	428	13.54	122
12.	Manipur	1	115	5	4.35	215
13.	Meghalaya	1	2051	14	0.68	133
14.	Orissa	1	452	74	16.37	101
15.	Punjab	3	2938	415	14.13	50
16.	Rajasthan	2	3165	318	10.05	58
17.	Tamil Nadu	7	1723	323	18.75	98
18.	Uttar Pradesh	6	6117	1065	17.41	8[illegible]
19.	West Bengal	5	6706	716	10.68	45
20.	Delhi	2	2817	343	12.18	64
	Total	71	58562	6976	11.91	[illegible]

Sources: Appendix II.

admission of students in the one year professional courses. But six of them (three States, two Deemed and eleven Central) did not mention the number of the SC students admitted in the courses. So only 71 universities (56 States, 12 Deemed and three Central) furnished information about the admission of total students as well as SC students in the first year professional courses, the details of which are given in Appendix II.

Statewise information on the number of the total students, number of SC students, percentage of SC students to total students and the coefficient of equality (C.E.), prepared from Appendix II, can be seen in Table 5.12.

Out of 58,562 students admitted during the year 1995-96, 6976 belonged to the Scheduled Castes. The C.E. was 72. Considering the fact that the C.E. in the Engineering Faculty was 40 and 55 in the Medical Faculty in 1995-96 (Tables 5.9 and 5.11), the C.E. of 72 appears to be quite good. In as many as six States, namely, Gujarat, Madhya Pradesh, Maharashtra, Manipur, Meghalaya and Orissa, the C.E. was as high as 167, 122, 122, 215, 133 and 101 respectively. The performance of another six States, viz., Tamil Nadu, Andhra Pradesh, Assam, Uttar Pradesh, Kerala and Haryana was also very satisfactory, the C.E. being 98, 93, 84, 83, 82 and 80 respectively. Only two States, Bihar and West Bengal gave a very poor account of themselves, the C.E. being 40 and 45 respectively.

This trend could have been evaluated much better if all the 203 universities had furnished the requisite information. Out of the 71 universities in 19 States and one U.T. for which data were available, the number of SC students exceeded the total reserved seats in 23 universities. In the rest of the universities, the C.E. ranged between 14 and 99. The position is summarised in Table 5.13.

It is heartening to find that in 32.39 per cent of the Universities reserved seats could be filled in far in excess of the share of Scheduled Caste population and in another 32.39 per cent cases the position was either very satisfactory or satisfactory. In 16.90 per cent of cases it was unsatisfactory and in the remaining 18.31 per cent cases it was either poor or very poor. So it can be said that 65 per cent of the universities gave a very good account of themselves in the matter of admission of the Scheduled Caste students in the first year professional courses, while 35 per cent of the universities were lagging far behind in this respect.

TABLE 5.13
DISTRIBUTION OF SCHEDULED CASTE STUDENTS ADMITTED AGAINST RESERVED SEATS IN UNIVERSITIES

Sl. No.	*Category Indicating C.E. of SC Students Admitted Against reserved Seats*	*Total No.of Univer- sities*	*Details of Universities*	*%age of col.3 to to total No. of Univ. Reported*
1	2	3	4	5
1.	More than 100	23	7 of Maharashtra, 3 of Tamil Nadu, 2 each of Andhra Pradesh and Madhya Pradesh, and 1 each of Assam, Bihar, Gujarat, Karnataka, Kerala, Manipur, Meghalaya, Orissa, and Rajasthan	32.39
2.	Between 75 and 100	23	5 of Andhra Pradesh, 3 of Tamil Nadu, 2 each of Gujarat, Haryana, Madhya Pradesh, Tamil Nadu and Uttar Pradesh, and 1 each of Assam, Bihar, Jammu & Kashmir, Maharashtra and West Bengal	32.39
3.	Between 50 and 75	12	2 each of Punjab, Uttar Pradesh, and West Bengal, and 1 each of Haryana, Himachal Pradesh, Karnataka, Kerala, Rajasthan and Delhi	16.90
4.	Between 30 and 50	6	2 each of Karnataka and Uttar Pradesh and 1 each of Andhra Pradesh and West Bengal	8.45
5.	Less than 30	7	2 of Bihar and 1 each of Maharashtra, Punjab, Tamil Nadu, West Bengal and Delhi	9.86

Source: AppendixII.

Indian Institute of Technology

At each of the six Indian Institutes of Technology (IIT) located at Mumbai, Delhi, Kanpur, Kharagpur, Chennai and Guwahati, 15 per cent of the seats are reserved for the Scheduled Castes and 7.5 per cent for the Scheduled Tribes in the various undergraduate courses. Direct admission of the SC/ST candidates who secured more than 50 per cent marks in the qualifying examinations was also made to these Institutes before 1979, besides admission through the Joint Entrance Examination (JEE) in which a cut-off value of marks to be obtained by the SC/ST candidates was prescribed at about two thirds of the cut-off value of marks prescribed for the general candidates. The method of direct admission of the SC/ST candidates was stopped from the academic year 1979 and since that year admission of candidates is made only through the JEE. The upper age limit for the SC/ST candidates is relaxable by five years. It was decided by the Government of India in 1980 to extend all the concessions available to the SC/ST candidates for admission to the I.I.Ts. to the Neo-Buddhists, who formerly belonged to the Scheduled Castes.[19]

With a view to improving the intake of the SC/ST students in the IITs, a special preparatory course of ten months duration was started. Those SC/ST students who fail to qualify the JEE Examination for admission in the IIT's but score a certain minimum percentage of marks are offered admission to the preparatory course. At the end of the preparatory course, the students are subjected to a qualifying test on the basis of which they are offered admission to the B.Tech Programme without having to appear in the JEE again. This has improved the position of intake of SC/ST students in the IITs. The SC/ST students also continue to get financial support from the institutes by way of pocket allowance, loans and discretion grant, apart from free messing.[20]

Due to the very high standard of academic performance expected from the students in these institutes, the performance of the SC/ST students has not been encouraging. Despite a carefully designed programme of special coaching after their admission, the SC/ST students who admitted were unable to complete the course requirements. Many of the students who had remained were in a precarious position. For, at the IIT, academic performance is evaluated on a ten point grading system. A student is expected to maintain a minimum Cumulative Performance Index (CPI) of 5.5 throughout. If a student fails to maintain this index, he is given a warning and a chance to improve his academic performance within a prescribed period.

It would appear from the above table that during the period

1973-80, a total number of 1370 SC/ST students were admitted to these institutes out of whom, 255 have graduated, so far, 762 were continuing their courses, 276 had left these institutes voluntarily, 74 were asked to discontinue due to their poor performance and they left, while 3 were transferred to other institutions. Thus, 350 or 22.5 per cent of the total number of the SC/ST students admitted to these institutes during these years, either left these institutes voluntarily, or were asked by the institutes to discontinue their studies.

A view has been expressed that if an SC/ST student who is admitted to an IIT, has passed the first year of his course successfully, it should be the responsibility of the IIT to help him by additional coaching, reduced work-load, etc., if necessary, but he should, on no account, be asked to discontinue his studies. This issue was discussed by the education minister with the directors of all the IIT's in July 1980, when they were asked to consider special steps to be taken to help the SC/ST students to improve their academic standards and also to follow a uniform policy in dealing with academically poor SC/ST students. In this connection, the IITs have taken the following steps to improve the standards of the SC/ST students so as to bring them at par with other students:—

(i) The period of the first 2 semesters may be extended from about 8 months to about 10½ months keeping the weaker students in separate batches for giving them extensive coaching.

(ii) Special coaching is given to weaker students during the first and second semesters.

(iii) The weaker SC/ST students are given reduced work-load, i.e., they are asked to take lesser number of subjects. This may lead to longer duration of courses, but will make it easier for the SC/ST students to get through.

(iv) After a review of performance of such students at the end of each year they may be put on regular stream depending upon their performance.[21]

Thus, in spite of the government policy of reservation of seats at all levels and in all courses at all educational institutions including Medical and Engineering Colleges and IITs, relaxation in minimum marks for admission and other educational facilities, the intake of the Scheduled Caste students in the Medical Colleges, IITs/ Engineering Colleges on the basis of JEE was very unsatisfactory. Not only was the performance of the Scheduled Caste students in the JEE not satisfactory [22], but the performance of the SC students admitted to such institutions was also a cause for great concern.

The Higher Education system in India has witnessed a steady growth since Independence. At the time of Independence in 1947, there were only 20 universities and 500 colleges in the country. In 1996-97, there were 166 Central/State Universities, 37 Deemed Universities and 9278 Colleges.[23] At the beginning of the year 1995-96, the total student enrolment in Universities and Colleges was 61.14 lakh, [24] which increased to 64.26 lakh in 1996-97.[25]

Out of ten students in higher education, four are in the faculty of Arts, enrolled for courses in social sciences and humanities which include History, Culture and Languages. Three, out of ten students, are enrolled for courses in Science, Engineering, Medicine, Agriculture and related disciplines. The faculty of commerce enrols two out of 10 students. Enrolment at the first degree level was 88.1 per cent out students. Enrolment at the first degree level was 88.1 per cent of the total enrolment; at the post-graduate level 9.5 per cent; at the research level 1.1 per cent, and at the diploma and certificate level 1.3 per cent.[26]

The massive expansion of higher education after Independence, albeit at the expense of the elementary education, has resulted in the emergence of sharp hierarchies in terms of courses and institutions; Medicine, Engineering and Technology are considered prestigious courses, leading to high income, high status occupations. Arts and Humanities are regarded as comparatively inferior. Similarly, in each city and in each field of study it is possible to identify 'elite' institutions which produce superior results, provide distinctive grooming and contribute subtly as an 'advantage' in the process of social selection. Admission to prestigious courses in elite institutions is ruthlessly competitive. So only a small fractionn gain admission to these institutions.

Taking the JEE and IIT Examination has become an essential part of the curriculum of all science-stream students at the Higher Secondary level, irrespective of their individual potential and attitude. Career decisions, even today, continue to hinge on a rather statutory ruling that all 'good' students should opt for the science stream after Secondary level and every science student should aspire to become an engineer or a doctor. There is a preconceived notion that unless one makes it to the IIT or JEE, his career is doomed and any other alternative career move that does not involve taking these competitive examinations is more often dubbed as a frivolous exercise, never quite worth the effort. thus, we find an increase of about 1/3rd in the number of candidates appearing for the JEE during the period 1991-95. A report[27] indicates that in West Bengal, 38,750 candidates appeared for the JEE in 1991 which increased to 51.222 in 1995, registering an increase of more than 32 per cent during this five-year period. The students are made to join in this mad rate race for admission to the various Engineering and Medical Colleges, because it is a general notion that a student having a B. Tech degree from an IIT or a reputed Engineering College, even with mediocre results, can get himself a job without much of a bother. A mere MBBS degree from a Medical College, however, will not enhance the marketability of a doctor unless he acquires a post-graduate degree as well. That is the reason why there is so much scramble for admission to post-graduate medical courses, which is quite absent in Engineering and Technology course. The Anti-resservation stir[28] in Gujarat in 1981 centred round the policy of admission to post-graduate courses in Medical Colleges.

But admission to Medical Colleges is not necessarily restricted to those qualified in the JEE. Even if one does not appear or qualify in the JEE, admission to a Medical College is possible provided one has the right connections. In some States, some seats are reserved as Chief Minister's quota or Donor's quota. For instance, in West Bengal 15 students are admitted to Medical Colleges every year under the Chief Minister's quota.[29] Those admitted under the Chief Minister's quota did not qualify in the West Bengal JEE, yet each one got a chance to be a doctor. They are the sons and daughters of politicians, bureaucrats, police officers, doctors, engineers, who are in the good books of the ruling party for their 'usefulness': The Chief Minister's quota results in denying meritorious students their admission to Medical Colleges for extraneous reasons.

There are cases when candidates were admitted by manipulating provisions for admission. In 1994-95, the MBBS Selection Committee of Tamil Nadu adopted the rule of reservation in the category reserved for sportsmen only to make way for the admission of the son of an IAS officer even though there was no such provision in the prospectus. Though the High Court did not set aside the selection, one year having been spent on this score, it imposed heavy penalty on those who were found responsible for this illegal action.[30]

The opportunities for higher education — general, technical and professional — to ambitious youngsters (boys and girls) who leave the formal education system, are numerous and varied. Pressure of enrolment will, however, make it far harder to get into the better colleges and there will be lively debate over who has a 'right' to higher education. Educating everyone up to the limit of his ability does not mean sending everyone to institutions imparting higher education. Presumably, college students should only be drawn from the group which is able to get through the Higher Secondary stage. So the question arises : "Should all HSC+2 students go to college for higher education"? As college education has gained extraordinary prestige, one is tempted to assume that the only useful learning and growth comes from attending such an institution, listening to professors talk from platforms and reproducing required information on evaluating occasions called examinations. This is an extremely constricting notion. The college or univeristy should not be regarded as the sole means of evaluating and establishing one's human worth. It should not be presumed as the unique key to happiness, self-respect and inner confidence. But the plain fact that college education is firmly associated with personal advancement, upward social mobility, marked value and salf-esteem is ingrained in the public mind.[31] Parents consider an investment in higher education of their wards as an investment for their future settlement and security.

The craze for 'degree', which broadens the scope of employment and higher grade jobs, especially white-collar jobs, has led to the emergence of many fake and unscrupulous educational institutuions. Many such institutions were found to have suffixed the word 'University', 'Vishwadayalaya' 'Vidyapith', to their names in violation of the University Grants Commission

Act, 1956 and had been advertising that they were empowered to award degrees. The UGC has listed [32] 20 institutions all over the country as 'fake' as in March 1996 and has warned the students and academic community that those dealing with the unrecognised institutions would be doing so at their own risk. These institutions had been operating from the cities and towns of U.P. (9), Delhi (4), Maharashtra (2), Bihar (1) Jammu & Kashmir (1), Madhya Pradesh (1), Kerala (1) and Tamil Nadu (1).

With the phenomenal increase in the number of those seeking university education going up to 64 lakhs per annum, the Vice-Chancellors of Southern Universities felt that the quality of education had suffered a setback.[33] Everybody admits that unless reform starts here and now, the system may altogether collapse before long. The blame for the decline of the system cannot be put on the schools alone, which justifiably complain that the quality of degree-holders the college and university system now turns out is so poor that they cannot make any better teachers than they are. The State is now caught up in a vicious circle of the Schools, Colleges and Universities unceasingly pulling one another's standards down.

The UGC has also failed to maintain, let alone improve, the standards of higher education at the national level. Nore often it has warned all concerned that too many colleges, not to speak of universities, do not raise their standards. But politicians neither at the Centre nor in the States have given any heed and thought to that, rather, pandering to political bosses institutions have come up where there is no real need. The Annual Report of the Department of Higher Education of the Government of West Bengal (1993-94) says that there are "some colleges with enrolment below 100 and some other colleges on the other hand with enrolments of 3,000 and above. The reasons behind poor enrolment of some colleges are weak infrastructure, teaching of pass courses in a few subjects, distances from localities, etc."[34]

In 21 constituent colleges under the Jai Prakash University, Chapra, Bihar, there were 5,908 students and the government spent a whopping Rs 8 crores annually on them. During 1993-94, in P.C. Vigyan College, Chapra under this University, there were five students whereas the government spent Rs 20.70 lakhs in one year on teachers' salaries and other heads. The average cost per student came to an unbelievable Rs 4.14 lakhs per year. Similarly, Narain College, Goriakothi under the same University, had enrolled only nine students and the government grant amounted to Rs 29.18 lakhs which came to Rs 3.24 lakhs per student in 1993-94.[35]

In West Bengal, in Coochbehar Maharaja Jagdipendra Narayan Rashtriya Sanskrit Mahavidyalaya, there is only one student for whose study about Rs 2 lakh is spent every year.[36]

There might be many more such colleges in the country. The existenceof over-crowded colleges simultaneously with the near-empty colleges is essentially a manifestation of preference for 'excellence'and 'quality'. It exposes the educational divide in our educational system.But our leaders are, apparently, oblivious of its consequences.

Higher education in India today is in a unique state : it has to face the challenge to maintain a fair balance between the indirect demand for better quality and direct demand for expansion in enrolment. It is, no doubt, a fact that both the Union and the State governments on their own find it difficult to go on subsidising the cost of education in the universities and colleges. The tuition fees in the majority of these institutions — either managed directly or aided by the government — are, to say the least, extremely low with no relation whatsoever to the prevailing cost. Almost a decade ago educationists have sounded a note of warning that the government funding was not adequate to sustain the momentum generated by various social and economic factors like greater intake and a wide variety of courses made available to the students. The World Bank and other international leading agencies have time and again pointed out this factor of over-subsidising higher education at the cost of the school education sector. But the fact remains that the authorities in charge of education have been reluctant to take a hard decision on the enhancement of tuition fees in the colleges and universities for obvious reasons. The Justice Punnayya Committee (1992-93) had identified possible sources for income generation by the universities. These include an upward revision in the tuition, hostel and mess fees, renting out facilities like auditoria, classrooms, computer services, playgrounds, guest houses, etc. and seeking support from a wide spectrum of sponsors for research programmes and consultancy. In addition, it suggested resource mobilisation from the alumni association[37]. It is a known fact that the products of the IITs/Engineering Colleges/Medical Colleges are the highest paid professionals in this country. Even if it is conceded that it would cause tremendous hardship on the parents if they are asked tos bear the entire expenses incurred by these Institutions for the education of their wards, there cannot be any dissenting voice if these students are asked to pay back the entire cost of their education within a span of 10-15 years after graduation which could be kept aside as a corpus fund and utilised for the improvement of these institutions. All this sounds good but bold steps and pragmatic actions on several fronts should be taken in order to improve the situation.

So far as the enrolment of the Scheduled Castes in the institutions of higher education is concerned, the policy of 'reservation' ensures that a fixed percentage of seats are reserved in all the institutions of higher education for students belonging to the SC/ST. Admission is granted to them in this quota as long as they fulfil the basic qualifying requirements, regardless of their position vis-a-vis the total body of applicants competing for admissions.

It would, however, not be proper to assume that all the states and all the districts of the various states and all the castes among the Scheduled Castes have registered uniform progress in the matter of enrolment for higher education. Even as early as 1969, the Commissioner for Scheduled Castes and Scheduled Tribes observed that "different castes and different districts within the same State have been developing in education at very uneven rates".[38] We have noticed that some states recorded a higher enrolment ratio in some courses while many others lagged behind. For instance, during the year 1995-96, the co-efficient of equality of enrolment for the Scheduled Castes was as high as 174 in Assam, 137 in Tripura and 107 in Pondicherry in graduate Engineering courses, 138 in Goa and 146 in Manipur in graduate Medical courses and 215 in Manipur, 167 in Gujarat, 133 in Meghalaya, 122 in Madhya Pradesh and Maharashtra, and 101 in Orissa in first year professional courses, while it was as low as 3 in Uatter Pradesh, 18 in West Bengal and 28 in Karnataka in graduate Engineering courses, 12 in Uatter Pradesh in graduate Medical courses and 45 in West Bengal and 50 each in Himachal Pradesh and Punjab in first year professional courses.

While it is much easier for the Central States Governments to ensure that the SC/ST candidates are given admission to the various educational institutions and in all the courses and in all the faculties/departments by strictly enforcing the 'reservation policy', strangely enough, they have not, as yet, applied their mind to the larger and more vexed question of equality of opportunity and of enrolment. N.K. Bose, Commissioner for Scheduled Castes and Scheduled Tribes, pleaded in 1969 for 'making educational facilities available to those who have been largely neglected over the years'.[39] His pleadings fell on deaf ears. Neither the Central Government nor the State Governments have addressed themselves to the problem that all the castes listed as the Scheduled Castes do get proportionate share in enrolment according to their population size and that all the regions/districts of the states develop uniformly in the educational field so that no regional imbalance sets in. Though it is a well-known fact that 'the progress of education among Scheduled Caste and Scheduled Tribe communties is not taking place uniformly among various communities and males and females',[40] unifortunately leaders of the Scheduled Castes/Scheduled Tribes, have apparently a more wide spread concern about the interests of the educated minority,[41] than those who have remained outside the realm of education. The vocal minority is cornering all the benefits of the Governments' 'protective policy', much to the chagrin of the silent majority.

Another question directly related to admissions in higher educational institutions is the quality of performance of those admitted against reserved quota. As we have seen in earlier paragraphs. The performance of those admitted under the quota system was far from satisfactory. Consideration of caste or ethnicity or even a heavy dose of relaxed condition of admission might have been essential for the purpose of admission according to the 'reservation policy'. Once a student gets admitted it is his performance which matters. Special and extensive coaching after admission, lesser workload, extra classes, prolongation of duration of semesters, etc., all aim at improving the standard and quality of performance. The mere fact that such assistance is being provided is, in a way, an admission of the fact that the education given in schools during regular hours is of a deficient nature.[42] As is well known, no edifice can be built on a weak foundation. If the foundation is weak, no amount of palliatives in the latter period can undo the wrong. What is needed is better schooling facilities, if not for all, at least for a selected few who are expected to come up to a particular grade.

At this point it is necessary to reflect upon the objectives of education in our country, especially for the listed classes. As it appears, the purpose of imparting education is to enable the SC/ST people "to slip into white-collar occupations for the sake of social prestige[43] or to ensure that they get admission in Engineering/Medical/professional Colleges or IIT and such other institutions of higher education, at least according to their population ratio. If it is so, the best way of achieving this is to equip the students from the very formative stage of their life and give them all help in the form of "Scholarships and other help in right amounts and at the appropriate time"[44] . Since and socially and educationally backward groups and families require more promotional avenues at the beginning of their education, it has been suggested that a cess may be levied for creating a special fund to provide free boarding and lodging. tution and other allied expenditure in full, to support those deserving student's who, for economic reasons, cannot afford education at any level including specialised technical and medical education.[45] As a matter of fact, the State should take upon itself the task of giving them the best education possible so that they can compete with others on equal terms and conditions educationally, culturally, psychologically and physically also. This would, in the long run, take care of many of the burning problems of the day — sub-standard quality of education, poor quality of performance, need to provide crutches at all stages of life and, above all, reservation in educational institutions/services on the basis of caste.

It is not difficult for the State Governments to spot the SC/ST children at the school level — say, at IX, X or XI Classes or even earlier — and to give them special training so that these children are generally prepared for higher education. This intensive and specialised coaching will prepare them to compete on equal terms with children of other castes in all examinations, be it for admission to IITs/Engineering Colleges/Medical Colleges or for services.

Since no government can spend such an enormous amount on each and every SC/ST child, thouth it would have been the ideal one, this scheme will not be able to ecompass all the SC/ST children. To begin with, it may cover, say, around 1,000 students in every major state, with number increasing according to available resources.

Dr. B.R.Ambedkar also held the same view while submitting his evidence before the First Backward Classes Commissions:

> "I think that the means that have to be adopted for the purpose of bringing these people up are not that we should have primary schools and secondary schools for those people. Out of 100 boys 20 remain and 80 go away. My idea is something fantastic. I would suggest that schools should be opened for them in their own locality or some central place. I would suggest to collect the best boys from the primary schools and give them food, shelter and education in that very place, away from their parents. Up to the Matriculation Examination you give them education there. As soon as they pass the Matriculation Examination, send them in a college and give them tuition fee. After that select a number of students from amongst them and send them to Europe, Germany, France, America and similar other foreign countries where they can get the best of education. After that give them service in the Government Departments. I would be quite prepared to spend one crore of rupees for the Scheduled Castes and one crore for the Scheduled Tribes for 10 years and probably the Scheduled Castes are becoming vocal now. Thus you will create a few people with high qualification and place them in high posts. That will be 2000 times better than the 200 boys educated in Marathi or Gujarati.[46]

At a meeting of the Directors of the IITs with the Education Minister in July 1977 to discuss the various problems faced by the SC/ST students admitted to these Institutes, the following decision[47], among others, was taken:

> A common examination for SC/ST students who desire entry in all professional courses like Engineering. Medicine, etc., should be arranged while they are in schools, to organise special training for them specially in English, Mathematics and Physical Sciences. Such a training should be a part of the preparation of school education and be the responsibility of the state Governments. For this purpose, a scheme should be drawn up by the Ministry of Education in consultation with the Ministry of Home Affairs.

The Comissioner for SC/ST also welcomed this decision to locate, at school stage, talented SC/ST students desirous of entry to professional courses like Engineering and medicine and to organise special training for preparing them for entry to these professional courses and recommended that steps should be taken immidiately to start the scheme for such fraiming.[48]

Neither this scheme of the Directors of the IITs nor the recommendations of the Commissioner for Scheduled Castes and Scheduled Tribes nor the suggestion of Dr. B. R. Ambedkar has been acted upon. A bold and pragmatic step is called for to give a new orientation to the present policy of educational development of the Scheduled Castes — both in regard to their enrolment as well as achievement in Higher Education including professional and technical education.

In other words, the student is kept on probation. If the student fails to improve his performance within the prescribed period, he is advised to leave the institute. Date furnished by five IITs (all except Delhi) regarding the number of the SC/ST students admitted to IITs, expelled therefrom, etc. for the years 1973-80, is summarised in Table 5.14.

TABLE 5.14

STATUS PARTICULARS OF SCHEDULED CASTE STUDENTS IN VARIOUS IIT'S DURING 1973-80

Sl. No.	*Year*	*Number of SC/ST students in various IIT's*					
		Admitted	*Graduated*	*Continuing for graduation*	*Left voluntrily*	*Asked to discontinue due to poor performance*	*Transferred to other IITs*
1	2	3	4	5	6	7	8
1.	1973	168	80	16	45	26	1
2.	1974	218	96	54	47	19	2
3.	1975	218	67	78	69	4	-
4.	1976	195	12	120	53	10	-
5.	1977	207	-	160	36	11	-
6.	1978	133	-	114	15	4	-
7.	1979	89	-	81	8	-	-
8.	1980	142	-	139	3	-	-
	Total	1370	255	762	2767	4	3

Source: p.191 of 27th Report of the Commissioner for SC/ST (1979-80).

References

1. *Annexure Table VIII.*
2. *Select Educational Statistics*, 1996-97, Ministry of Human Resource Development, Department of Education, pp. xxvii and 31.
3. *Ibid.*, p. 56.
4. *Ibid.*, p. 56.
5. *Ibid.*, p. 56.
6. *Fifth All India Educational Survey*, Vol. I, 1986, NCERT, p. 82.
7. *Select Educational Statistics*, 1996-97, p. xxvii.
8. *RCSCST*, twenty-seventh (1979-81), para 6.45, p. 171.
9. *Facilities to Scheduled Castes and Scheduled Tribes in Universities and Colleges*, 1982, University Grants Commission, p. 19.
10. *RCSCST*, twenty-fifth (1977-78), para 6.30, p. 111.
11. *RCSCST*, twenty-seventh (1979-81), para 6.58, p. 175.
12. *Ibid.*, para 6.58, p. 179.
13. *Ibid.*, para 6.69, p. 180.
14. *RCSCST*, twenty-Sixth (1978-79), para 6.54, p. 177.
15. *RCSCST*, twenty-seventh (1979-81), para 6.63, p. 177.
16. *Ibid.*
17. *Ibid.*, para 6.70, p. 180.
18. *Ibid.*, para 6.72, p. 181.
19. *Ibid.*, para 6.101, p. 190.
20. *Annual Report*, Ministry of Human Resource Development, Department of Education, 1996-97, para 7.2.6, p. 118.
21. *RCSCST*, twenty-seventh (1979-81), para 6.108, p. 192.
22. *Ibid.*, para 6.120, pp. 190-191.
23. *Annual Report*, Ministry of Human Resource Development, Department of Education, 1996-97, p. 6.
24. *Ibid*, 1995-96, p. 71.
25. *Ibid.*, 1996-97, p. 6.
26. *Ibid.*, 1995-96, p. 71.
27. *The Telegraph*, September 25, 1995, p. 14.
28. *RCSCST*, twenty-seventh (1979-81), pp. 184-85.
29. *The Telegraph*, September 27, 1995, p. 10.
30. *The Hindu*, September 29, 1995, p. 4.
31. Chellappa, Paul. Is College Education 'Everyone's Right' ? *The Hindu*, September 5, 1995, p. 26.
32. *Annual Report, University Grants Commission*, 1995-96, pp. 9-10.
33. *The Hindu*, September 14, 1995.
34. Quoted by Sunanda Sanyal, Advising State-I, Higher Education Gone Astray, *The Statesman*, June 16, 1995, p. 6.
35. *The Telegraph*, July 20, 1995, p. 8.
36. *Ananda Bazar Patrika*, September 13, 1995, p. 8.
37. Investing in Higher Education, editorial in *The Hindu*, August 31, 1995, p. 12.

38. *RCSCST*, eighteenth (1968-69), para 1.20, p. 4.
39. *Ibid.*, para 1.25, p. 4.
40. *RCSCST*, twenty-fifth (1977-78), para 1.13, p. 3.
41. *RCSCST*, nineteenth (1969-70), para 1.187, p. 12.
42. *RCSCST*, seventeenth (1967-68), para 1.50, p. 10.
43. *RCSCST*, eighteenth (1' 68-69), para 1.24, p. 4.
44. *RCSCST*, nineteenth (1969-70), para 18, p. iv.
45. *The Hindustan Times*, September 28, 1990.
46. *Report of the Backward Classes Commission*, Vol. III, 1956, pp. 73-75.
47. *RCSCST*, twenty-fifth (1977-78), para 6.40, p. 113.
48. *Ibid.*, para 6.41, p. 113.

6
Educational Inequalities

A major aim in providing the Scheduled Caste students with the special educational facilities is to make the unequal educational attainments of these castes even with the rest of the population.

There is no doubt that the Scheduled Castes have made considerable progress in education since Independence. Their literacy rate has increased from 10.27 in 1961 to 37.41 in 1991 and in some States/UTs, the SC literacy rate either has exceeded or compares favourably with the general literacy rate. The literacy gap between the SC and the non-SC population nevertheless shows an increasing trend in the successive Censuses during the period 1961-91. This gap is wider when we compare these figures in respect of rural and urban areas or in relation to women. Their enrolment ratio 1995-96 has exceeded the general enrolment ratio in primary sections but is considerably lower in upper primary stage. The rural-urban imbalances and gender disparities in the matter of enrolment have been reduced considerably. In respect of location of primary and upper primary schools within habitations or at a certain distance, the predominantly Scheduled Caste habitations do not compare favourably with general habitations in all cases. While near-parity situation exists in respect of certain categories of habitations, the position is comparatively worse in relation to other habitations. The drop-out rates at the elementary stage of education have declined over the years but it is still higher than that of general students. The overall position would have been appreciably better had not the inter-State and inter-regional disparities been so prominent, specially in the traditionally educationally backward States like Bihar, Uttar Pradesh, Rajasthan, Madhya Pradesh, and Orissa.

Though the trend of enrolment of the SC students at the Secondary/Higher Secondary stage of education revealed a substantial improvement over the years, yet it was still not proportionate to their total population in the country. There is, however, a sharp reduction in the all-India enrolment ratio as one moves up the education ladder. As Table 5.4 has revealed, there is almost 34 per cent reduction at the Higher Secondary stage. This implies that the rates of wastage and stagnation among the SC students are considerably higher than those among the non-SC/ST students.

The trend of enrolment of the SC students at graduate and postgraduate levels for general, professional and technical education was unsatisfactory. Moreover, their weak foundation at the lower level of education had its impact at the higher levels of education. Due to the high standard of academic performance expected from the students at graduate and postgraduate levels of different courses, specially professional and technical education, the performance of the SC students has not been encouraging. Considering the protective discrimination that have been afforded to them since Independence, the educational progress of the Scheduled Castes, is rather disappointing — a finding consistent with the results of several other studies in different regions.[1]

Another disturbing finding of studies about the educational problem of the Scheduled Castes is the uneven degree of educational level achieved by different Scheduled Castes. We have seen in Chapter II that even in 1981 there were a number of Scheduled Castes which did not boast of a single literate person, while there were a number of castes which had attained a literacy rate much above the literacy rate of the non-SC/ST communities in those States. A study[2] was conducted in the early 70s at the behest of the Indian Council of Social Science Research to find out, amongst others, the castewise distribution for the Scheduled Caste school and college students in 15 States (actually 14 States because Uttar Pradesh was divided into East Uttar Pradesh and West Uttar Pradesh) accounting for 86 per cent of the total Scheduled Caste population of the country. The most striking feature about this distribution was the preponderance of one or two castes in, each State. Percentage of the different Scheduled Castes in the total Scheduled Caste population of these States according to the 1971 Census and their percentage in the School and College samples, as revealed in this study, is given in the Annexure Table XV reveals that the students belonging to the Mala caste constitute 57 per cent of the school sample in Andhra Pradesh. In Gujarat, the

Mahyavanshi group of castes account for 52 per cent of the school sample and 66 per cent of the college sample. In Kerala, the Pulayans predominate both at school (55 per cent) and at college (28 per cent). Similarly in Maharashtra, the Mahars account for 72 per cent of the school sample and 66 per cent of the college sample. In Punjab, it is the Ad-Dharmis both at school (39 per cent) and at college (55 per cent) and in Tamil Nadu, the Adi-Dravidas account for 51 per cent at the school level and 39 per cent at the college level. In Haryana, the Chamars alone constitute 46 per cent of the school sample and 67 per cent of the college sample, as also in Madhya Pradesh (53 per cent of the school sample), in Uttar Pradesh (78 per cent of the school sample and 68 per cent of the college sample) and in Rajasthan (39 per cent at school and 38 per cent at college).

If it is not a single caste that predominates, as in the foregoing instance, it is a small cluster of castes. Not infrequently, this cluster is composed of castes that hold different positions in the ritual hierarchy. For instance, in Assam, the Kaibartas, Malis, Namasudras and Patnis account for 74 per cent of the school sample and 73 per cent of the college sample. In Bihar, the Chamars, Dusadhs, Pasis and Dhobis together account for 92 per cent of the school sample and 95 per cent of the college sample. In Karnataka, the Adi-Dravidas, Adi-karnatakas and Holeyas together account for 64 per cent of the school sample and 58 per cent of the college sample. In Orissa, the Panos, Dhobas, Kandaras and Namasudras constitute 65 per cent of the school sample and 49 per cent of the college sample.

This predominance of a single caste or a small group of castes is particularly striking, in view of the fact that caste or castes that predominate are not invariably the ones that are numerically the most prominent in the concerned States. Even if they do happen to be the castes that are numerically prominent, their representation in the sample is more often than not noticeably larger than their percentage-wise representation in the Scheduled Caste population in the State.This point may be illustrated with reference to some States.

The Malas who predominate in the school sample in Andhra Pradesh represent only 37 per cent of the total SC population of the State. The Kaibartas or Jalias who predominate in the college sample in Assam (51 per cent) constitute only 32 per cent of the Scheduled

Caste population of that State. The Mahyavanshis who constitute 66 per cent of the college sample and 52 per cent of the school sample in Gujarat are the largest group within the Scheduled Caste population of the State, but their representation in this population is noticeably smaller (41 per cent) than their representation in the samples. In Karnataka, the Adi-Dravidas constitute only 11 per cent of the SC population of the State, but they comprise 30 per cent of the college sample and 20 per cent of the school sample. In Kerala, Pulayans or Cheramans constitute only 33 per cent of the SC population of the State, but they comprise 55 per cent of the school sample and 28 per cent of the college sample. In Maharashtra, the Mahars who constitute just 35 per cent of the SC population account for 72 per cent of the school sample and 66 per cent of the college sample. In Punjab, Ad-Dharmis constitute only 13 per cent of the SC population, but account for 55 per cent of the college sample and 39 per cent of the school sample. In Uttar Pradesh, the Chamars who predominate both in school sample (78 per cent) and college sample (68 per cent), do happen to hold a majority (55 per cent) within the SC population of the State but their representation at school and college is totally out of proportion to their representation in the SC population of the State.

This fact of over-representation of some castes may probably be even better appreciated with reference to the underrepresentation of others. In Andhra Pradesh, the Madigas constitute 44 per cent of the Scheduled Caste population of the State but account for only 11 per cent of the school sample. In Assam, the Namasudras, who comprise 33 per cent of the population, account for only 16 per cent of the college and 20 per cent of the school samples. In Bihar, the Musahars account for 15 per cent of the Scheduled Caste population of the State, but their share in the school sample is a mere one per cent and 0.4 per cent in the college sample. In Gujarat, the Bhangis, constitute 13 per cent of the Scheduled Caste population but only five per cent of the college sample and six per cent of the school sample. In Haryana, the Balmikis constitute 20 per cent of the Scheduled Caste population of the State but their share in the school and college samples is a mere five per cent and seven per cent respectively. In Karnataka, the representation of the Adi-Karnatakas who constitute 36 per cent of the Scheduled Caste population is substantially smaller both in the school (27 per cent) and the college (28 per cent) samples. In Maharashtra, the Mangs constitute a bare five per cent of the college sample and ten per cent of the school sample in spite of the fact that their representation in the Scheduled Caste population of the State (30 per cent) is almost equal to that of the Mahars (35 per cent), who, as has been pointed out above, constitute 72 per cent of the school sample and 66 per cent of the college sample. In Punjab, the Mazhabis account for 29 per cent of the Scheduled Caste population but only two per cent of the college sample and seven per cent of the school sample. Annuexure Table XV explains in details this predominance as well as underrepresentation of some castes in education in 14 States.

A similar picture emerges in a study[3] conducted in Gujarat during the same period. Eleven castes which together account for 92.50 per cent of the total Scheduled Caste population of the State in the 1971 Census figure in this study. The castewise distribution of the State's Scheduled Caste population is given in Table 6.1 indicates that Mahyavanshis, Garodas, Nadias, Turis, Mahars and Bawas are overrepresented while Bhambis or Chamars and Bhangis are under represented. Such sizeable groups as Meghvals and Shenvas are not at all represented.

TABLE 6.1

SCHEDULED CASTE COLLEGE STUDENTS AND THEIR CASTE IN GUJARAT

Sl. No.	*Scheduled Caste*	*State Population percentge 1971*	*Students*
1.	Mahyevanshi, Dhed, Vankar	41.09	66.34
2.	Bhambi, Chamar, Rohit, Khalpa	22.75	19.60
3.	Bhangi	12.76	5.03
4.	Meghval	8.16	-
5.	Shenva, Sedma	2.61	-
6.	Garoda, Garo	2.51	3.52
7.	Nadia or Hadi	1.21	2.51
8.	Turi	0.65	1.00
9.	Bava	0.28	0.50
10.	Tirgar or Tirbanda	0.23	-
11.	Mahar	0.26	1.00
12.	Others not specified above (19 caste groups and unclassified ones)	7.50	-

Source: Shah, B.V. and Thakar, J.D., *Scheduled Caste and Scheduled Tribe College Students in Gujarat,* Vallabh Vidyanagar, 1978, p. 36.

In West Bengal, a study was conducted by the Cultural Research Institute to assess the progress of Post-matric education among the Scheduled Castes for the year 1971-72. The study[4] reveals that out of 16,464 Scheduled Caste college students, 15,693 or 95.33 per cent of the total Scheduled Caste college students belong to 11 Scheduled Castes which accounted for 73.33 per cent of the total Scheduled Caste population in the 1971 Census. The rest 4.67 per cent of the students belong to 41 communities which account for 26.67 per cent of the total Scheduled Caste population. The communitywise distribution of the Scheduled Caste college students and their share in the total Scheduled Caste population of the State is given in Table 6.2. It will appear therefrom that the Namasudras, Poundras, Sunris, Dhobas, Jalia Kaibarttas, Malos and Tiyars are overrepresented while the Rajbanshis, Bagdis, Muchis and Bauris are underrepresented.

TABLE 6.2
SCHEDULED CASTE COLLEGE STUDENTS AND THEIR CASTE IN WEST BENGAL

Sl. No.	*Name of Scheduled Caste*	*No. of Students*	*Percentage of Population of Each Caste to the Total SC Students of the State*	*Percentage of Population of Each Caste to the Total SC Population of the State in 1971 Census*
1	2	3	4	5
1.	Namasudra	5,744	34.89	11.12
2.	Poundra	3,099	18.82	11.06
3.	Rajbanshi	2,180	13.24	15.36
4.	Sunri	1,986	12.07	1.89
5.	Dhoba	672	4.08	2.17
6.	Jalia Kaibartta	632	3.84	2.32
7.	Bagdi	511	3.10	14.64
8.	Malo	349	2.13	1.02
9.	Muchi	224	1.36	5.76
10.	Tiyar	163	0.99	0.91
11.	Bauri	133	0.81	7.08
	Total	15,693	95.33	73.33
	Source:	a	a	b

Source: a : Bulletin of the Cultural Research Institute, West Bengal, Vol. X, Nos. 1 and 2, 1974, pp.125-26.

b : Census of India, 1971, Vol. 23, West Bengal

This aspect of the problem was also analyzed[5] in Punjab with reference to 11 large and medium-sized castes accounting for 94.15 per cent of the Scheduled Caste population of the State. Educational achievement of these 11 castes in 1961-71 is presented in Table 6.3. The coefficient of equality is calculated by dividing the proportion of literate and better-educated persons among those belonging to a given Scheduled Caste by the proportion of literate and better-educated persons in the rest of the population of the Scheduled Castes and by multiplying the result by 100.

TABLE 6.3

EDUCATIONAL ACHIEVEMENT OF LARGE AND MEDIUM-SIZED SCHEDULED CASTE IN PUNJAB (1961-71)

Sl. No.	*Name of Scheduled Caste*	*Population in 1971 Census*	*1961*		*1971*	
			% Literate and Better Educated Persons	*Coeff-icient of Equity*	*% Literate and Better Educated Persons*	*Coeffi-ent of Equity*
1	2	3	4	5	6	7
1.	Ad-Dharmi	4,39,632	16.01	175	27.27	189
2.	Balmiki	4,01,960	7.76	72	13.84	84
3.	Bauria	42,713	5.36	52	5.99	37
4.	Bazigar	75,092	3.18	31	6.61	40
5.	Chamar	9,81,471	12.01	125	19.83	136
6.	Dhanak	27,910	7.66	74	10.97	68
7.	Dumna	91,685	9.31	90	17.47	109
8.	Kabirpanthi	37,625	16.99	167	29.63	186
9.	Mazhabi	9,62,546	6.52	56	8.31	43
10.	Megh	52,608	11.90	116	23.53	147
11.	Sansi	39,084	8.20	79	11.01	68

Source: D'Souza, Victor S., "Educational inequalities among the Scheduled Castes—A case-study in the Punjab," Panjab University, Chandigarh, 1980, p. 7.

Table 6.3 indicates the growth of wide disparities in the educational achievements of the Scheduled Castes. It also shows that the castes high on the coefficient of equality scores in 1961 like Ad-Dharmi, Chamar, Kabirpanthi, Megh have not only maintained their higher position but have also improved upon them further; on the other hand, castes lower down on the scores have, on the whole, climbed down even further. Thus, the gaps existing between castes with higher educational achievement and those with lower achievement in 1961 widened further in 1971. This evidence about the Scheduled Castes of the Punjab State is also in agreement with similar trends in other States of India.

Another aspect of educational development, which also shows a systematic relationship with other variables, is the spread and growth of higher education. Wide disparities among various Scheduled Castes in this regard was revealed in a Punjab study.[6] Table 6.4 shows a comparison between the coefficient of equality among various Scheduled Castes in respect of literate and better-educated persons, on the one hand and those with matriculation and higher education, on the other, for the years 1961 and 1971.

TABLE 6.4

COEFFICIENTS OF EDUCATIONAL EQUALITY OF THE SCHEDULED CASTES IN PUNJAB IN 1961 AND 1971 RELATING TO :(A) LITERATE AND BETTER-EDUCATED PERSONS, AND (B) MATRICULATES AND ABOVE.

Sl. No	*Name of Scheduled Castes*	*Coefficient of equality in 1961*		*Coefficient of equality in 1971*	
		(a) Literate and Better-Educated	*(b) Matriculates and Above*	*(a) Literate and Better Educated*	*(b) Matriculates and Above*
1	2	3	4	5	6
1.	Ad-Dharmi	175	233	189	230
2.	Balmiki	72	40	84	71
3.	Bauria	52	7	37	12
4.	Bazigar	31	7	40	31
5.	Chamar	125	144	136	156
6.	Dhanak	74	40	68	51
7.	Dumna	90	68	109	88
8.	Kabirpanthi	167	155	186	218
9.	Mazhabi	56	47	43	27
10.	Megh	116	146	147	154
11.	Sansi	79	42	68	54
	Other Scheduled Castes				133

Source: D'Souza, Victor S., "Educational inequalities among Scheduled Caste— A case study in the Punjab," Punjab University, Chandigarh, 1980. p. 9.

Thus, whereas the disparities among the various Scheduled Castes with regard to literate and better-educated persons are very

Castes with regard to literate and better-educated persons are very wide both for 1961 and 1971, they are still wider with regard to persons with higher education. Just as the disparities between the population of the Scheduled Castes and the rest of the population widen more and more with the increasing level of education, so is the case in respect of the disparities among the Scheduled Castes themselves. Thus, there is a clear indication that the prospects of higher education for the Scheduled Castes are very much related to the degree of their education at the lower levels. The advantage gained at the lower levels has a snow-balling effect on the higher education.

Not only are there great disparities in the educational achievements among different Scheduled Castes, but also the use made by them of the educational facilities which are highly disproportionate to their population strength. As an example, we may consider the post-matriculation government scholarships utilized by different castes.

With a view to finding out as to which Caste/Tribes were receiving more benefits from the Government of India Post-Matric Scholarships Scheme, and whether it would be necessary to take specific steps to make these scholarships available in larger numbers to the communities to whom, either the benefit of the Scheme did not accrue at all, or it was proportionately much less as compared to the percentage of their population to the total Scheduled Caste/Tribe population in the State, the Commissioner for the Scheduled Castes and Scheduled Tribes collected community wise figures of post-matric scholarships awarded to the SC/ST students in various States in 1966-67 and 1967-68. The information[7] received from the States revealed quite interesting facts.

In Andhra Pradesh, out of the total number of 60 Scheduled Caste communities, the students of 16 communities were able to get more than proportionate awards of scholarships as compared to their population during 1967-68.

TABLE 6.5

COMMUNITIES IN ANDHRAPRADESH GETTING MORE THAN PROPORTION OF AWARDS OF SCHOLARSHIPS AS COMPARED TO THEIR POPULATION

Sl. No.	*Name of Scheduled Caste*	*Percentage of Population to Total SC Population in the State in 1961 Census*	*Percentage of Awards Received by the Community*
1	2	3	4
1.	Adi-Andhra	11.96	27.33
2.	Arwa Mala	0.08	2.10
3.	Beda (Budga) Jangam	0.04	0.23
4.	Bindla	0.10	0.12
5.	Chamar or Mochi, Muchi	0.15	0.79
6.	Ellamalwar (Yellammalawandla)	0.01	0.07
7.	Godari	0.01	0.02
8.	Jambuvulu	0.19	0.67
9.	Kolupulvandlu	0.01	0.05
10.	Madasi Kuruva or Madari Kuruva	0.01	0.04
11.	Madiga Dasu and Mashteen	0.08	0.21
12.	Mala	35.09	42.87
13.	Mala Dasu	0.54	0.71
14.	Mala Jangam	0.11	0.12
15.	Mehtar	0.06	0.32
16.	Samagara	0.02	0.09
	Total	48.55	76.00

Source: pp. 116-17 of Eighteenth Report of the Commissioner for SC/ST

These 16 communities constituted 48.55 per cent of the total Scheduled Caste population in the State and received 76.00 per cent scholarships. The maximum benefit of the Scheme was derived by the students of Adi-Andhra and Mala communities constituting 11.96 per cent and 35.09 per cent population, which got 27.33 per cent and 42.87 per cent awards respectively. These two communities also registered an appreciable increase in the percentage of awards over the earlier two years. Some communities got awards less than proportionate to their population. For instance, Madigas constituting 43.19 per cent population, got only 22.80 per cent awards during 1967-68, where as the students of 23 communities, did not receive even a single award during that year.

In Gujarat, out of 37 Scheduled Caste communities, 23

communities availed of the benefits under the scheme of post-matric scholarships during 1963-64, while during 1965-66 and 1966-67 the students of 24 communities availed of the benefits. The percentages of population of the communities which availed of benefits of the scheme as well as the percentage of the scholarships awarded to them are given in Table 6.6

TABLE 6.6

SC COMMUNITY TO SC POPULATION PERCENTAGE IN GUJARAT AND SCHOLARSHIPAWARDED PER CENT DURING 1963-67

Sl.	*ScheduledCastes*	*Percentages of Population of Community to the Total SC Population*	*Percengage of Awards Received by the Community*		
			1963-64	*1965-66*	*1966-67*
1	2	3	4	5	6
1.	Bawa (Dedh) or Dedh-Sadhu	0.23		0.03	0.02
2.	Bhambi, Bhambhi, Asadaru, Asodi Chamadia, Chamar, Chambhar, Chamgar, Haralayya, Harali, Khalpa, Machigar, Mochigar, Madar Madig, Telegu Mochi, Kamati Mochi, Ranigar, Rohidas, Rohit or Samgar, Chamadia, Nalia or Rohit	22.41	19.70	23.10	20.09
3.	Bhangi or Rukhi, Mehtar, Olgana, Malkana, Halalkhor, Lalbegi, Balmiki, Korar or Zadmalli	13.71	3.00	3.10	2.50
4.	Dangashia	0.12	-	0.04	0.03
5.	Garmatang	0.05	0.06	0.03	-
6.	Garoda or Garo	2.55	4.65	5.12	6.48
7.	Hadi	0.48	-	0.04	0.08
8.	Mahar, Taral or Dhegu Megu Mahyavanste, Dhil, Vanuar or Maru	0.20	0.20	0.30	0.23
9.	Mahyavanshi, Dhed, Vankar or Maru Vankar, Dhedh or Antyaj	42.57	69.09	65.91	68.08
10.	Mang, Matang or Mini Madaig	0.07	0.06	-	-
11.	Meghwal or Menghvar	10.95	1.00	0.80	1.00
12.	Nadia or Hadi	0.79	0.80	0.60	0.41
13.	Shenva, Chenva, Sedma or Rawat, Senva	2.68	0.62	0.52	0.50
14.	Tirgar or Tirbanda	0.21	0.20	0.12	0.05.
15.	Turi	0.71	0.40	0.38	0.41
16.	Turi-Barot or Dedh Barot	0.13	-	-	-

Source: pp. 117-18 of Eighteenth Report (1968-69) of the Commissioner for SC/ST.

It would be seen from the above Table that two communities, namely,(1) Mahyavanshi, Dhed, Vankar or Maru Vankar, Dhedh or Antyaj, and (2) Garoda or Garo, derived maximum benefits from the scheme. They constituted 45.12 per cent of the total SC population of the State but received 73.74 per cent of the total awards in 1963-64 71.03 per cent of the awards in 1965-66 and 74.56 per cent of the total awards in 1966-67. Major communities, like (1) Bhangi or Rukhi, Mehtar, Olgana, etc. (2) Meghwal or Menghvar derived much less benefits from the scheme as compared to their population. They constituted 24.66 per cent of the total Scheduled Caste population but received only 4.00 per cent of the awards in 1963-64, 3.90 per cent of the awards in 1965-66 and 3.50 per cent of the awards in 1966-67. As many as 11 communities did not receive a single scholarship in any of the three years, namely, 1963-64, 1965-66, and 1966-67.

In Maharashtra, the total number of post-matric, scholarships awarded to the Scheduled Caste students in the State during 1963-64 was 9384 which increased to 12,148 during 1965-66 and 15,144 during 1967-68.

The percentages of scholarships received by the various communities and the percentage of their population to the total population in the State are given in Table 6.7.

It would be seen from the Table 6.7 that out of the 57 Scheduled Caste communities in the State, three main communities, viz., Mahar, Mang and Chambhar constituting 90.17 per cent of the total population in the State received 96.61 per cent of scholarships during 1967-68. The remaining 3.39 per cent scholarships were shared by 13 communities while 41 communities did not receive any scholarships.

The Mahar community derived the maximum benefit from the scheme. It constituted 35.11 per cent of the population, and was able to receive 82.83 per cent of the Scholarships in 1967-68. In contrast, the Mang and Chambhar communities constituting 33.00 per cent and 22.06 per cent of the total Scheduled Caste population in the State, received only 3.87 per cent and 9.91 per cent of the scholarships respectively.

TABLE 6.7
SC COMMUNITYTO SC POPULATION PERCENTAGE IN MAHARASHTRA AND SCHOLARSHIPS AWARDED PERCENTAGE DURING 1963-68

Sl. No.	*Name of Community*	*Percentage of Population to the Total SC Population in the State*	*Percentage of Scholarships Awarded* 1963-64	1965-66	1967-69
1	2	3	4	5	6
1.	Mahar	35.11	82.62	84.17	82.83
2.	Mang	33.00	4.16	3.34	3.87
3.	Chambhar	22.06	10.22	8.76	9.91
4	Bhangi	2.80	0.13	0.53	0.44
5.	Holar	1.20	0.07	0.10	0.11
6.	Madgi	0.70	-	0.02	0.01
7.	Dhor	2.00	1.64	1.75	1.76
8.	Khatik	0.60	0.26	0.52	0.30
9.	Mahyavanshi	0.53	0.37	0.35	0.36
10.	Meghval	0.40	0.42	0.23	0.21
11.	Basor	0.02	0.02	-	-
12.	Balahi	0.12	-	0.02	-
13.	Madiga	0.10	-	0.02	0.02
14.	Kaikadi	0.08	-	0.01	0.01
15.	Pasi	0.06	-	0.02	0.01
16.	Ellamalwar	0.02	0.05	0.03	0.07
17.	Kori	0.02	0.03	0.07	0.07
18.	Chalvadi	0.01	0.01	0.03	0.01
19.	Bedar	-	-	0.01	-

Source: Pp. 119-20 of Eighteenth Report (1968-69) of the Commissioner for SC/ST.

In Rajasthan, 19 communities constituting 9.22 per cent of the total Scheduled Caste population in the State received more than proportionate awards of scholarships in 1967-68, as compared to thier population. The total percentage of awards received by all these communities was 24.44 as detailed in Table 6.8.

TABLE 6.8
SC COMMUNITY TO SC POPULATION PERCENTAGE IN RAJASTHAN AND SCHOLARSHIPS AWARDED PERCENT DURING 1967-68

Sl. No.	*Name of Scheduled Caste*	*Percentage of Population to Total SC Population in the State*	*Percentage of Awards Received by the Community*
1	2	3	4
1.	Aheri	0.06	0.28
2.	Bairwa of Berwa	0.26	3.88
3.	Baori	0.06	0.11
4.	Bhand	0.13	0.50
5.	Dabgar	0.04	0.05
6.	Dhanuk	0.06	1.33
7.	Dhobi	0.17	0.39
8.	Dom	0.01	0.33
9.	Garancha, Mehtar on Gancha	0.05	0.50
10.	Garoda	0.01	0.33
11.	Jingar	0.05	0.44
12.	Khandgar	0.01	0.05
13.	Khatik	3.11	5.66
14.	Koli or Kori	3.97	6.66
15.	Mehar	0.57	1.05
16.	Mehtar	0.37	1.22
17.	Rawal	0.14	0.33
18.	Salvi	0.10	1.16
19.	Santia	0.05	0.17
	Total	9.22	24.44

Source: P. 122 of Eighteenth Report (1968-69) of the Commissioner for SC/ST.

It would be seen from the Table 6.8 that notable communities in this category are Bairwa or Berwa, Dhanuk, Khatik, Koli or Kori.

13 communities received less than proportionate awards as compared to their population. Such communities included Chamar, Balai and Megh or Meghwal, who constituted about 62 per cent of the total Scheduled Caste population in the State. Out of the 73 Scheduled Caste communities in the State, 36 communities constituting 6.87 per cent of the total Scheduled Caste population did not receive a single scholarship.

In Tamil Nadu, out of 67 Scheduled Caste communities in the State, students from 45 communities took advantage of the scheme in 1967-68 and the remaining 22 communities did not get a single scholarship. About 65 per cent of the scholarships were awarded to students of two communities alone, viz., Adi-Dravida and Pallan, constituting 42.60 per cent of the total Scheduled Caste population in the State, while another 17 per cent of the scholarships were bagged by Parayan community which accounted for 25 per cent of the Scheduled Caste population. Thus, these three communities received 82 per cent of the scholarships whereas their total population was only 67.60 per cent of the Scheduled Caste population of the State. The remaining 18 per cent of the awards were shared by 42 communities accounting for 32.40 per cent of the total Scheduled Caste population in the State. The position is illustrated in the Table 6.9.

TABLE 6.9

SC COMMUNITY TO SC POPULATION PERCENTAGE IN TAMIL NADU AND SCHOLARSHIPS AWARDED PERCENTAGE DURING 1967-68

Sl. No.	*Name of Scheduled Caste*	*Percentage of Population to the SC Population in the State*	*Percentage of Awards Received by the Community*
1	2	3	4
1.	Adi-Dravida	27.00	39.00
2.	Pallan	15.60	26.00
3.	Parayan	25.00	17.00
4.	Chakkiliyan	12.80	2.00
5.	Arunthathiyar	1.60	2.00
6.	Valluvan	1.00	2.00
7.	Sambavan	2.20	2.00
8.	Other 38 Communities	14.80	9.00

Source: p. 124 of Eighteenth Report (1968-69) of the Commissioner for SC/ST.

Some communities with sizeable population, like Thoti, Kudumban, etc., constituting 6.70 and 4.08 per cent of the total Scheduled Caste population respectively, could derive only 0.03 and 0.05 per cent benefit from the scheme respectively, which is only negligible.

A number of communities could not get a single scholarship during the year. Notable among these communities were the

Pannadi and Vettiyan having 0.05 per cent and 0.10 per cent of the total Scheduled Caste population in the State. The population of other communities not getting any scholarship was small.

A study[8] conducted by the Cultural Research Institute, West Bengal, of the communitywise distribution of the post-matric awards to the Scheduled Caste students in the State of West Bengal during the years 1959-60 and 1966-67 revealed that, 82.08 per cent of the total post-matric awards went in 1966-67 to the students of six Scheduled Caste communities which constituted about 29.79 per cent of the total Scheduled Caste population in the State, while two Scheduled Caste communities, namely, Rajbanshi and Bagdi constituting 33.36 per cent of the total Scheduled Caste population had only 11.91 per cent of the total awards. The position is illustrated in Table 6.10.

TABLE : 6.10

SC COMMUNITY TO SC POPULATION PERCENTAGE IN WEST BENGAL AND SCHOLARSHIP AWARDED PERCENT DURING 1959-67

Sl. No.	*Name of Scheduled Caste*	*Percentage of Population to Total SC Population in the State*	*Percentage of Awards Received by the Community*
1	2	3	4
1.	Namasudra	10.58	37.18
2.	Poundra	12.71	24.66
3.	Sunri	1.55	11.88
4.	Dhoba	2.25	3.42
5.	Jalia Kaibartta	1.70	3.08
6.	Malo	1.00	1.86
	Total	29.79	82.08
1.	Rajbanshi	17.44	9.82
2.	Bagdi	15.92	2.09
	Total	33.36	11.91

Source : p. 63 of Seventeenth Report (1967-68) of the Commissioner for SC/ST.

The rest six per cent awards were shared by 42 Scheduled Caste communities, who constituted about 36 per cent of the total Scheduled Caste population in the State, while there were no students at post-matric stage among the remaining 13 communities.

In 1959-60 also the same six communities mentioned above, dominated in number of awards shared at post-matric level. The only improvement during 1966-67 was that while during the year 1959-60, 21 communities did not send any students for post-matric studies, the number of such communities came down to 13 during 1966-67.

In a study[9] made in Punjab on the basis of data pertaining to the years 1969-70 to 1973-74, it was revealed that at graduate level Ad-Dharmis and Ramdasias constituting 17.01 per cent and 29.65 per cent of the Scheduled Caste population in the State got 40.73 per cent and 36.77 per cent awards respectively. On the other hand, Balmikis and Mazhabis constituting 15.78 per cent and 24.74 per cent of the Scheduled Caste population in the State got only 5.46 per cent and 5.60 per cent awards respectively. The position of these communities was almost similar at postgraduate level also. In professional courses, Ramdasias and Ad-Dharmis got 51.85 per cent and 26.10 per cent awards while Mazhabis and Balmikis got only 7.76 and 2.48 per cent awards respectively. Another study[10] conducted in nine colleges of Haryana during 1975-76 revealed that the maximum advantage of the post-matric scholarships scheme was derived by students belonging to Chamar/Jatav community who constituted 52.97 per cent of the Scheduled Caste population in the State and got 76.12 per cent of the total awards. The Balmikis and Kabirpanthis constituting 19.77 per cent of Scheduled Caste population only got 8.30 per cent and 0.60 per cent awards respectively. In yet another study[11] made on the basis of data pertaining to 1969-70, five communities of Uttar Pradesh, viz., Chamar, Kori, Dhobi, Khatik and Pasi or Tamali constituting 72.83 per cent of the total Scheduled Caste population in the State got 92.02 per cent scholarships while all the remaining Scheduled Caste communities constituting 27.17 per cent of the Scheduled Caste population got only 7.98 per cent awards. In Karnataka, it was revealed in a sample study[12] conducted in Mysore and Mandya districts of the State that 85.7 per cent of the Scheduled Caste students awarded post-matric scholarships belonged to the Adi-Karnataka community, while only 14.3 per cent belonged to the remaining Scheduled Caste communities.

The Commissioner for the Scheduled Castes and Scheduled Tribes conducted another study in Punjab[13] with reference to the award of scholarships during 1976-77. The communitywise break-up of the scholars in graduate, postgraduate and professional courses as revealed in the study is given in Table 6.11. It would be seen therefrom that the communities like Ramdasia, Ad-Dharmi, etc., were able to derive much benefit from the scheme, while students belonging to some economically more backward communities like Mazhabi and Balmiki could derive much less benefit from the scheme.

TABLE 6.11

STATEMENT SHOWING COMMUNITY-WISE BREAK-UP OF POST-MATRIC SCHOLARSHIP AWARDED TO SCHEDULED CASTE STUDENTS IN PUNJAB DURING 1976-77

Sl. No.	*Name of Scheduled Caste*	*Population*	*Name of Scholars at*					
			Graduate		*Post-graduates*		*Professional/ Technical*	
			Total No.	Per 10,000 Population	Total No.	Per 10,000 Population	Total No.	Per 10,000 Population
1	2	3	4	5	6	7	8	9
1.	Ramdasia	9,81,471	2,545	26	130	13	467	5
2.	Ad-Dharmi	4,39,632	2,041	46	128	29	511	12
3.	Mazhabi	9,62,546	392	4	14	1	90	1
4.	Megh	52,608	273	52	13	25	51	10
5.	Kabirpanthi/Julaha	37,625	61	16	7	19	21	6
6.	Dumna,Mahasha,or Doom	91,685	112	12	2	2	22	2
7.	Balmiki	4,01,960	388	10	14	3	60	1
8.	Sansi/Bhedkut/ Manesh	39,084	37	9	6	13	6	1
9.	Bazigar	75,092	29	4	-	-	4	N
10.	Sarora	5,969	20	34	1	17	6	10
11.	Bauria or Bawaria	42,713	1	..	1	2		...
12.	Dhanak	27,910	12	4	..	..	1	N
13.	Khatik	5,943	9	15	..	..	4	7
14.	Bhanjra	1,907	4	21	..	..	..	..
15.	Kori/Koli	2,057	..	..	..	..	1	5
16.	Batwal	6,210	7	11	1	16	1	2
17.	Barar,Burar or Berar	1,911	3	16	..	..	1	5
18.	Sikriband	1,948	10	51	..	..	4	21
19.	Passi	1,713	3	18	..	..	..	..
	Total	31,79,534	5,947	19	317	1	1,250	4

Source: Appendix LII, p. 117 of Twenty-fifth Report (1977-78) of the Commissioner for SC/ST, Part II.

In another study[14] on Educational Development of the Scheduled Castes and the Scheduled Tribes of Madhya Pradesh since Independence till 1973, it was found that among the Scheduled Castes, the Mahar group received the maximum advantage whereas the Gandas lagged behind among the Scheduled Castes.

All these studies indicate that there are huge disparities in the degree of utilization of scholarships by different Scheduled Castes. The distribution of post-matric scholarships is an indicator of the progress made in higher education by the students belonging to different Scheduled Caste communities. There is a high degree of correlation between the coefficients of equality and the level of higher education and those of the utilization of post-matric scholarships as revealed in a study[15] in Punjab. Coefficients of equality among the Scheduled Castes in Punjab relating to : (a) persons with higher education in 1971, and (b) post-matriculation scholarships in 1970-71 given in Table 6.12 indicate that there are huge disparities in the degree of utilization of the scholarships by different Scheduled Castes.

TABLE 6.12

COMMUNITY-WISE BREAK-UP OF COEFFICIENTS OF EQUALITY FOR HIGHER LEVEL EDUCATION AND POST-MATRIC SCHOLARSHIPS AND NUMBER OF SCHOLARSHIPS DURING 1971 IN PUNJAB

Sl. No.	*Name of Scheduled Castes*	*Coefficients of Equality* (a) *level of higher Education*	(b) *post-matric higher scholarships*	*Number of scholarships*
1	2	3	4	5
1.	Ad-Dharmi	230	467	2,279
2.	Balmiki	71	50	367
3.	Bauria	12	12	10
4.	Bazigar	31	12	16
5.	Chamar	156	140	2,054
6.	Dhanak	51	47	21
7.	Dumna	88	59	95
8.	Kabirpanthi	218	112	68
9.	Mazhabi	27	14	332
10.	Megh	154	219	183
11.	Sansi	54	65	44
12.	Other Scheduled Castes	133	16	56
	Total	100	100	5,525

Source : D'Souza, "Educational Inequalities among Scheduled Castes : A case study in the Punjab" Panjab University, 1980, p.11.

They range from scores of 12 to 467. The range of disparities in the utilisation of the scholarships is even wider than the range of disparities in the spread of higher education. At the same time, there is a high degree of correlation between the coefficients of equality on the level of higher education and those on the utilization of post-matric scholarships. Thus, the differences in the educational levels of the Scheduled Castes account for their different use of educational facilities provided under 'protective discrimination'

One also notices caste imbalance in the utilization of hostel facilities. Table 6.13 reveals that in most States one or two castes predominate either in the school hostel sample or in the college hostel sample or in both samples. It implies that the castes which have advanced in educational attainments have also enjoyed the benefits of hostel facilities. It has also been found in a Madhya Pradesh study[16] that in the matter of hostels for the Scheduled Caste boys and girls, some districts (Shajapur, Khargone, Hoshangabad) appeared to have been benefited disproportionately while some other districts like Jabalpur, Guna and Sidhi deserved more hostels.

It is thus evident that although the facilities for the education of the Scheduled Caste have succeeded in drawing the Scheduled Caste youth from uneducated homes and rural occupation backgrounds to education, the benefits of the facilities are not evenly distributed. Their poor representation could be due to their own lack of motivation. It could even be due to their relative backwardness that makes for inability to hold out in the mad scramble of competition for facilities like scholarships and hostel facilities. Or it could be due to other positive constraints to their advancement like acute poverty of the households, the attitude of elders in the family, lack of facilities for study at home, uncaring attitude of the teachers or apathetic school environment. It also suggests a series of inter-state imbalances in the progress of the Scheduled Castes. For instance, although the Scheduled Caste women are generally ill-represented , their underrepresentation is more pronounced in the northern States than in the southern States. There are serious rural-urban imbalances within a State or inter-district imbalances. The identification of inequalities between the different sections of the Scheduled Caste community, therefore, assumes importance from the point of working towards the even

TABLE 6.13
STATEWISE CASTES IN SC PREDOMINATING COLLEGE/ SCHOOL HOSTELS

Sl. No.	*Name of State*	*Name of Scheduled Caste*	*% of SC Population in 1971 Census*	*% Among School Hostelers*	*% Among College Hostelers*
1.	Andhra Pradesh	Mala	36.60	57	Not covered
2.	Assam	Kaibartta, Jalia	32.30	None in the sample	80
3.	Bihar	Chamar	29.97	None in the sample	51
4.	Gujarat	Mahyavanshi	41.09	51	81
5.	Haryana	Chamar	52.98	None in the sample	90
6.	Karnataka	(i) Adi-Karnataka	36.49	Not over represented	31
		(ii) Holeya, Holar, Holvar/ Not represented at all Baked, Chelvadi/Thigla		9.72	17
		(iii) Banjara, Lambani Not over represented		4.81 25	
7.	Kerala Sambavar/ Paraya		8.62	None in Sample	26
8.	Madhya Pradesh	All Chamar castes	56.62	82	data not available
9.	Maharashtra Mahar	35.40	71	82	
10.	Orissa	(i) Dandasi	1.42	11	Not over represented
		(ii) Dhoba	9.73	15	25
		(iii) Gokha	2.48	Not over represented	18
		(iv) Namasudra	1.50	23	Not over represented
11.	Punjab Adi-Dharmi		13.33	None in sample	93
12.		(i) Chamar/Bhambi/ Jatava/ Mochi/Raigar	39.32	43	45
		(ii) Balai	8.31	Not over represented	24
		(iii) Meghwal	15	30	10
13.	Tamil Nadu	(i) Adi-Dravida	34.82	66	33
		(ii) Pallan	18.14	22	46
		(iii) Paraiyan	20.96	Not over represented	19
14.	Uttar Pradesh	(i) Chamar/Jatav	54.57	None in sample	68
		(ii) Dhobi	6.23	None of sample	13

Source : Chitnis, Suma, *A Long Way to go*, Allied Publishers, 1981, Table 193, pp. 302-303.

development of the Scheduled Castes.

In extending the benefits of welfare programmes— especially educational benefits — the differences in the level of educational, social, political and economic development between the different communities brought together under the category of 'Scheduled Castes' are not recognized. As a result, a few castes have been moving ahead to the exclusion of others in the educational field. The uneven educational progress among the different Scheduled Castes is in agreement with the general observation that when development takes place the inequalities existing among different segments actually tend to increase rather than diminish.[17] But the reasons for such a strange tendency are not so very clear.

Another important fact is that relatively better-off sections among the Scheduled Castes have taken most of the advantages of the welfare programmes and the more backward sections have virtually remained where they were, if they have not actually deteriorated.[18] The real problem is how to bring this vast deprived groups within the fold of education. It appears that it is the hard core of population which has been left out.[19]

This problem was visualized as far back as 1959 by the Study Team on Social Welfare and Welfare of Backward Classes, when it recommended for the application of economic criterion within the groups of the Scheduled Castes and Scheduled Tribes so as to ensure that more benefits would go to those who were economically less advanced.[20]

Being appalled by the findings of several field studies conducted by its field officers which suggested an uneven growth of education among the Scheduled Castes, the Commissioner for the Scheduled Castes and the Scheduled Tribes has warned in many reports that the benefits of the scheme of Post-matric scholarships had not accrued equitably to the more backward communities among the Scheduled Castes and the Scheduled Tribes. While some better placed communities among them had derived much more than proportionate benefits from the scheme, some backward communities had not received even a single scholarship.

It was, therefore, recommended in the Commissioner's reports 1975-77[21], 1977-78[22], 1978-79[23] and 1979-81[24] that urgent steps should be taken to identify the economically more backward communities among the Scheduled Castes and the Scheduled Tribes in all the States Union Territories and special programmes at the pre-matric level, like special coaching classes, increased rates of pre-matric stipends, special incentives like supply of free books, uniforms, mid-day meals, special residential schools on the lines of ashram schools, etc., should be taken up in order to encourage more students among these communities to reach the level of post-matric education, to enable them to derive benefits from the post-matric scholarships scheme.[25]

Not only the Commissioner for the Scheduled Castes and the Scheduled Tribes, but the Commission for the Scheduled Castes and the Scheduled Tribes also warned as far back as 1980 that the benefits of the post-matric scholarships scheme were not percolating down to the more deserving backward sections among the Scheduled Castes/Tribes. Based on the studies conducted by its field officers, the Commission for the Scheduled Castes and the Scheduled Tribes observed that the benefits of the post-matric scholarships scheme were not accruing equitably to all the Scheduled Castes and the Scheduled Tribes. In order to ensure that the benefits of the scheme accrued to all sections and especially to the deserving backward sections among the Scheduled Castes/ Scheduled Tribes, the Commission recommended that it was necessary to identify such communities and take up schemes for promoting pre-matric education among them so that sufficient number of students from these backward sections could come up for post-matric scholarships scheme.[26]

Much before the Commissioner for the Scheduled Castes and the Scheduled Tribes made these recommendations, the Ministry of Education and Social Welfare had warned against such a trend in 1972 in "a paper prepared for the consideration of the Central Advisory Board of Education on education in the Fifth Five-Year Plan, 1974-79." While defining National Scholarships Policy, it felt that the main changes required in the system of award of scholarships to the Scheduled Castes and the Scheduled Tribes were:

> The scholarships are largely being utilised by certain sub-castes amongst the Scheduled Castes and by some tribes, while there are several Scheduled Castes and a large number of tribes which have received little benefit from

> this programme during the last 25 years. An effort will have to be made to identify these more neglected groups even among those underprivileged sections and to see that they receive the benefit of these scholarships to a much larger extent than in the past.

This review even went to the extent of suggesting the introduction of a programme of scholarships for the most underprivileged sections of the society, such as landless agricultural labourers, who deserved a similar programme of scholarships but had no such facilities, "What is even more important is that we must look forward to a time when backwardness could be defined without reference to caste or birth and all deserving backward class students so defined should be eligible for a general scholarships programme from the middle school stage to the university," it observed.

It suggested a programme meant for the most underprivileged sections of the society (other than Scheduled Castes and Scheduled Tribes), defined on socio-economic considerations, unrelated to caste or birth or religion, could operate side by side with that for the Scheduled Castes, and the Scheduled Tribes.

It may be possible, at some later stage, to merge both the programmes together, and create a common programme of National Scholarships, from the middle school to the university stage, for all underprivileged sections of the society, including the Scheduled Castes and the Scheduled Tribes. For some time, a special consideration may have to be shown to the Scheduled Castes and the Scheduled Tribes even in this programme. But ultimately there would emerge only a common programme for the most underprivileged groups defined on the basis of socio-economic criteria, unrelated to caste, religion or birth.[27]

If this was the view of the Government of India in 1972, one fails to understand what stood in the way of introducing such a programme.

The UGC, after making an analysis of the actual admissions made by universities and colleges to various courses of studies from among the students belonging to the Scheduled Caste communities during the period 1978-79, recommended in 1985 that:

There is also need for evolving indicators so that facilities reserved for these communities are not utilized by a particular stratum among these very communities denying benefits to several others who are not so articulate and knowledgeable but they belong to these very communities.

One of the factors that has not received adequate attention is the need to give weightage to these communities for social, economic and educational deprivation. This can be decided on the basis of district wise indicators as applicable and a uniform policy for the country as a whole may not be feasible because of the varied conditions and attitudes prevalent in different districts.

There is a felt need to identify these neglected groups among these communities.

It may be suggested in this connection that highest weightage has to be provided for the neglected sections having the lowest level of educational attainments, as also to first generation learners.[28]

There is a section of opinion in the country which believes that the separation of the Scheduled Caste issue from the broader issue of poverty and backwardness, detracts from the force of a concerted movement on behalf of the economically under-privileged. In fact, some argue that the protective discrimination provided to the Scheduled Castes, destroys their motivation to join common movement of the economically underprivileged.[29] This implies, of course, that the Scheduled Castes are baited away by provision of special facilities that enable them to move ahead, in a situation wherein others from similar socio-economic backgrounds cannot. It, however, cannot be denied that these special facilities have led to the emergence of a privileged social clan among the Scheduled Castes, who have cornered all the educational benefits, amenities and facilities to the detriment of the interest of the really needy, deprived and under privileged communities among the Scheduled Castes who may not even know what they are entitled to.

Such a condition has arisen because as a NIEPA publication suggests the policy of protective discrimination overlooks the concept of mobility which operates once the percentage of first generation learners start dominating. It has also failed to curtail the existing intra-caste gaps in terms of literacy, rather has aggravated them.[30]

Sadly enough, in spite of the concrete recommendations of so many authorities, no well-thought-out programme has yet been evolved to ensure that the educationally backward and disadvantaged communities among the Scheduled Castes have a better access to educational facilities and incentives for an equitable progress in education comparable at least to their more advanced brethren among the Scheduled Castes, if not to the most advanced among the non-SC communities. Unless this trend is arrested, not only the main aim in providing special educational facilities to the Scheduled Caste students for ushering in 'equality through education'[31] will be defeated, but it will also precipitate social tension and conflict, even violence, due to the increased disparities and inequalities among different communities brought under 'Scheduled Castes'. Quick action in the right direction will perhaps avert a major crisis that is brewing in our body politic.

References

1. D'Souza, Victor S., 1980, *"Educational Inequalities among Scheduled Castes — A case study in the Punjab,"* p. 6., Department of Sociology, Panjab University.
2. Chitnis, Suma, 1981. 'A Long Way to Go' Report of a survey of SC High School and College Students in Fifteen States of India, Bombay : Allied Publishers.
3. Shah, B.V. and Thakar, J.D., 1978, *Scheduled Caste and Scheduled Tribe College Students in Gujarat*, Vallabh Vidyanagr.
4. Saha, Ramendra Nath 1974, *Achievements of the Scheduled Tribes and Scheduled Castes in Post-matric Education*, Bulletin of the Cultural *Research Institute*, Vol. X, Nos. 1 & 2, Government of West Bengal, pp. 119-27.
5. D'Souza, op. cit., pp. 7-8.
6. *Ibid.*, pp. 9-10.
7. Eighteenth *RCSCST* (1968-69), pp. 116-24.
8. Seventeenth *RCSCST* (1967-68), pp. 63-64.
9. Twenty-fourth *RCSCST* (1975-77), p. 96.
10. *Ibid.*
11. *Ibid.*
12. *Ibid.*
13. Twenty-fifth *RCSCST* (1977-78), p. 108.
14. Tripathi, C.B., 1986, Educational Development of the Scheduled Castes and Scheduled Tribes of Madhya Pradesh since Independence to 1973, In *Third Survey of Research in Education, 1978-83*, NCERT, Sl. 321, p. 235.

15. D'Souza, op. cit., pp. 10-11.
16. Tripathi, *C.B.*, op cit.,
17. D'Souza, op. cit., p. 2.
18. Dubey, S.N., 1976, "Deprivation, Welfarism and Predominant Adaptation Reforms of Backward Classes in India: Implication of Social Policy," In *Social Work Education and Development of Weaker Sections*, p. 116. *Ed.* T. Krishna Nair, Association of Schools of Social Work in India.
19. Nautiyal, K.C. and Sharma, Y.D. 1979, *Equalisation of Educational Opportunities for Scheduled Castes and Scheduled Tribes*, NCERT, P. 27.
20. *Committee on Projects, Report of the Study Team on Social Welfare and Welfare of Backward Classes*, Vol. I, 1959, p. 329.
21. Twenty-fourth *RCSCST* (1975-77), p. 96.
22. Twenty-fifth *RCSCST* (1977-78), p. 108.
23. Twenty-sixth *RCSCST* (1978-79), p. 174.
24. Twent-seventh *RCSCST* (1979-81), p. 206.
25. *Ibid.*
26. *Second Report of the Commission for Scheduled Castes and Scheduled Tribes*, 1979-80, pp. 167-68.
27. *Education in the Fifth Five-Year Plan 1974-79*, Ministry of Education, 1972, pp. 46-47.
28. Facilities to Scheduled Castes and Scheduled Tribes in Universities and Colleges relating to the periods 1978-79, University Grants Commission, 1985, p. 19.
29. Chitnis, op. cit., p. 37.
30. Aggarwal, Yash and Sibou Sarika, 1994, *Educating Scheduled Castes, A study for Inter District and Inter caste Differentials*, NIEPA . p. 116.
31. Goyal, Bhagat Ram, 1981, *Educating Harijans*, p. 36. *Gurgaon :* The Academic Press.

7

Reservations in Educational Institutions

Since India gained independence, the Government of India has been giving high priority to efforts to ameliorate the conditions, of the Scheduled Castes. They are provided all opportunities for the full growth of their personality to enable them to walk hand in hand with various other groups in society. The Government of India grants them liberal concessions in the field of education because education will play the most important role in the advancement of the Scheduled Caste people, as also in the removal of their social and economic disabilities.

The provision of educational facilities and incentives, including reservation of seats in educational institutions for the Scheduled Castes, is based on the idea that merit in an elitist society is not something inherent but is the consequence of environmental privileges enjoyed by the members of certain communities, specially the higher castes. To correct this anomaly in environmental privileges, the disadvantaged sections of the population—the Scheduled Castes, should be given all infrastructural facilities and be helped in all possible ways, in order that in course of time, they may attain parity with the other members in respect of educational, economic, social and cultural aspects of life. It was thought that the policy of reservation along with the other educational facilities given to the Scheduled Castes will bring these communities quantitatively as well as qualitatively to the level of other sections of the society. It is a matter of great regret that the administration, at the appropriate levels, national and state, did not or could not arrive at a decision to implement the policy of reservation against a time-frame, and that is why, after more than 45 years of the commencement of the Constitution, we are still discussing the issue and are bogged down with the problem.

Of all the facilities extended to the Scheduled Castes for their educational advancement, the policy of reservation of seats in the educational institutions has attracted public opprobrium the most. One often encounters reactions to the effect that students of much lower calibre are getting preference in admission in educational institutions, specially in higher educational and professional institutions, while some hundreds of other candidates with excellent performance to their credit are denied admission because they do not fit into a particular category. Caste instead of merit has become the sole criterion for getting easy admission. One also often hears comments that, reservation is a retrogade step, as it discourages hard work and initiative and encourages inaction and parasitism. The policy of reservation is making them dependent and incapable of open competition and advancement. All over the world the stress is on talent and merit. On the other hand, the Scheduled Castes feel that though the policies and privileges have benefited them greatly, much remains yet to be done. They still cling to protection and favour continuation, improvement and effective implementation of the government policy of protective discrimination.[1] They have argued that since there is a strong bias against them, the policy of reservation is not properly implemented and the full quota is never filled up. The report of the Basumatari Committee lists a variety of ways in which the policy of reservation is rendered ineffective. In fact, it illustrates the shortcomings of the policy by quoting cases of non-Scheduled Caste persons obtaining admissions to medical and engineering colleges posing as Scheduled Caste persons.[2] The political leadership of the Scheduled Castes has been constantly clamouring for proper implementation of the reservation policy and continuation of the protection and privileges.

The Basumatari Committee submitted its report more than two decades ago. The position has changed perceptibly since then. Since the Government has an obligation to provide adequate incentives to help alleviate the sufferings of the educationally depressed sections of the population, the Central Government and the State Governments have been more demanding and vigilant over the years with respect to the implementation of the policy of reservation. Massive concessions in terms of lower admission requirements are also offered to the SC/ST students in order to enable them to utilize these reserved seats. The enrolment of the Scheduled Caste students in the institutions of higher education, both professional and non-professional, has increased and the full quota of seats reserved for the Scheduled Castes The States are trying to fill up the full cota of seats reserved for the Scheduled Castes at any cost. As a result, some distortions have crept in the system as evidenced in the recent Madhya Pradesh episode.

In Madhya Pradesh, a ST candidate who scored just one mark out of 900 marks in the Pre-Engineering Test has secured a place on the merit list under the ST military personnel quota. Twenty seats were reserved for students of this category, but only eight candidates appeared for the examination and all were taken. The remaining twelve seats could not be filled up for dearth of candidates. Those who secured 33 and 114 marks become eligible for admission under the SC Freedom Fighters category. In the case of general category candidates, the minimum marks required for admission were 546 out of 900. Those with lower marks were either placed on the waiting list or rejected outright. For the Medical college it was no better. An aspirant to a medical career has found a place in the merit list for the pre-medical test in Madhya Pradesh in the quota earmarked for ST Freedom Fighters by scoring only four per cent, i.e., 49 marks out of the total marks of 1200. In this particular category, there were 4 reserved seats but only 3 students appeared and all of them got through. A student with 328 marks which works out to only 27.33 per cent, is the highest scorer in this category. An SC candidate finds himself on the way to becoming a doctor having secured 167 marks, i.e., only 13.9 per cent marks. This is in sharp contrast to the general category, where students figure in the waiting list despite getting 73.25 per cent, or a total of 879 marks. The highest marks secured by a student in this category were 1085 out of 1200, i.e., 90.41 per cent. It was possible for those scoring very low marks to succeed and appear even on the merit list as the Professional Examination Board which conducts those examinations in Madhya Pradesh has specified that there are no minimum qualifying marks in any category. It was because of this practice that students were able to enrol in engineering/medical courses scoring as little as 1 mark or 49 marks.[3]

The Madhya Pradesh case might be an aberration or a very extreme case and yet it will have to be said that the entire scheme of reservation as is being practised today has become distorted.[4] The real danger lies in the fact that the politicians who are after vote banks, may follow the Madhya Pradesh model and similar episodes might occur in other States as well. This kind of anomaly could be rectified if in the case of entry into professional institutions, at least a minimum be prescribed and clearly enforced so that what happened in Madhya Pradesh may not be repeated elsewhere. What would be the minimum would, however, depend on the attitude and political compulsions of the ruling parties in the States.

The present policy of reservation of seats, in educational institutions ensures that some percentage of seats, generally proportionate to the population of the Scheduled Castes in a State, are earmarked for the Scheduled Caste students in every course and in every stage of education. Many States reserve seats at the school level as well. Those States which have not reserved seats at the school level seem to have been swayed by the argument that since the State is obliged to provide elementary education to all, no matter what might be the caste composition of the students, it is rather illogical to reserve seats at the elementary level as well. Moreover, allotment of seats on the basis of quota and admissions of students at the lowest stage of education on the basis of caste only serves to emphasize caste origins and may create a lasting impression at that formative stage of life about the advantages and disadvantages of being born in a caste and thus will make them caste conscious.

Issues raised by Reservation

The policy of reservation raises two very pertinent issues which need to be addressed soon. There is, first of all, the question of how far we are going to reward merit, and how far to make allowance for need, i.e., who should be the actual beneficiaries of the reservation policy.There is also the equally important question of how long this reservation policy should continue.

It is an acclaimed fact that the Scheduled Caste is not a caste in itself but comprises of a conglomeration of heterogeneous castes which have been placed in a Schedule for the purpose of enjoying the various constitutional benefits and safeguards for their overall development. It is unrealistic and misleading to think that of the problems of educational development of the Scheduled Caste are uniform throughout the country. There are educational development problems of wide inter-state and intra-state variations in terms of poverty, uneducated home backgrounds, educational level of the parents, access to schooling facilities, quality of the teachers, outlook and the like. As a result, there are some castes which enjoy the maximum advantages of the reservation policy while many others lag behind with still some others being totally deprived.

For admission to various higher education courses at college/ university level, entrance tests are held for preparing a merit list. Students up to a certain position in the merit list are admitted in the courses. Scheduled Caste students obtaining marks above the level up to which general category students are admitted, are not counted towards reserved quota at all and are included in the general merit list of admissions. The reserved quota is filled up from the SC candidates who have obtained marks below the marks secured by the last candidates from the general category, placed in the order of merit occuring in the SC merit list *inter se*. In case, no entrance test is held, the SC students are admitted on the basis of marks obtained in the last qualifying examinations.[5] Some States, however, fix minimum qualifying marks, though there is still a tendency to lower down the qualifying marks. For instance, in West Bengal, an SC candidate would be eligible for admission into general and professional colleges if his marks in the previous qualifying examination were not lower by more than 25 per cent.[6] Incidentally, this order became effective from 1995, in consequence of the recommendation of a one-man Committee, constituted by the State Government, to make a study on the problems of admission of the SC/ST students in various educational institutions specially for higher studies in general/technical and engineering education. Earlier the grace marks were restricted to 10 per cent.

All the empirical studies indicate that the SC students qualifying in the general category merit list, and in the SC merit, list more often than not, belong to the educationally advanced Scheduled Caste communities. The students belonging to the educationally backward Scheduled Caste communities do not virtually figure in any of these lists, being unable to compete either with the students belonging to non-SC communities or with the students belonging to the educationally advanced Scheduled Caste communities.

In a sense, the policy of reservation for the Scheduled Castes in higher education, anticipates this situation. The children from the less-advanced communities who are likely to lose out in the competition for gaining admission to institutions of higher education, should be the beneficiaries of this policy. It is primarily for this section of the population that this policy of reservation was conceived, but unfortunately, these very sections of the population are deprived of this benefit. The evaluation of results of the reservation policy show the emergence of a separate class within the Scheduled Castes.[7] As the benefits of our economic policies have hardly reached the poor, similarly, the reservation policy has not been implemented with the desired intention of uplifting the illiterate generations. No one denies that there has been a massive "creaming off" of the benefits by the favoured few[8] who monopolize the benefits of reservations, while the rest of the communities remain exactly where they were. Only some castes who are better educated than the others from the very beginning have enjoyed the benefits in every State, as we have seen in Chapter VI. They might be Chamars, Koris and Pasis in Uttar Pardesh; Ad-Dharmis, Ramdasias, Meghas and Kabirpanthis in Punjab; Chamars and Mahars in Madhya Pardesh; Mahyavarnshis, Garodas, Hadis and Mahars in Gujarat; Mahars in Maharashtra; Adi-Dravidas, Adi Karnatakas and Holeyas in Karnataka; Pulayans in Kerala; Adi-Dravidas in Tamil Nadu; Adi-Andhras and Malas in Andhra Pradesh; Panos, Dhobas, Kandaras and Namasudras in Orissa; Chamars, Dusadhas, Dhobis and Pasis in Bihar; Namasudras, Poundras, Sunris, Dhobas and Jaliya Kaibarttas in West Bengal and Namasudras, Patnis, Kaibartta or Jaliyas and Malis in Assam or some such castes, who have reaped the benefits of the reservation policy since inception. To the extent that these communities have taken advantage of the special facilities offered to the Scheduled Castes, their more backward brethren have been denied these.

The percentage of reservation for the Scheduled Castes is fixed in every State in accordance with the percentage of the Scheduled Caste population among the total population of that State. In the quota of seats fixed for the Scheduled Castes in the educational institutions, the population consists not only of the educationally advanced Scheduled Caste communities, but also of the educationally backward Scheduled Caste communities. Since the lion's share of the reservation quota is grabbed by the few educationally advanced Scheduled Caste communities thereby depriving the less advanced; should not these ill-fated communities be protected?

Should not a mechanism for periodic review and revision of the list of beneficiaries and the nature of preferences be built to rearticulate the reservation/preference arrangement? Should not reservation begin from the poorest and those who are the most handicapped? Should not the quota be earmarked for the various communities according to their population strength, so that their share is not appropriated by other castes?

Population Proportionate Reservation

As a matter of fact, some castes have been agitating for some time, to earmark the quota in proportion to their share in the total Scheduled Caste population of the State. At least in one State orders have been issued to this effect. From now on, in Haryana, the Balmikis and 35 other related communities, which account for half of the State's Scheduled Caste population, would get 50 per cent quota in Government jobs out of the reservation earmarked for the Scheduled Castes in that State.[9] This system of compartmental reservation has been introduced in Tamil Nadu for the most backward classes (MBCs) for admissions in educational institutions. Of the 50 per cent seats reserved for those socially and educationally backward, there is a compartmental reservation of 20 per cent for 39 castes and 68 denotified communitised categorized as MBCs. The idea was to provide a better opportunity for the most deprived among the backward castes to secure the benefits of reservation. It is, however, a different matter that as many as 66 castes out of the 107 communities in the MBC list drew a blank in respect of admissions in engineering and other professional colleges in 1990. More significantly, Vanniyars, Maravars and Piramalai Kallars, accounted for 708 seats in 1267 seats reserved for MBCs, in the professional colleges offering degree courses in—medicine, engineering, law, agriculture and veterinary sciences. This triggered an agitation by Thevars, Kongu Vellalas and other dominant communities seeking reservations in proportion to their population.[10]

Reservation of SC/ST Girls

Again, there is the question of gender bias in educational matters. The girl students are in a disadvantageous position so far as their enrolment is concerned. Seeing the plight of the girls, especially of those belonging to the Scheduled Caste communities, it is safe to presume that a very few of them advance to higher education level. Already 30 per cent of the seats have been reserved for the women in the Panchayati Raj Institutions and the Municipalities. The share of the Scheduled Caste women is coming from the quota reserved for the Scheduled Castes. There is a move to allocate a portion of the reserved quota in the defence services for the women. The natural corollary of it is its extension to the educational field as well. So, should the quota be fixed on the basis of population of each community constituting the Scheduled Castes and again on the basis of gender? These are the questions which are to be pondered over.

The question may be examined from another angle. There are great intra-state variations. Some districts are educationally advanced while others are not. Again, the institutions of higher learning are city-centred. The women, poor and rural students cannot enjoy the benefits of higher education unless they come out of their traditional moorings. They are in a disadvantageous position to pursue higher education in an uncongenial environment. How can we solve their specific problems? Should we take recourse to earmarking a separate quota for these disadvantaged groups and regions as well?

Some Wrong Assumptions of Reservation Policy

And, last of all, there is the equally important question of how to balance the claims of the individual with those of the group or community. It has to be viewed with concern that the policy of protective discrimination which sets out to decrease the inequalities between castes and communities, end by increasing the inequalities between individual members of each caste and community. It would be a mistake to believe that by making concessions to castes and communities the needs of all, or even the most deserving, individual members would be automatically satisfied.[11] It would be equally wrong to argue that in providing for equal opportunity, or even the equalization of opportunities among those unequally placed, we should always give priority to the group over the individual. Such a course might be justified if all the groups with which we are concerned were absolutely homogeneous on every significant scale of inequality. But we know perfectly well that they are not. Firstly, a caste which has a low ritual status may be materially well off, secondly, individual members of most castes vary considerably in their actual material condition, irrespective of the traditional ritual status of their caste.It is only at the very lowest end of the scale that the assumption of uniform deprivation holds true to a large extent.[12] This society made a terrible mistake in the past in believing that merit was an attribute not of individuals but of groups, that being born a Brahmin was in itself a mark of merit. We shall make the same kind of mistake if we act on the belief that need, too, is always, and not just in special cases, an attribute of groups rather than of individuals.[13]

But any change in the reservation policy will be vehemently resisted by the 'privileged groups' among the Scheduled Castes who have so long been benefited by the reservation policy. They have developed a vested interest in perpetuating the present system because they enjoy the benefits to which they might not be entitled otherwise. They will naturally see the 'black hand' of the 'reactionary forces' who are bent upon dividing the 'solidarity' of the Scheduled Castes. Their protests would not be so much for division among the cluster of communities grouped under the rubric 'Scheduled Castes' which is in any case, a historical and sociological fact, but for abrogation of the benefits so long enjoyed by them at the cost of others. The more developed would try to preserve their existing position, while the less developed would fight for more opportunities. Hence, a casteist or communal type of grouping becomes inevitable for those who feel threatened by any change in the present reservation policy.

The effectiveness of reservation as a means of preference is being questioned by those who instead regard it as, improvement of social environment, added educational facilities and removal of inequalities. In fact, it cannot be disputed that reservation as a social engineering device cannot be viewed as a permanent feature but only as a short-term measure. If this sound principle is accepted, there is an urgent need to adopt long-term measures for raising literacy and education, health and better living conditions. Inaction or even insufficient attention on the part of Government to these issues will necessarily lead to the institutionalization of reservation.

Implementation of Affirmative Action in USA for the African Americans

A parallel may be drawn with the policy of affirmative action, the principle that disadvantaged minorities deserve preferential access to the work place and higher education, which is the touchstone of American liberalism for the last three decades. The great civil rights victories of the 1960s removed discrimination against the black population in law, if not always in practice. That was followed by efforts to compensate the victims for the oppression of the past. It was clear that African-Americans who had originally been brought here as slaves, remained so disadvantaged that they were in no position to compete on equal terms with the rest of the population. To start creating a level playing field, offering equal opportunity to both black and white Americans, the black had to be given something of a kick-start. Affirmative action was the answer given by President Jhonson 30 years ago. By an executive order, he directed institutions of the Federal Government to give preference in jobs and contracts to the under represented blacks or preferential access to higher education. His lead was followed, in varying formulations, by many States and public bodies.

Affirmative action has long been a sacred but contradictory element in the US self-image. Americans like to think of themselves as champions of the underdog. But equally, the nation is founded on the belief that success should be the direct reward for talent and hard work, without regard to race, gender or class. This, in turn, explains why most Americans consider affirmative action iniquitous, un-American and moribund.

By definition, affirmative action was meant to address specific and historical discrimination against the African-Americans; and that it was meant to be temporary. The implementation of this moral programme turned out to be an extremely troublesome affair. It soon became glaringly evident that an advantage given to blacks in employment meant that whites were passed over for jobs. If universities set aside a quota of places or gave special scholarships for blacks, it followed that white students with better qualifications would lose out. Recently, the US Supreme Court has confirmed a district Court of Appeal ruling given in October, 1994 that the granting of scholarships by the University of Maryland to 40 African- Americans each year was unconstitutional because it was limited to African-Americans.

Opposition to affirmative action is growing in the USA both as an expression of the current conservative mood and because it is increasingly seen as reverse discrimination against whites. They perceive affirmative action as a violation of majority rights and because it causes damage to the self-esteem of the blacks to know that they have been preferred, not through merit, but just to satisfy a quota. If underrepresented groups are to be given equality then the answer lies not in awarding opportunities to distinct racial groups, irrespective of ability, in an effort to create an artificially diversified workforce, but in tackling the problem at a more fundamental level: specifically by improving education and rebuilding a sense of community and family in the USA's ravaged ghettos.

Yet the proponents of affirmative action are equally prone to hiding their intentions behind euphemistic language: 'diversity goals' 'admission preferences; 'special consideration, 'compensatory time-table,' all adding up to that dreaded, forbidden word 'quotas'.

Opposition to Affirmative Action

Racism is subtle, supple and usually covert, but only by attacking it at the root can minorities take, with pride, the place in American society, merited by their individual talents— as women have begun to do. Rather than bringing the USA's races closer together, affirmative action has pushed them further apart, as indignation at preferential racial policies has reached a critical level among whites. More than 80 per cent of whites and a majority of non-whites oppose it. Spurred by mounting public anger, a long overdue reassessment is under way. The reopening of this debate is likely to be acrid and ugly. The main two political parties— the Republicans and the Democrats— had made it an issue in the 1996 elections.[14]

India's Protective Discrimination Vs USA's Affirmative Action

Though the fall-out of the affirmative action in the USA and of the protective discrimination in India is more or less the same, there is a basic difference between the two policies. The former aims at alleviating the condition of the racial minorities whereas the latter has set its target on those who are neither racial minorities nor linguistic minorities nor a minority on the basis of religion but some communities considered to be suffering from educational and social disabilities due to their birth in some castes. Reservations in the educational institutions for them, are based on the theory that, by certain members of a particular caste, getting well-educated and thereby holding public office, the level of the whole caste will be raised; this theory has proved to be wrong. Individual members of the caste getting admission in the higher educational institutions or government service on a preferential basis has had little effect on raising community standards. What has happened instead was polarization in Indian society on the basis of caste, which is fraught with disastrous consequences, affecting the integrity of the country.

There is another difference in their approach to this problem. While in the USA the process of assessment and reassessment of the policy is underway, in India no effort has been made to critically analyse the effect of 50 years of reservation and the extent to which this has helped improve the lot of the Scheduled Castes in this country. As M.N. Buch has pointed out, "the Government has deliberately and with malice aforethought refused to carry out any exercise to ascertain who are the main beneficiaries of the reservation so far."[15]

Hangover of Reservation

When India became independent, countries such as Japan, Germany, etc., were in a woeful state. Today if they are in an enviable position it is only because of hard work and dedication, whereas we have not yet recovered from the hangover of reservation. If there is no perceptible change despite the fact that the reservation policy has been in existence for nearly five decades now, there must be something wrong somewhere. While, the reservationists are disappointed and frustrated with the progress, results and achievements, on the other hand, anti-reservationists are losing patience and annoyed at the extensions of reservation. This is because of the misconceived, self-defeating approach to the solution of the problem. It is time we take an objective view of the policy and initiate suitable corrective measures.

Sub-standard over Merit

It is often alleged that in the name of reservation, the Government is making a mockery of our education system.[16] It is no doubt that the reserved communities do possess excellence. Otherwise, how is it that their names figure in the general merit list as well. As no study has yet been conducted to find out what is their representation in the general category merit list, the relative performance of the Scheduled Caste students could not, therefore, be assessed. But the fact is that the search for excellence is not properly pursued, leading to sub-standard stuff stealing a march over merit. If the quota-based reservation system becomes the practice and criterion for admission in any educational institution, what motivation will such a student have to work hard for better performance? Will he not expect the school, college and university to confer on him the degree just for appearance in the examination? Would not his expectation be the same in the matter of employment and promotion? What can the society expect of him? This situation is not good either for the nation as a whole or for the reserved communities themselves."To check this situation the foremost and the most important requirement", suggests the Scheduled Castes and the Scheduled Tribes Commissioner, "is to bring about a change in the thinking of all concerned, both at the governmental and the people's level."[17]

If, instead of following this policy of giving preference to backwardness in performance and merit, proper attention was paid in making the Scheduled Caste students equal in academic performance, if instead of giving emphasis to quota, due emphasis was given to improving their performance, then the present system of reservation in educational institutions and even in jobs would not have been necessary. They could have competed on an equal footing not only for their admissions in educational institutions, but for securing jobs as well. They cannot be helped to stand on their own feet by keeping reservations alive for a whole century even, because as Prof S.L. Saksena told the Parliament: "If you continue these privileges, these disabilities or this backwardness will never disappear, because crutches will never enable the backward classes to come up".[18] No community can prosper by remaining dependent on government handouts.

A Commissioner for the Scheduled Castes and Scheduled Tribes once commented in his report:

> Sometimes one feels that a person belonging to a down-trodden neglected community would not mind if he is not offered various concessions and verbal sympathy: but if he is only recognised as a 'man', we will find that he will

> not only stand like a 'man' but would march ahead of others. Incidentally, it may be mentioned that in the international circles our country is sometimes put in an awkward position with reference to the problems of the Harijans when we point out to the treatment of the Blacks at the hands of the white people in other countries.[19]

Politicization of Reservation, An Irreversible Situation

The Constitution of India allows reservation of seats in educational institutions, along with several other social welfare measures, as one of the potential means of reducing inequalities. Pandit Nehru, who piloted the Bill for amendment of Article 15 of the Constitution in 1951, which enables the State to pursue the policy of reservation in educational institutions, perhaps could realize the folly of the reservation policy at quite a late stage of his tenure as the Prime Minister of India. On June 27, 1961, that is after holding the office of the Prime Minister of India for nearly 14 years uninterruptedly, he, in a letter addressed to the Chief Ministers, deprecated the policy of reservation in no uncertain terms. He wrote:

I have referred above to efficiency and to our getting out of our traditional ruts. This necessitates our getting out of the old habit of reservations and particular privileges being given to this caste or that group. The recent meeting we held here, at which the Chief Ministers were present to consider national integration, laid down that the help should be given on economic considerations and not on caste. It is true that we are tied up with certain rules and conventions about helping the Scheduled Castes and Tribes. They deserve help but, even so, I dislike any kind of reservation, more particularly in services. I react strongly against anything which leads to inefficiency and second-rate standards. I want my country to be a first class country in everything. The moment we encourage the second-rate, we are lost.

> The only real way to help a backward group is to give opportunities of good education, this includes technical education which is becoming more and more important. Everything else is provision of some kind of crutches which do not add to the strength or health of body. We have made recently two decisions which are very important;

> one is universal elementary education, that is the base; and the second is scholarships on a very wide scale at every grade of education to the bright boys and girls, and this applies not merely to literacy education but, much more so to technical, scientific and medical training. I lay stress on the bright and able boys and girls because it is only they who will raise our standards. I have no doubt that there is a vast reservoir of potential talent in this country if only we can give it opportunity.
>
> But if we go in for reservations on communal and caste basis, we swamp the bright and able people and remain second-rate or third-rate. I am grieved to learn of how far this business of reservation has gone based on communal considerations.[20]

There was need to avoid populist decisions in the interest of the ultimate good of the nation. Resorting to populism may sometimes be politically expedient and pay electoral dividends, but it is only for a short time, and in the long run it may prove to be disastrous. Kennedy in his *Profiles in Courage,* gave seven instances in US history when the President took unpopular decisions and did not mind staking his popularity, but ultimately saved the nation. Such is the stuff of which statesmanship is made, for it thinks not merely of today but also of tomorrow and the day-after.[21] Sadly enough, Pandit Nehru, though he realized the mistake in providing for reservation on the basis of caste, did not initiate any action for doing away with the quota-based reservation system. Neither constitutionally nor administratively, such an atmosphere was created which would have precluded any recourse to the quota-based reservation system. Was it because he was really afraid to take such a bold decision?

It is certainly nobody's case that the Scheduled Castes, at least the educationally disadvantaged communities among them, should not be helped, but many sharply differ on the strategy for alleviation of the conditions of the Scheduled Castes. Immediately after partition, Punjab and West Bengal faced an identical problem: rehabilitation of millions of refugees who were forced to come over to this side of the border due to the communal holocaust. The methods applied for the solution of this gigantic problem however differed. In Punjab, cultivable land and agricultural inputs were allotted to those who wanted to live on agriculture and a lump sum of money and other incentives and concessions to those who wanted to be traders or small-scale industrialists. The refugee problem in Punjab was solved in no time. In West Bengal, an altogether different method was followed. The refugees from East Pakistan were put in hastily constructed refugee camps where they were given paltry doles which allowed them to survive but not to live like human beings. The refugee problem still lingers in West Bengal. For solution of the educational problem of the Scheduled Castes, what was needed was to follow the Punjab model. But the West Bengal model was followed instead. As aptly put by Lelah Dushkin, "the logic of the special treatment policy requires that the greatest amount be given at the beginning and that it then tapers off as the need for it becomes less acute. In practice, the reverse has happened."[22]

The result is what we see today. This policy, however, suits the politicians well, who have developed a vested interest in perpetuating the backwardness. They would like to win the favour of particular sections of the community and reservation is seen as a tool of patronage which will bring them some electoral benefits. They really never liked to solve this problem permanently. Otherwise a different strategy for alleviation of the conditions of the Scheduled Castes would have been formulated. As pointed out in an editorial in *The Telegraph:*[23]

To despair over the abuse of the reservation policy is to admit Indian politics is at its cynical worst. Cynicism over the fate of institutions that are burdened with quota criteria, cynicism over the repeated sacrifices to which the merit principle is subjected and cynicism over the farce that allows an already comparatively privileged group — Scheduled Castes and Scheduled Tribes who are double, or more, beneficiaries of reservations and the other backward classes in general — to "progress" under relaxed norms of judgement.

While politicians of all hues may not mind sacrificing the future of the nation to safeguard their own, what about the Scheduled Castes themselves, specially the educated ones and their leaders? A member of the Committee on Untouchability, Economic and Educational Development of the Scheduled Castes has observed that "the existence and continuation of caste system in India is essential for the survival of some individuals and organisations. Such persons are there not only among caste Hindus but also among the Scheduled Castes." He was of the opinion that the Scheduled Caste leaders, getting liberal grants from the government, were trying "to keep the Harijans downtrodden forever."[24]

One may draw a lesson from the attitude of the emerging black middle class in the USA which is not sold wholly on the affirmative action as an antidote to the ills of the blacks. Mr Michael Williams, Chief of civil rights enforcement at the US. Department of Education, boldly gave a ruling against race-designated scholarships in federally-funded educational institutions.Though the decision was reversed by President Bush, the guts of this intrepid black administrator were widely admired. It is now increasingly felt by high achievers among blacks that discriminatory treatment of blacks as a community is castrating, both intellectually and psychologically. It demeans their legitimate achievements and degrades them to a genre of inferior human beings.[25]

Since the disadvantages suffered by the Scheduled Caste students at school and college do not seem to be substantially different from those suffered by others who are economically or culturally disadvantaged, one may question the justification of protective discrimination for the Scheduled Castes in education. In fact, one may take the position that continued protection is likely to make for continued dependency and is, therefore, inadvisable. There may be a good case for continuation of protective discrimination for the Scheduled Castes in areas of life in which caste *per se* continues to be a problem, but as far as education is concerned, it may be more advantageous to merge their cause with that of other disadvantaged sectors.[26]

There is a growing awareness among the public that the distortions and anomalies that have enveloped the quota-based reservation system — not only in the educational field but in other spheres of public life like employment and representation in legislatures as well — could have been avoided if from the very beginning greater attention was paid for removal of educational backwardness by providing more facilities on a war footing. In fact, such demand is being raised from different quarters, specially the intelligentsia who, unlike the politicians, have no interest in keeping the country poor, illiterate, uneducated and inefficient for all time.

The caste concessions granted to the Scheduled Castes are all supposed to be temporary. No one has opposed this as a statement of principle. The most common characterization of special treatment for the Scheduled Castes is that it is a " crutch" which, if continued to be used too long, will only weaken its users. Special treatment is also commonly called a "necessary and evil." Although there are all sorts of subtle variations of emphasis on the words "necessasry" and "evil," the consensus that it is temporary in principle is universal. Temporary concessions, like temporary taxes, have a way of becoming permanent unless something is done to ensure that they remain temporary. This is the weakest part of the present system of caste benefits, for little has been done in this direction.[27] It is true that in spite of sounding warnings time and again, no serious thought was devoted to the problem of ensuring that special treatment would be temporary in fact as well as in principle. On the other hand, increasing politicization of reservation and the related politics of accommodation have resulted in a situation when it may even be "too unrealistic to talk of scrapping reservation in all spheres now".[28] Unfortunately, reservation is being regarded as a right and its original purpose, as envisaged by Dr. Ambedkar, is ignored. The process appears to be irreversible but it may not be altogether impossible to do away with reservations in educational institutions.

As a possible solution to the institution of reservation, B.K. Nehru, eminent civil servant and former Governor of Gujarat, suggested the following measures in 1988, i.e., much before the country was embroiled in fresh controversy over extension of this system to the Other Backward Classes. This is what he suggested:

> The State should establish residential schools of the standard of the best public school — the products of which start with an enormous advantage in all fields and not only in the public services — in every district of the country. Admissions to these should be limited to the economically disadvantaged people, the vast majority of whom belong to the backward and landless sections of the community. All costs should be borne completely by the State. It is obvious that the I.Q of a child belonging to, no matter how suppressed and backward, a caste is as high as that of a child of the upper castes; the distribution of natural talent

has nothing whatever to do with the caste into which one is born.

The upper castes have an advantage of learning; if the same conditions are given to children of the backward castes, there is absolutely no reason why the product should not equal that of the best of the privileged classes. If we had vision enough originally to foresee this situation , we could have solved this problem, that still bothers us and divides us, for all time to come in the courses of one generation. There would probably have been more members of the Scheduled Castes and the Scheduled Tribes and backward classes in the government services than there are at present with all the reservations to back them up and they would undoubtedly have been of greater competence. We would have succeeded in eliminating one of the many factors that hinder our integration as a nation.

The scheme of the Navodaya Schools is a step very much in the right direction. If I were a member of a backward class I would stop agitating for more reservation; I would agitate instead for a rapid implementation of the scheme and would be vigilant to see that it is not hijacked on the way by the rich or the strong.[29]

Let us give the best of education to those listed in the Schedule, apart from the general education to the children born in those castes. Let us give them abundant financial aid to pursue their studies and encourage them by giving large numbers of scholarships and other encouragements. It would be a proud day in the history of this country if we can produce a number of Ambedkars in different fields on the strength of their own talent and merit. That would be the best way to uplift the members of the Scheduled Castes. The backwardness of these castes is a great stigma on our national polity.

In fact, there should be a demand for such facilities from the communities themselves. Whether or not it would at all be possible to withdraw the reservation in education, will depend to a large extent on the Scheduled Castes themselves. Even as the existing government policies are reconsidered and revised, efforts have to be made to give a firm lift to the Scheduled Caste cause from within the Scheduled Caste community. Somewhere, somehow the consciousness of the Scheduled Caste communities needs to be sparked from within. They have a long way to go and their movement for advancement is not likely to make substantial gains in the future unless something happens to generate and mobilize forces for change from within.[30] Moreover, it is important that the Scheduled Castes themselves decide whether they wish to keep a separate identity of theirs or whether they wish to merge their cause with all the others, irrespective of caste, creed and religion. On their actions and deeds will largely depend the future course of the Indian society-whether it will continue to remain a 'casteist' society or a 'casteless' society. Let us wait for the day when the Scheduled Castes themselves refuse to receive 'benefits' under reservation, rather than stay permanently incapacitated under their load.

Other Backward Classes and Mandal Commission

Till 1990,the Scheduled Castes and the Scheduled Tribes were the only beneficiaries of the policy of reservation. From 1990, another tier of reservation has come to be added. This time it is for 'Other Backward Classes' (OBCs), though in a few States OBCs were given reservation benefits much earlier. Once there was an effort to determine backwardness on the basis of income. During Nehru's regime, a Commission headed by Kaka Kalelkar assessed whether the earnings could form the basis but it was found that such a criterion would declare 90 per cent of people in India backward. The economic yardstick was dropped.[31] But the pressure to identify backward classes did not ease; it ultimately got spelt into what came to be known as the Mandal Commission Report. It identified 52 per cent of the population as backward. Though the Mandal Commission considered some sub-castes among the 'higher castes' or among casteless religions like Christianity or Islam also as backward, the main criterion for identification of the 'backward classes' was the caste. But 'class' and 'caste' are different things. Class is an economic concept; caste is not. Caste is a kinship concept; it is exactly that which is our objective to eliminate from our body politic. But the compulsions of electoral necessity, under our present political system, are so overwhelming that class has been equated with caste and the courts have been pleased to accept this interpretation. The Supreme Court's ruling in *Indra Sawhney vs. Union of India* delivered in November, 1992 is one such erroneous judgment which breathes a new life into our anachronistic caste system fracturing the Indian society right from the village upwards.[32] Articles 15 and 16 of the Constitution provide for a casteless, creedless society and prohibits discrimination on the ground of caste or creed. As an exception, the Constitution provides: for the Scheduled Castes/ Scheduled Tribes and to certain 'socially and educationally backward classes of citizens'. The Framers of the Constitution could have easily substituted the phrase by "backward castes". Instead, they chose to call it "backward classes". Is its ethical on the part of the Supreme Court to interpret the word 'classes' as 'castes'? Not only did they equate 'castes' with 'classes' but asked all the State Governments to constitute permanent Commissions for the purpose of inclusion in, and deletion from, the list of "Backward Classes". Since the Framers did not visualize, and, therefore, did not provide for such a contingency, this direction of the Supreme Court amounted to virtually framing a new law. But unlike a new enactment, the Supreme Court directive did not contain any guidelines for the benefit of these Commissions. Should the "Backward Classes (read Castes)" be determined solely on the basis of social and educational backwardness? What is the criterion of social and educational backwardness? How to determine the social and educational backwardness? Which should be the reference group in relation to which a particular class is to be considered backward? What should be the yardstick for such a categorization? If the causes of educational backwardness are:

(a) traditional apathy for education on account of the social and environmental conditions or occupational handicaps;
(b) poverty and lack of educational institutions in rural areas; and
(c) living in inaccessible areas; then the yardstick for measuring it will vary from region to region, district to district, and even from *taluk* to *taluk*. Should these factors be taken into consideration for fixing a yardstick? How to obtain the relevant data? Since the Census do not compute caste-wise date, will the Commission wait till a caste-wise data is available or will it give credence to the written statements/ sworn affidavits of the interested groups who claim for recognition as a backward class? One would like a detailed survey to be done on the extent of social, educational, cultural or economic handicap from which all these castes claiming to be included in the OBCs, suffer. Such a survey might be conducted by a separate agency. Should such a survey precede such a determination? "Was it proper to give such a

direction without ascertaining relevant statistics? If the Commissions arrive at a decision without such basic data like the number of population; literacy rate, drop-out rate and educational attainment; dependence on traditional occupations like cultivation, artisan, etc., economic conditions including those living below poverty level, marriage age; representation in Government and semi-Government service; can these decisions be construed as rational and scientific? All these questions remain unanswered.

Again, there is another dichotomy. Commissions have been set up at the national as well as State levels. The list prepared by the State Commission is applicable for obtaining the State benefits, while the list prepared by the National Commission is-valid for enjoying the Central benefits. Since the methodology followed for arriving at a decision is not uniform, it is quite likely that these two lists would differ. If there is really an anomaly between these two lists — a caste figuring in one list and not in the other — it will give rise to tensions and conflicts and even enlarge the scope for political manoeuvre.

The absence of any guidelines does not, however, prevent the State Commissions from declaring a caste backward. Though the Commission is vested with the power of deletion from the list of OBCs, it is more likely to be a one-way traffic, like that of the Scheduled Castes, all would aspire to be included and none would like to go away. The best course would have been to frame a detailed guideline for these Commissions to function in a uniform and meaningful manner — the criterion for social and educational backwardness which should be taken into consideration for inclusion in, and deletion from, the list and the procedure and methodology to be followed for that purpose, if the Backward Classes (Castes?) were at all to be listed.

Since no leader of any accredited political party can openly take up the cause of a single caste, because, after all, how could he align himself with the aspirations of a single caste when he is to depend on the votes of other castes as well, the task of mobilizing the caste members and representing their case before the Commission have been taken up by the elites among the individual caste group. They have taken up this task with a zeal, apparently for the benefit of all the members of his caste, but the real purpose of taking up this cudgel is to ensure a safe berth for their sons and daughters, who may not be equally fortunate to attain the same educational and economic level in the future. It is mostly this section of the Backward Classes like that of the educationally advanced Scheduled Castes, who will be profited by reservation policy. It is a long term investment for the rainy days. However, it is quite likely that the mantle of leadership of the respective caste may be thrust upon them, which means more power, more prestige and more clout for them, if the battle lines are drawn on the basis of caste.

Due to legislation, the caste system has undergone considerable change. Rather than being diluted, there is an apparent increase in caste loyalties and interests which have political dimensions, with restructuring of caste loyalties and identities. There is a proliferation of caste *sabhas*, which reminds one of the 1930s when the caste *sabhas* became a way of life. But there is a difference between the two situations. The caste *sabhas* in the 1930s worked for the elevation of social conditions of the caste members and in many cases, were able to persuade the census authority to accord them higher position in the caste hierarchy. Nowadays, the caste *sabhas* are mainly concerned to see that their caste members are recognized as members of the Scheduled Castes, or at least as members of the Backward Classes or the More Backward Classes, and to ensure[33] quota implementation.

One sees the resurgence of what the Tamil Nadu First Backward Classes (Sattanathan) Commission, 1970 called the "claims for down-grading." These include the recent demands by the Tamil Nadu Brahmin Association (TAMBRAS) for 20 per cent educational reservation for the Forward Castes, by Vellala, for inclusion in the Backward Classes list, by Nadar, Reddy, Sengunthar, Veerasaivar, and Yadava, already in the Backward Classes list; for inclusion in the Most Backward Classes list, by PMK; for raising the quota in the State for the BCs-MBCs combine from 50 per cent to 68 per cent, for the SCs from 18 per cent to 22 and for 10 per cent reservation for the Forward Communities, and by organizations of the SCs and STs for 31 per cent reservation, reservation for all posts, in all departments and in promotions, and restoring the carry forward system.[34]

The mobilization of men on the basis of caste has made the task of Commissions more difficult. If they do not concede the demand of a caste, they are subjected to massive public criticism. If they include, they face the charge of fragmenting the society on the basis of caste. Was it necessary to give that much importance to caste in a country where the danger of caste war already looms large? All that the Court had been able to do is to mount a rear-guard action in ruling that reservation of more than 50 per cents negates the principle of non-discrimination itself. The ruling is widely disregraded; reservations in excess of this arbitrary limit are common; the States are 'managing' to circumvent the order. And should obstacle by way of legal proscriptions come in the way, the Constitution is there to be amended. In fact, the shape of things to come is indicated when Tamil Nadu's legislation protecting the 69 per cent quota regime found its way into the Ninth Schedule of the Constitution, which is supposed to provide it immunity against judicial scrutiny, and this is virtually an open invitation to the other States to emulate that example and hike the quotas. It is outrageous that the Constitution has been played with in such a cavalier fashion to satisfy certain political needs.

By entering into the percentage controversy, the Court has allowed the exception to become the rule and made a mockery of the constitutional clause prohibiting discrimination on grounds of caste. Even today, there are States like West Bengal where the Hindu community is cohesive and has been brought up to think along international Marxist lines. The court's order inflicts the curse of casteism even on such homogeneous societies.[35] The Court had once declared: "Threats of mob hysteria should not deflect the court from its true accountability to the Constitution."[36] One only wishes that this was followed literally.

And if we have to have reservations on the basis of birth, why stop at caste? Why not include religion—the Muslims, for example, in many parts of the country loudly proclaim their backwardness. "Dalit Christians", "Dalit Muslims", have already been included in the list of OBCs in many States and they now demand for inclusion in the list of the Scheduled Castes.[37] And why stop at religion? Should we not have reservation for all the linguistic groups, regions and sub-regions as well? And do we really hope that on this basis we will create a united India? Very clearly, it is patent that the continuous extension of reservations is designed to attract votes. The test for being included in the favoured category is no longer backwardness, it is number.[38] Perhaps, in keeping with this spirit of reservation, there is a thinking amongst a section of the ruling Left Front in West Bengal to reserve seats in educational institutions for the Nepali speaking people.[39]

The backwardness of certain groups arises from their inability to compete in a modern competitive society, either because their religious and social environment has impeded this ability, or because they have been too poor to take advantage of the facilities for advancement that modern India offers. The solution then, is to create an environment for as large a number as possible, of these deprived sections, where they will have from infancy the same advantage as only the rich enjoy today so that by the time they grow up, they will be able to compete on their merits with anybody else.

Our national life today is plagued and imperilled by a number of divisive forces and internal conflicts. The need of the hour is to pull down the barriers that divide the people, resolve the conflicts and bring about fusion and unity with a view to fostering national integration. We must remember that each generation is the custodian of the well being of the nation, the sentinel of its destiny and the trustee of its future. It is for them to ensure that it leaves a better and stronger nation, compared to what it inherited. It would be a sad day for the present generation if we leave to posterity an India ridden with dissensions and conflicts.

References

1. Shah, B.V., *Sociology of education, a Trend Report, Third Survey of Research in Education, 1978-83*, NCERT, 1986, p. 96.
2. *Fourteenth Report of Parliamentary Committee on the Welfare of Scheduled Castes and Scheduled Tribes*. Fourth Lok Sabha, Lok Sabha Secretariat, SCTC No. 17, December, 1970, pp. 17-19.
3. *The Telegraph*, June 19, 1995, p. 5.
   The Hindu, June 29, 1995, p.1.
   The Statesman, June 30, 1995 , p. 3.
4. Reservation Anomalies, editorial in the *Hindu*, June 17, 1995. p. 8.
5. D.O. No. F. 1-6/89(SCT) of Additional Secretary, University Grants Commission dated July 30, 1989. See Appendix I.
6. Government of West Bengal, Higher Education Department Establishment Branch, Memo. No. 906-Edn(Esst) dated August 8, 1995.

7. See Sachidananda ,"*Research on Scheduled Castes with Special Reference to Change*" in *Survey of Research in Sociology and Social Anthropology*, Vol. I, Popular Prakashan, Bombay, 1974, pp. 276-319; Brij Raj Chauhan and G. Narayana, *Problems of Education among Scheduled Castes Students in Uttar Pradesh in Social Change, 1976; pp. 13-18; G. Narayana"Social Background of Scheduled Caste MPs in the Fifth Lok Sabha — A Comparative Study"*, in *CDPR Digest*, Vol. 5, No. 2, 1974.
8. Ramanujachari, T.C.A., "Cornering the benefits", *Indian Express*, October 3, 1990.
9. *The Hindu*, October 20, 1994, p. 2.
10. The *Times of India*, October 12, 1990, p. 9.
11. Beteille, Andre, *The Backward Classes and the New Social Order*, Oxford University Press, 1981, p. 30.
12. *Ibid.*, pp. 42-43.
13. *Ibid.*, p. 49.
14. Macintyre, Ben, "Quota norms fight for survival in USA, *The Statesman*, March 14, 1995, p. 9.
Frankel, W:lliam, "No Blacks—Only Scholarship," *The Statesman*, June 3, 1995, p. 8
The Hindu, July 25, 1995, p. 7.
15. Buch, M.N., "The Futility of Reservations," *Indian Express*, October 11, 1990, p. 8.
16. Satyamurty, Letters to the Editor, *The Hindu*, June 22, 1995, p. 8.
17. Twentieth *RCSCST* (1970-71), p. 3.
18. *Parliamentary Debates* (Part II- Proceedings other than Questions and Answers), Volume XII, 1951, (15th May, 1951 to 6th June, 1951), Third Session (Second Part) of Parliament of India, 1951, dated June 1, 1951, Col. 9820.
19. Mane, Shankarrao, Twenty-third *RCSCST* (1974-75), para 1.68 pp. 19-20.
20. Nehru, Jawaharlal, *Letters to Chief Ministers, 1947-64*, Vol. 5, Oxford University Press, 1989, pp. 456-57.
21. Khanna, H.R., "Education, the Better Way," *The Hindustan Times*, September 14, 1990, p.13.
22. Dushkin, Lelah, "Future of Special Treatment", *The Economic Weekly*, November 18, 1961, p. 1729.
23. "Ladder Among Men", editorial in The *Telegraph*, June 2, 1995, p.10.
24. Achutan, R., Member, In: *Report of the Committee on Untouchability, Economic and Educational Development and other Connected Documents*, 1969, pp.viii-ix.
25. Khatkhate, Deena,"Reservation: Need to Remove Crutches",The *Times of India*, January 31, 1991.
26. Chitnis, Suma, *A Long Way to Go*, op. cil p. 165.
27. Dushkin, Lelah, op. cit., p. 1729.

28. "Reservation Anomalies", editorial in The *Hindu*, June 17, 1995, p. 8
29. Nehru, B.K., "Do we still need reservation? " *Indian Express Magazine*, April 17, 1988, p. 6.
30. Chitnis, Suma, op. cit., p. 65.
31. Nayar, Kuldip, Politics plagues Reservation, *The Statesman*, October 10, 1995, p. 6.
32. Ramanujam, T.C.A. and Sangeetha, T.C.A. "Guardian of the Law?" *The Hindu*, July 9, 1995. p. IV.
33. *The Indian Express*, October 21, 1990, p. 3.
34. Radhakrishan, P., "The quota conundrum, "*The Hindu Magazine*, February 19, 1995, p. IV.
35. Ramanujam, T.C.A. and Sangeeta, T.C.A., *The Hindu*, July 9, 1995, p. IV.
36. 1981, ASC, p. 301.
37. *The Hindu*, November 29, 1995, p. 13.
    The Telegraph, November 29, 1995, p. 5.
    The Telegraph, November 30, 1995, p. 7.
38. Nehru, B.K., *Express Magazine*, April 17, 1988, p. 6.
39. *Ananda Bazar Patrika*, February 25, 1996, p. 6.

8
Educational Development and Social Integration

In all societies of the world, education as an instrument of socialization is also considered as a powerful catalyst for social change. It is also considered as sine qua non of attaining a better socio-economic status in society. It adds dignity, grace and prestige to ones social personality. It directly influences one's attitudes, opinions and behaviour patterns. It is also considered a powerful medium for reducing prejudices and discriminations in societies, torn by communal and racial conflicts. It is also considered important for generating both horizontal and vertical mobility. Even proponents of conflicting uses of education share a common belief that education makes a difference and thus is worth personal and collective investment.[1]

In the Indian context, education has an added importance. Social reformers have put considerable faith in education not only for the speedy abolition of untouchability, thereby leading to the socio-economic progress, but also as the most effective change-agent and the pivotal factor for the upkeep of the democratic set-up and emotional integration of the country, so very essential for our nation torn by casteism and caste conflicts.

The framers of the Constitution also thought that provision of better educational facilities would not only improve the socio-economic conditions of the Scheduled Castes but would also be helpful in the removal of the bane of untouchability and, indirectly, in the elimination of alienation amongst them. Educational requirements are a pre-requisite for entry into higher prestige jobs and into higher income categories. It is a prerequisite for their mobility through both occupation and income. Therefore, a series of measures have been taken both at the level of the Central Government and the State Governments to spread education and literacy among the Scheduled Castes mentioned in Chapter IV, so that through educational advancement the other two disabilities, social and economic, may also be resolved. The Commission for the Scheduled Castes and the Scheduled Tribes also commended as far back as 1982 that Government of India and the State Governments had been making progress in educational development of the Scheduled Castes and the Scheduled Tribes by making liberal financial allocations for a variety of educational schemes in various Five -Year Plans.[2]

With all the opportunities and constitutional safeguards provided, it was expected that the Scheduled Castes would feel a reduced sense of alienation and segregation, which will ultimately pave the way for social integration in all its facets. Now the question arises as to what extent education provided so far has been able to achieve the cherished goals of influencing the attitudes and behaviour patterns of the Scheduled Castes, and consequently of helping them in eliminating or reducing their social inequalities, disabilities, discrimination and feelings of alienation, as well as in promoting social integration based on a sense of equality.

Social scientists conducted many studies during the post-independence period to evaluate the effect of educational development of the Scheduled Castes. A brief review[3] of these studies reveal that the educational efforts of the Government and some other agencies have contributed positively to uplift the status of the Scheduled Castes. It has been observed by such scholars that increase and spread of education among the Scheduled Castes has provided them with more opportunities for political participation; they have gained greater economic independence and higher status; they have come to occupy elite positions; there is perceptible improvement in their socio-economic status and so on. But the impact of educational development has not been felt equally by all the communities among the Scheduled Castes. Some Scheduled Castes have been benefited more to the exclusion of others. Education has led to the emergence of a new elite group among the Scheduled Castes and also to the alienation of the educated elite from their own community. It has created new inequalities and new areas of social inequality.

A number of researches have been conducted in the field of

sociology of education by scholars either for their Ph.D. thesis or as Research Projects. It is found that the sixties have yielded only 62 studies whereas the seventies brought out as many as 204. This means that the interest of social scientists in this field has increased a great deal during the seventies. Though the figure for the eighties is unavailable, it is very probable that the same trend has continued during the eighties also as is indicated by the 44 studies during the first two years of the eighties. Of the 198 researches, both published and unpublished, during 1978-83, a trend report of which was made by the National Council of Educational Research and Training, about 20 papers deal with the educational problems of the Scheduled Caste school and college students. They cover most of the States. These studies mostly indicate that the Scheduled Caste students have encouraging parents and that they have high aspirations. However, they are found lower than non-Scheduled Caste students in utilizing the available educational facilities, intellectual ability, school adjustment, participation in co-curricular activities, scholastic achievement, etc. The rates of non-attendance, stagnation and wastage are still higher among them. They still possess a feeling of inferiority and diffidence. They lack study facilities at home. Only the elites from among them have been able to show ability to overcome the handicap of the segregated home environment and come up to the school, college and university level.[4]

These studies, most of them empirical, were conducted a few years earlier and some of them are even more than 20 years old. These studies, nevertheless, show the trend and in the absence of latest findings, the old data have been relied upon. The trends emerging from these studies have, therefore, been advantageously employed in analysing the prevailing trends in social mobility, and social integration of the Scheduled Castes due to the effect of educational development.

Encouragement and Motivation

One of the major objectives in instituting scholarships, freeships and other incentives for the education of backward groups is to enkindle the motivation for education that is missing. The programmes and the facilities provided not only aim at removing the extraneous restrictions to the education of individuals belonging to the educationally disadvantaged sections, but also aim at motivating them to be educated and thus enabling them to overcome their own resistance, inertia or indifference to education. Unlike the Scheduled Tribes, the Scheduled Castes have used the resources allocated to them much more effectively. This suggests that the Scheduled Castes are not wanting in motivation.

Modern secular education is playing a central role in the efforts of the Scheduled Castes to improve their position. They know that education and education alone can help them to come up to the levels of other forward castes in India. Education is one of the important factors, in fact the most important factor, for determining mobility and occupational success of the members of the Scheduled Castes. They, therefore, constantly express a desire for more education and attribute their low position to lack of education. The Scheduled Caste parents value education as an important means of moving away from the traditionally low caste-based occupations and of raising the socio-economic status of their children. A study[5] shows that, contrary to the general notion that uneducated parents are unable to motivate their children, most of the parents provide not only ample encouragement and emotional support but also financial support for the education of their children. It was revealed in another study[6] that though most of the parents were either illiterates or less educated, they had a positive attitude towards education of their children. Another study[7] indicates that though far less educated and of poor economic means, needing immediate financial help from the grown up members of the family, nearly nine-tenths of the students got encouragement from their father, mother and brother. Thus, it can be said that the members of the older generation, irrespective of their own educational level, have understood the value of education in raising their socio-economic status and are, therefore, encouraging the younger members of the family to take to education. This factor can be expected to accelerate the educational advancement of Scheduled Castes. Not only encouragement but financial support is also extended by the members of family. A study[8] shows that only 13 per cent of the students depend wholly on scholarships/freeships as the only source of finance for pursuing their studies, while 76 per cent depend partly on the financial support of their parents/brother and partly on scholarships/ freeships.

A study[9] conducted in the Punjab concluded that `urge to

improve status' was the most important motivating force among the Scheduled Castes pursuing education. Another study[10] conducted in Poona revealed that due to higher education the Scheduled Caste women achieved a high status which was hitherto unknown in their families and community. Ninety per cent of the respondents felt that education made them realize that they should change their way of life. It was due to education that the Scheduled Caste women had been accepted, at least in urban society, on par with the members of the higher classes.

It was found[11] that while two-thirds of the Scheduled Caste elite (i.e... those who use intellect and rational judgment while participating in the decision-making process and occupy some position of trust and responsibility) in Andhra Pradesh identified education as the main factor for their rise to their present position, actually no less than four-fifths of them owed it to education. If a Scheduled Caste has education, automatically the constitutional provisions of reservation of seats in educational institutions for higher education including professional institutions and in legislatures and in public service, enable him to get an elite position in society. Family reputation also counts in several cases in getting to the elite position but it might not be an essential factor in case of the Scheduled Castes.[12] Sachidananda also found[13] that the elite in Bihar have been most active in propagation of education through which, they think, social change can be brought among the Scheduled Castes.

Aspirations

Education influences the levels of aspirations of Scheduled Castes in the sense that once Scheduled Caste children succeed in getting entry into institutions of higher learning they begin to idertify themselves with the goals set by other children belonging to non-Scheduled Castes. They make the non-Scheduled Caste groups as their normative groups.They compete with non-Scheduled Caste students in the attainment of those goals which were earlier forbidden to them. They like to take full advantage of the secular education and make use of the special privileges granted to them. They are fully aware of the fact that they can easily get entry into prestigious public services and grab many of the opportunities to which they had hitherto no access.

This conclusion is supported by the data collected from 14 States by a study team.[14] It is found that both the school and college respondents suggest that the Scheduled Caste students who have made it to high school and college aspired for higher education. It is possible that the aspirations of students from educationally backward sections take a shape and begin to rise only when they move along to higher levels of education.

Similarly, a study[15] shows that the higher education of the father, the higher was the education of the son, showing that the chances of the sons of less educated fathers achieving higher education were much fewer than the chances of sons whose fathers had higher education. Another study [16] indicates that the students' aspirations are somewhat conditioned by their caste status among the Scheduled Castes. There is a distinct difference in the aspirations of castes at the top and at the bottom of the caste groups. Most of the students belonging to the caste at the top of status hierarchy among the Scheduled Castes (e.g. Garoda in Gujarat) have medium (Post-graduate) or high (doctoral degree/technical/professional degree) educational aspirations, while the students belonging to castes at the bottom of the status hierarchy like Bhangi evince low educational (graduate degree) aspirations. A broad hierarchical pattern of educational aspirations, therefore, can be noticed with castes at the top in the middle and at the bottom.

A study[17] reveals that majority (49.2 per cent) of the Scheduled Caste elite in Andhra Pradesh desired that their children should pursue professional courses like Medicine, Engineering, Technology, etc., 23 per cent of them desired post -graduate education for their children; while 15.7 per cent desired that their children should not only go for professional courses but also for postgraduate degrees. The higher the position of the father, the higher is the aspiration level of education for their children. On the whole, the utilization of educational facilities was much slower among the sons of poorly educated fathers than among those of well-educated fathers.

Thus, those who have achieved greater socio-economic status tend to have higher educational aspirations for the educational and occupational careers of their children than those with lower education. The educated Scheduled Castes realize the importance of education because it helps in occupational mobility which, in turn, leads to better economic conditions and better social status. The higher the level of education, the greater is the chance of moving away from caste-based occupations, which are generally low and inhibit higher status in the society. Therefore, education becomes a means to forsake all those occupations which are considered degrading. A study [18] indicated that as formal education increased in standards and numbers gradually from one generation to another, there was more mobility from traditional occupations to liberal occupations and from liberal occupations to professional occupations. Another study [19] revealed professional mobility among the educated. Scheduled Caste youth, which was a post-Independence achievement and had been possible through education. A study [20] conducted in Andhra Pradesh shows that the majority of the Scheduled Caste elite moved from one position to another because of their educational attainments. It was revealed in another study [21] that the Scheduled Caste elite in Bihar are experiencing upward mobility. They are no more in their caste occupations.

Another study [22] shows that almost all the respondents would wish to see their sons and daughters reach an educational standard higher than their own; only a few respondents in the higher education categories have preferred that the educational level of their wards be of the same as their own level or even slightly lower.

Status Determinants in Society

It may be observed that the socio-economic stratification in almost all societies is operationalized through such indicators as education, occupation and income. An analyst has asserted [23] that among these three variables, education is the most efficient index of socio-economic status. Education is a prerequisite for the mobility of the Scheduled Castes through both occupation and income. While differences in family background have their repurcussions on educational attainment, education also determines an individual's evaluation of his social status. Social status of an individual has two dimensions: (i) status which he receives from his own personal characteristics, and (ii) status which he receives from the group to which he belongs. In other words, the social status of an individual is influenced not only by his individual properties, but also by the social status of the group to which he belongs.

It is found that the Scheduled Caste's own assignment to the different status levels depends on the level of education of the individual. The level of education of an individual is a good indicator of his social class and the evaluation of status criteria varies according to the educational background of the subjects. The more educated tend to place themselves in the upper and middle classes while the illiterates and less educated regard themselves as belonging to the lower and working classes. This shows that their class consciousness is in accordance with the changes in their educational levels and consequent socio-economic status attained.[24]

This finds corroboration in another study [25] which indicates that the father's education and caste are the two factors which influence the Scheduled Caste's perception of his own status. The fathers of the Scheduled Caste youth, who feel that the status of the Scheduled Castes has improved, are educated and belong to high status castes while the fathers of those who think that the status of the Scheduled Castes has not improved, are either illiterates or less educated and belong to lower status castes. The subjective opinion of the respondents regarding the improvement in the status of the Scheduled Castes varied according to the educational level of the respondents, that is, the educated respondents perceive a great deal of improvement in the status of the Scheduled Castes as compared to the illiterates and less educated respondents.

A great majority of those with education till the matric level and above, opined that there was great deal of improvement in the status of the Scheduled Castes and only a few among them considered that there was only a slight improvement. It will be observed that among the educated respondents, no one considered that there was a deterioration in the status of the Scheduled Castes or that there was no change. On the other hand, everyone perceived some improvement in the status as compared to the past.

Yet another study [26] shows that barely 13 per cent of the school students and 4 per cent of the college students believe that the status of the Scheduled Castes has improved to a point where they are now equal in status to caste Hindus. The majority—74 per cent of the school students and 89 per cent of the college students—either believe that their status has not improved at all, or that although their status has improved, as compared to what the status of the Scheduled Castes was in the past, it is not yet equal to that of the other castes. It shows that education does not seem to have been fully effective in developing a positive and confident self-image on the part of the Scheduled Castes.

Another study[27] reveals that about 70 per cent of the Scheduled Caste pupils in Tamil Nadu categorically derived any improvement in their social status. This is, no doubt, a severe indictment of the government policy, despite the various facilities and special privileges doled out to them by the Central and State Governments.

What about the general attitude of the upper castes towards the Scheduled Castes. A study[28] conducted in the rural and urban areas around Agra, Delhi and Varanasi in 1968 revealed that 80 per cent of the members of the upper castes believed that one's own achievements, rather than one's caste, determined one's status in society.

Those who move up are more likely to be oriented towards the higher caste groups. As the level of education increases, the tendency to dissociate from their own caste groups increases, because while, on the one hand, they improve their socio-economic conditions through their own achievements. On the other, the status of the group to which they belong remains the same, which, infact, lowers their own social standing and as a result, they tend to dissociate themselves from their own caste groups.[29] Social mobility, thus, minimizes one's contacts with one's own group, which, infact, again means that when the Scheduled Castes improve their occupational and educational status they are prone to dissociate from their own caste groups and manifest a degree of alienation in terms of social isolation.[30] Some of the educated Scheduled Castes who have risen high in the social hierarchy have snapped their ties with their past[31] and there are instances of the fellow illiterate villagers being ill-treated by their educated Scheduled Caste fellows.[32] Sachidananda has found that, by and large, a great number of the Scheduled Caste elite in Bihar have taken little interest in bettering the lot of their less fortunate brethren.[33]

While the Scheduled Castes have improved their educational and occupational status, they feel that their improved educational and occupational status have not received adequate and commensurate social recognition because of their lowly social origin, thus leading to status incongruence.

A study [34] has demonstrated that secular education is playing a central role in Chamars' efforts to improve their position. It shows that two Chamars who teach in a village school in Uttar Pradesh are accorded much more respect than their less educated caste fellows in the same village. It is also emphasized in that study that these two Chamar school teachers who have acquired the highest education have not been accorded the full degree of respect which is granted to teachers of the higher castes which indicates "while education is an individual achievement, even educated Chamars cannot escape an awareness that mobility for them, too must be a group phenomenon"[35]. Lipset and Bendix have rightly suggested that "as a man advances his economic fortunes, he may find himself excluded from certain social groups because of his lowly social origin or his ethnic background. [36]

The reason for this relatively lower status of the educated Scheduled Caste is evident if we consider the fact that the social status of an individual is influenced not merely by his individual possessions, but the social status of the group which he belongs. Unless a mechanism is found by which an educated Scheduled Caste ceases to be a part of the lowly placed castes grouped under the Scheduled Castes this incongruence in social position cannot be obviated. This is all the more necessary so that the process of integration with the higher castes can gain momentum.

Transformation in Interaction Pattern of the Scheduled Castes

It has been widely recognized that status is achieved by associating with those of equal or greater social attainment. Therfore as a consequence of educational attainment, the interaction pattern of the Scheduled Castes has undergone a change. The educated Scheduled Castes seek to move upward and have contacts with the elite sections of the society.[37] They tend to change their membership of organizations and their choice of leaders and friends and may also move to a new neighbourhood in keeping with their newly gained position. The consequences of educational development may directly be felt in interpersonal relations between the Scheduled Castes and other higher castes.

As the level of education increases, the tendency to dissociate castes with names increases. The association between education and the tendency to dissociate from caste names is highly significant. A study[38] showed that the educated members among the Scheduled Castes pointed out that they did not like to use their caste names, because if they did, the outlook of the people would change and they would be looked down upon as inferiors. So to avoid rejection by the other castes, they did not use their caste names. It was also gathered from talks with members of the educated Scheduled Castes who felt that while during work the question of castes did not arise, in their private lives it mattered a lot. If a man belonged to a Scheduled Caste in spite of his high occupational status, the non-Scheduled Caste would not mix with him freely. They would keep a little aloof even though they did not show their aloofness too openly. For these very reasons, the educated Scheduled Castes in many cases did not like to advertise the fact that they belonged to the Scheduled Castes.

It is found that a majority among the illiterate and less-educated Scheduled Castes are not only members of the caste associations but are also active participants and office-bearers of these organisations, whereas the majority among the educated Scheduled Castes are members of non-Scheduled Caste organizations and even those who have joined the Scheduled Caste organizations play a second fiddle in the organization by remaining in the capacity of ordinary members. A great majority of the illiterate and less-educated Scheduled Castes favour these caste organizations because these origanizations solve their varied problems and also work for community welfare. On the other hand, educated Scheduled Castes do not regard these organizations as constructive for the society because they spread communalism and segregation. Moreover, these organizations work for their selfish interests ignoring the larger interests of the society.[39] But the Scheduled Caste elite, being aware of their mutual interdependence, are not averse to joining such caste associations. They are mostly members in such caste organizations, in the capacity of Secretary, etc.[40] A study [41] of the Bihar elite also showed a similar trend. Most of the elite are anxious to foster caste solidarity because they feel that only by a united stand as a community can they act as a pressure group, gain political rights and improve their economic condition. They organized caste meetings or participated in such meetings. Sometimes caste meetings have been organized to highlight the newly found corporate status of the caste. On other occasions, the emphasis has been upon uniting the caste members to safeguard their economic interests.

Effect of Education on Family Size of Scheduled Castes

Education has repercussions on the family patterns of the Scheduled Castes. With the rise in educational level, the family pattern undergoes a change towards a decrease in size of the family. Education strongly influences fertility behaviour. Primary education by providing basic fundamental literacy and numeracy, enhances women's status within and outside their family and increases their exposure to the information and ideas disseminated through printed material. This brings changes in their general behaviour involving breast-feeding, the use of contraceptive and fertility. In addition, staying longer in schoal raises their age at marriage. In other words, advancement of female education can be expected to influence fertility behaviour.[43] Analysis of data of 15 major States, accounting for 96 per cent of the total population of the country, shows that female literacy and education are positively associated with population growth rates.[44]

A micro level study in Allahabad city shows that education is one of the most important determinants of fertility. Illiterate couples have the highest number of children ever born. The birth-rate decreases with the increase in the educational status of males and females.[45]

Effect of Education on Marriage of Scheduled Castes

Not only does the family pattern undergo a change, but the institution of marriage, too witnesses a change as a result of education. The traditional norms and values change as a consequence of education. The shift from ascribed occupation to occupation by choice means lengthening of the period of education and at times an uncertain future, thus making them hesitant to marry and raise a family until they are well-settled in life.[46] Education tends to exercise pressure for a higher age at marriage for men and, consequently for women too. Furthermore, the educated Scheduled Castes preferred a higher age at marriage for sons and daughters, as compared to the illiterate and less-educated Scheduled Castes. In the majority of cases, the ages specified for boys and girls are appreciably higher than the age traditionally regarded as appropriate.[47] The higher the level of education the lower is the proportion of opposition to intercaste marriage. A study[48] shows that there is not a single case opposing intercaste marriage among postgraduates, whereas an insignificant percentage among graduates, i.e., 3.1 opposed intercaste marriage. The highly educated Scheduled Castes and those who have an elevated social standing form an exclusive group to move upward by seeking marital relations with the upper castes.[49] Although they have been leaning towards intercaste marriages, a study[50] inidcates, they are not willing to marry their girls to caste Hindu boys. Curiously enough, the majority of the students seemed to be inclined towards endogamy, by choice. A study[51] showed that 76 per cent of school students and 64 per cent of college students said that it was either `important' or `very important' for them to marry the person of their own caste. Another study[52] revealed that 72 per cent of college students regarded `sameness of castes' either as `very important' or 'important'. Education may grant more freedom of choice in marriage in the sense that it gives men and women some right to choose their mates. But a study [53] shows that nearly two-thirds of the students accept parental authority in the matter of their marriage even though it may be against their personal choice. Among graduates and post-graduates not more than 14 per cent think that marriages should be decided upon by the boy and girl concerned.[54] A study[55] reveals that love marriages are still quite unknown among the educated Scheduled Castes. Only 1.5 per cent of the respondents have love matches. This may be attributed to the fact that among the Scheduled Castes, spread of education and modern attributes are only a recent phenomenon.

In India, in the lower stratabride-price is paid for the bride at marriage, whereas in the higher sections a dowry, i.e., a sum of money or property is given to the daughter at the time of marriage. A study[56] indicates that educated youths have started accepting dowry. At present, for educated Scheduled Castes who are gainfully employed, the acceptance of dowry has become a symbol of prestige.[57] Another study[58] shows that a fairly large number of the Scheduled Caste illiterates or those having education up to the primary level, have paid the bride-price. But this percentage decreases considerably for the under matriculates and matriculates, whereas it is totally absent in the higher educational categories. It shows that education has replaced bride-price by dowry among the educated Scheduled Castes as well. The winds of changes, though negative in this case, have been so great that even a rumour of someone alleged to have taken bride-price would be severely dealt with by the elders of the community. In some cases both the bride's and groom's families have had to appear before the Caste Council and declare, on oath, that neither of the parties had encouraged the custom of bride-price behind the curtain.[59]

Effect of Education on Choice of Friends of Scheduled Castes

If it is expected that liberating individuals from the confines of caste is one of the effects of education, one may ask how far and to what extent education has achieved that objective in the matter of choice of friends of the Scheduled Caste students. A study[60] indicates that as many as 57 per cent of school students and 46 per cent of college students say that all three of their best friends either belong to their own caste or some other Scheduled Caste. In fact, 28 per cent of the school students and 21 per cent of the college students say that all their friends belong to their own caste, while only 10 per cent of school students and 12 per cent of the college students say that all their best friends belong to the non-Scheduled Castes. Another study[61] revealed that a majority of the less educated counted among their best friends persons from their own caste groups while a majority of the educated Scheduled Castes did not specify their friends from any group. However, of the small percentage among them who specified their friends, a majority had their friends from the non-Scheduled Caste community. Again, where there is a greater concentration of Scheduled Caste students, they interact among themselves much more than with others and hence, develop high homophily in larger proportion. When the concentration is low , there are less chances of inter-mixing with one's own group and hence, they develop low or no homophily in larger proportion. This also means that high concentration of the Scheduled Caste students in an area or an institution may develop a greater group consciousness among them.[62] It is also found that the students coming from the higher stratum of Scheduled Castes are more able to give up homophily than the others in their friendship pattern. A study[63] reveals that lower the caste status, the lower is the proportion of students showing low homophily and higher is the proportion of students showing `high homophily'. The converse is also found equally true. Thus, the students coming from `Garoda' caste, who are priests of Scheduled Castes in Gujarat, are more able to give up homophily than others in their friendship pattern. Higher the status of the family, the greater are the chances of reduction of homophily among its wards.

On the basis of homophily observed, it would be justifiable to assert that at least as far as the Scheduled Caste students are concerned, schools and colleges have not functioned effectively as melting pots for caste boundaries in the matter of friendship.

Caste Restrictions and Discriminations

Reformers have put considerable faith in education as one of the principal agents for the removal of caste restrictions and the promotion of interaction. They expected the schools and colleges to function as melting pots for caste difference, and hoped that mingling of children from different castes in these institutions will eventually lead to the dissolution of caste in social life. They believed that education generated liberalism and humanism and led to the emancipation of individuals from the confinement of caste and the resultant vices of caste consciousness and caste discrimination. What is the experience of the Scheduled Caste students in the respect? According to a study[64] the majority of the college students stated that most of their classmates knew them as Scheduled Castes but it did not at all affect their behaviour towards them. Four-fifths of the students themselves or their family members had not experienced any ill-treatment from any non-Scheduled.Caste persons. However, one-fifth of them had experienced ill-treatment. Those who experienced ill-treatment largely belonged to the families with no or low level of education.

As per another study[65] as many as 78 per cent of the school students and 71 per cent of the college students say that neither they themselves nor their relatives have personally experienced caste discrimination or ill-treatment associated with their caste status. Further, majority of both school (72 per cent) and college (63 per cent) students say that most of their classmates know that they belong to the Scheduled Castes and majority of the school students (57 per cent) and a large percentage of the college students (43 per cent) say that the behaviour of their classmates at school and college is not affected by their knowledge.

It is interesting to observe that the percentage of those who say that most of their classmates know that they belong to the Scheduled Castes is distinctly larger at school than at college. It is possible that students grow to be less aware of caste by the time they get to college. It, however, does not necessarily mean that the college students are less caste conscious in the sense that they are less likely to let their awareness of the caste identity of their classmates affect their behaviour towards their classmates. In fact, the data indicate just the opposite.

The finding that the percentage of those who feel that the behaviour of their classmates is affected by awareness of their caste is larger at college than at school is disturbing. Do caste identities and caste resentment get aggravated by the time school students enter college? As aptly pointed out by a perceptive social scientist :

> In examining the variation between school and college students it is necessary to view resentment shown by college students in the context of the liberal scholarships and reservation facilities provided to the Scheduled Caste students in higher education. These facilities make for protective discrimination and privilege and it is possible that this state of affairs breeds resentment among the non-Scheduled Caste students who are economically disadvantaged or who for other reasons have had difficulty in gaining access to higher education. Under the circumstances, it could well be that caste-conscious behaviour is rooted not in discrimination as conveniently understood, but in the inability to see the justice of the policy of protective discrimination for the Scheduled Castes.[66]

Vertical Mobility

Social mobility is the transition of an individual from one social position to another. Vertical and horizontal social mobilities can be defined as a certain kind of movement from group to group or stratum to stratum. While horizontal social mobility could be understood as a transition of an individual from one social group to another on the same level, vertical social mobility is the transition of an individual from one social stratum to another. According to the direction of transition, vertical mobility can be described as upward or downward vertical mobility. In the Indian context, vertical mobility among the Scheduled Castes is generally a group phenomenon which is experienced by the members of the entire community belonging to a particular caste or sub-caste or sub-sub-caste, while horizontal mobility is generally restricted to the individual level.

Education is generally considered as an important means for generating both horizontal and vertical mobility. How far has it been able to effect vertical mobility among the Scheduled Castes? Education does not seem to have been instrumental in generating vertical mobility. Many studies have shown that education, specially the present-day westernized education is ill-equipped to help in ushering vertical or group mobility. Mahar notes[67] that in a village in North-Western Uttar Pradesh, secular education is proving an important avenue for mobility. She says that the unit of advancement seems to have become individual rather than of the group. While discussing the value of education as a determinant of social status, Srinivas[68] observes that in a Mysore village a local untouchable servant or tenant may be treated as an inferior by a peasant while an untouchable official will be shown respect `although grudgingly'. J. Singh[69] has concluded that the vertical social mobility consistently decreased with the increase in the educational level. Another study[70] has shown that among the educated Scheduled Castes there is a strong reluctance to change the traditional social status and occupational structure. The educated instead of getting Sanskritized in the rituals, practices, etc., of the high castes, aspired to imitate the elite sections of any caste, class or culture in urbanized and westernized values. They made little efforts to internalize Sanskritic values. It appears[71] that their exposure to the new socio-economic order has made them believe that any award of change in custom to imitate the upper castes is irrelevant for social transformation. The less educated Scheduled Castes, on the other hand, have mostly tried to acquire the traditional symbols of high status, namely the customs, rituals, ideas, beliefs, and way of living of the higher castes to raise their social status, i.e., in the words of Srinivas, they are becoming

Sanskritized. But, modernization is more operative among the educated and upwardly mobile Scheduled Castes, i.e., they are trying to improve their status by improving their economic status and standard of living and by acquiring education.[72] Elite emulation was the basis for structural mobility rather than cultural and ritual mobility through Sanskritization.[73]

Inequalities among the Scheduled Castes

There are several studies that have characteristically observed on the basis of their investigations that, in India today, lower caste subjects are unable to move up the social ladder through the process of socialization but classes within castes are developing and it is more true in the case of lower caste groups. Among the Scheduled Caste groups, on account of educational facilities, inequalities on caste and class basis are growing.[74]

Even if theoretically it is possible for all the members of the Scheduled Castes to receive any amount of education and achieve mobility, in actual practice, advancement in this field is gradual. There is every reason to believe that while the expansion of facilities has opened the door to social mobility for the Scheduled Castes, a large majority of them are still unable to avail themselves of such facilities. We have observed in Chapter VI that apart from the plethora of empirical studies, the Commissioner of Scheduled Castes and Scheduled Tribes and the Ministry of Education of the Government of India were aware of the fact that post-matric scholarships had been creating new inequalities among the Scheduled Castes and that caste patterns had played a big hand in their utilization. But this inequality is not confined to post-matric scholarships alone. In the matter of availing other educational facilities, inequalities among the Scheduled Castes are being created, as reflected in educational attainments at all levels. There are severe intra-caste disparities in literacy status as well. The very fact that a group of people among the same castes listed as Scheduled Castes have been able to attain a higher educational and occupational status and a hither economic class status goes to support the `from caste to class' hypothesis.

The upwardly mobile Scheduled Castes who have attained higher standards of education and are occupying high posts are now a class by themselves. They are becoming modernized and are following the pattern of living of the higher classes in all respects. Having secured higher posts, they have become members of another class. They are different from their fathers and forefathers. They do not mix with members of the other Scheduled Castes. Olsen's[75] observation that education is as much of an indicator of alienation in society as it is of socio-economic status seems to be relevant in this context. Chauhan[76] has also observed that the spread of education among the Scheduled Castes may have consequences of creating social classes among them on the lines parallel to those existing in higher society.

A study[77] about caste composition of the elite in Andhra Pradesh reveals that though there are 59 castes/groups of castes in the Schedule for Andhra Pradesh, members from only five castes are found forming the elite group and in that the majority belong to the Mala Caste (47 per cent). Next to them are Madigas (30.5 per cent), Adi-Andhra (13.2 per cent), Muchi (3.00 per cent) and Mala Dasu (2.1 per cent). That means that 54 castes/groups of castes are not found in any of the elite positions, i.e., IAS/IPS, Doctors, Engineers, MLA/MP, Lecturers/Professors, etc. The preponderance of only five castes in the elite position to the exclusion of other castes may lead to the fact that "among the Scheduled Caste those who are economically well off may still become better while those who are economically poor may still grow worse."[78]

As there are differences among the various Scheduled Castes, so there are differences in the utilization of educational facilities and consequently, in achieving social mobility. Disparities among the Scheduled Castes themselves in the matter of literacy, educational development, social position, economic condition existed even before they were grouped together by the Britishers to form the Scheduled Castes in 1935 and these disparities in the same form prevail, with the only difference that have widened in some respects. The lower strata among the Scheduled Castes continued to remain at the bottom while those who enjoyed higher literacy, better access to educational facilities and higher social and economic status, registered better progress during the last fifty years after Independence. Thus a class among the Scheduled Castes emerged who availed of all the benefits of protective discrimination in the field of education. It is immaterial whether they are termed as `creamy layer', `elite group', `more privileged among the privileged',

'privileged' 'underprivileged' and the like. And this is true for all the States/Union Territories.

It is apparent that mere expansion of educational facilities and external facilities like — free books, uniforms and mid-meals — may not be sufficient for resolving the problems of uneven spread of education. On the contrary, expansion of such educational facilities may make the situation more complex. As Philip Foster[79] has rightly observed:

Quite obviously, formal education in so far as it is unevenly distributed contributes to the process of structural differentiation. But substantial problems arise if privileged groups `capture' the educational system in such a manner as to use it as an instrument for maintaining existing status differentials.

Unequal participation of the different Scheduled Castes Communities in the existing programme of education and the close correlation between their lower position in the hierarchical structure and educational achievement surely corroborates this point.

Such a condition has arisen mainly due to the failure of the policy of protective discrimination in two ways.[80] Firstly, all the SCs are considered as a homogeneous category and it ignores the inter-caste differentials. Secondly, it encourages the accrual of the advantages to a relatively better off caste groups, while the weaker caste groups keep struggling for the tangible opportunities for their self-betterment. To break this nexus, many new initiatives will have to be undertaken to develop a congenial atmosphere for raising the educational level of the disadvantaged sections among the Scheduled Castes and for creating an urge within them to acquire education.

References

1. Sinha, R.K.,1986 *Alienation Among Scheduled Castes*, p. 129. Delhi : Manas Publications.
2. *Fourth Report of the Commission for Scheduled Castes and Scheduled Tribes*, 1981-82. para 4.6 p. 61
3. Sinha, op. cit., pp. 43-44.
4. *Third Survey of Research in Education*, 1978-83, 1986 NCERT, pp. 91-96.
5. Chitnis, Suma, *A Long Way to Go*, op. cit., p. 163.
6. Joshi, S.D., "Educational Problems of the SC/ST of Baroda District", 1980 in *Third Survey of Research in Education*, op. cit. Sl. 163, p. 143.

7. Shah, B.V. and Thaker, J.D., op. cit., p. 90.
8. *Ibid.*, p. 147.
9. Kusum K. Premi, 1974 "*Educational Opportunities for the Scheduled Castes: Role of Protective Discrimination in Equalisation* Nov. p.1905. *Economic and Political Weekly*, Vol. 9, Nos. 45-46.
10. Tribhuvan, U.D., 1977 "*A study of Educated Scheduled Caste Women in an Urban Setting*, In *Third Survey of Research in Education*, op. cit., Sl. 320, p. 234.
11. Abbasayulu, Y.B., 1978, p.75. *Scheduled Caste elite: a study of Scheduled Caste elite in Andhra Pradesh*, Hyderabad, Department of Sociology, Osmania University.
12. *Ibid.*, p. 78.
13. Sachidananda, *The Harijan Elite*, 1976, pp. 130-31 Thomson Press (India) Ltd.
14. Chitnis, op. cit., p. 50.
15. Malik, Suneila, 1979, p. 50. *Social Integration of Scheduled Caste*, : New Delhi : Abhinav Publications.
16. Shah and Thaker, op.cit., pp. 83-85.
17. Abbasayulu, op. cit., pp. 89-90.
18. *Ibid.*, pp.93-95.
19. Prajapati, G.K., "*Impact of Education on Social, Economic and Political Changes among Scheduled Castes: A case study of Danapur Sub-division*, 1982, In *Third Survey of Research in Education*, *op. cit.* Sl. 218, p. 173.
20. Abbasayulu, op. cit., p. 95.
21. Sachidananda; op. cit., p. 96.
22. Malik, op.cit., p. 100.
23. *Ibid.*, p. 64.
24. *Ibid.*, p. 46.
25. Shah and Thaker, op. cit., p. 26.
26. Chitnis, op. cit., pp. 283-84.
27. Ramanath, S., "*Educational Problems of Scheduled Castes and Scheduled Tribes*, " In *Social Work Education and Development of Weaker Section*, p. 78.
28. Anant, Santokh Singh, *The Changing Concept of Caste in India*, Vikas Publications, 1969, p. 47, 57.
29. Malik, *op.cit.*, p. 167.
30. Sinha, *op.cit.*, p. 132.
31. Abbasayulu, op. cit., p. 26.
    Sachidananda, op. cit., p. 83
32. Prajapati, G.K., op. cit.,
33. Sachidananda, op. cit. pp. 132-33.
34. Cohn, B.S., 1955 "The Changing Status of a Depressed Caste," In (Ed). Mekim Marriot, *Village India*, 1955 p.74. The University of Chicago Press.

35. *Ibid.*
36. Lipset, M., and Bendix, R., 1959, *Social Mobility in Industrial Society*, p. 6. University of California Press.
37. Pandey, P.N., "*Education and Social Mobility among Scheduled Castes,*" 1979, *In Third Survey of Research in Education*, Sl. 207, pp.166-67.
38. Malik., op. cit., p. 55.
39. *Ibid.*, pp. 62-67.
40. Abbasayulu, op.cit., p. 133.
41. Sachidananda, op.cit., p. 70.
42. *Ibid.*, p. 140.
43. Jain, Anrudh K., and Nag, Moni, 1987, "*Importance of Female Primary Education for Fertility Reduction in India,*" In *Education and the Process of Change*, Ratna Ghosh and Mathew Zachariah, (eds.) p. 175 New Delhi: Sage Publications.
44. *Education for All, The Indian Scene, A Synopsis*, 1992, p. 23. Ministry of Human Resource Development, Education Department.
45. Mishra, J.P., "*A Study on the Impact of Education on Fertility in Allahabad City,*" 1978. In *Third Survey of Research in Education*, Sl. 191, p. 157.
46. Sachidananda, op.cit., p. 31.
47. Malik, op. cit., p. 171.
48. *Ibid.*, p.134.
49. Pandey, P.N., op. cit.
50. Prajapati., G.K., op. cit.
51. Chitnis, op. cit., p. 103.
52. Shah and Thaker, op. cit., p. 112.
53. *Ibid.*, pp. 111-12.
54. Malik., op. cit., p. 136.
55. Sachidananda, op. cit., p. 33.
56. Prajapati, G.K., op. cit.,
57. Sachidananda, op. cit., p. 33.
58. Malik. op. cit., p. 141.
59. Trivedi, H.R., 1976 *Scheduled Caste Women, Studies in Exploitation with Reference to Superstition, Ignorance and Poverty,*. p. 31. New Delhi: Concept.
60. Chitnis, op. cit., pp. 85-86.
61. Malik, op. cit., p. 168.
62. Shah and Thaker, op. cit., p. 120.
63. *Ibid.*
64. *Ibid.*, 116, 261.
65. Chitnis, op. cit., pp. 278-81.
66. *Ibid.*, p. 93.
67. Mahar, Pauline, M., 1960 "Changing Religious Practices of an Untouchable Caste, p. 28. "In *Economic Development and Social Change*.
68. Srinivas, M.N., 1955 "The Social System of a Mysore Village," In

Mekim Marriot, In *Village India*, p. 26. (ed). The University of Chicago Press.

69. Singh, J., "*Impact of Education on Vertical Social Mobility as Measured by Income, Occupation and Social Status*," 1978. In *Third Survey of Research in Education*, Sl. 283, p. 213.
70. Pandey, P. N., op. cit.,
71. Sachidananda, op. cit. p. 141.
72. Malik, op. cit., pp. 168-169.
73. Pandey, P. N., op. cit.
74. Sinha, R.K., op. cit., pp. 162-63.
75. Olsen, Marvin, E., 1965 "*Political Assimilation, Social Opportunities and Political Alienation*," Unpublished Doctoral Dissertation, (University of Michigan), quoted by Sinha, Ibid., p.163.
76. Chauhan, (eds.) B.R., 1967 Special Problems of Education of the Scheduled Castes. In M.S. Gore and I. P. Desai *Papers in Sociology of Education*,
77. Abbasayulu, op. cit., pp. 55-56.
78. *Ibid*.
79. Foster, Philip, 1971, In Don Adoms (ed) *Access to Schooling* in *Education in National Development*, Routledge and Kegan Paul, London, p. 29.
80. Aggarwal, Yash and Sibou, Sarika, *1994 Educating Scheduled Castes, A study of Inter District and Intra Estate Differentials*, p. 116. NIETA .

9
Looking Ahead

The social and religious consequences of colonial rule in India are many and varied. If the encouragement to communalism by sowing seeds of dissension between the Hindus and the Muslims, and between one region and the other in order to perpetuate its rule, is regarded as the major one, the destruction of the old educational system based on moral values is another. The educational system in ancient India was highly beneficial to the society and it attracted the praise even of foreign scholars like Hieun-Tsang and Al-Beruni. The Turk, Pathan and Mughul rulers tried their best to supplant this system by their own system of education but even the old system continued with its full vigour especially in villages. In those days in every village there was a Sanskrit school where education was imparted free of charge. Consequently, illiteracy was nominal and this was admitted by early British historians.[1] There are records to show that, even a century and a half ago, the whole country was dotted with small village schools as well as schools of oriental learning which were more or less within easy reach of the children sent to these schools.[2]

The progress of education among the 'lowest' castes was, however, marred by many difficulties. The schools in ancient India were located in temples and the absence of right to enter the temples due to acute untouchability practised in those days, deprived these people of the facilities to attend schools. In some States, in olden days the society considered education of low caste children as a social offence. As a result, education was denied to the Scheduled Castes or otherwise called the depressed classes, and they remained illiterate and backward throughout those years.[3]

The British uprooted the old system and instead introduced a new system of education on English lines. The British colonial rulers were, however, not committed to schooling the masses and consciously subscribed to what was known as the "downward filtration theory", namely, that education percolated or filtered from the higher to the lower stage. Very few schools and colleges were opened by the government of the day and mostly the educational institutions were run by the Christian missionaries. The new system of education was highly expensive. Therefore, very few people benefited from it. Even the functional literacy which Hindus and Muslims could pick up in their own schools, disappeared almost completely, thereby plunging the country into the darkness of almost absolute illiteracy.[4] Moreover, the new educational system was completely divorced of high ancient ideals, history and culture, Sanskrit literature, learning, knowledge and traditions. It taught only Western literature, history and traditions and science. Consequently, the English educated people forgot their glorious history, traditions and culture and began to take pride in everything that was Western. This retarded the growth of Indian nationalism for sometime.[5]

Formerly, the purpose of education in pre-British days was commonly accepted in terms of character-building and spiritual awakening. The process of education in ancient India, as Professor Kabir has said, "reached its culmination in achieving *Ananda,* poise and joy, arising from the harmonious and successful control and exercise of all the other faculties and elements and the contemplation of the true, the beautiful and the good."[6] In the new situation, education could lead to employment education became associated with the specific skills that the narrow sphere of the civil service within which colonial education, could lead to employment, education because assocised with the specific scills that civil service required. And the highest image of the educated man became that of the Administrator. As administration was the only elite role to which education could be expected to lead,[7] the only aim of the British education system was to churn out people fit enough to man the different civil service jobs under the British Government.

Even when the Indians were ready for Western education, the British Government was not ready to open adequate number of schools. Moreover, whatever schools were opened were concentrated in urban areas. As a result, rural and less-affluent people were denied access to education. Being content with imposing restrictions on access to educational facilities, they brought in religion and caste as criteria for admission to these institutions, though in the name of equity. Thus, the dragon's teeth of communal and caste divide were and caste divide were sown not only in our body politic for the first time but also in the educational sphere,which in course of time engulfed our whole national fabric. In Independent India the role of education as an instrument of social change was visualized and an effort was made to give a new orientation to education so that it became instrumental in developing physical, mental and social mobility.

Independent India was saddled with the task of providing education to all citizens. Education was not viewed as the exclusive preserve of a chosen few. It was thought that access to education was not to be hindered on consideration of caste, race, sex, place of birth or religion, etc. Education Commissions and Committees have been set up from time to time by the Government of India to examine the status of educational development and advise the Government on future policies, programmes and strategies. Prominent among them have been the University Education Commission (headed by Dr S. Radhakrishnan, 1948); the Secondary Education Commission (headed by Sir A.L. Mudaliar, 1952-53); and the Education Commission (headed by Dr D.S. Kothari, 1964-66). There have also been reports on Language Policy and Emotional Integration (Dr Sampurnanand Committee); Moral and Religious Education (Sri Prakasha Committee); Vocational Education (Ishwarbhai Patel Committee) and Work Experience in Schools (Malcolm Adiseshaiah Committee, Kulandaivalu Committee). In addition, such national bodies as CABE (Central Advisory Board of Education); NCERT (National Council of Educational Research and Training); NIEPA (National Institute of Educational Planning and Administration); AICTE (All India Council of Technical Education); ICMR (Indian Council of Medical Research); CSIR (Council of Scientific and Industrial Research) and UGC (University Grants Commission) have been advising and assisting the Union and State Governments on education on a regular basis.

Decisions regarding the organization and structure of education are largely the concern of the States. Within the overall policy framework, each State determines independently the educational structures to be adopted. The Indian Parliament was empowered through the 42nd Amendment of the Constitution to legislate on education concurrently with the States. The concept of 'concurrency' was given an operational meaning by the National

Policy on Education (NPE), 1986. This policy envisages concurrency as a "meaningful partnership between the Centre and the States" and places on the Union government a clear responsibility regarding the national and integrative character of education, quality and standards, manpower planning, research and advanced study, culture, human resource development and the international aspects of education. The Central Advisory Board of Education (CABE), set up during the pre-Independence period in 1935, continues to play a lead role in the evolution and monitoring of educational policies and programmes, the most notable of which are the National Policy on Education (NPE), 1986, Programme of Action (POA), 1986 and a revised NPE and POA, 1992.

Tremendous expansion at all levels of education, specially at higher education level, has taken place since 1950 (Table 9.1).

The literacy rate has risen from 16.6 per cent in 1951 to 52.21 per cent in 1991. The number of educational institutions as well as that of teachers and students has grown rapidly. While the elementary education system of India has expanded into one of the largest in the world, the country also possesses the dubious distinction of having the world's largest number of out-of-school children (22 per cent of the global total) and adult illiterates (30 per cent of global population). The largest group of the endeavour to achieve Education for All (EFA) in India constitutes about 19 to 24 million children in the age group of 6-14 of whom 60 per cent are girls, and 122 million adult illiterates in the age group 15-35 of whom 62 per cent are women. Given the demographic pressure, the numbers are likely to increase further.[8] The outlay on education in the national Five-Year Plans has gone from Rs 1530 million in the First Five-Year Plan (1951-56) to Rs 196,000 million in the Eighth. Five-Year Plan (1992-97),[9] i.e., an increase of 128 times within a 40-year period. Yet, the availability of educational facilities does not ensure their utilization. The major reasons are socio-economic and cultural constraints, which result in educational constraints.

The growth rate of student enrolment in higher education has been phenomenal . India has the largest university population in the world. The number of universities has increased from 27 in 1950-51 to 226 in 1995-96. The proportion of women enrolment at the collegiate level rose from 10 per cent in 1950-51 to 28 per cent

TABLE 9.1
ACHIEVEMENTS AND TARGETS AT DIFFERENT LEVELS OF EDUCATION, 1950-96

Particulars	*1950-51*	*1978-79*	*1989-90*	*1995-96*
Enrolment Figures Number of				
Pupils in Class I to V (lakh)*	191.5	689.6	973.2	1097.34
Percentage thereof to total Population in Age Group 6 to 11	42.6	81.6	99.96	104.3
Number of Pupils in Class VI to VIII (lakh)	31.2	181.8	321.8	410.14
Percentage thereof to total Population in Age Group 11 to 14	12.7	38.0	59.15	67.6
Number of Pupils in Class IX to XI/XII (lakh)	12.2	84.1	199.70	248.89
Percentage thereof to Total Population in Age Group 14 to 17	5.3	18.3	26.5	32.58**
Number of Pupils at the University Stage-- Arts, Science and Commerce (lakh)	3.6	38.2	36.4	64.26
Percentage thereof to Total Population in Age Group 17 to 23	0.8	4.9	3.67	
Institutions				
Number of Primary/Junior Basic Schools	209,671	472,519	550,700	590,421
Number of Middle/Senior Basic Schools	13,596	112,801	143,747	171,216
Number of High/Higher Secondary Schools	7,288	46,874	76,119	98,134
Number of Arts, Science, (including Research Institutions) and Commerce Colleges	542	2,141	4,803	7,293
Number of Universities+	27	125	207	226
Teachers				
Number of Teachers in High/Higher Secondary Schools	126,506	818,507	1,264,249	1,493,251
Number of Teachers in Universities, Arts, and Science Colleges	18,648	249,399	NA	3,10,000

* 1 lakh=1,00,000 ** for the age group 14-18

\+ Includes those deemed to be universities and institutions of national importance.

Source: *India, 1984*, p. 59 and *India, 1992*, p. 83, Publications Division, Ministry of Information and Broadcasting, Government of India.

and p. 87, pp. 260.2 and p. 270 of Annual Report Ministry of Human Resource Development, Department of Education, 1996-97.

in 1982-83, yet, the main problem of the educated is unemployment. In 1977-78, 45.94 per cent of the Art graduates and 23.66 per cent of the Science graduates were unemployed.[10] It is clear that the direction of expansion in higher education has not been related to the needs and capacity of national development. In the developed nations even the son of the richest person cannot simply get into college unless he passes the entrance examinations. But in India for want of anything better to do, everybody drifts to college. Naturally, the atmosphere in the colleges is devoid of any real commitment.[11] As very aptly pointed out by Dr Raja Ramanna, the noted scientist and educationist, after independence was achieved there was a clamour for everybody to go and take a BA degree. All sorts of BA's, B.Scs, were uselessly floating around, unable to do any job. Higher education was destroyed. What was wrong with education, he wondered.[12] What was needed, it was felt, was universalization of elementary education, vocationalization of secondary education and rationalization and strengthening of university education.[13]

This expansion in education has unfortunately been accompanied by an erosion in standards. Leading educationists and others have been complaining that the quality of Indian education is low; there are no national or State level Schools Achievement Tests. The International Educational Achievement (IEA) throws some light on what our children learn in schools. According to reports of the IEA, Indian pupils at the age of 10 learn only 50 per cent as much science and 48 per cent as much reading as those in Japan, Europe and America. The gap in the knowledge of science between Indian students and those in industrial countries is larger at the secondary level than at the primary level. At the upper secondary level, Indian students learn only 28 per cent as much in science and 14 per cent as much in reading as children from industrial countries. The gap between Indian students and others increases despite the fact that the transition ratio from primary to secondary is higher in industrial countries than in India.[14]

The poor quality of students coming out of our schools, colleges and universities, however, has nothing to do with the innate capacity of the Indian population because, after all, good private schools and select institutes of higher learning turn out good scholars.

The adverse impact of poor education on society and the economy, it is leading to an increase in the unequal distribution of opportunities, the beneficiaries being those possessing wealth or political privileges. What was an aberration limited to a miniscole protion of Indian population decades ago has now assumed vastly alarming proportions. There are literally thousands of Indian children (not NRIs) in the best schools of Europe and America where school fees can go up to $ 20,000 a year. Similarly, there are thousands of full fee paying students from India at the Australian, Canadian, British and American universities doing undergraduate studies. Even within India, there is a great divide. The smallest clusters of villages have developed a dual education system. There are the government-run schools. The teachers are relatively better paid, though the schools are poorly maintained and the quality of education imparted in most of these schools is of a low quality. Hence, most people prefer to send their wards to the privately-owned, relatively better-run so-called "English-Medium" schools.[15] Anybody who passes out of such a school automatically enjoys an advantage in entrance examinations for all categeries of institutions of higher education. Upwardly mobile parents aspire to give their children the "spit-and-polish" of an English-medium education. A few such schools have found practical activities a good way to teach Science as well as English. Though many of these schools are commercial in their approach and have classes of sixty and seventy children, parents are not kept so much at arm's length as in Government schools, where teachers are simply not accountable to them.[16]

Improvement is required in literally every aspect of our educational system — from the unhygienic condition of the urinals in our schools to the jobs of defining the basic objective of the entire national education system. As highlighted by Dr P.K. Ponnusamy, Vice-Chancellor, Madras University, our curricula and syllabi are not in tune with the demands of the society : they do not enthuse our students and tap their hidden potentials: they remain static without any kind of flexibility.[17] It is high time the éducational planners, administrators, the public and the teaching fraternity show determination to realize the responsibility left in their own hands.If education is to be purposive and meaningful, the education sector in India has to contend simultaneously with meeting the educational needs of a burgeoning population while striving for sustained improvement in the quality of education.

Education, in order to be effective, has to cover four distinct dimensions of the human personality, beginning with the physical body, the development of intellectual and aesthetic sensibilities, the development of socially desirable moral values, and finally the inner dimension of spiritual growth. It is not enough to look upon education as an academic endeavour which enables young people to pass examinations and then get gainful employment, or remain unemployed, as the case may be. It is much deeper, a much fuller understanding.[18]

The provision of a basic, minimum quantum of knowledge and skills as well as the development of a healthy and desirable set of attitudess, appreciations and values is a *sine qua non* of the development of a nation. It is a fundamental right as well as a societal and national duty. The UNESCO has recognized this human right at the international level, by its mandate on Universalisation of Primary Education and Literacy for all on this planet. Our Constitution has, however, gone one step further than the UNESCO Declaration. It has provided free and compulsory education for all children up to 14 years under Article 45 of the Constitution.

It is a fact that education is an individual achievement. It may start from an individual and then spread to the family, lineage and then to group as well. We have inherited a social order based on status, one in which the individual did not count very much. Therefore, the advancement in education is measured not in terms of progress made by everybody but by the community as such, because, it was thought that when all the communities are brought to the same level in the matter of education, differences of status in the Indian society would disappear.[19]

The concern for the removal of educational backwardness of the communities brought under the rubric 'Scheduled Castes', a term coined by the Britishers, generated in the Indian society during the freedom struggle, resulted in provisions being included in the Constitution of free India to enable the Government to provide for special educational facilities which included reservation of seats in educational institutions as well, for removal of the gigantic problem. The educational measures not only appropriate the major portion of the budget allocation under the welfare of the Scheduled Castes, but also are regarded as constituting the crucial mechanism for removal of caste restrictions and the promotion of interaction as well as for bringing about social and occupational mobility among the persons belonging to these castes. The educational progress of the Scheduled Castes, therefore, can be regarded as the most important index of their general growth and development. The most single indicator in this regard is the literacy rate which is estimated as a part of the Census operations once in every decade.

The literacy rate of the Scheduled Castes has increased from 10.27 per cent in 1961 to 37.41 per cent in 1991. Though the SC literacy rate has registered almost a four-fold increase during the period 1961-91, the literacy gap between the SC and the non-SC/ST population has rather been widening, though marginally, in successive Censuses. The gap between the SC and the non-SC/ST population was 17.59 in 1961 which has increased to 20.28 in 1991. This gap in literacy rate as well as the existence of a vast army of illiterates, which is projected to be about 500 million by AD 2000, according to a World Bank estimate, is a sad commentary on our ability to implement the Constitutional obligation of providing free compulsory education to all children up to the age of 14, enshrined as a Directive Principle in Article 45 of the Constitution. Universalization of education has been accepted as a goal in all formal forums including the successive Five Year Plans. Nevertheless, the pace of universalization of elementary education has been extremely slow.

The question that arises concerns the respective performances of the Centre and of the States with regard to the universalization of elementary education in India. Compulsory Primary Education Act had been enacted by almost all the States by 1962. Attendance officers were also appointed in many of the states of the States to eusure enrolment and regular attendance of children. Compulsion, however, did not succeed as parents offered stiff resistance for various apparently justifiable reasons such as poverty, the need for child labour to supplement family income or to save on expenditure by using family labour, care of the young and household management including water-supply from distant resources, etc. This resistance was also defended on account of individual liberty. Finally, the word 'compulsory' in the Compulsory Education Act was reinterpreted to mean: it is compulsory for the Government to provide facilities for primary education, if the parents so choose to provide such education for their children. But it is not compulsory for parents to send their children if they do not choose to do so.

An analysis of the pattern of expenditure at various levels of education in India reveals that it is the elementary education that has suffered in the course of time. For the masses of the Indian people, education means elementary education. As a proportion to the total expenditure on education, the expenditure on primary education has gone down from 56 per cent in the First Plan to 33 per cent in the Sixth Plan and is expected to reach 47 per cent of the total budget of the Education Sector by the end of the Eighth Plan (1992-97).

Though the level of literacy of the SC people has not reached the non-SC/ST level, it would not be proper to infer that all the States/UTs are guilty of this dismal performance As many as 15 States/UTs—Himachal Pradesh, Assam, Chandigarh, Pondicherry, Manipur, Maharashtra, Tripura, Arunachal Pradesh, Delhi, Goa, Gujarat, Dadra and Nagar Haveli, Mizoram, Daman and Diu and Kerala, recorded a literacy rate above the general literacy rate of 52.21 per cent and the last six of them even crossed the non-SC/ST literacy rate of 57.69 per cent in the 1991 census in the matter of the SC literacy. The six States of Bihar, U.P., Rajasthan, Madhya Pradesh, Andhra Pradesh and Orissa, which together account for 54.79 per cent of the country's total SC population registered an SC literacy rate below the All-India SC literacy rate of 37.41 per cent. Incidentally, these six States are also below the All-India literacy of 52.21 per cent in respect of general literacy. It is observed that if the general literacy rate is higher in any State/UT, the SC literacy rate is correspondingly higher in that State/UT, and if the general literacy rate is low, the SC literacy rate is also low in that State/UT.

There are tremendous inter-State disparities in the spread of literacy among the SC males and SC females. The progress made in this respect is not uniform among the SC males and SC females. Some States have achieved a high level of literacy status for both the SC males and the SC females, some have achieved progress only in respect of either of them, while others are lagging behind.

Similarly, there are perceptible rural-urban variations. The number of States/UTs in the lower literacy category is more in urban areas than in rural areas and the number of States/UTs in the high literacy category is more in rural areas than in urban areas. This improvement in respect of rural literacy among the SCs is a good sign, specially because the majority of the SC people live in rural areas. Intra-State disparities have also been noticed. About 200 districts have been identified in the entire country as educationally backward which require special attention for eradication of illiteracy.

Again, it will not be proper to assume that all the castes among the Scheduled Castes have registered uniform progress in literacy level. Not only were the inter-State variations in literacy rates of the Schduled Castes very sharp, there was also a big gap in the literacy rates amongst the different Scheduled Caste communities within the same State/UT. The traditional educationally backward States tended to show a higher differential ratio between the maximum literacy and the minimum literacy, whereas the educationally advanced States/UTs registered a lower ratio. This shows that as the overall literacy level of the Scheduled Castes in any unit increases, the gap between the maximum literacy and minimum literacy tends to get narrowed down.

It has been observed that as many as 100 castes/groups of castes registered a literacy rate above the non-SC/ST literacy rate, and another 433 castes groups of castes recorded a literacy rate above the SC literacy rate of the respective units in the 1981 census, i.e., about 50 per cent of the castes/groups of castes had crossed the average SC literacy rate in 1981. In terms of population, these 533 castes/groups of castes accounted for 59.39 per cent of country's total SC population. It is noteworthy that 100 Scheduled Caste communities, constituting 1.67 per cent of the total SC population, had even performed better than the non-SC/ST communities in 1981 itself.

It may so happen that a caste might register a better literacy rate in only one census. But if we analyse the level of literacy reached by each Scheduled Caste community in the three censuses of 1961, 1971 and 1981 (census data for 1951 were not computed castewise and those for 1991 are yet to be published), a trend would emerge. As many as 341 castes/groups of castes had maintained a higher literacy rate in all these three census operations. A clear picture would have emerged if the literacy rate of each sub-caste or sub-sub-caste had been tabulated separately. In any case, 341 castes/groups of castes accounting for 32 per cent of the total number of castes/groups of castes, constituting 50.08 per cent of the country's SC population in 1981, had maintained a standard above the standard of the average Scheduled Castes in the respective State/UT continuously over a thirty-year period. It is quite likely that the same trend would be revealed in the 1991 census as well. Another trend revealed from this study is that most of the 'very large' and 'large' categories of the Scheduled Castes had maintained this higher standard.

It is also observed that most of the castes, which represented in the thirties for a higher social status but ultimately found themselves in the list of the Schduled Castes, have maintained a higher literacy rate during the last three censuses.

Enrolment Ratio

Another important indicator of the educational development of the Scheduled Castes could be their enrolment ratio. If the proportion of their enrolment in any given category of education, to the enrolment of other communities, is not the same as the proportion of their population to the population of other communities, it may be inferred that the Scheduled Caste communities are lagging behind the other communities. The data collected from different Government publications are presented in Table 9.2 showing the coefficients of equality of the SC for enrolment at primary, middle, high/higher secondary and university levels of education during 1965-66, 1976-77 and 1985 and 1995.

It is seen from this Table that the coefficient of equality for Scheduled Castes has moved up during the above mentioned stages of education in 1976-77 as compared to that in 1965-66 and again in 1985 as compared to that in 1976-77, indicating that the enrolment of these communities has increased at all these stages of education, and at the primary stage it has even exceeded the non-SC/ST communities enrolment ratio. The maximum increase was at the university stage. It would also be seen that though a lot of educational development has taken place among the Scheduled Castes, yet they have still a fairly long way to go to even up with the educational development of the general population at the higher education stage.

TABLE 9.2
COEFFICIENT OF EQUALITY OF SC FOR ENROLMENT AT DIFFERENT LEVELS OF EDUCATION (1965-95)

Sl. No.	*Stage of Education*	*Coefficients of Equality for the SCs*			
		1965-66	*1976-77*	*1985*	*1995*
1.	Primary Jr. Basic schools	84.5	91.0	108.70	102.10
2.	Middle/Senior Basic schools	57.8	72.4	93.27	86.59
3.	High/Higher Secondary Schools	45.5	61.8	80.44	81.61
4.	Universities and Colleges for General education	26.2	51.2		54.49
	Source	a	a	b	c

Source: a — *27th report of the Commissioner for SCs and STs*, 1979-8 para 1.35 p.8.
b — *Vth All-India Educational Survey, 1985*, NCERT, Vol.II, pp. 1206-07.
c — Annual Report, 1996-97. *Ministry of HRD, Department of Education*, p. 261, p. 263

One more salient point which emerges from the above Table is that there is a sharp reduction in the coefficient of equality (C.E.) as one moves up in the education ladder. For instance, while the C.E. at the primary stage was 102.10 in 1955, it came down to 54.49 at the university/college level. If the rates of wastage and stagnation among the Scheduled Castes were to be the same as those among the general population, the C.E. at the middle, high /higher secondary and University stages should also have been the same as that at the primary stage. This implies that the rates of wastage and stagnation among the Scheduled Castes are considerably higher than those among the other communities. It is thus evident that in spite of the incentives/facilities like pre-matric and post-matric scholarships, backward classes hostels, Ashram Schools, book banks, supply of uniforms and stationery, mid-day meals, etc., apart from reservation of seats, there is a wide educational gap between these communities and the rest of the population and the spread of higher education among them was not commensurate with the investments made since Independence. Taking India as a whole, the overall progress achieved in the enrolment or the SC students was quite impressive when compared to the position prevalent at the time of Independence. However, the progress is not uniform throughout the country. The position in regard to educational attainment of SCs differ from State to State. Even within the same State, there is a variation from area to area and also among the various communities. As a matter of fact, the position has not improved, rather it has deteriorated since 1969 when N.K.Bose, the then Commissioner for Scheduled Castes and Scheduled Tribes observed that "different castes and different districts within the same State have been developing in education at uneven rates."[20]

Up-to-date caste-wise data on enrolment of Scheduled Caste students at different stages of education is not available. Whatever data are there relate to the 70s. Though there is no dearth of studies, projects, analysis, assessments, and so on and so forth, it is not known to the general public what the findings were. Even the various published reports of the different departments of the Central and State Governments, not to mention of the autonomous institutions like the NCERT, UGC, have become scarce commodities, as if these reports and studies are a closely guarded secret, not to be divulged except to a chosen few. Otherwise, how does one explain the fact that not a single copy of the reports published by them, specially in the late 80s and early 90s, was sent to the National Library, the repository of all published materials. As one rightly said, though jocularly, these reports cannot be divulged unless one belongs to the same fraternity. Even the first report of the National Commission for Scheduled Castes and the Scheduled Tribes for the year 1992-93 is yet to see the light of day. The Commissioner for Scheduled Castes and Scheduled Tribes published only three reports in the 80s— 27th report(1979-81); 28th report (1986-87) and 29th report(1987-89) before this office was replaced by a multi-member National Commission with increased functions and powers. The National Commission took office on 12 March 92. The first annual report for the period 12.3.92 to 12.3.93 has been prepared and submitted to the President of India but it could not be made public as the same has not been laid on the table of the Parliament. As it appears, not only is there a distinct dearth of published materials on this score but also a positive disinclination on the part of the powers that be in analysing and assessing the effect of educational facilities on the different communities among the Scheduled Castes as reflected in their enrolment, achievement, performance, etc., lest the actual position is revealed. This tendency of not calling a spade a spade is also manifested in the reports of the Commissioner for Scheduled Castes and Scheduled Tribes, who refrained from delving into this aspect after the 27th report (1979-81).

Available data, mostly relating to the 70s, indicated that certain castes or cluster of castes in every State had better access to education at school and college levels. Preponderence of some castes and under-representation of others suggest an uneven growth of education among the several castes that are administratively grouped together as the Scheduled Castes.

There are wide disparities in the spread and growth of higher education among the Scheduled Castes. Just as the disparities betwen the Scheduled Caste population and the rest of the population widen more and more with the increasing level of education, so is the case in respect of the disparities among the Scheduled Castes themselves. There is a clear indication that the prospect of higher education for the Scheduled Castes are very much related to the degree of their education at the lower levels. The advantage gained at the lower levels has a snowballing effect on their higher education.

The differential educational attainment of the Scheduled Castes is related to their variation in socio-economic status. The factors identified as being responsible for the advance of certain castes seem to be:

1. Early head start for mobility, i.e., contact with the British and entry into the railways and the army meant exposure to education and the opening up of new ambitions and horizons, as happened in the case of the Mahars of Maharashtra;

2. Political awareness and power including economic power (opening of new market for the leather goods meant better economic condition for the Charmars);

3. Initial caste status (Garoda being the priests of the other Scheduled Castes of Gujarat) and migration to other States and to urban areas in their own States;[21]

4. High literacy rate;

5. Absence of opportunity in traditional occupation (Bhangis being tied down to its traditional occupation even in urban areas resulted in their low progress);

6. Industrialisation;

7. General advancement or backwardness of a region in which a particular caste is concentrated;[22] and the like on the other hand, segregation and deprivation, illiteracy, poverty, domination of higher castes, ineffective government machinery[23] and ignorance of the parents[24] are found to be responsible for their backwardness.

And yet, all the Scheduled Castes are bracketed together in the matter of granting of assistance and are considered to be equally deserving of protection.

Inequalities Among Scheduled Castes

It is better to remember that the castes referred to as the 'Scheduled Castes' and grouped together as a single category are in fact castes that stand at different points on the scale of ritual status and on the scale of deprivation, discrimination and backwardness. The 'Scheduled Castes' are not a single community. They comprise several groups, each of which has its own identity, traditions and a definite place in the hierarchical order. Thus, within the Scheduled Caste cluster there are several caste groups forming a hierarchy within the general hierarchical order. The caste restrictions as regards inter-marriage and inter-dining are observed far more strictly among the different groups on castes known as 'untouchables', than among the 'higher' castes. Both the British Government, who prepared a list of Depressed Classes, later termed as the 'Scheduled Castes' in 1935 for political purposes, and the Government of India in post-Independence India, who continue to prepare the schedule for protective discrimination, have, no doubt, considered untouchability and ritual status as one of the key factors responsible for their backwardness. If it is construed that lack of political power and other 'secular' features characteristic of the castes identified for eligiblity to special benefits are considered to accrue from their low status in the ritual hierarchy, then it follows that the caste that stands lowest in the ritual herarchy could also be expected to be the poorest, the most backward and the least able to advance in politics or in education.

Or rather, one would at least expect a large measure of correspondence between the placement of the castes on the ritual scale and their advance with respect to the several items on the secular scale,like wealth, landholding, position of the castes occupation in the economy of this community ? Political awareness or organization, and rural/urban location. Correspondingly, one would expect the castes that are higher up in the ritual scale, to advance ahead of those who stand lower in the caste hierarchy. But is this in fact the case, at least so far as educational advancement is concerned ?

We have seen in a separate study* that many castes were treated as Depressed Classes in 1930-35, and later included in the list of the Scheduled Castes in 1935, who were, strictly speaking, not untouchables according to the twin criteria fixed by the Lothian Committee in 1932. In Independent India, the same trend continued and many castes and groups of castes/sub-castes were included in the list of the Scheduled Castes in 1950/51, 1956 and 1976 by the Government of India, who were not 'untouchables' and therefore, did not stand in the lowest of the ritual hierarchy. In 1911, an attempt was made during the Census operations to classify the castes according to certain disabilities suffered by them and two of these disabilities, viz., (i) denial of access to interior of Hindu temples, and (ii) causing pollution by (a) touch, or (b) approach, were later adopted by the Lothian Committee in 1932 as the criteria of untouchablity. Since many of the castes included in the list of 'Scheduled Castes' in 1935 by the British Government and later in 1950/51, 1956 and 1976 by the Government of India did not conform to these twin criteria fixed by the Lothian Committee, it is fit and proper to find out, how many of these castes considered 'untouchable' in 1911 and included in the list of Scheduled Castes have since advanced in education. Though no study has been made on this line so far, an idea can be had from the field data collected in early 70s for the purpose of a Project sponsored by the Indian Council of Social Science Research (ICSSR), New Delhi. It is seen that many of the castes considered 'Depressed' in 1911 because of their low status in the Hindu hierarchical society which denied them access to the interior of temples and considered them polluting, did not

* See volume III of *Scheduled Castes* in India by the author.

figure in the sample drawn from the 14 States whose Scheduled Caste population constituted 86 per cent of the total Scheduled Caste population of the country.

It appears that of these 14 States, Karnataka, Kerala and Rajasthan were not included in the erstwhile British Indian Provinces. In the remaining 11 States, i.e., those forming part of the then British Indian Provinces, untouchable castes, conforming to the twin criteria of untouchability settled by the Lothian Committee, could be identified in the 1911 Census. The Provincial Governments also drew up lists of untouchables in 1917. From these two lists of Untouchables, as many as 141 castes later found place in the lists of 'Scheduled Castes' of 1956/1976 as well. It is observed as many as 76 castes, which are more than half of these 141 castes, did not figure in the samples drawn from these States, the largest number being in Punjab (16), followed by Haryana (15), Orissa (11), Tamil Nadu (7), U.P (6), Bihar and Maharashtra, (5 each) Andhra Pradesh and Gujarat(4 each) and Madhya Pradesh (3). The detailed list is given in Annexure Table XVI. Since the various castes among the Scheduled Castes of a State are not proportionately spread over the different areas of a State, there is a possibility that these castes were not represented in the area from where the samples were drawn. Therefore, it would not be proper to come to a conclusion that these castes have not progressed at all in educational development. It only draws our attention to the fact that the level of educational attainment of more than half of the castes identified as 'untouchables' in 1911/1917 could not be properly assessed. To find out their actual level of development in the field of education, a further detailed probe is called for.

It is perhaps worthwhile to find out in this connection, how far the remaining 65 castes had progresed at the educational level, whether all of them had registered uniform progress or whether there was a different level of development. It is found that 16 castes had larger representation both in the school and college samples, and 24 castes had larger representation, either in the school sample or in the college sample than their population strength warranted, while 25 castes had lagged far behind both in the school and college samples.

The forty castes that register larger representation are:

TABLE 9.3

Mala	of Andhra Pradesh
Dhubi	of Assam,
Chamar, Dhobi,Dushadh, Ghasi, Pan and Pasi	of Bihar,
Dhed, Mahar and Turi	of Gujarat,
Chamar, Khatik and Pasi	of Haryana,
Dhobi, Katia, Kori, Mahar, Mehar and Mang	of Madhya Pradesh,
Dhed, Dhor and Mahar	of Maharashtra,
Chamar, Dhoba, Ghasi, Gokha, Kandara, Pan, Siyal and Tior	of Orissa,
Batwal, Chamar, and Megh	of Punjab,
Pallan and Valluvan	of Tamil Nadu,
Balai, Chamar, Dhobi and Khatik	of U.P.

The twenty-five castes whose progress were not commensurate with their popoulation are:

TABLE 9.4

Madiga	of Andhra Pradesh,
Muchi	of Assam,
Bauri, Dom, Mehtar and Musashar	of Bihar,
Bhangi and Chamar	Gujarat,
Dhanak and Kori	of Haryana,
Balahi, Chamar, Ganda and Mehtar	of Madhya Pradesh,
Bhangi and Mang	of Maharashtra,
Bauri, Ganda and Kela	of Orissa,
Mazhabi	of Punjab,
Chhakkiliyan	of Tamil Nadu, and
Bahelia, Dhanak, Kori and Tarmali	of U.P.

It is evident from these two lists of castes that like Chamar, Dhobi, Mahar/Mehar, Dhed, Balai/Balahi, have progressed in all the States, the only exceptions being the Chamars of Madhya Pradesh and Gujarat. Similarly, the castes which traditionally enjoyed low status in the ritual hierarchy, like Bauri, Bhangi/Mehtar, Dhanak, Dom, etc., have hardly achieved any progress in education. The lists of Scheduled Castes, their percentage in the States Scheduled Caste population in the 1971 census and their representation in the School/College samples, given in Annexure Table XVI , will explain the matter in detail.

Thus, the educational level of 101 (76+25) castes, which accounted for more than 70 per cent of the 141 castes identified as 'untouchables' in 1911/1917 were either below the educational level achieved by other Scheduled Castes or their educational level could not even be assessed due to their not figuring in the samples. Thus, the hard core of the real 'untouchable' population who were at the lowest rung of the ritual hierarchy and beyond the pale of education and enlightenment have been left out of the fold of education. The benefits of the reservation policy and other incentives which have been devised primarily for the purpose of raising the level of education of these disadvanteged sections of the society, have not percolated down to them. The 'privileged section' among the Scheduled Castes have availed of the advantages of all the welfare programmes since Independence, while the more backward sections have virtually remained where they were, if not further deteriorated. The majority of the 'lower castes' are paradoxically facing oppresion in a traditionally caste-structured society on the one hand and, on the other, from among a new elite in their own group who monopolise the benefits of protective discrimintion.

A study[25] of the educational growth of the Scheduled Castes in the State of Punjab found two major reasons for widening of the inequalities among the Scheduled Castes. Firstly, the different Scheduled Castes living in a given geographical area form a hierarchy on the indexes of modernization, and the castes which are at a higher level, advance faster than those at lower levels. Secondly, the different castes are spread in different geographical areas: those residing in the more developed areas advance faster than those living in the backward areas. As a result of these two trends, the caste at the apex of the Scheduled Caste hierarchy in the geographical area which is most advanced will advance most rapidly and the caste which is at the bottom of the Scheduled Caste heirarchy in the geographical area which is least developed will grow most tardily. Thus, the gulf between the most advanced and the least advanced castes keeps on widening.

The real problem is how to turn the tide and bring the vast oppressed group within the fold of education.

Disparities in the Educational Attainments

Not only are there great disparities in the educational

attainments among different Scheduled Castes but also in the use made by them of the various educational facilities like post-matric scholarships scheme, hostel facilities, which are highly disproportionate to their population strength.

Available information clearly indicates that in the districts with higher levels of educational attainment, the Scheduled Castes availed themselves of the financial aid in far higher proportions. In the districts with educational levels lower than the average for the State, the utilization of the aid by them falls far short of their expected share.[26]

We have seen in Annexure Table IX that not only expenditure under the Post-Matric Scholarships Scheme has been rising steadily but an increasing number of the SC/ST students has been reaching post-Matric stage of education and are enjoying the benefit of the scheme. As many as 2.03 crores (20.3 million) of the Scheduled Castes scholars have been benefited by this scheme till now. Some Communities, however, derived maximum benefit of this scheme, while many communities derived far lesser advantage compared to their population. There are many communities whose students did not receive even a single scholarship. Similarly, in the matter of utilization of hostel facilities, some castes have advanced over the others. It implies that the castes which have advanced in educational attainments either due to their own efforts or due to the reservation policy, have also enjoyed the benefits of other educational incentives including post-matric scholarships and hostel facilities. As a result, some castes among the Scheduled Castes have moved ahead to the exclusion of others in education.

Welfare measures, in addition to creating inequality among Scheduled Castes, and between them and other groups, have also heightened a sense of relative deprivation among them. Increasingly, they tend to feel that they have been consciously and deliberately denied the rights and access to resources and opportunities to which they are entitled to. Further, there is a growing feeling that the welfare measures provided in the Constitution and legislative statutes are being deliberately thwarted by the ruling elite in the Government.[27]

As suggested by Patwardhan, the capacity of the Scheduled Castes to socially move upward differs from person to person or from group to group[28] because every person or group is likely to have a different set of values and standards of reference for his status. In terms of social change every endogamous social group of the Scheduled Castes can have common yardsticks to measure change and accept an identical reference group for the same. The social and religious factors can, however, have an influence on the aspiration of the people depending on their economic and educational background. However, since most of the Scheduled Caste communities suffer from the latter disabilities, they are not able to change as fast as they would like to. It is the latter group of the Scheduled Castes who need special attention and help so as to enable them to enjoy the fruits of Independence with others. But which are these communities that are still lagging behind and therefore, in need of special measures for their educational development? They have to be identified.

The need to identify the more neglected communities among the Scheduled Castes and to take up schemes in order to encourage more students from these communities to reach the level of post-matric education had repeatedly been stressed by all the officials and institutions related to the SC and ST. But, curiously enough, neither the Government of India nor the Commissioner for Scheduled Castes and Scheduled Tribes have undertaken this task themselves. They gave sufficient indications as to which were these castes, but refrained from saying so in concrete terms.

There has been a big gap between the past and the present status of the Scheduled Castes. One way to look at it, is to consider macro-level changes in the status of the Scheduled Caste communities themselves. As discussed earlier, a rise in the level of literacy and educational attainment of a class of people is a relative indicator of change in their status. As many as 32 per cent of the Scheduled Caste communities accounting for 50 per cent of the country's Scheduled Caste population had recorded a literacy rate above the respective State's SC literacy rate in three consecutive censuses during the period 1961-81.

Similarly, some castes have been benefited most by the reservation policy as revealed in their enrolment in post-matric stage of education. There may be some others who have not been identified in those studies. Though no efforts have been made by the Government to conduct a systematic study on this score, yet it is not at all difficult to find this out from the Government records. The records of disbursement of post-matric scholarships and other scholarships awarded at higher level of education and of the enrolment of the Scheduled Caste students at different levels of post-matric education would reveal the beneficiaries who have enjoyed the benefits of 'protective discrimination' most. Apparently, the same set of castes who have consistently shown a higher rate of literacy in the last three censuses are the beneficiaries, with minor variations here and there. The coefficients of literacy, enrolment at different stages of education and beneficiaries of other facilities/ incentives would, however, clearly indicate the people who are deprived of these benefits.

As very rightly pointed out by N.K.Bose, the Commissioner for Scheduled Castes and Scheduled Tribes:

> Everyone will agree that one part of the nation cannot be made free from social inequality and exploitation if other parts are allowed to remain in that condition. If a whole village is suffering from an epidemic of cholera, it is never possible to free one house, or a number of houses belonging to one particular community by differential treatment if the rest of the village remains as it is. Exploitation arises out of a system; and if it has to be ended for one community, it has to be ended for all.[29]

Unless radical measures are taken on a priority basis, and all out effots made in the right direction for proper development of the most neglected and deprived sections among the Scheduled Castes, the problem may assume the form of a crisis.

But how to ensure that the benefits of the policy of reservations, concessions and other facilities do percolate down to the most disadvantaged sections among the Scheduled Castes? The best way of bringing about a more even course of development is to make more money available for education of these sections who did not catch up with their advanced bretheren. This could be the ideal solution. But India has limited resources and what is spent on education is a smaller proportion of the national income than in many other countries of the modern world. Considering the inherent constraints, it is hardly possible to allocate considerably larger proportions of the Gross National Product to only meet the increased demand of this sector.

The other alternative is to make equitable distribution of the existing resources. If the relatively less priviledged classes of society are no to be denied the educational facilities, then ways and means have to be devised for making education available to them, because, after all, the key to their uplift largely lies in the field of education. And in this great task the leadership of the Scheduled Castes has a significant role to play, much more than the leadership of other communities. What should be the right approach for this purpose cannot be explained better than in the words of the late Prime Minister, Shrimati Indira Gandhi herself. She said:

> As in a family, the parents look upon their children with equal affection but a sick child gets additional attention, similarly, in society the weaker sections have to be nursed by giving some preferential treatment and the privileged sections should make sacrifices willingly for the welfare of the have-nots.[30]

It is fit and proper that the 'privileged' section among the Scheduled Castes should willingly come forward and make sacrifices for really downtrodden sections among them. Unless this section of the population is given extra help and assistance, they are not likely to advance. What is needed is more and more help to them. The non-SC/ST communities have not grudged the suffering, rather they willingly did so, during the fifty years of Independence for the educational advancement of the Scheduled Castes/Tribes to enable them to catch up with all round progress and development. Similarly, in the fitness of things, the advanced sections among the Scheduled Castes, who have, taken advantage of the policy of 'protective discrimination', and have registered higher progress in educational attainments during the last fifty years, compared to all other SC/ST groups taken together, should now come forward and extend a helping hand to the most neglected and disadvantaged communities among the Scheduled Castes so that they could share the benefits of 'protective discrimination' equitably and prosper. This is, no doubt, a momentous decision but such a decision, if not taken, may create a sense of deprivation and separatism amongst these communities, because they have been lagging behind while some communities have reaped the benefits at their cost. They can legitimately claim a better deal, at least they must have an equal share of the cake of 'protective discrimination', if not more to make up the leeway as fast as possible.

Shishir Kumar, the Commissioner for Scheduled Castes and Scheduled Tribes had the same thing in view when he observed in 1980:

> But a time is often reached in a nation's history when a historical need having been completed, the hitherto less emphasised or inadequately stressed aspects of the national commitment, if not attended to or neglected further, may pose a threat to the very edifice of the system. We seem to have reached a stage where a more meaningful and viable advancement of the weaker sections and the dispossessed can be considered a necessary condition for the stability of the nation and its political system. The responses, so far, to the challenges of time have not been as adequate despite the emphasis, in later years, on growth with social justice.[31]

In fact, he was very emphatic in recommending "a positive discrimination in favour of the educationally less advanced Scheduled Caste/Scheduled Tribe communities in giving them educational facilities and employment opportunities."[32]

Inequalities Among Scheduled Castes

In every society some men are recognized as superiors and others as inferiors like the ruler and the ruled, the twice-born and the once-born, the aristocrats and the commoners, the masters and the slaves, the upper class and the lower class. Everywhere there are some to rule and others to obey. The contrast between the higher and the lower, the rich and the poor, the powerful and the powerless constitute the substance of social differentiations or social stratification. This kind of ranking of the people from the high to low is done according to the values of the society. The factors of social stratification are so complex and multifaceted that they have been described and interpreted in many diverse ways.[33]

The distinction between societies which assign priority to the group in their classifications and those which assign priority to the individual corresponds in large measure to the distinction made famous by Hery Maine betweeen societies based on status and those based on contract.[34] Indian social order being based on caste status, the Indian model for eliminating the social differentiations has been providing a set of measures known as protective discrimination; which aims at remedying the long-standing effects of discrimination suffered in the past by certain castes, called Scheduled Castes. It rests on a recognition of existing social disparities as well as their historical basis. There is also a sense of making reparation for ancient wrongs, of compensating whole groups and classes for the injuries they have suffered in the past. Sociologists like Andre Beteille, however, believe[35] that protective discrimination can and should seek to satisfy present needs; it can do nothing to repair past injuries.

A host of educational facilities which include a quota of seats in educational institutions as well, have been provided to the communities clubbed together under the 'Scheduled Castes' so that they can have equal access to educational opportunities. Strictly speaking, the complete equalization of educational opportunities is an utopia if not a myth. In this heterogeneous world it is not easy to create situations under which such equalization could become a reality. However, equality in society is desirable, not only for its own sake but, as an essential pre-requisite for the total social development, removal of social unrest, tensions and other accompanying train of vices in the society. Although perfect equality may be unattainable, it is always possible to reduce the disparities and promote a desirable order of equality amongst all sections of the population so that no community, specially the weaker sections of the society, remains in a disadvantageous position *vis-a-vis* other communities in the matter of educational opportunities.[36] Equality of opportunity will, however, mean very little if at every turn the individual is shadowed by the caste or the community into which he was born. Justice must be rendered to the castes and communities which have in the past been denied justice, but, as Beteille points out, if we do this without any regard at all for the cost to the individual, instead of moving forward into the new social order promised by the makers of our Constitution, we might move backward into the Middle Ages.[37]

The education policy relating to the Scheduled Castes is embroiled into attaining two conflicting goals — one of providing free compulsory elementary education to all in pursuance of the constitutional obligation and the other of implementing the Ambedkarian theory of 'excellence of a few'. Ambedkar thought that the different status in society would disappear only by advancement of education. If a community had a good number of highly educated and professional men, say 10 barristers, 20 doctors, 30 engineers then that community would be regarded as rich in education, although everyone of that community was not educated. According to Ambedkar, it was 2000 times better to produce a few people with high qualification and to place them in high posts than to have 2000 boys educated in primary education in vernacular language. He was in favour of this policy of giving highest education to a few individuals because that would enhance the status of the community and thus, ultimately pave the way for disappearance of different status in the society.[38]

Ambedkar's prescription for disappearance of social status through highest education to a few individuals has been followed since Independence and in the process, the country has not been able to fulfil the constitutional obligation of providing free elementary education to all. So far there has been a heavy stress upon granting financial and material assistance to those aspiring for higher education, graduation level included. A large number of doctors, engineers, lawyers, professors, lecturers, technocrats, bureaucrats even outstanding national political leaders have come up during the last fifty years. The emergence of this elite group in almost all the States did not, however, help in the obliteration of caste distinctions in our society, because these special provisons can directly satisfy only a few individual members of groups that are made up of many. Such opportunities are too few in number to materially alter the conditions of any caste as a whole and as Beteille has said, "there is little reason to believe that the personal advancement of an individual and the social betterment of the caste into which he was born have very much to do with each other."[39]

The Ambedkarian theory of 'excellence of a few' could neither obliterate distinctions in caste status nor raise the level of education of all the Scheduled Caste communities. On the other hand, it has accentuated the hold of caste and has also given rise to a situation in most States where a section of the Scheduled Caste communities has eduationally advanced far beyond the rest of the Scheduled Caste communities.Out of that, other consequences flow- their predominance in the services, in the educational institutions, their ability to secure seats in technical institutions and professional colleges, etc. This creates a vicious circle. Just as vibrant rivers flow steadily into the ocean, the educationally advanced Scheduled Caste communities get more and more forward and the educationally backward Scheduled Caste communities recede further backward. As it appears, about one-third of the Scheduled Caste communities accounting for about half of the total Scheduled Caste population have not only usurped almost all the educational benefits meant for the entire Scheduled Caste population, but have also appropriated to a large measure the educational benefits extended to the Scheduled Tribes, though by default. Thus, the present policy gives unfair advantage to a section of the Scheduled Castes who have been thrice benefited. As in the traditional hierarchical society there were basically two groups of communities — the privileged twice-born and the under-privileged Sudras, — similarly, the post-Independence India saw the emergence of the 'neo-Brahmin' privileged group among the Scheduled Castes who have cornered the advantages of the protective policy of the State, depriving the less-privileged sections among the Scheduled Castes and the Scheduled Tribes

The underlying spirit of all the educational safeguards is that the Scheduled Castes shall be brought to the level of the rest of the advanced communities.[40] By implication it means discontinuancy of these benefits to those who have reached the level of the rest of the advanced communities or have progressively advanced in relation to other Scheduled Caste communities. The framers the of constitutional benefits or its misuse by those who were not educationally backward and aired their views in the Constitutent Assembly. Though no specific provision was embodied in the Constitution, they thought that these benefits would automatically cease once the Scheduled Caste communities attained a comparable level in the matter of education. Future course of events, however, belied this hope of the framers. There is no move on the part of those who have reached elite positions in the society to forego their claims to protective discrimination. Rather, having entrenched themselves in power, they want perpetuation of the same system for furtherance of the interests not so much for their caste members as for their kith and kin.

The policy framed for the educational growth and development of the Scheduled Castes has brought changes among the communities who are receptive to change. The ability to absorb the new facilities depended on the already existing level of education of the Scheduled Caste communities. It was assumed that the benefits which would first accrue to the more advanced sections, would eventually trickle down to the underprivileged communities. But the trickle down to the bottom layers does not ensure that the bottom layers have the same opportunities as the upper layers. In effect, the difference between the 'upper' and the 'bottom' layers among the Scheduled Castes actually increased, thus giving rise to a negative correlation between the development of these two groups of the Scheduled Castes in some cases. The apparent failure of ieducationists, policy makers and planners to formulate effective strategies to put a stop to this lopsided educational development among the Scheduled Castes, calls for a rethinking for developing a more pragmatic attitude in our entire approach to the educational development of the Scheduled Castes. If one of the objectives of 'protective discrimination' is to provide equal opportunities of advancement for the under privileged, then they should be given favoured treatment through target-group planning which can be made effective, as D'souza points out, only when the development idea of 'putting the last first' is made the sheet-anchor of planning.[41] These sections need exclusive development treatment with a view to giving them an added push for developing their capabilities and upgrading their skills. The ends of justice are hardly met if our vain endeavour to bring about equality between castes leads only to the increase of inequality among the castes.

The country has travelled a long way since the day when Ambedkar fell a victim to caste discrimination. The situation has changed perceptibly during the last fifty years since Independence. Undoubtedly, Hindu social order is based on hierarchy and caste was one of the predominant factors during pre-constitution period. Unfortunately, instead of dissipating its incursion it is being needlessly accentuated, perpetuated and stratification is given legitimacy for selfish ends instead of being discouraged and put an end to by all measures, including administrative and legislative. The fact that people are identified by their caste is a reality, so much so that caste is reflected in relevant entries in the public records or school or college admission register.[42] This warning being administered by the Supreme Court has got to be viewed with concern. But, as long as caste remains the only basis for special support by way of affirmative action, such support needs identification by caste.

No society starts on a clean slate; every society has its own historical legacy. Age-old disparities must be taken into account if the equality in the new social order is to be real and not merely formal. At the same time, we must ensure that in destroying old inequalities we do not create new ones. Discrimination is a dangerous instrument, no matter how pure are the intentions of those who use it. Our own history ought to teach us how infectious the use of discrimination can be, and how careful we have to be in using it even for a desirable end.[43]

Time has now come to deeply ponder whether discrimination based on caste, which had in past been a source of so much evil can, by being inverted, be made a source of good for the society at large. If the present policy of affirmative actions being followed in the education field had at all had any effect of raising the social, educational and economic standards of the community as a whole for the benefit of which they were ostensibly made, the number of castes listed in the Schedule should by now have shown some reduction. The facts, on the other hand, are that the number of these castes goes on increasing without a single deletion. It may be remembered that even in 1917, when the tendency on the whole was for the lower castes to edge themselves here and there into a higher scale by the assumption of new names and privileges, sometimes a whole community declared itself to be depresssed (forerunner of the Scheduled Castes) with a view to reaping special concessions of education or appointment.[44] If this was the situation eighty years earlier, it is no wonder that it has reached this level today. The benefits of educational facilities being accorded primarily on the basis of caste have propelled the demand for inclusion of more castes either in the list of the Scheduled Castes or in the list of Other Backward Classes and more and more groups are clamouring for being declared backward. The whole country seems to be engaged in a rat race to move backwards instead of forwards.

If the larger objective of a more homogeneous political community based on social and economic equality is to be achieved,[45] keeping the larger interest of the country and fuller opportunities to all classes and communities in view;[46] if there ought to be social justice among all the communities;[47] if it is our objective not only to give opportunity to each individual in India to grow but also to build up a united nation where each individual does not think so much of his particular group or caste but thinks of the larger community;[48] if we are anxious to avoid that premium should not be put upon a caste or a community;[49] if the real purpose is to help the really backward communities also to see that the provision of discrimination is not abused[50] or misused by any Government for perpetuating any class discrimination[51] or to ensure that backwardness is not crystallized or perpetuated;[52] if the really backward classes who are poor and who cannot get opportunities to come up and raise themselves shall all be helped[53] as visualised by the framers of our Constitution, then serious attempts should be made by all right-thinking people to put a stop to the incursion of casteism in the education field, more so because educational backwardness has nothing to do with caste superiority or inferiority at the present juncture.

Eradication of Child Labour

With a view to eradicating child labour by 2002 AD, as declared by the Prime Minister of India on August 15, 1995, the Centre has formulated a scheme aimed at checking child labour by drawing working children into schools with a stipend. As the then Prime Minister, P.V.Narasimha Rao, said: "Child labour is a sad reality of our world. Whereever it is practised it has to be eliminated. Inducing children to education is clearly the means of this objective."[54] The working children will be paid Rs 100 per month and given a daily meal worth Rs 2.50, if they attend schools specially set up for them for at least 26 days a month. The scheme proposes to cater to about 2000 children through 40 schools in each district. Each school must have a minimum of 50 students. The schools will impart vocational and non-formal education.[55] The Government has targeted two million children for the special schools, as a part of Rs 850 crore government scheme for eradication of child labour. The project will cover 100 districts in States with a high concentration of child labour.[56]

The formulation of this policy, though belated, for motivating child labour towards education is itself an admission of the reality that education of this section of children is hindered because of their poverty and not due to their caste. Poverty is a great leveller and does not distinguish between 'high caste', 'low caste', creed, community or religion.

The Government of India also introduced from the academic year 1977-78 a centrally sponsored scheme for the award of post-matric scholarships exclusively for the children of those persons who are not members of Scheduled Castes and Scheduled Tribes and who are engaged in unclean occupations,viz. (i) scavenging of dry latrines, (ii) tanning, and (iii) flaying. The expenditure of the scheme is met from the funds provided by the Central Government for the centrally sponsored scheme of post-matric scholarships to the Scheduled Castes and the Scheduled Tribes though the Commissioner for Scheduled Castes and Scheduled Tribes recommended for meeting the expenditure from a separate budget head.[57] This scheme was introduced because it was thought that children belonging to this category also needed special attention for their educational advancement. This also shows that one's educational progress is not related so much to his caste status as to his present occupational and economic disabilities. The introduction of this scheme for the educational advancement of the children belonging to the non-SC/ST communities is no doubt an attempt at breaking the caste-barrier in providing educational facilities.

The official view of caste in India is perfectly straightforward. According to the Constitution of India, no discrimination can be exhibited toward citizens, "on grounds only of religion, race, caste,sex, (or) place of birth...(in) access to shops, public restaurants, hotels and places of public entertainment, or ...(in) the use of wells, tanks, bathing ghats, roads and places of public resort maintained wholly or partly out of State funds or dedicated to the use of the general public."In addition, untouchability "is abolished and its practice in any form is forbidden." Legally, then, the caste system can no longer serve as the basis for regulating social relationships. No discerning observer, however, would agree that the effects of the caste system have in fact disappeared. In fact, while abolishing discrimination, the Constitution itself has contributed to a new caste awareness, though perhaps on a broader geographic scale than had been known in the past.[58] Nearly fifty years after 1947, the stranglehold of caste is virtually undiminished.

Independent India, while eloquently decrying this evil practice, nonetheless uses the language of caste when it comes to wooing the electorates. And reservation, meant to eradicate centuries of injustice, only increases the hold of caste identity and hierarchy Dr B.R. Ambedkar in *Annihilation of Caste* wrote:

> The effect of caste on the ethics of the Hindus is simply deplorable. Caste has killed public spirit. Caste has destroyed the sense of public charity. Caste has made public opinion impossible. A Hindu's public is his caste. His responsibility is only to his caste. His loyalty is restricted only to his caste. Virtue has become caste-ridden and morality has become caste-bound. There is no sympathy to the deserving. There is no appreciation of the meritorious. There is no charity to the needy. Suffering as such calls for no response. There is charity but it begins with the caste and ends with the caste. There is sympathy but not for men of other castes. Would a Hindu acknowledge and follow the leadership of a great and good man? The case of a Mahatma apart, the answer must be that he will follow a leader if he is a man of his caste. A Brahmin will follow a leader only if he is a Brahmin, a Kayastha if he is a Kayastha and so on. The capacity to appreciate merits in a man apart from his caste does not exist in a Hindu. There is appreciation of virtue but only when the man is a fellow caste-man. The whole morality is as bad as tribal morality. My caste-man, right or wrong; my caste-man, good or bad. It is not a case of standing by virtue and not standing by vice. It is a case of standing or not standing by the caste. Have not Hindus committed treason against their country in the interests of their caste?[59] ... Anything that you will build on the foundations of caste will crack and will never be a whole.[60]

What Ambedkar wrote about sixty years back is perhaps more relevant in the present situation than before. The moot point for consideration is whether caste and caste alone should be the sole identity of the Indians and continue to guide the destiny of the nation, or we should work steadfastly towards its gradual obliteration in all walks of life, especially in the educational sphere so that a strong, secular, casteless, united India can emerge. Cannot a beginning be made?

Issues and Suggestions Related to Past Experiences

Over the last fifty years of Independence, the educational experience of the Scheduled Castes in the country has posed two major issues. They are :

(i) eradication of illiteracy and providing elementary education; and

(ii) improving the quality of education comparable to that of the non-SC communities.

So far as eradication of illiteracy and providing elementary education is concerned, it may be remembered that the constitutional obligation of providing compulsory elementary education to all children up to the age of 14 years of the commencement of the Constiltution,i.e., by 26th January, 1960, has not been fully implemented till now. If this constitutional commitment was honoured, the country would have got rid of illiteracy much earlier. So the first priority should be of providing free elementary education to all children, irrespective of caste, creed, sex, religion or the like, because even if a small segment of population — be it a Scheduled Caste or a Scheduled Tribe or any other section of population — remains uncovered, the national goal of education for all would not be achieved.

Suggestions for ProvidingElementary Education to All

The following steps for providing elementary education to all should be taken:

(i) Proper enforcement of the Compulsory Education Act at the Primary level and specially to make the parents admit their children to the 1st standard at the proper age;

(ii) Some sort of counselling and guidance for the parents making them aware of their responsibilities and developing in them some ability to understand their role *vis-a-vis* their ward as a student;

(iii) Special schemes to enrol girls at the primary and upper primary levels;

(iv) Special incentives to those below the poverty level and engaged mostly as agricultural labourers, subsistence farmers, artisans, collectors of minor forest produce and urban slum dwellers to enlist and sustain their children for compulsory education;

(v) Payment of cash compensation in the form of opportunity cost to those parents who for economic and social constraints cannot send their children to schools;

(vi) Schemes like payment of monthly stipend to child labourers, pre-matric scholarships to children of those engaged in unclean occupations like scavenging of dry latrines, tanning and flaying, should be broad-based;

(vii) Establishment of educational institutions in rural areas in such a manner that they are within easy reach of the downtrodden people;

(viii) Study centres and reading rooms within easy reach of students'residences should be provided. Some class rooms of the school may be kept open during early morning and late evening hours for the benefit of those who do not have suitable place to study at home;

(ix) Extra coaching classes should be organized free of cost for the deficient students during week-ends and holidays;

(x) Extra-curricular activities should be strengthened in schools and all the students should be encouraged to participate more and more actively; and

(xi) There should be a time-bound programme of free compulsory literacy and free elementary education for all people. This will open the gates of education, progress and prosperity to all people. Free and quality education will ensure equal opportunities for all, without restriction, enabling every one to fight for self esteem and progress.

For improvement of the quality of education of the Scheduled Caste students so that they can stand on their own legs without any crutch, certain corrective and ameliorative measures are required to be taken at the elementary stage of education. The main emphasis so long was on giving financial and other incentives at post-matric stage of education, oblivious of the fact that no good building can be erected on a weak foundation. If the foundation is weak, the entire edifice would crumble, no matter what extra props are provided later. The performance at the level of higher education entirely depends on the quality of education at the elementary level. Before going further one is compelled to reflect upon the objectives of education in the country *vis-a-vis* the Scheduled Castes. Education for the sake of education is considered as a "luxurious pastime"[61] for the Scheduled Castes. The major objectives of receiving education seems to be to secure a job anyhow and thereby escape the traditional occupations involving manual labour.[62] At best, it could prepare the Scheduled Caste students to face the struggles of life with self-confidence and a certain amount of skill of the head as well as of the hand.[63] Such being the objectives of education, it is necessary to examine whether it is realistic to try and combine within the system, the conflicting goals of excellence and social justice,[64] as we have been trying to do over the past decades. It is necessary, further, to examine carefully whether and how education could be used effectively as an instrument of social change.

That education has failed to usher in the deserved social change is borne out by the fact that the educated Scheduled Castes have formed an elite group who aspire for a position commensuarate with their educational and occupational achievements where caste would not be a factor but at the same time they are not willing to come out of the caste system. Education has no doubt loosened family and caste ties but the educated Scheduled Castes are still in favour of the caste system. The main reason for such a feeling among the Scheduled Castes is the advantage they are getting from the reservation policy. Evidently, something has gone awry in our entire approach to improve the educational level of the Scheduled Castes.

The planners have also realized the changed role of education. The Seventh Five Year Plan has acknowledged the dependence of economic development on education. With the growing importance of technology which itself has been changing at a very fast rate, education came to be acknowledged as a crucial investment for economic development. It is a big change from the earlier attitude when education was perceived merely as an instrument of social change. Besides social change, education has a close connection with development and modernization. This official confirmation of the obvious is significant for all.

Despite the Government's efforts to provide extra educational facilities to the Scheduled Caste students, the clear perception of the man-in-the-street is that the performance level of the Scheduled Caste students has not reached a level commensurate with the investments made on them so far. The Scheduled Caste students being sheltered under the Government umbrella for education as well as job, are not developing a healthy attitude to fair competition. India is passing from a non-competitive mode of production into a competitive open system when progressively more and more use is made of modern technology.[65] India has liberalized its economy and opened its economy to foreign capital and increased competition. Unless one is able to adapt itself to the changing environment, the chance of survival is not very bright.

Suggestions to Improve Qualitative Performance of Scheduled Castes

For qualitative improvement of the performance of the Scheduled Caste students the following measures should be taken:

(i) establishment of best schools in predominantly Scheduled Caste habitations so that the Scheduled Caste students can go forward to higher courses properly equipped;[66]

(ii) special efforts should be made to draw the Scheduled Caste students from their homes into hostels where the best of education be given for those who lag behind;[67]

(iii) more, better and cheaper hostel facilities for the Scheduled Caste students should be provided;

(iv) the Hostel Superintendent should be such as would be able to take on the role of parents in supervising, directing, guiding and counselling the Scheduled Caste students in performing their students role. If necessary, a person with special training should be appointed for the task;

(v) the minimum amount of scholarships should be increased. The amount of the scholarship should be granted starting from the minimum so that the students showing better results get more;

(vi) the formal procedure of securing benefits should be simplified as much as possible;

(vii) provision of benefits to the Scheduled Caste students should be so devised as to encourage merit. Incentives should be provided for those who show greater merit;

(viii) instead of providing a lower limit for admission to

educational institutions, remedial measures should be organized and implemented to raise their level of performance; and

(ix) talented Scheduled Caste students to be spotted from class V and the State should take full responsibility of their education up to a certain level, say up to the higher secondary level. These students should get the best of education in best environment with proper emphasis for their physical, mental and cultural development.

We have seen that the governmental assistance for educational development of the Scheduled Castes have created inequalities between different States as well as between different Scheduled Caste communities within a State. Some States and some Scheduled Castes within a State have progressed much more than the others. It is quite likely that these measures for qualitative improvement of the Scheduled Castes, suggested above, will not percolate down to the really disadvantaged sections among the Scheduled Castes unless some ways and means are devised. In order to ensure that these benefits do not accrue to the 'privileged sections, among the Scheduled Castes, it is suggested that the following steps be taken:

Suggestions to Ensure Effective Implementation to Needy

(i) Criteria should be devised on the basis of which concessions and benefits could be tapered off or stopped altogether for those communities that reach a particular level of economic and educational development;

(ii) Castes registering a comparatively higher level of educational development *vis-a-vis* other sections of the Scheduled Castes be descheduled for the purpose of obtaining educational facilities so that the benefits of 'protective discrimination' accrue to the really educationally backward communities among the Scheduled Castes.

(iii) A comparative study of the social background, educational and occupational aspirations, level of literacy, co-efficient of equality in enrolment at different stages of education and academic performance at higher secondary, college/university levels including Medical and Engineering courses of each and every caste/sub-caste should be conducted periodically in each State with a view of taking remedial measures for the improvement of educational level or the really educationally backward sections amongst the Scheduled Castes.

Today India is at the crossroads, where the integrated community hangs by a thread, ready to break up and split. Problems of casteism, communalism, regionalism, linguism, orthodoxy and obscurantism — these are the vicious products of a dark period of Indian history. Indian disunity which frequently had tempted foreign powers to seek their fortunes has been sedulously fostered by the agents of those powers and by the forces of disruption and disintegration. These have to be fought relentlessly and without respite till the end.

Education is the most powerful weapon with which we can fight these forces and curb them. Our educational system should be the catalyst to achieve the goal of a strong, united, casteless, creedless India. Educationists, Planners, Administrators, and above all, the politicians should realize that unless a practical strategy is evolved to make education a vehicle for achieving this goal, the forces of disintegration will continue to rear their ugly heads in every nook and corner of the country and India will continue to face the threat of agression, both internal and external, as at present. One should look beyond today and tomorrow and ensure that education does not divide the society. What is required is a bold and pragmatic step to give a new orientation to the present policy of educational development of the Scheduled Castes, if we are really interested in ushering in equality through education.

References

1. Agarwal, R.C., 1988, *Constitutional Development and National Movement of India*, pp. 31-32. Eighth Edition, S.Chand & Company,
2. Sen, Khagendra Nath, 1970, *Education and the Nation*, p.262. University of Calcutta.
3. *Report of the Committee on Untouchability, Economic and Educational Development of the Scheduled Castes and Connected Documents*, Department of Social Welfare, Government of India, 1969, p.179.
4. Sen, Khagendra Nath, op. cit., p.264.
5. Agarwal, R.C., op. cit., p. 32.
6. Kabir, Humayun, 1961 *Indian Philosophy of Education*, pp.172-73. Asia Publishing House

7. Kumar, Krishna, 1987 "Reproduction or Change? Education and Elites in India," In *Education and the Process of Change,* p.33. Ratna Ghosh and Mathew Zachariah eds. Sage. Publications Delhi :
8. *Education For All, The Indian Scene, A Synopsis,* Department of Education. Ministry of Human Resource Development, Government of India, December 1993, p.3.
9. Table 3.17.
10. Ghosh, Ratna, *Education and the Process of Change,* p.17. op. cit
11. Singh, Karan, *Patel, Memorial Lectures, 1988,* Publications Divisions, Ministry of Information and Broadcasting, Government of India, 1990, p.1, 5.
12. Samayak, V.K., 1993, *India Beyond Today and Tomorrow,* p.126. Allied Publishers,
13. *Ibid.,* p.87.
14. Gounden, A.M. Nalla, "Education and Economic Growth," In *Education and the Process of Change,* ed. op. cit., pp.121-22.
15. Ambirajan, S., 1995 "Check the Educational Divide," *The Hindu,* June 29, p.8.
16. Surya Vasantha, 1995, "The Lure of the English Medium," *The Hindu,* June 4, p.V.
17. Dr. P.K. Punnusamy while delivering the 91st commemoration address of Dr Rajah Sir M.A. Muthiah Chettiar at Annamalai University, *The Hindu,* August 11, 1995, p.17.
18. Singh, Kanra, op. cit., pp.9-10.
19. *Report of the Backward Classes Commission,* Volume III, 1956, pp.73-75 (*Chairman, Kalelkar*).
20. Eighteenth *RCSCST,* 1968-69, p.4.
21. Chitnis, Suma, *A Long Way to Go,* op. cit., pp.18-19.
22. Shah, B.V. and Thakar, J.D., op. cit., pp.37-38.
23. Shah, B.V., 1986, *Third Survey of Research in Education,* NCERT, p.96.
24. Nineteenth *RCSCST,* 1969-70, p.iv.
25. D'Souza, Victor, S., 1980 *Development Planning and Structural Inequalities- The Response of the Underprivileged,* 1990, p.190. Sage Publications.
26. D'Souza, Victor. S., *Educational Inequalities among Scheduled Castes -A Caste Study in the Punjab,* op. cit., p.28.
27. Dubey, S.N., 1975 "*Deprivation, Welfarism and Predominant Adaptation Response of Backward Classes in India: Implication for social policy,*" In T. Krishna Nair, *Social Work Education and Development of Weaker Sections,* p. 118 (ed.) Association of Schools of Social Work in India.
28. Patwardhan, M.V., 1959, *The Mirage of a Classes Society,* p. 244. Bombay, Chetna.
29. Nineteenth *RCSCST,* 1969-70, para 1.46 p.6.
30. Twentieth *RCSCST,* 1970-71, para 1.20 p.3.

31. Twenty-sixth *RCSCST*, 1978-79, para 1.3 p.1.
32. *Ibid.*, para 1.31 p.8.
33. Abbasayalyu, op. cit., pp.13-14.
34. Maine, H.S., 1950 *Ancient Law*, Oxford University Press,
35. Beteille, Andre, 1981 *The Backward Classes and the New Social Order*, p.25. Oxford University Press,
36. Nautiyal, K.C., and Sharma, Y.D., 1979, *Equalisation of Educational Opportunities for Scheduled Castes and Scheduled Tribes*, p. 26. NCERT.
37. Beteille, 1981 *The Backward Classes and the New Social Order*, op. cit., p. 32.
38. *First Backward Classes Commission Report*, Vol.III, 1956, pp. 73-75.
39. Beteille, 1981, *The Backward Classes and the New Social Order*, op. cit., p. 47.
40. *Report of the Committee on Untouchability etc.*, op. cit., p. 181.
41. D'Souza, 1990, *Development Planning and Structural Inequalities*, op. cit., p.203.
42. *Kumari Madhuri Patil and another v. Additional Commissioner, Tribal Development and others, AIR 1995 SC 94.*
43. Beiteille, 1981 *The Backward Classes and the New Social Order, op. cit*, pp.25-26.
44. *Progress of Education in India, 1912-17, Seventh Quinquennial Review*, 1919, Vol.I, p.206.
45. D'Souza, Rev. *Parliamentary Debates, Volume XII, 1951, Third Session, of Parliament of India*, 1951, dated 30-5-51, Col. 9689.
46. Shankaraiya, *Ibid.*, dated 17-5-51, col. 9001.
47. Ramalingam Chettiar, *Ibid.*, dated 18-5-51, Col.9040.
48. Jawaharlal Nehru, *Ibid.*, dated 1-6-51, Col. 9617.
49. H.V. Kamath, *Ibid.*, dated 1-6-51, col. 9828.
50. S.P. Mookherjee, *Ibid.*, dated 30-5-51, Col.9710.
51. Views of the Select Committee, *Ibid.*, Col. 9619.
52. Pandit Thakurdas Bhargava, *CAD*, Vol. VIII, dated 16-6-49 p.946.
53. S.L. Saxena, *Parliamentary Debates*, op. cit., dated 1-6-51, Col.9819.
54. *The Hindu*, July 23, 1995, p.viii.
55. *The Statesman*, August, 6, 1995, p.5.
56. *The Telegraph*, September, 1995, p.7.
57. Twenty-fifth *RCSCST*, 1977-78, p.109.
58. Tilman, Robert, O., 1973 "The Influence of Caste on Indian Economic Development," In *Administration and Economic Development in India*. p. 211 *Ralph Braibanti and Joseph J. Spengler, (eds)*. Cambridge University Press.
59. *Dr. Babasaheb Ambedkar: Writings and Speeches*, Vol.I, Government of Maharashtra, 1979, pp. 56-67.
60. *Ibid.*, p.66.
61. Twentieth *RCSCST*, 1970-71, para 2.4, p.4.

62. *Ibid.*
63. Eighteenth *RCSCST*, 1968-69, para 1.24 p.4.
64. Chitnis, Suma, "*Education and Social Stratification- An illustration from a Metropolitan City,*" In *Education and the Process of Change*, op. cit., p.99.
65. Nineteenth *RCSCST*, 1969-70. para 1.45 p.6.
66. Seventeenth *RCSCST*, 1967-68. para 1.51 p.10.
67. Eighteenth *RCSCST*, 1968-69, para 1.20 p.4.

ANNEXURE TABLE I
LITERACY RATES FOR TOTAL POPULATION AND SCHEDULED CASTE POPULATION BY SEX, 1991.

Sl. No.	*States/ UTs*	*Total Population*			*Scheduled Caste Population*		
		All Persons	*Males*	*Females*	*All Persons*	*Males*	*Females*
1	2	3	4	5	6	7	8
1.	Andhra Pradesh	44.09	55.13	32.72	31.59	41.88	20.92
2.	Arunachal Pradesh	41.59	51.45	29.69	57.27	66.25	41.42
3.	Assam	52.89	61.87	43.03	53.94	63.88	42.99
4.	Bihar	38.48	52.49	22.89	19.49	30.64	7.07
5.	Goa	75.51	83.64	67.09	58.73	69.55	47.51
6.	Gujarat	61.29	73.13	48.64	61.07	75.47	45.54
7.	Haryana	55.85	69.10	40.47	39.22	52.06	24.15
8.	Himachal Pradesh	63.86	75.36	52.13	53.20	64.98	41.02
9.	Jammu & Kashmir		Not	Available			
10.	Karnataka	56.04	67.26	44.34	38.06	49.89	25.95
11.	Kerala	89.81	93.62	86.13	79.66	85.22	74.31
12.	Madhya Pradesh	44.20	58.42	28.85	35.08	50.51	18.11
13.	Maharashtra	64.87	76.56	52.32	56.46	70.45	41.59
14.	Manipur	59.89	71.63	47.60	56.44	65.28	47.41
15.	Meghalaya	49.10	53.12	44.85	44.27	54.56	31.19
16.	Mizoram	82.27	85.61	78.60	77.92	77.54	81.25
17.	Nagaland	61.65	67.62	54.75	-	-	-
18.	Orissa	49.09	63.09	34.68	36.78	52.42	20.74
19.	Punjab	58.51	65.66	50.41	41.09	49.82	31.03
20.	Rajasthan	38.55	54.99	20.44	26.29	42.38	8.31
21.	Sikkim	56.94	65.74	46.69	51.03	58.89	42.77
22.	Tamil Nadu	62.66	73.75	51.33	46.74	58.36	34.89
23.	Tripura	60.44	70.58	49.65	56.66	67.25	45.45
24.	Uttar Pradesh	41.60	55.73	25.31	26.85	10.80	10.69
25.	West Bengal	57.70	67.81	46.56	42.21	54.55	28.87
26.	A & N Islands	73.02	78.99	65.46	-	-	-
27.	Chandigarh	77.81	82.04	72.34	55.44	64.74	43.54
28.	Dadra & N. Haveli	40.71	53.56	26.98	77.64	88.03	66.61
29.	Daman & Diu	71.20	82.86	59.40	79.18	91.85	67.62
30.	Delhi	75.29	82.01	66.99	57.60	68.77	43.82
31.	Lakshadweep	81.78	90.18	72.89	-	-	-
32.	Pondicherry	74.74	83.88	65.63	56.26	66.10	46.28
	India	52.21	64.13	39.29	37.41	49.91	23.76
	Source	a	a	a	a	a	a

Source : Census of India, 1991, Series -1, India, Paper 1 of 1993, p. 14.

ANNEXURE TABLE II

LITERACY RATE OF SCHEDULED CASTES FOR AGE-GROUP 7 YEARS AND ABOVE IN DIFFERENT STATES/UTs IN THE 1991 CENSUS, BY SEX AND RESIDENCE

Sl. No.	Name of States/Uts	Total population			Total Male population			Total Female population			Sources
		All Persons	Rural	Urban	All Persons	Rural	Urban	All Persons	Rural	Urban	
1	2	3	4	5	6	7	8	9	10	11	12
1.	Andhra Pradesh	31.59	26.80	54.10	41.88	37.02	64.88	20.92	16.19	43.03	
2.	Arunachal Pradesh	57.27	55.29	61.99	66.25	65.02	69.39	41.42	37.25	50.40	
3.	Assam	53.94	51.95	65.71	63.88	62.19	73.72	42.99	40.72	56.66	
4.	Bihar	19.49	17.49	39.23	30.64	28.30	52.74	7.07	5.54	22.90	
5.	Goa	58.73	56.05	61.76	69.55	67.67	71.69	47.51	43.94	51.53	
6.	Gujarat	61.07	55.59	70.06	75.47	71.21	82.35	45.54	38.96	56.53	
7.	Haryana	39.22	37.67	46.42	52.06	50.62	58.69	24.15	22.48	31.89	
8.	Himachal Pradesh	53.20	52.00	70.32	64.98	63.95	78.87	41.02	39.78	60.16	
9.	Jammu & Kashmir	Not	Available								
10.	Karnataka	38.06	31.42	59.18	49.69	43.21	70.05	25.95	19.23	47.64	
11.	Kerala	79.66	78.55	84.47	85.22	84.22	89.56	74.31	73.09	79.60	
12.	Madhya Pradesh	35.08	30.22	52.26	50.51	45.70	67.29	18.11	13.30	35.38	
13.	Maharashtra	56.46	50.27	67.07	70.45	65.86	78.17	41.59	33.99	54.94	
14.	Manipur	56.44	56.69	56.22	65.28	65.43	65.14	47.41	47.52	47.32	
15.	Meghalaya	44.27	37.11	53.05	54.56	47.28	63.34	31.19	24.35	39.70	
16.	Mizoram	77.92	75.76	82.30	77.54	74.81	83.24	81.25	85.00	75.00	
17.	Orissa	36.78	35.45	47.80	52.42	51.22	62.10	20.74	19.39	32.30	
18.	Punjab	41.09	37.05	47.04	49.82	48.54	54.76	31.03	29.20	38.14	
19.	Rajasthan	26.29	22.06	43.35	42.38	37.63	61.37	8.31	4.73	22.83	

1	2	3	4	5	6	7	8	9	10	11	12
20.	Sikkim	51.03	47.53	76.58	58.69	55.28	84.20	42.77	39.13	68.70	
21.	Tamil Nadu	46.74	42.50	62.24	58.36	54.47	72.58	34.89	30.30	51.68	
22.	Tripura	56.66	55.24	64.06	67.25	66.07	73.43	45.45	43.69	54.40	
23.	Uttar Pradesh	26.85	24.76	42.30	40.80	38.87	54.79	10.69	8.47	27.36	
24.	West Bengal	42.21	39.98	53.98	54.55	52.72	63.90	28.87	26.32	42.71	
25.	Chandigarh	55.44	48.57	56.48	64.74	57.55	65.88	43.54	35.79	44.63	
26.	Dadra & N. Haveli	77.64	77.17	79.90	88.03	87.42	90.75	66.61	66.52	67.03	
27.	Daman & Diu	79.18	82.22	74.29	91.85	94.32	88.02	67.62	71.48	61.15	
28.	Delhi	57.60	55.50	57.86	68.77	68.99	68.74	43.82	38.50	44.49	
29.	Pondicherry	56.26	50.07	65.05	66.10	59.89	74.67	46.28	39.94	55.30	
	India	37.41	33.25	55.11	49.91	45.95	66.60	23.76	19.46	42.29	
	Source	a	b	b	a	b	b	a	b	b	
	All Categories	52.21	44.69	73.08	64.13	57.87	81.09	39.29	30.62	64.05	c
	Non-SC/ST	57.69	49.87	75.93	69.53	63.42	83.40	44.82	35.38	67.48	d

Source : a– Census of India, 1991, Paper 1 of 1993, p. 14.
b- calculted on the basis of figures at pp.18-36 of Paper 1 of 1993, Census of India, 1991.
c - Census of India, 1991, Paper 2 of 1992, pp. 210 – 211.
d- calculated on the basis of figures at pp. 18-63 of Paper 1 of 1993 and pp. 210-216 of Paper 2 of 1992.

ANNEXURE TABLE III
SCHEDULED CASTES WITH ZERO LITERACY RATE BY SEX AND RESIDENCE, 1981.

Sl. No. State/Union Territory	Male		Female	
	Rural	Urban	Rural	Urban
1 2	3	4	5	6
1. Andhra Pradesh	-	-	1. Ellamalawar, Yellammalawandlu 2. Mang Garodi	
2. Arunachal Pradesh	1. Jalkeot 2. Lalbegi	1. Dugla, Dholi 2. Hira	1. Dugla, Dholi 2. Lalbegi 3. Mahara	1. Brittial Banta, Bania 2. Dugla, Dholi 3. Hira 4. Lalbegi 5. Mahara
3. Goa	-	-	1. Bhangi, Hadi	-
4. Gujarat	1. Mukri	-	1. Halleer 2. Mukri	- -
5. Haryana		1. Sansoi	1. Dagi 2. Darain 3. Dhogri, Dhangri, Siggi 4. Gagra 5. Marija, Marecha 6. Perna 7. Pherera 8. Sanhai 9. Sarera	1. Pherera 2. Sansoi
6. Himachal Pradesh	1. Sapela 2. Sirki-band	1. Gagra 2. Gandhila, Gandil Gondola 3. Perna 4. Sanhal 5. Sirkiband	1. Gagra 2. Sirkiband	1. Bazigar 2. Darain 3. Gagra 4. Gandhila, Gandil, Gondola 5. Nat 6. Sanhal 7. Sansi, Bhedkut, Manesh: 8. Sansoi 9. Sirkiband

1	2	3	4	5	6
7. Jammu & Kashmir		-	-	1. Watal	-
8. Karnataka		1. Mala Masti		1. Mahya-vanshi Dhed, Vankar, Maru 2. Mala Hannai 3. Mala Masti 4. Mavilan 5. Meghval, Menghvar 6. Panniandi 7. Sapari 8. Sindhollu, Chindollu	1. Adiya 2. Mala Sale, Netkani Maru 3. Meg-hval, Meng-hvar 4. Sapari
9. Kerala		-	1. Ajila 2. Bellara 3. Chandala 4. Hasla 5. Panchama	-	1. Bellara 2. Chand-ala 3. Goda-gali 4. Hasla 5. Mun-dala 6. Panchama
10. Madhya Pradesh		-	-	1. Muskhan	-
11. Maharashtra		-	-	1. Byagara	-
12. Manipur		-	1. Yaithibi	1. Sutradhar	-
13. Meghalaya		1. Dugla, Dholi 2. Jalkeot	-	1. Bansphor 2. Dugla, Dholi 3. Jalkeot	-
14. Mizoram		-	-	1. Bansphor 2. Bhuinmali, Mali 3. Namasudra	-
15. Orissa		-	1. Bajikar 2. Chachati	1. Audhelia 2. Panchama	1. Bajikar 2. Bavuri 3. Ghogia 4. Sabak-hia
16. Punjab		1. Sapela	-	1. Sanhai 1. Sapela	-

1	2	3	4	5	6
17.	Rajasthan	-	-	1. Mang, Matang, Minimadig 2. Mang Garedi, Mang Garudi	1. Bidakia
18.	Tamil Nadu	1. Koosa	-	1. Bellara 2. Godagali 3. Koosa 4. Mavilan 5. Nalakeyava 6. Raneyar	1. Ajila 2. Jamb-uvulu 3. Mavi-lan 4. Mun-dala 5. Sama-gara
19.	Tripura	-	1. Bhunar 2. Gur 3. Kalindi 4. Kanda 5. Keot 6. Musahar 7. Sabar	1. Dhenuar	1. Bhunar 2. Gur 3. Kalindi 4. Kan-ugh 5. Koir
20.	Uttar Pradesh	-	-		1. Banmanus
21.	Chandigarh	1. Bangali 2. Barar, Burar, Berar 3. Bhanjra 4. Gandhila, Gandil Gondola	1. Dagi 2. Nat 3.Sapela	1. Batwa 2. Bauria, Bawaria 3. Dhanak	1. Dagi 2. Darain 3. Gandhi-la, Gandil Gondola 4. Nat 5. Sapela 6. Sirk-iband
22.	Delhi	1. Bazigar 2. Madari 3. Sirkiband	-	1. Gharrami 2. Kachhandha 3. Kanjar, Giarah 4. Lalbegi 5. Mazhabi 6. Meghwal 7. Naribut 8. Sirkiband	-
23.	Pondicherry	1. Madiga	1. Mala, Mala Masti	-	1. Mala, Mala Masti 2. Vetan

Seurce : Main Table

ANNEXURE TABLE 4
LITERACY RATEAMONG SC/NON SC COMMUNITIES AND NAMES OF SC/NON SC COMMUNITIES

Sl. No.	*Literacy rate in the 1981 Census of* Non SC/ST communities	*Literacy rate in the 1981 Census of* SC communities	*Names of SC communities having a literacy rate above the literacy rate of* Non SC/ST communities	*Names of SC communities having a literacy rate above the literacy rate of* SC communities
1	2	3	4	5
			1. Andhra Pradesh	
	33.91	17.65	1. Anamuk (37.6)	1. Adi Andhra (27.5)
			2. Arwa Mala (36.8)	2. Adi Dravida (20.6)
			3. Chamar, Mochi, Muchi (34.2)	3. Aray Mala (31.9)
			4. Dhor (37.6)	4. Bariki (18.7)
			5. Mala Dasu (63.8)	5. Beda Jangam, Budga Jangam (18.5)
			6. Mitha Ayyalvar (37.6)	6. Chalavadi (19.0)
			7. Samagara (37.1)	7. Chambhar (20.0)
				8. Chandala (19.6)
				9. Ellamalawar, Yellammalawandlu (20.1)
				10. Godari (18.5)
				11. Holeya (20.4)
				12. Holeya Dasari (19.6)
				13. Kolupulvandlu (21.6)
				14. Madasi Kuruva, Madari Kuruva (32.4)
				15. Madiga Dasu, Mashteen (26.8)
				16. Mahar (18.8)
				17. Mala Hannai (20.0)
				18. Mala Dasari (31.6)
				19. Mala Hannai (20.0)
				20. Mala Jangam (27.3)
				21. Mala Sale, Netkani (19.1)

1	2	3	4	5
				22. Mala Sanyasi (21.6) 23. Mehtar (28.4) 24. Paky, Moti, Thoti (18.9) 25. Pambada, Pambanda (23.7) 26. Relli (24.2) 27. Sapru (21.4) 28. Sindhollu, Chindollu (26.3)
			2. Arunachal Pradesh	
	36.30	37.14	Nil, the rate being lower than the SC literacy rate	1. Brittial Bania, Bania (58.8) 2. Hira (55.5) 3. Jhalo, Malo, Jhalo-Malo (44.0) 4. Kaibartta, Jaliya (44.5) 5. Mahara (53.8) 6. Namasudra (39.0) 7. Patni (63.6) 8. Sutradhar (48.0)
			3. Assam	
			Not Available	
			4. Bihar	
	30.17	10.40	Nil	1. Bauri (11.1) 2. Chamar, Mochi (11.5) 3. Dabgar (22.2) 4. Dhobi (18.6) 5. Dusadh, Dhari, Dharhi (12.4) 6. Ghasi (14.6) 7. Halalkhor (19.3) 8. Hari, Mehtar, Bhangi (16.4) 9. Kanjar (11.2) 10. Kurariar (10.4) 11. Lalbegi (18.2) 12. Pan, Sawasi (27.0) 13. Pasi (17.6)

1	2	3	4	5
			5. Goa	
	57.69	36.10	1. Chambhar (58.90)	1. Bhangi, Hadi (44.7)
	57.69			2. Mahyavanshi, Vankar (38.6)
			6. Gujarat	
	48.14	39.79	1. Garoda, Garo (56.9) 2. Holaya, Holer (51.0) 3. Lingader (57.4)	1. Ager (47.6) 2. Bhambi, Bhambi, Asadaru, ... Rohit, Samgar (39.8) 3. Chalvadi, Channayya (43.1) 4. Chenna Dasar, Holeya Dasar (45.3) 5. Halsar, Haslar, Hulasvar, Halasvar (46.7) 6. Mahyavanshi, Dhed, Dhedh, Vankar, Maru Vankar, Antyaj (44.2) 7. Turi (46.6)
			7. Haryana	
	39.90	20.15	Nil	1. Ad-Dharmi (31.78) 2. Bangali(29.22) 3. Barar, Burar, Berar (21.21) 4. Chamar, Jatia Chamar, Rehgar, Raigar, Ramdasi, Ravidasi (23.58) 5. Chanal (22.52) 6. Kabirpanthi, Julaha (31.6) 7. Khatik (32.58) 8. Kori, Koli(26.48) 9. Megh (28.40) 10. Pasi (33.37)

1	2	3	4	5
				11. Pherera(20.83) 12. Sanhai (27.11) 13. Sanhal (26.71)
			8. Himachal Pradesh	
	47.37	31.50	1. Chhimbe, Dhobi (52.22)	1. Ad Dharmi(39.51)
			2. Gagra (50.0)	2. Balmik, Bhangi, Chuhra, Chura, Chuhre (45.85)
			3. Gandhila, Gandil Gondola (100.0)	3. Bandhela(33.33)
			4. Kamoh, Dagoli (61.85)	4. Patwal (34.88)
			5. Khatik (49.89)	5. Chamar, Jatia Chamar, Rehgar, Raigar, Ramdasi, Ravidasi, Ramdasia, Mochi (34.20)
			6. Phrera, Pherera (64.19)	
			7. Sanhal (83.33)	
				6. Darai, Daryai (35.27) 7. Dhanak(35.29) 8. Jogi (35.91) 9. Julaha, Julahe, Kabirpanthi, Keer (39.32) 10. Karoack (34.04) 11. Lohar (38.17) 12. Marija, Marecha (41.67) 13. Mazhabi (34.39) 14. Od (31.92) 15. Pasi (38.05) 16. Perna (33.33) 17. Sanhai (42.51) 18. Sansoi (37.36) 19. Sarde, Sarera, Sarare, Siryare, Sarehde (41.59) 20. Teli (33.01) 21. Thathiar, Thathera (43.3)

1	2	3	4	5
			9. Jammu & Kashmir	
	27.05	22.44	1. Basith (29.14) 2. Chamar or Ramdasia (27.87)	1. Jolaha (26.68) 2. Megh or Kabirpanthi (23.28)
			10. Karnataka	
	42.95	20.59	1. Anamuk (68.33) 2. Bant (61.97) 3. Ager 3. Bandi (64.06) 4. Ellamalwar, Yellammala-wandlu (53.40) 5. Kotegar, Metr (50.00) 6. Mundala (43.37) 7. Pallan (43.35) 8. Pambada (50.21) 9. Samban (50.70) 10. Valluvan (57.19)	1. Adi Andhra (36.74) 2. Adi Dravida (36.73) (33.29) 4. Ajila (26.13) 5. Aray Mala(34.39) 6. Arunthathiyar (25.36) 7. Baira (27.42) 8. Bakad (26.67) 9. Bakuda(39.48) 10. Bathada(26.12) 11. Beda Jangam, Budga Jangam (27.61) 12. Bellara (25.73) 13. Chalavadi, Chalvadi, Channayya (22.39) 14. Channa Dasar, Holaya Dasar (26.01) 15. Ganti Chores (29.73) 16. Garoda, Garo (29.46) 17. Godda (29.30) 18. Halleer (22.54) 19. Halsar, Haslar, Hulasvar, Halasvar(28.70) 20. Dhor, Kakkayya, Kankayya(37.69) 21. Holeya Dasari (23.34) 22. Kolupulvandlu (22.43)

1	2	3	4	5
				23. Korama (24.73) 24. Kudumban (41.50) 25. Kuravan (22.55) 26. Lingader (33.81) 27. Machala (34.34) 28. Mahar, Taral, Dhegu Megu (32.01) 29. Mahyavanshi, Dhed, Vankar Maru, Vankar (38.39) 30. Mala (31.11) 31. Mala Dasari (29.73) 32. Mala Hannai (22.50) 33. Mala Jangam (25.43) 34. Manne (21.26) 35. Masthi (32.50) 36.Meghval, Menghvar(31.82) 37. Moger (23.10) 38. Mukri (22.10) 39. Nadia, Hadi (32.2) 40. Nalkadaya (22.98) 41. Nalakeyava (24.55) 42. Nayadi (28.10) 43. Panchama (30.06) 44. Paraiyan, Paraya (23.06) 45. Paravan (20.70) 46. Raneyar (29.76) 47. Samagara (33.45) 48. Sindhollu, Chindollu (31.70) 49. Tirgar, Tirbanda (42.77)

1	2	3	4	5
			11. Kerala	
	72.50	55.96	1. Bharatar (79.76) 2. Paravan (73.10) 3. Pathiyan (74.34) 4. Perumannan (72.63) 5. Raneyar (72.97) 6. Velan (76.86)	1. Arunthathiyar (62.54) 2. Ayyanvar(68.62) 3. Bandi (66.67) 4. Chamar, Muchi (66.44) 5. Chandala (62.22) 6. Gosangi (65.54) 7. Kakkalan (59.80) 8. Kudumban(56.22) 9. Malayan (58.58) 10. Mannan (67.70) 11. Mundala (57.04) 12. Padannan (67.38) 13. Pambada (59.05) 14. Panan (56.02) 15. Paraiyan, Paryan, Sambavar (57.64) 16. Pulayan, Cheramar(61.52) 17. Pulaya Vettuvan (58.33) 18. Puthirai Vannan (67.50) 19. Samban (61.83) 20. Semman (72.42) 21. Thandan (63.94) 22. Valluvan (57.12) 23. Vannan (71.62) 24. Vettuvan (57.91)
			12. Madhya Pradesh	
	36.15	18.97	1. Pasi (42.68)	1. Audhelia (22.44) 2. Bahna, Bahana (24.41) 3. Beldar, Sunkar (20.07) 4. Bhangi, Mehtar, Balmik, Lalbegi, Dharkar (24.93) 5. Chadar (24.29) 6. Chitar (22.66)

1	2	3	4	5
				7. Dahait, Dahayat, Dahat (23.20) 8. Dhobi (20.78) 9. Dom, Dumar, Dome, Domar, Doris (33.06) 10. Ganda, Gandi (19.96) 11. Kanjar (22.02) 12. Katia, Patharia (29.54) 13. Khatik (34.82) 14. Koli, Kori (26.33) 15. Khangar, Kanera, Mirdha (20.25) 16. Mahar, Mehra, Mehar (31.67) 17. Mang, Mang Garodi, Mang Garudi, Dankhni Mang, Mang Mahasi, Madari, Garudi, Radhe Mang (27.58) 18. Moghia (22.0) 19. Silawat (22.10)
			13. Maharashtra	
	50.90	35.55	1. Aray Mala (51.29) 2. Arwa Mala (58.09) 3. Bakad, Bant (60.19) 4. Beda Jangam, Budga Jangam (59.44) 5. Khatik, Chikwa, Chikvi (54.96) 6. Mahyavanshi, Dhed, Vankar, Maru Vankar (69.79)	1. Ager (46.65) 2. Anamuk (43.97) 3. Bahna, Bahana (50.49) 4. Basor, Burud, Basar, Bansodi (45.69) 5. Bhambi, Bhambhi, Asadaru... ...Surjyaraamnaml (41.74) 6. Bhangi, Mehtar, Olgana... ....korar, Zadmalli (41.28) 7. Bindla (44.55)

1	2	3	4	5
			7. Mala (51.51)	8. Chenna Dasar, Holeya Dasari (37.68)
			8. Mala Jangam (55.66)	9. Dhor, Kakkayya, Kankayya, Dohor (48.51)
			9. Meghval, Menghvar (59.10)	
			10. Mitha Ayyalvar (58.42)	10. Dom, Dumar (43.90)
			11. Turi (58.18)	11. Ellamalvar, Yellammala-wandlu (44.47)
				12. Ganda, Gandi (40.81)
				13. Garoda, Garo (36.93)
				14. Ghasi, Ghasia (47.10)
				15. Halsar, Haslar, Hulasvar, Halasvar (50.41)
				16. Katia, Patharia (38.70)
				17. Khangar, Kanera, Mirdha (41.84)
				18. Kolupulvandlu (41.20)
				19. Kori (39.63)
				20. Lingader (50.50)
				21. Mahar, Mehra, Taral, Dhegu Megu (38.38)
				22. Mala Hannai (44.29)
				23. Mala Masti (46.67)
				24. Manne (37.21)
				25. Mashti (46.43)
				26. Nadia, Hadi (44.58)
				27. Pasi (45.76)
				28. Sansi (36.16)
				29. Tirgar, Tirbanca (48.27)

1	2	3	4	5
			14. Manipur	
	42.11	33.63	1. Dhupi, Dhobi (58.06) 2. Muchi, Ravidas (47.15)	1. Namasudra (39.66) 2. Patni (40.74)
			15. Meghalaya	
	44.97	25.78	1. Brittial Bania, Bania (55.65) 2. Hira (66.66) 3. Kaibartta 3. Jhalo, Malo (28.80) Jaliya (59.16) 4. Lalbegi (50.00) 5. Patni (46.30)	1. Bhuinmali, Mali (43.28) 2. Dhupi, Dhobi (39.61) 3. Jhalo-Malo 4. Sutradhar (41.85)
			16. Mizoram	
	63.53	84.44	1. Bhuinmali, Mali (66.67) 2. Dugla, Dholi (75.0) 3. Namasudra (83.33) 4. Patni (75.0)	1. Brittial Bania, Bania (100.00) 2. Dhupi, Dhobi (84.[illegible]) 3. Hira (100.00) 4. [illegible] Malo, [illegible] (100.00) [illegible], [illegible] (100.00) 6. [illegible] (100.00) 7. Mehtar, Bhangi (100.00) 8. Muchi, Rishi (93.33)
			17. Orissa	
	44.22	22.41	1. Bauti (47.23) 2. Musahar (58.62)	1. Adi Andhra (22.81) 2. Bari (32.64) 3. Bariki (31.17) 4. Bavuri (24.00) 5. Beldar (22.99) 6. Bhata (36.82) 7. Chakali (23.72) 8. Chamar, Mochi, Muchi, Satnami (23.75) 9. Chandala (23.49)

1	2	3	4	5
				10. Chandhai Maru (25.00)
				11. Cherua, Chhelia (25.56)
				12. Dewar (37.22)
				13. Dhoba, Dhobi (31.30)
				14. Dosadha(37.80)
				15. Ghogia (28.51)
				16. Godagali (29.17)
				17. Gokha (24.98)
				18. Haddi, Hadi, Hari (22.96)
				19. Irika (40.00)
				20. Kandra, Kandara (27.59)
				21. Katia (30.67)
				22. Kela (22.44)
				23. Khadala (22.67)
				24. Kodalo, Khodalo (23.94)
				25. Kori (26.57)
				26. Kurunga (22.90)
				27. Mahuria (24.40)
				28. Mala, Jhala, Malo, Zala (25.97)
				29. Mehtar, Bhangi (29.25)
				30. Nagarchi (32.89)
				31. Namasudra (30.13)
				32. Paidi (23.91)
				33. Pan, Pano (22.84)
				34. Pantanti (26.73)
				35. Pasi (37.43)
				36. Patial, Patikar, Patratanti, Patua (27.64)
				37. Samasi (25.45)
				38. Sanei (25.27)
				39. Sapari (23.26)
				40. Sinduria (34.46)
				41. Siyal (36.11)
				42. Tiar, Tior (30.65)
				43. Valamiki, Valmiki (22.91)

1	2	3	4	5
			18. Punjab	
	34.87	23.86	1. Ad Dharmi (40.43) 2. Chanal (35.97) 3. Dagi (61.11) 4. Kabirpanthi, Julaha(39.32) 5. Dumna, Mahasha, Doom (28.37) 6. Sarera (41.44)	1. Batwal(26.93) 2. Bhanjra (34.66) 3. Chamar, Jatia Chamar, Rehgar, Raigar, Ramdasi, Ravidasi (28.72) 4. Darain (28.20) 5. Sanhal (35.94) 6. Kori Koli (24.98) 7. Megh (30.89) 8. Pasi (24.98) 9. Pherera (27.96) 10. Sansoi (31.25)
			19. Rajasthan	
	29.31	14.04	1. Ad Dharmi (35.26) 2. Bargi, Vargi, Birgi (31.33) 3. Dabgar (33.10) 4. Jingar (37.86) 5. Pasi (33.93)	1. Aheri (15.68) 2. Bairwa, Berva (15.13) 3. Balai (14.49) 4. Bedia, Beria (19.65) 5. Bhangi, Chura, Mehtar, Olgana, Rukhi, Malkana, Halalkhor, Lalbegi, Balmiki, Valmiki Kodrra Zadmalli (15.29) 6. Chamar, Bhambhi, Bambhi.....Rohit, Samgar (15.33) 7. Chandal (28.42) 8. Dhanak, Dhanuk (15.43) 9. Dhankia(25.52) 10. Dhobi (19.23) 11. Dholi (20.52) 12. Dome, Dom (16.47) 13. Gandia(23.90) 14. Garancha, Gancha (20.82)

1	2	3	4	5
				15. Garo, Garura, Gurda, Garoda (21.53) 16. Kamad, Kamadia (19.25) 17. Khangar (21.20) 18. Khatik (23.84) 19. Koli, Kori (22.02) 20. Koria (19.18) 21. Mahar, Taral, Dhegu Megu (27.11) 22. Mang, Matang, Minimadig (25.73) 23. Mang Garodi, Mang Garudi (15.82) 24. Mehar (22.49) 25. Rawal (20.54) 26. Salvi (25.15) 27. Sarbhangi (16.48) 28. Sargara (14.32) 29. Turi (14.06) 30. Bhand (19.21)
			20. Sikkim	
	34.37	28.06		1. Damai (Nepali) (30.97)
			21. Tamil Nadu	
	51.01	29.22	1. Ajila (57.14)	1. Adi Andhra (35.46)
			2. Ayyanavar (64.79)	2. Adi Dravida (32.07)
			3. Bharatar (65.53)	3. Adi Karnataka (29.94)
			4. Chamar, Muchi (74.55)	4. Bakuda (31.82
			5. Chandala (72.97)	5. Bandi (38.89)
			6. Godagali (58.33)	6. Bellara (29.55)
			7. Godda (69.83)	7. Chalavadi (44.27)
			8. Kakkalan (66.67)	8. Cheruman (48.95)
			9. Karimpalan (55.56)	9. Devendrakulathan (46.69)

1	2	3	4	5
			10. Kavara (63.73)	10. Gosangi (29.30)
			11. Mannan (59.85)	11. Kanakkan, Padanna (43.75)
			12. Panan (77.90)	12. Koliyan (42.50)
			13. Paravan (61.87)	13. Kootan, Koodan (40.82)
			14. Pathiyan (60.87)	14. Maila (48.94)
			15. Semman (58.87)	15. Mundala (50.00)
			16. Vallon (54.81)	16. Pallan (30.32)
			17. Valluvan (52.66)	17. Palluvan (31.79)
			18. Vannan (64.50)	18. Pambada (40.22)
			19. Vetan (67.83)	19. Paraiyan, Paryan, Sambavar (30.92)
			20. Vettuvan (74.83)	20. Pulayan, Cheramar (30.41)
				21. Puthirai Vannan (36.10)
				22. Thandan (49.03)
				23. Tiruvalluvar (50.37)
				24. Vathirivan (50.99)
				25. Velan (41.82)
			22. Tripura	
	53.93	33.89	1. Kora (85.71)	1. Bhuimali (36.34)
				2. Dhenuar (46.15)
				3. Dhoba (39.54)
				4. Jalia Kaibarta (36.20)
				5. Kahar (39.46)
				6. Kan (37.50)
				7. Kanugh (51.85)
				8. Mahisyadas (41.99)
				9. Mali (36.39)
				10. Patni (35.99)
			23. Uttar Pradesh	
	30.45	14.96	1 Bhantu (48.78)	1. Baiswar (28.30)
			2. Ghasiya (31.87)	2. Balai (15.37)
				3. Barwar (19.28)
				4. Beriya (23.32)
				5. Bhuyiar (20.17)
				6. Boria (21.01)

1	2	3	4	5
				7. Chamar, Dhusia, Jhusia, Jatava (15.98) 8. Dabgar (23.11) 9. Dhangar (20.48) 10. Dhanuk (15.82) 11. Dhobi (15.76) 12. Gharami (26.18) 13. Gond (14.96) 14. Gual (16.63) 15. Habura (16.07) 16. Hela (24.48) 17. Karwal (15.16) 18. Khairaha (17.55) 19. Khatik (17.90) 20. Kori (15.24) 21. Korwa (15.61) 22. Majhwar (17.35) 23. Mazhabi (23.71) 24. Patari (15.99) 25. Rawat (15.38) 26. Sanaurhiya (30.12) 27. Sansiya (27.55) 28. Shilpkar (25.90)
			24. West Bengal	
	48.12	24.37	1. Sunri (excluding (Saha) (54.95)	1. Baiti (32.92) 2. Damai (Nepali) (37.46) 3. Dhoba, Dhobi (38.79) 4. Gonrhi (25.20) 5. Halalkhor (29.89) 6. Jalia Kaibarta (30.16) 7. Jhalo Malo, Malo (25.51) 8. Kadar (25.50) 9. Kami (Nepali) (34.70) 10. Kandra (31.49) 11. Khatik (30.00) 12. Konwar (45.69) 13. Kurariar (25.14) 14. Lalbegi (25.87) 15. Namasudra (35.87)

1	2	3	4	5
				16. Nat (31.25) 17. Pan, Sawasi (27.25) 18. Pasi (26.79) 19. Patni (25.44) 20. Pod, Poundra (34.48) 21. Rajbanshi (24.65) 22. Sarki (Nepali) (27.32) 23. Tiyar (25.33)
			25. Chandigarh	
	69.33	37.07	1. Dhogri, Dhangri, Siggi (71.43) 2. Perna (83.33) 3. Pherera (75.00)	1. Ad Dharmi (65.41) 2. Bangali (63.27) 3. Batwal (53.66) 4. Bhanjra (57.00) 5. Chamar, Jatia Chamar, Rehgar, Raigar, Ramdasi, Ravidasi (45.25) 6. Dumna,Mahasha, Doom (54.46) 7. Gagra (40.54) 8. Kabirpanthi, Julaha (44.05) 9. Khatik (41.28) 10. Marija, Marecha (55.26) 11. Mazhabi (56.78) 12. Od (37.14) 13. Sanhai (68.54) 14. Sanhal (43.37) 15. Sarera (61.40)
			26. Dadra & Nagar Haveli	
	64.41	51.20	—	1. Mahyavanshi, Dhed (61.08)
			27. Daman & Diu	
	48.96	54.43	—	1. Mahar (83.33) 2. Mahyavanshi, Vankar (60.89)
			28. Delhi	
	66.44	39.30	Nil	1. Adi Dharmi (62.16)

1	2	3	4	5
				2. Agria (41.88) 3. Chamar, Chanwar, Chamar, Jatav or Jatav Chamar, Mochi, Ramdasia, Ravidasi, Raidasi, Rehgarh or Raigar (43.31) 4. Chohra (Sweeper) (40.56) 5. Dhobi (43.56) 6. Gharrami (41.07) 7. Julaha (Weaver) (45.37) 8. Kabirpanthi (42.73) 9. Lalbegi (47.01) 10. Mallah (43.74) 11. Mazhabi (59.56) 12. Perna (40.16) 13. Sansi or Bhedkut (40.12)
			29. Pondicherry	
	60.32	32.36	1. Madiga (61.54)	1. Adi Andhra (41.06) 2. Chakkiliyan (35.88) 3. Valuvan (49.26)

Source : *Census of India, 1981*, Series 1 to 32, Part IX (1), SC I.

ANNEXURE TABLE V

LIST OF SCHEDULED CASTES WHOSE LITERACY RATES WERE HIGHER THAN THE RESPECTIVE UNIT'S SC LITERACY RATE AND NON-SC/ST LITERACY RATE IN THE 1981 CENSUS, THEIR POPULATION AND THE CATEGORY TO WHICH THEY BELONG.

Scheduled Castes whose Literacy Rate was Higher than the non-SC/ST Literacy Rate				*SCs whose Literacy Rate was Higher than the SC Literacy Rate but lower than the non-SC/ST Literacy Rate*			
Sl. No.	*Name of Scheduled Caste*	*Population*	*Category*	*Sl. No.*	*Name of Scheduled Caste*	*Population*	*Category*
1	2	3	4	5	6	7	8
			Andhra	**Pradesh**			
1.	Anamuk	85	V	1.	Adi Andhra	698,857	II
2.	Arwa Mala	22,443	III	2.	Adi Dravida	95,340	II
3.	Chamar, Mochi, Muchi	12,881	III	3.	Aray Mala	1,395	III
				4.	Bariki	11,835	III
4.	Dhor	2,443	IV	5.	Beda Jangam Budga Jangam	12,024	III
5.	Mala Dasu	13,384	III				
6.	Mitha Ayyalvar	2,777	IV	6.	Chalavadi	1,740	IV
7.	Samagara	1,845	IV	7.	Chambhar	520	V
		55,885	(.70%)	8.	Chandala	184	V
				9.	Ellamalawar, Yellammalawandlu	358	V
				10.	Godari	835	IV
				11.	Holeya	664	V
				12.	Holeya Dasari	620	V
				13.	Kolupulvandlu	966	IV
				14.	Madasi Kuruva Madari Kuruva	3,550	IV
				15.	Madiga Dasu, Mashteen	4,419	IV
				16.	Mahar	11,437	III
				17.	Mala	2,896,642	I
				18.	Mala Dasari	18,416	III
				19.	Mala Hannai	70	VI
				20.	Mala Jangam	4,897	IV
				21.	Mala Sale, Netkani	81,270	II
				22.	Mala Sanyasi	300	V
				23.	Mehtar	4,553	IV
				24.	Paky, Moti, Thoti	7,826	IV
				25.	Pambada, Pambanda	2,333	IV
				26.	Relli	77,324	III
				27.	Sapru	495	V
				28.	Sindhollu, Chindollu	2,383	IV
					3,941,253	(49,50%)	

1	2	3	4	5	6	7	8
				2. Arunachal Pradesh			
					1. Brittial Bania, Bania	102	II
					2. Hira	9	III
					3. Jhalo, Malo, Jhalo-Malo	75	II
					4. Kaibartta, Jaliya	764	I
					5. Mahara	13	III
					6. Namasudra	540	I
					7. Patni	11	III
					8. Sutradhar	100	II
						1,614	(55.29%)
				3. Assam			
					Not Available		
				4. Bihar			
					1. Bauri	103,114	II
					2. Chumar, Mochi	2,978,562	I
					3. Dabgar	5,508	IV
					4. Dhobi	553,380	II
					5. Dusadh, Dhari, Dharhi	2,655,832	I
					6. Ghasi	84,756	III
					7. Halalkhor	5,463	IV
					8. Hari, Mehtar, Bhangi	156,349	II
					9. Kanjar	1,780	IV
					10. Kurariar	4,449	IV
					11. Lalbegi	932	V
					12. Pan, Sawasi	28,931	III
					13. Pasi	463,601	II
						7,042,657 (69.44%)	
				5. Goa			
	1. Chambhar	6,438	I		1. Bhangi, Hadi	355	II
		6,438			2. Mahyavanshi, Vankar	119	III
		(31.22%)				474 (2.30%)	
				6. Gujarat			
	1. Garoda, Garo	52,549	II		1. Ager	151	V
	2. Holaya, Holer	92	V		2. Bhambi, Bhambhi... ...Rohit, Samgar	664,086	I
	3. Lingader	94	V				
		52,735			3. Chalvadi, Channayya	58	VI
		(2.16%)			(2.1690)		

1	2	3	4	5	6	7	8
				4.	Chenna Dasar, Holeya Dasar	139	V
				5.	Halsar, Haslar, Hulasvar, Halasvar	154	V
				6.	Mahyavanshi, Dhed,Dhedh, , Vankar, Maru Vankar, Antyaj	1,049,837	I
				7.	Turi	12,846	III
						1,727,271 (70.84%)	
			7. Haryana				
				1.	Ad-Dharmi	689	IV
				2.	Bangali	674	IV
				3.	Barar, Burar, Berar,	957	IV
				4.	Chamar, Jatia Chamar, Rehgar, Raigar, Ramdasi Ravidasi	1,297,339	I
				5.	Chanal	293	IV
				6.	Kabirpanthi, Julaha	31,503	II
				7.	Khatik	32,259	II
				8.	Kori, Koli	34,303	II
				9.	Megh	11,265	III
				10.	Pasi	6,748	III
				11.	Pherera	24	VI
				12.	Sanhai	59	V
				13.	Sanhal	35	V
						1,416,148 (57.47%)	
			8. Himachal Pradesh				
1.	Chhimbe, Dhobi	12,166	II	1.	Ad Dharmi	15,098	II
2.	Gagra	6	VI	2.	Balmiki, Bhangi, Chuhra, Chura, Chuhre	19,764	II
3.	Gandhila, Gandil	6	VI				V
	Gondola			3.	Bandhela	30	V
				4.	Batwal	10,290	III
4.	Kamoh, Dagoli	249	IV	5.	Chamar, Jatia Chamar,		
5.	Khatik	449	IV		Rehgar, Raigar, Ramdasi, Ravidasi, Ramdasia,		
6.	Phrera, Pherera	1,109	III		Mochi	286,668	I
7.	Sanhal	12	V	6.	Darai, Daryai	6,385	III
		13,997 (1-33%)		7.	Dhanak	34	V

1	2	3	4	5	6	7	8
				8.	Jogi	11,183	II
				9.	Julaha, Julahe, Kabirpanthi, Keer	102,838	II
				10.	Karoack	47	V
				11.	Lohar	112,389	I
				12.	Marija, Marecha	12	V
				13.	Mazhabi	221	IV
				14.	Od	639	IV
				15.	Pasi	226	IV
				16.	Perna	21	V
				17.	Sanhai	1,675	III
				18.	Sansoi	1,052	III
				19.	Sarde, Sarera, Sarare, Siryare, Sarehde	9,663	III
				20.	Teli	3,768	III
				21.	Thathiar, Thathera	709	IV
						582,712 (55.29%)	

9. Jammu & Kashmir

1	2	3	4	5	6	7	8
1.	Basith	9,962	II	1.	Jolaha	371	IV
2.	Chamar or Ramdasia	122,292	I	2.	Mehg or Kabirpanthi	199,242	I
		132,254 (26.59%)				199,613 (40.13%)	

10. Karnataka

1	2	3	4	5	6	7	8
1.	Anamuk	60	V	1.	Adi Andhra	29,516	III
2.	Bant	1,746	IV	2.	Adi Dravida	518,860	II
3.	Bandi	2,958	IV	3.	Ager	4,815	IV
4.	Ellamalwar, Yellammalawandlu	103	V	4.	Ajila·	1,301	IV
5.	Kotegar, Metri	16,675	III	5.	Aray Mala	189	V
6.	Mundala	20,623	III	6.	Arunthathiyar	899	IV
7.	Pallan	745	IV	7.	Baira	4,223	IV
8.	Pambada	683	IV	8.	Bakad	990	IV
9.	Samban	71	V	9.	Bakuda	1,525	IV
10.	Valluvan	1,002	IV	10.	Bathada	1,026	IV
		44,666 (.80%)		11.	Beda Jangam, Budga Jangam	3,035	IV
				12.	Bellara	1,263	IV
				13.	Chalavadi, Chalvadi, Channayya	103,596	II
				14.	Channa Dasar, Holaya Dasar	17,732	III

1	2	3	4	5	6	7	8
				15.	Dhor, Kakkayya, Kankayya	22,432	III
				16.	Ganti Chores	3,020	IV
				17.	Garoda, Garo	129	V
				18.	Godda	1,280	IV
				19.	Halleer	2,790	IV
				20.	Halsar, Haslar, Hulasvar, Halasvar	7,902	III
				21.	Holeya Dasari	2,939	IV
				22.	Kolupulvandlu	107	V
				23.	Korama	79,167	II
				24.	Kudumban	147	V
				25.	Kuravan	1,335	IV
				26.	Lingader	139	V
				27.	Machala	99	V
				28.	Mahar, Taral, Dhegu Megu	50,620	III
				29.	Mahyavanshi, Dhed, Vankar Maru, Vankar	719	IV
				30.	Mala	10,1439	III
				31.	Mala Dasari	2,193	IV
				32.	Mala Hannai	40	VI
				33.	Mala Jangam	291	V
				34.	Manne	174	V
				35.	Masthi	80	VI
				36.	Meghval, Menghvar	22	VI
				37.	Moger	45,113	III
				38.	Mukri	7,669	III
				39.	Nadia, Hadi	118	V
				40.	Nalkadaya	483	V
				41.	Nalakeyava	4,928	IV
				42.	Nayadi	1,434	IV
				43.	Panchama	785	IV
				44.	Paraiyan, Paraya	2,307	IV
				45.	Paravan	2,227	IV
				46.	Raneyar	2,553	IV
				47.	Samagara	54,433	III
				48.	Sindhollu, Chindollu	41	VI
				49.	Tirgar, Tirbanda	173	V
						996,648 (17.81%)	
					11. Kerala		
1.	Bharatar	1,892	IV	1.	Arunthathiyar	1,308	IV
2.	Paravan	42,884	II	2.	Ayyanvar	10,079	III
3.	Pathiyan	9,508	III	3.	Bandi	24	VI
4.	Perumannan	34,940	II	4.	Chamar, Muchi	298	IV

1	2	3	4	5	6	7	8
5.	Raneyar	148	V	5.	Chandala	90	V
6.	Velan	58,796	II	6.	Gosangi	769	IV
		148,168		7.	Kakkalan	5,487	III
		(5.81%)		8.	Kudumban	3,368	III
				9.	Malayan	11,561	III
				10.	Mannan	51,902	II
				11.	Mundala	291	IV
				12.	Padannan	5,015	III
				13.	Pambada	105	V
				14.	Panan	40,964	II
				15.	Paraiyan, Paryan, Sambavar	189,241	II
				16.	Pulayan, Cheramar	845,604	I
				17.	Pulaya Vettuvan	1,008	IV
				18.	Puthirai Vannan	280	IV
				19.	Samban	2,486	IV
				20.	Semman	1,142	IV
				21.	Thandan	202,064	II
				22.	Valluvan	13,488	III
				23.	Vannan	34,068	II
				24.	Vettuvan	111,436	II
						1,532,078	
						(60.10%)	

12. Madhya Pradesh

1	2	3	4	5	6	7	8
1.	Pasi	30,310	III	1.	Audhelia	2,794	IV
		30,310		2.	Bahna, Bahana	1,835	IV
					(0.41%)		
				3.	Beldar, Sunkar	17,618	III
				4.	Bhangi, Mehtar, Balmik Lalbegi, Dharkar	222,039	II
				5.	Chadar	41,527	III
				6.	Chitar	428	V
				7.	Dahait, Dahayat, Dahat	37,706	III
				8.	Dhobi	22,318	III
				9.	Dom, Dumar, Dome, Domar, Doris	39,874	III
				10.	Ganda, Gandi	205,166	II
				11.	Kanjar	8,553	III
				12.	Katia, Patharia	95,647	II
				13.	Khatik	75,068	II
				14.	Koli, Kori	379,138	II
				15.	Khangar, Kanera, Mirdha	96,529	II

1	2	3	4	5	6	7	8
				16.	Mahar, Mehra, Mehar	577.240	II
				17.	Mang, Mang Garodi, Mang Garudi, Dankhni Mang, Mang Mahasi, Madari, Garudi, Radhe Mang	17,738	III
				18.	Moghia	21,289	III
				19.	Silawat	23,832	III
						1,886,539 (25.64%)	

13. Maharashtra

1	2	3	4	5	6	7	8
1.	Aray Mala	232	V	1.	Ager	3,846	IV
2.	Arwa Mala	241	V	2.	Anamuk	116	V
3.	Bakad, Bant	736	IV	3.	Bahna, Bahana	303	V
4.	Beda Jangam, Budga Jangam	27,994	III	4.	Basor, Burud, Basar, Bansodi	34,206	III
5.	Khatik, Chikwa, Chikvi	55,036	II	5.	Bhambi, Bhambhi... ...Surjyaramnami	865,500	I
6.	Mahyavanshi, Dhed, Vankar, Maru Vankar	13,555	III	6.	Bhangi, Mehtar... ... Korar, Zadmalli	133,386	II
7.	Mala	11,890	III	7.	Bindla	303	V
8.	Mala Jangam	17,595	III	8.	Chenna Dasar, Holaya Dasar, Holeya Dasari	613	IV
9.	Meghval, Menghvar	29,310	III	9.	Dhor, Kakkayya, Kankayya, Dohor	68,509	II
10.	Mitha Ayyalvar	202	V	10.	Dom, Dumar	6,070	III
11.	Turi	275	V	11.	Ellammalavar, Yellammalavandlu	12,484	III
		157,066 (3.51%)		12.	Ganda, Gandi	615	IV
				13.	Garoda, Garo	352	V
				14.	Ghasi, Ghasia	1,983	IV
				15.	Halsar, Haslar, Hulasvar, Halasvar	123	V
				16.	Katia, Patharia	3,207	IV
				17.	Khangar, Kanera, Mirdha	858	IV
				18.	Kolupulvandlu	517	IV
				19.	Kori	17,506	III
				20.	Lingader	64,975	II
				21.	Mahar, Mehra, Taral, Dhegu Megu	1,648,269	I

1	2	3	4	5	6	7	8
				22.	Mala Hannai	70	VI
				23.	Mala Masti	60	VI
				24.	Manne	1,752	IV
				25.	Mashti	112	V
				26.	Nadia, Hadi	249	V
				27.	Pasi	11,995	III
				28.	Sansi	531	IV
				29.	Tirgar, Tirbanda	1,154	IV
						2,879,664	
						(64,28%)	
			14. Manipur				
1.	Dhupi, Dhobi	186	II	1.	Namasudra	2,423	I
2.	Muchi, Ravida	193	II	2.	Patni	2,793	I
		379				5,216	
		(2.13%)				(29.38%)	
			15. Meghalaya				
1.	Brittial Bania, Bania	115	II	1.	Bhuinmali, Mali	201	II
2.	Hira	48	III	2.	Dhupi, Dhobi	313	II
3.	Kaibartta, Jaliya	191	II	3.	Jhalo, Malo, Jhalo-Malo	1,062	I
4.	Lalbegi	30	III	4.	Sutradhar	270	II
5.	Patni	54	III			1,836	
		438				(33.43%)	
		(7.98%)					
			16. Mizoram				
1.	Bhuinmali, Mali	3	II	1.	Brittial Bania, Bania	2	II
2.	Dugla, Dholi	4	II	2.	Dhupi, Dhobi	33	I
3.	Namasudra	6	II	3.	Hira	3	II
4.	Patni	4	II	4.	Jhalo, Malo, Jhalo-Malo	1	III
		17		5.	Kaibartta, Jaliya	5	II
		(12.59%)		6.	Mahara	6	II
				7.	Mehtar, Bhangi	10	II
				8.	Muchi, Rishi	15	I
						75	
						(55.56%)	
			17. Orissa				
1.	Bauti	307	V	1.	Adi Andhra	3,621	IV
2.	Musahar	29	VI	2.	Bari	144	V
		336		3.	Bariki	12,357	III
		(.0087%)		4.	Bavuri	50	V
				5.	Beldar	2,440	IV
				6.	Bhata	4,508	III
				7.	Chakali	215	V

1	2	3	4	5	6	7	8
				8.	Chamar, Mochi, Muchi, Satnami	109,576	II
				9.	Chandala	5,581	III
				10.	Chandhai Maru	28	VI
				11.	Cherua,Chhelia	759	IV
				12.	Dewar	4,250	III
				13.	Dhoba, Dhobi	418,383	I
				14.	Dosadha	455	IV
				15.	Ghogia	656	IV
				16.	Godagali	24	VI
				17.	Gokha	116,226	II
				18.	Haddi, Hadi, Hari	133,625	II
				19.	Irika	270	V
				20.	Kandra, Kandara	316,367	II
				21.	Katia	1,200	IV
				22.	Kela	13,344	III
				23.	Khadala	50,965	II
				24.	Kodalo, Khodalo	330	V
				25.	Kori	286	V
				26.	Kurunga	2,371	IV
				27.	Mahuria	4,286	III
				28.	Mala, Jhala, Malo, Zala	6,118	III
				29.	Mehtar, Bhangi	2,332	IV
				30.	Nagarchi	225	V
				31.	Namasudra	76,316	II
				32.	Paidi	343	V
				33.	Pan, Pano	806,514	I
				34.	Pantanti	27,210	III
				35.	Pasi	537	IV
				36.	Patial, Patikar, Patratanti, Patua	34,774	III
				37.	Samasi	1,214	IV
				38.	Sanei	1.005	IV
				39.	Sapari	129	V
				40.	Sinduria	177	V
				41.	Siyal	18,677	III
				42.	Tiar, Tior	20,140	III
				43.	Valamiki, Valmiki	1,960	IV
						2,199,988 (56.91%)	
				18. Punjab			
1.	Ad Dharmi	680,132	I	1.	**Batwal**	9,367	II
2.	Chanal	139	V	2.	**Bhanjra**	3,557	III

1	2	3	4	5	6	7	8
3.	Dagi	54	V	3.	Chamar, Jatia Chamar, Rehgar, Raigar, Ramdasi, Ravidasi	1,221,145	I
4.	Kabirpanthi, Julaha	56,888	II				
5.	Sanhal	192	V	4.	Darain	156	V
				5.	Dumna, Mahasha, Doom	124,924	II
6.	Sarera	10,238	III	6.	Kori, Koli	5,625	III
		747,643		7.	Megh	78,405	II
		(16.57%)		8.	Pasi	5,593	III
				9.	Pherera	279	V
				10.	Sansoi	320	V
						1,449,398	
						(32.12%)	
				19. Rajasthan			
1.	Adi Dharmi	780	IV	1.	Aheri	2,736	IV
2.	Bargi, Vargi, Birgi	3,725	IV	2.	Bairwa, Berwa	429,625	II
				3.	Balai	462,925	II
3.	Dabgar	1,166	IV	4.	Bedia, Beria	2,361	IV
4.	Jingar	12,327	III	5.	Bhand	12,058	III
5.	Pasi	943	IV	6.	Bhangi, Chura... Korar, Zadmalli	263,565	II
		18,941	...	7.	Chamar, Bhambhi... ...Rohit, Samgar	1,872,133	I
		(0.32%)		8.	Chandal	1,105	IV
				9.	Dhanak, Dhanuk	82,234	II
				10.	Dhankia	6,477	III
				11.	Dhobi	104,252	II
				12.	Dholi	72,282	II
				13.	Dome, Dom	3,692	IV
				14.	Gandia	159	V
				15.	Garancha, Gancha	5,168	IV
				16.	Garo, Garura, Gurda, Garoda	28,888	III
				17.	Kamad, Kamadia	6,270	III
				18.	Khangar	4,320	IV
				19.	Khatik	215,089	II
				20.	Koli, Kori	265,767	II
				21.	Koria	2,794	IV
				22.	Mahar, Taral, Dhogu Magu	7,635	III
				23.	Mang, Matang, Minimadig	241	V
				24.	Mang Garodi, Mang Garudi	177	V
				25.	Mehar	31,450	III

1	2	3	4	5	6	7	8
				26.	Rawal	12,649	III
				27.	Salvi	19,409	III
				28.	Sarbhangi	613	IV
				29.	Sargara	77,169	II
				30.	Turi	2,041	IV
						3,995,284	
						(68.43%)	
					20. Sikkim		
				1.	Damai (Nepali)	5,980	I
						5,980	
						(32.71%)	
					21. Tamil Nadu		
				1.	Adi Andhra	50,391	III
1.	Ajila	35	VI	2.	Adi Dravida	3,831,152	I
2.	Ayyanavar	1,224	IV	3.	Adi Karnataka	30,073	III
3.	Bharatar	1,790	IV	4.	Bakuda	198	V
4.	Chamar, Muchi	165	V	5.	Bandi	486	V
5.	Chandala	37	VI	6.	Bellara	44	VI
6.	Godagali	24	VI	7.	Chalavadi	131	V
7.	Godda	116	V	8.	Cheruman	1,673	IV
8.	Kakkalan	66	VI	9.	Devendrakulathan	33,528	III
9.	Karimpalan	9	VI	10.	Gosangi	157	V
10.	Kavara	3,711	IV	11.	Kanakkan, Padanna	176	V
11.	Mannan	274	V	12.	Koliyan	7,509	III
12.	Panan	209	V	13.	Kootan, Koodan	147	V
13.	Paravan	1,634	IV	14.	Maila	47	VI
14.	Pathiyan	23	VI	15.	Mundala	26	VI
15.	Semman	992	IV	16.	Pallan	993,070	I
16.	Vallon	104	V	17.	Palluvan	151	V
17.	Valluvan	63,253	III	18.	Pambada	624	V
18.	Vannan	4,566	IV	19.	Paraiyan, Paryan, Sambavar	824,337	I
19.	Vetan	774	IV	20.	Pulayan, Cheramar	6,581	IV
20.	Vettuvan	143	V	21.	Puthirai Vannan	17,962	III
		79,149		22.	Thandan	2,466	IV
		(1.07%)		23.	Tiruvalluvar	3,828	IV
				24.	Vathiriyan	302	V
				25.	Velan	318	V
						5,805,377	
						(78.16%)	
					22. Tripura		
1.	Kora	14	V	1.	Bhuimali	798	III
		14(.0045%)		2.	Dhenuar	13	V
				3.	Dhoba	34,274	I
				4.	Jalia Kaibarta	52,612	I

1	2	3	4	5	6	7	8
				5.	Kahar	223	IV
				6.	Kan	8	V
				7.	Kanugh	81	IV
				8.	Mahisyadas	53,751	I
				9.	Mali	28,643	II
				10.	Patni	3,268	II
						173,671 (55.95%)	
				23. Uttar Pradesh			
1.	Bhantu	6,663	IV	1.	Baiswar	16,145	IV
2.	Ghasiya	4,531	IV	2.	Balai	1,321	V
		11,194 (.048%)		3.	Barwar	12,001	IV
				4.	Beriya	19,504	IV
				5.	Bhuyiar	12,630	IV
				6.	Boria	2,004	V
				7.	Chamar, Dhusia, Jhusia, Jatava	12,914,218	I
				8.	Dabgar	3,202	V
				9.	Dhanuk	340,473	II
				10.	Dhangar	20,027	IV
				11.	Dhobi	1,423,574	II
				12.	Gharami	615	V
				13.	Gond	204,638	III
				14.	Gual	7,491	IV
				15.	Habura	3,529	IV
				16.	Hela	29,837	IV
				17.	Karwal	12,154	IV
				18.	Khairaha	809	V
				19.	Khatik	496,944	II
				20.	Kori	1,381,588	II
				21.	Korwa	1,734	V
				22.	Majhwar	12,978	IV
				23.	Mazhabi	6,781	IV
				24.	Patari	1,257	V
				25.	Rawat	53,727	III
				26.	Sanaurhiya	249	V
				27.	Sansiya	657	V
				28.	Shilpkar	514,877	II
						17,494,964 (74.59%)	
				24. West Bengal			
1.	Sunri (lexcluding Saha)	252,331	II	1.	Baiti	10,034	IV
		252,331 (2.10%)		2.	Damai (Nepali)	18,842	III
				3.	Dhoba, Dhobi	251,737	II
				4.	Gonrhi	14,832	III
				5.	Halalkhor	1,348	IV

1	2	3	4	5	6	7	8
				6.	Jalia Kaibarta	318,344	II
				7.	Jhalo Malo, Malo	154,557	II
				8.	Kadar	9,782	IV
				9.	Kami (Nepali)	42,493	III
				10.	Kandra	65,183	III
				11.	Khatik	4,862	IV
				12.	Konwar	2,841	IV
				13.	Kurariar	1,416	IV
				14.	Namasudra	1,692,233	I
				15.	Lalbegi	1,179	V
				16.	Nat	3,376	IV
				17.	Pan, Sawasi	9,328	IV
				18.	Pasi	21,367	III
				19.	Patni	22,466	III
				20.	Pod, Poundra	1,536,197	I
				21.	Rajbanshi	2,258,760	I
				22.	Sarki (Nepali)	11,292	IV
				23.	Tiyar	82,108	III
						6,534,577 (54.45%)	
	25. Chandigarh						
1.	Dhogri, Dhangri, Siggi	21	IV	1.	Ad Dharmi	1,431	II
				2.	Bangali	49	IV
2.	Perna	18	IV	3.	Batwal	41	IV
3.	Pherera	12	IV	4.	Bhanjra	207	III
		51	(.80%)	5.	Chamar, Jatia, Chammar, Rehgar, Raigar, Ramdasi, Ravidasi	20,128	I
				6.	Dumna, Mahasha, Doom	112	III
				7.	Gagra	37	IV
				8.	Kabirpanthi, Julaha	2,109	II
				9.	Khatik	1,170	II
				10.	Marija, Marecha	38	IV
				11.	Mazhabi	856	II
				12.	Od	35	IV
				13.	Sarfhai	89	III
				14.	Sanhal	19	IV
				15.	Sarera	215	III
						26,536 (41.71%)	
	26. Dadra & Nagar Haveli						
				1.	Mahyavanshi, Dhed	943	I
						943 (46.20%)	
	27. Daman & Diu						
				1.	Mahar	6	IV

1	2	3	4	5	6	7	8
				2.	Mahyavanshi, Vankar	1,759	I
						1,765 (62.74%)	
					28. Delhi		
				1.	Adi Dharmi	4,882	III
				2.	Agria	1,139	III
				3.	Chamar, Chanwar, Chamar, Jatav or Jatav Chamar, Mochi,Ramdasia, Ravidasi, Raidasi, Rehgarh or Raigar	411.316	I
				4.	Chohra (Sweeper)	3,272	III
				5.	Dhobi	59,675	II
				6.	Gharrami	280	IV
				7.	Julaha (Weaver)	43,024	II
				8.	Kabirpanthi	4,334	III
				9.	Lalbegi	134	IV
				10.	Mallah	17,344	II
				11.	Mazhabi	858	IV
				12.	Perna	371	IV
				13.	Sansi or Bhedhut	5,915	III
						552, 544 (49.26%)	
					29. Pondicherry		
1.	Madiga	39	IV	1.	Adi Andhra	2,148	II
		39	(.04%)	2.	Chakkiliyan	1,558	II
				3.	Valuvan	2,783	II
						6,489 (6.71%)	

Category I- Very Large communities having 10% or more of total SC population.

Category II - Large communities having a population between 10% and 1% of total SC population.

Category III - Small communities having a population between 1% and .1% of total SC population.

Category IV - Very small communities having a population between .1% and .01% of total SC population.

Category V - Negligible communities having a population between .01% and .001% of total SC population.

Category VI - Most negligible communities having a population less than .001% of total SC population.

Source : Census of India, 1981, Series 2 to 32, part IX (1), SCI.

ANNEXURE TABLE VI

LIST OF SCHEDULED CASTES WHOSE LITERACY RATES WERE HIGHER THAN THE RESPECTIVE STATE'S SC LITERACY RATE IN ALL THE THREE SUCCESSIVE CENSUSES OF 1961-81, THEIR POPULATION ACCORDING TO THE 1981 CENSUS AND THE CATEGORY TO WHICH THEY BELONG

Sl. No.	Name of Scheduled Castes	Population According to the 1981 Census	Category No.
1	2	3	4
	1. Andhra Pradesh		
1.	Adi Andhra	698.857	II
2.	Arav Mala	1,395	IV
3.	Arwa Mala	22,443	III
4.	Chalavadi	1,740	IV
5.	Chamar, Mochi, Muchi	12,881	III
6.	Dhor	2,443	IV
7.	Godari	835	IV
8.	Holeya Dasari	620	V
9.	Kolupulvandlu	966	IV
10.	Madasi Kuruva, Madari Kuruva	3,550	IV
11.	Madiga Dasu, Mashteen	4,419	IV
12.	Mala	2,896,642	I
13.	Mala Dasari	18,416	III
14.	Mala Dasu	13,384	III
15.	Mala Jangam	4,897	IV
16.	Mala Sanyasi	300	V
17.	Mehtar	4,353	IV
18.	Mitha Ayyalvar	2,777	IV
19.	Paky, Moti, Thoti	7,826	IV
20.	Pambada, Pambanda	2,333	IV
21.	Relli	77,324	III
22.	Samagara	1,845	IV
23.	Sindhollu, Chindollu	2,383	IV
	Total	3,782,629 (47.51%)	
	2. Arunachal Pradesh		
1.	Brittial Bania, Bania	102	II
2.	Hira	9	III
3.	Jhalo, Malo, Jhalo-Malo	75	II
4.	Mahara	13	III
5.	Namasudra	540	I
6.	Patni	11	III
7.	Sutradhar	100	II
	Total	850 (29.12%)	

1	2	3	4
	3. Assam		
	Not Available		
	4. Bihar		
1.	Chamar, Mochi	2,978,562	I
2.	Dabgar	5,508	IV
3.	Dhobi	553,380	II
4.	Dusadh, Dhari, Dharhi	2,655,832	I
5.	Ghasi	84,756	III
6.	Halalkhor	5,463	IV
7.	Hari, Mehtar, Bhangi	156,349	II
8.	Lalbegi	932	V
9.	Pan, Sawasi	28,931	III
10.	Pasi	463,601	II
	Total	6,933,314	(68.36%)
	5. Goa		
1.	Bhangi, Hadi	355	II
2.	Chambhar	6,438	I
3.	Mahyavanshi, Vankar	119	III
	Total	6,912	(33.52%)
	6. Gujarat		
1.	Garoda, Garo	52,549	II
2.	Lingader	94	V
3.	Mahyavanshi, Dhed, Dhedh, Vankar, Maru Vankar, Antyaj	1,049,837	I
4.	Turi	12,846	III
	Total	1,115,325	(45.74%)
	7. Haryana		
1.	Barar, Burar, Berar	957	IV
2.	Chamar, Jatia Chamar, Rehgar, Raigar, Ramdasi, Ravidasi	1,297,339	I
3.	Chanal	293	IV
4.	Kabirpanthi, Julaha	31,503	II
5.	Khatik	32,259	II
6.	Kori, Koli	34,303	II
7.	Megh	11,265	III
8.	Pasi	6,748	III
9.	Sanhal	35	V
	Total	1,414,702 (57.41%)	
	8. Himachal Pradesh		
1.	Ad Dharmi	15,098	II
2.	Balmiki, Bhangi, Chuhra, Chura, Chuhre	19,764	II
3.	Bandhela	30	V

1	2	3	4
4.	Batwal	10,290	III
5.	Chamar, Jatia Chamar, Rehgar, Raigar, Ramdasi, Ravidasi, Ramdasia, Mochi	286.668	I
6.	Chhimbe, Dhobi	12,166	II
7.	Darai, Daryai	6,385	III
8.	Jogi	11,183	II
9.	Julaha, Julahe, Kabirpanthi, Keer	102,838	II
10.	Kamoh, Dagoli	249	IV
11.	Khatik	449	IV
12.	Lohar	112,389	I
13.	Marija, Marecha	12	V
14.	Mazhabi	221	IV
15.	Od	639	IV
16.	Perna	21	V
17.	Phrera, Pherera	1,109	III
18.	Sanhai	1,675	III
19.	Sansoi	1,052	III
20.	Sarde, Sarera, Sarare, Siryare, Sarehde	9,663	III
21.	Teli	3,768	III
22.	Thathiar, Thathera	709	IV
	Total	596,378 (56.58%)	

9. Jammu and Kashmir

1.	Chamar or Ramdasia	122,292	I
2.	Jolaha	371	IV
3.	Megh or Kabirpanthi	199,242	I
	Total	321,905 (64,72%)	

10. Karnataka

1.	Adi Andhra	29,516	III
2.	Adi Dravida	518,860	II
3.	Ager	4,815	IV
4.	Arunthathiyar	899	IV
5.	Bakad	990	IV
6.	Bant	1,746	IV
7.	Bakuda	1,525	IV
8.	Bandi	2,958	IV
9.	Chalavadi, Chalvadi, Channayya	103,596	II
10.	Chenna Dasar, Holaya Dasar	17,732	III
11.	Dhor, Kakkayya, Kankayya	22,432	III
12.	Halleer	2,790	IV
13.	Halsar, Haslar, Hulasvar, Halasvar	7,902	III
14.	Kolupulvandlu	107	V
15.	Korama	79,167	II
16.	Kotegar, Metri	16,675	III

1	2	3	4
17.	Kuravan	1,335	IV
18.	Lingader	139	V
19.	Mahar, Taral, Dhegu Megu	50,620	III
20.	Mahyavanshi, Dhed, Vankar Maru, Vankar	719	IV
21.	Mala Dasari	2,193	IV
22.	Mala Hannai	40	VI
23.	Meghval, Menghvar	22	VI
24.	Mundala	20,623	III
25.	Nayadi	1,434	IV
26.	Pambada	683	IV
27.	Panchama	785	IV
28.	Raneyar	2,553	IV
29.	Samagara	54,433	III
30.	Sindhollu, Chindollu	41	Vi
31.	Tirgar, Tirbanda	173	V
	Total	947,503 (16.93%)	

11. Kerala

1.	Arunthathiyar	1,308	IV
2.	Ayyanavar	10,079	III
3.	Bandi	24	VI
4.	Bharatar	1,892	IV
5.	Kakkalan	5,487	III
6.	Malayan	11,561	III
7.	Mannan	51,902	II
8.	Mundala	291	IV
9.	Padannan	5,015	III
10.	Panan	40,964	II
11.	Paraiyan, Parayan, Sambavar	189,241	II
12.	Paravan	42,884	IV
13.	Pathiyan	9,508	III
14.	Perumannan	34,940	II
15.	Pulayan, Cheramar	845,604	I
16.	Pulaya Vettuvan	1,008	IV
17.	Puthirai Vannan	280	IV
18.	Samban	2,486	IV
19.	Semman	1,142	IV
20.	Thandan	202,064	II
21.	Vannan	34,068	II
22.	Velan	58,796	II
23.	Vettuvan	111,436	II
	Total	1,661,980 (65.19%)	

12. Madhya Pradesh

1.	Audhelia	2,794	IV

1 2	3	4
2. Bahna, Bahana	1,835	IV
3. Bhangi, Mehtar, Balmik, Lalbegi, Dharkar	222,039	II
4. Chadar	41,527	III
5. Dahait, Dahayat, Dahat	37,706	III
6. Dom, Dumar, Dome, Domar, Doris	39,874	III
7. Ganda, Gandi	205,166	II
8. Holiya	3,363	IV
9. Katia, Patharia	95,647	II
10. Khatik	75,068	II
11. Khangar, Kanera, Mirdha	96,529	II
12. Koli, Kori	379,138	II
13. Mahar, Mehra, Mehar	577,240	II
14. Mang, Mang Garodi, Mang Garudi, Dankhani Mang, Mang Mahasi, Madari, Garudi, Radhe Mang	17,738	III
15. Pasi	30,310	III
Total	1,825,974 (24.81%)	

13. Maharashtra

1 2	3	4
1. Ager	3,846	IV
2. Aray Mala	232	V
3. Arwa Mala	241	V
4. Bakad, Bant	736	IV
5. Basor, Burud, Basor, Bansodi	34,206	III
6. Bhambi, Bhambhi, Asadaru, Asodi, Chamadia, Chamar, Chamari, Chambhar, Chamgar, Haralayya, Harali, Khalpa, Machigar, Mochigar, Madar, Madig, Mochi, Telegu Mochi, Kamati Mochi, Ranigar, Rohidas, Nona, Ramnami, Rohit, Samgar, Samagara, Satnami, Surjyabanshi, Surjyaramnami	865,500	I
7. Bhangi, Mehtar, Olgana, Rukhi, Malkana, Halalkhor, Lalbegi, Balmiki, Korar, Zadmalli	133,386	II
8. Dhor, Kakkayya, Kankayya Dohor	68,509	II
9. Dom, Dumar,	6,070	III
10. Ghasi, Ghasia	1,983	IV
11. Khatik, Chikwa, Chikvi	55,036	II
12. Kori	17,506	III
13. Lingader	64,975	II
14. Mahyavanshi, Dhed, Vankar, Maru Vankar	13,555	III
15. Mala	11,890	III
16. Mala Hannai	70	VI
17. Mala Jangam	17,595	III
18. Meghval, Menghvar	29,310	III
19. Pasi	11,995	III
20. Turi	275	V
Total	1,336,976 (20.84%)	

1	2	3	4
	14. Manipur		
1.	Dhupi, Dhobi	186	II
2.	Muchi, Ravidas	193	II
3.	Patni	2,793	I
	Total	3,172 (17.87%)	
	15. Meghalaya		
1.	Bhuinmali, Mali	201	II
2.	Brittial Bania, Bania	115	II
3.	Dhupi, Dhobi	313	II
4.	Kaibartta, Jaliya	191	II
5.	Sutradhar	270	II
	Total	1,090 (19.85%)	
	16. Mizoram		
1.	Brittial Bania, Bania	2	II
2.	Jhalo, Malo, Jhalo-Malo	1	II
3.	Kaibartta, Jaliya	5	II
4.	Mahar	6	II
Total		14 (19.37%)	
	17. Orissa		
1.	Bariki	12,357	III
2.	Bavuri	50	V
3.	Beldar	2,440	IV
4.	Bhata	4,508	III
5.	Chamar, Mochi, Muchi, Satnami	109,576	II
6.	Chandhai Maru	28	VI
7.	Dewar	4,250	III
8.	Dhoba, Dhobi	418,383	I
9.	Ghogia	656	IV
10.	Gokha	116,226	II
11.	Irika	270	V
12.	Kandra, Kandara	316,.367	II
13.	Katia	1,200	IV
14.	Kori	286	V
15.	Mahuria	4,286	III
16.	Mehtar, Bhangi	2,332	IV
17.	Namasudra	76,316	II
18.	Pan, Pano	806,514	I
19.	Pantanti	27,210	III

1	2	3	4
20.	Patial, Patikar, Patratanti, Patua	34,774	III
21.	Siyal	18,677	III
22.	Tiar, Tior	20,140	III
	Total	1,976,846 (51.14%)	
	18. Punjab		
1.	Ad Dharmi	680,132	I
2.	Batwal	9,367	II
3.	Bhanjra	3,557	III
4.	Chamar, Jatia Chamar, Rehgar, Raigar, Ramdasi, Ravidasi	1,221,145	I
5.	Chanal	139	V
6.	Dagi	54	V
7.	Darain	156	V
8.	Dumna, Mahasha, Doom	124,924	II
9.	Kabirpanthi, Julaha	56,888	II
10.	Kori, Koli	5,652	III
11.	Megh	78,405	II
12.	Pasi	5,593	III
13.	Pherera	279	V
14.	Sanhal	192	V
15.	Sarera	10,238	III
	Total	2,196,721 (48.69%)	
	19. Rajasthan		
1.	Adi Dharmi	780	IV
2.	Aheri	2,736	IV
3.	Bairwa, Berwa	429,625	II
4.	Bedia, Beria	2,361	IV
5.	Bhand	12,058	III
6.	Bhangi, Chura, Mehtar, Olgana, Rukhi, Malkana, Halalkhor, Lalbegi, Balmiki, Valmiki, Korar, Zadmalli	263,565	II
7.	Chandal	1,105	IV
8.	Dabgar	1,166	IV
9.	Dhanak, Dhanuk	82,234	II
10.	Dhankia	6,477	III
11.	Dhobi	104,252	II
12.	Dholi	72,282	II
13.	Dome, Dom	3,692	IV
14.	Garancha, Gancha	5,168	IV
15.	Garo, Garura, Gurda, Garoda	28,888	III
16.	Jingar	12,327	III
17.	Kamad, Kamadia	6,270	III
18.	Khangar	4,320	IV
19.	Khatik	215,089	II
20.	Kori, Koli	265,757	II

1	2	3	4
21.	Mahar, Taral, Dhegu Megu	7,635	III
22.	Mang, Matang, Minimadig	241	V
23.	Mang Garodi, Mang Garudi	177	V
24.	Mehar	31,450	III
25.	Pasi	943	IV
26.	Salvi	19,409	III
27.	Turi	2,041	IV
	Total	1,582,058 (27.10%)	

20. Sikkim

Nil

21. Tamil Nadu

1	2	3	4
1.	Adi Andhra	50,391	III
2.	Adi Dravida	3,831,152	I
3.	Ajila	35	VI
4.	Ayyanavar	1,224	IV
5.	Bandi	486	V
6.	Bellara	44	VI
7.	Bharatar	1,790	IV
8.	Cheruman	1,673	IV
9.	Devendrakulathan	33,528	III
10.	Kakkalan	66	VI
11.	Karimpalan	9	VI
12.	Kavara	3,711	IV
13.	Koliyan	7,509	III
14.	Mundala	26	VI
15.	Pallan	993,070	I
16.	Palluvan	151	V
17.	Panan	209	V
18.	Paraiyan, Parayan, Sambavar	824,337	I
19.	Paravan	1,634	IV
20.	Pathiyan	23	VI
21.	Pulayan, Cheramar	6,581	IV
22.	Puthirai Vannan	17,962	III
23.	Semman	992	IV
24.	Thandan	2,466	IV
25.	Tiruvalluvar	3,828	IV
26.	Valluvan	63,253	III
27.	Vannan	4,566	IV
28.	Vathiriyan	302	V
29.	Velan	318	V
30.	Vetan	774	IV
31.	Vettuvan	143	V
	Total	5,852,253 (78.79%)	

1	2	3	4
	22. Tripura		
1.	Dhoba	34,274	I
2.	Jalia Kaibartta	52,612	I
3.	Mahisyadas	53,751	I
4.	Mali	28,643	II
	Total	169,280 (54.54%)	
	23. Uttar Pradesh		
1.	Baiswar	16,145	IV
2.	Balai	1,321	V
3.	Barwar	12,001	IV
4.	Beriya	19,504	IV
5.	Bhantu	6,663	IV
6.	Chamar, Dhusia, Jhusia, Jatava	12,914,218	I
7.	Dabgar	3,202	V
8.	Dhangar	20,027	IV
9.	Dhanuk	340,473	II
10.	Dhobi	1,423,574	II
11.	Gual	7,491	IV
12.	Hela	29,837	IV
13.	Khatik	496,944	II
14.	Korwa	1,734	V
15.	Mazhabi	6,781	IV
16.	Sanaurhiya	249	V
17.	Shilpkar	514,877	II
	Total	15,815,041 (67.43%)	
	24. West Bengal		
1.	Damai (Nepali)	18,842	III
2.	Dhoba, Dhobi	251,737	II
3.	Jalia Kaibartta	318,344	II
4.	Jhalo Malo, Malo	154,557	II
5.	Kami (Nepali)	42,493	III
6.	Kandra	65,183	III
7.	Khatik	4,862	IV
8.	Konwar	2,841	IV
9.	Lalbegi	1,179	V
10.	Namasudra	1,692,233	I
11.	Pasi	21,367	III
12.	Patni	22,466	III
13.	Pod, Poundra	1,536,197	I
14.	Sarki (Nepali)	11,292	IV
15.	Sunri (excluding Saha)	252,331	II
	Total	4,395,924 (36.63%)	
	25. Chandigarh		
1.	Ad Dharmi	1,431	II
2.	Batwal	41	IV

3. Bhanjra	207	III
4. Chamar, Jatia Chamar, Rehgar, Raigar, Ramdasi, Ravidasi	20,128	I
5. Dhogri, Dhangri, Siggi	21	IV
6. Dumna, Mahasha, Doom	112	III
7. Gagra	37	IV
8. Kabirpanthi, Julaha	2,109	II
9. Marija, Marecha	38	IV
10. Mazhabi	856	II
11. Od	35	IV
12. Pherera	12	IV
13. Sanhai	89	IV
14. Sanhal	19	IV
15. Sarera	215	III
Total	25,350 (39.85%)	

26. Dadra & Nagar Haveli

1. Mahyavanshi, Dhed	943	I
Total	943 (46.20%)	

27. Daman & Diu

1. Mahar	6	III
2. Mahyavanshi, Dhed	1,759	I
Total	1,765 (62.74%)	

28. Delhi

1. Adi Dharmi	4,882	III
2. Chamar, Chanwar Chamar, Jatav or Jatav Chamar, Mochi, Ramdasia, Ravidasi, Raidasi, Rehgarh, or Raigar	411,316	I
3. Julaha (weaver)	43,024	II
4. Kabirpanthi	4,334	III
5. Lalbegi	134	IV
6. Mallah	17,344	II
7. Mazhabi	858	IV
8. Sansi or Bhedkut	5,915	III
Total	487,807 (43.49%)	

29. Pondicherry

1. Adi Andhra	2,148	II
2. Valuvan	2,783	II
Total	4,931 (5.10%)	

Source : *Census of India, 1981*, Series 2 to 32, part IX (II SC I.)

ANNEXURE TABLE VII
EDUCATIONAL FACILITIES AND ENROLMENT AT DIFFERENT SCHOOL STAGES IN VARIOUS PLAN-PERIODS

Year	*Primary Education (I-V)*		*Middle Education (VI-VIII)*		*Secondary Education (IX-X/XI)*		Source
	No. of Schools	*Enrolment*	*No. of Schools*	*Enrolment*	*No. of Schools*	*Enrolment*	
1	2	3	4	5	6	7	8
1946-47 (At the time of Independence)	1,34,966	9,647,317	8,294	1,129,955	3,659	1,571,397	a
1951-52 (Beginning of First Five Year Plan)	184,123	16,288,960	12,124	1,880,726	7,538	2,968,043	a
1956-57 (Beginning of Second Five Year Plan)	287,298	23,922,667	24,486	4,392,223	11,805	5,186,941	a
1961-62 (Beginning of Third Five Year Plan)	351,530	29,474,377	55,915	12,136,018	19,306	8,429,721	a

1	2	3	4	5	6	7	8
1965-66 (Second All-India Educational Survey)	387,316 (465,681 Sections)	48,834,588	77,260 (96,932 Sections)	10,244,621	26,883	5,210,264	a
1973-74 (Third All-India Educational Survey)	455,729 (530,869 Sections)	61,255,250	90,681 (119,789 Sections)	14,387,748	42,621	7,714,095	b
1978-79 (Fourth All-India Educational Survey)	474,636 (570,010 Sections)	68,602,224	112,404 (147,250 (Sections)	17,958,477	36,675 (44,650 Sections)	8,872,141	c
1986 (Fifth All-India Educational Survey)	528,730 (631,308 sections)	85,913,478	139,016 (187,602 Sections)	27,272,336	52,560 (67,241 Sections)	11,519,996	d
1995-96	590,421	109,734,292	171,216	41.014,136	94,653	22,507,501	e

Source : a - p. 1. of Fourth All-India Educational Survey, 1978.
b - pp. 28, and p. 43 of Third All-India Educational Survey, 1973.
c - pp. 196-197 of Fourth All-India Educational Survey, 1978.
d - pp. 207-209 and 418-419 of Fifth All-India Educational Survey, 1986.
e - pp. 260-262. Annual Report 1996-97 MHRD Department of Education.

ANNEXURE TABLE IX

STATEMENT SHOWING THE POST-MATRIC SCHOLARSHIPS AWARDED TO SCHEDULED CASTES AND SCHEDULED TRIBES AND THE TOTAL EXPENDITURE INCURRED EVERY YEAR SINCE THE INCEPTION OF THE SCHEME.

Year	*Scheduled Castes*		*Scheduled Tribes*		*Total*	
	Awards	*Expenditure (Rs. in lakhs)*	*Awards*	*Expenditure (Rs. in lakhs)*	*Awards*	*Expenditure (Rs. in lakhs)*
1	2	3	4	5	6	7
1944-45	114	0.48	-	-	114	0.48
1945-46	292	2.12	-	-	292	2.12
1946-47	527	4.70	-	-	527	4.70
1947-48	655	5.39	-	-	655	5.39
1948-49	647	4.52	84	0.46	731	4.98
1949-50	879	5.16	186	0.95	1065	6.11
1950-51	1316	7.27	348	1.85	1664	9.12
Pre-first Plan Total	4430	29.64	618	3.26	5048	32.90
First Plan						
1951-52	1604	8.18	575	2.82	2179	11.00
1952-53	3404	14.36	1093	5.22	4497	19.58
1953-54	5954	26.86	1597	8.19	7541	35.05
1954-55	10034	45.81	2356	12.38	12390	58.19
1955-56	16081	63.78	2883	13.05	18964	76.83
First Plan Total	37077	158.99	8494	41.66	45571	200.65
Second Plan						
1956-57	21744	87.99	3482	16.78	25226	103.77
1957-58	26447	100.37	4300	18.97	30747	119.34
1958-59	32551	125.86	4821	20.76	37372	146.62
1959-60	38657	143.40	6112	23.89	44769	167.29
1960-61	42071	167.83	6877	30.96	48948	198.79
Second Plan Total	161470	625.45	25592	110.36	187062	735.81
Third Plan						
1961-62	49015	213.89	8548	36.78	57563	250.67
1962-63	55580	267.56	10249	44.37	65829	311.93
1963-64	60675	293.82	11836	50.28	72511	344.10
1964-65	75146	341.16	13500	60.62	88646	401.78

1	2	3	4	5	6	7
1965-66	78548	372.54	15,925	70.58	94,473	443.12
1966-67	90479	438.66	17,760	83.84	108,239	522.50
1967-68	107195	528.78	21,261	106.34	128,456	635.12
1968-69	130218	629.48	26,616	12,0.86	156,834	750.34
Third Plan Total	318964	1488.97	60058	262.63	379022	1651.60
Fourth Plan						
1969-70	151,413	747.50	31,324	136.89	182,737	884.39
1970-71	177,794	821.00	33,776	149.50	251,570	970.50
1971-72	204,463	1016.70	38,842	197.76	243,305	1214.46
1972-73	235,132	N.A.	44,668	N.A.	279,800	N.A.
1973-74	270,420	N.A.	51,368	N.A.	321,788	N.A.
Fourth Plan Total	1039,204	48,24.61	199,978	928.42	1,239,182	5,753.03 + 3700 of the state Sector

Source : pp. 64 and pp 274-75 of Twenty-first Report of the Commissioner for SC/ST (1971-72 and 1972-73).

Fifth Plan				
1974-75 2@	3.32 (in lakhs)	0.59 (in lakh)	3.91 (in lakhs)	10.09(in crores) (excluding committed expenditure)
1975-76$	2.90(do)	0.60 (do)	3.40 (do)	26.89 (in crore)
1976-77 $	3.17 (do)	0.59 (do)	3.76 (do)	29.72 (do)
1977-78 $	3.48 (do)	0.65 (do)	4.13 (do)	31.16 (do)
1978-79 $ *	3.89 (do)	0.72 (do)	4.61 (do)	34.20 (do)
1979-80 $ **	4.28 (do)	0.78 (do)	5.06 (do)	48.80 (do)
Fifth Plan Total	21.04 (lakhs)	3.831 (lakhs)	24.87 lakhs	180.86 crores (Both Central and State, Except for 1974-75)

* Provisional
** Estimated

Source : $ -- p. 166 of 2nd Report of the Commission for SC/ST (1979-80) @
* @ — P. 69 of 23rd Report of the Commissioner for SC/ST (1974-75)@

Sixth Plan		
1980-81	586,419	1073 lakhs
1981-82	657,120	2641 lakhs
1982-83	745,725	3165 lakhs
1983-84	823,287	3190 lakhs
1984-85	886,332	3987 lakhs
Sixth Plan Total	3,698,883	14056 lakhs

Source : Annexure I and II of the Note prepared by Shri R. K. Mukhi, Deputy Secretary, Ministry of Welfare (Memeographed).

ANNEXURE TABLE X

RFSERVATION OF SEATS IN EDUCATIONAL INSTITUTIONS AND OTHER RELAXATION IN ADMISSION CRITERION

Sl. No.	*Name of State/UT*	*Reservation Granted in*	*Percentage of Reservation for SC*	*ST*	*Relaxation in Eligibility Criterion for Admission*
1	2	3	4	5	6
1.	Andhra Pradesh	All recognised educations institutions	14%	4%	-
2.	Arunachal Pradesh		No need for separate reservation being predominantly inhabited by STs.		
3.	Assam	All recognised educational institutions above school level	7%	10% (Plains) 5% (Hills)	Concessions are provided for admission to Higher Education
4.	Bihar	No reservation at school level	-	-	
		General Higher, Professional, ITIs and Polytechnics	14%	10%	- -
5.	Gujarat	Colleges providing General, Professional & Technical Education	' 7%	13%	Relaxation is given in eligibility criterion for admission
6.	Haryana	General, Professional and Technical Education	20%	-	Relaxation is given to SC students for admission to various courses
7.	Himachal Pradesh	No reservation at school and college level, general education relaxation is given in eligibility			

1	2	3	4	5	6
		Professional and Technical education	22%	5%	criterion for admission to higher education
8.	Jammu & Kashmir	Colleges providing general, professional and technical education		8% for SC/ST	Concession of 10% marks is given in the eligi! ility criterion for admission.
9.	Karnataka	All recognised educational institutions	15%	3%	Concessions in marks are given to SC/ST students for admission to Higher Education.
10.	Kerala	Institutions providing technical and professional education	8%	2%	Relaxed conditions of eligibility.
		Under-graduate and post-graduate courses in general education	15%	5%	-do-
11.	Madhya Pradesh	Recognised educational institutions above school level	15%	18%	Relexation of 5% marks for admission to colleges for general education and of 15% marks for Medical, Engineering and other professional courses including ITIs/Polytechnics
12.	Maharashtra	Secondary schools and colleges providing general and professional education	13%	- 7%	
13.	Manipur	No reservation at school level and for general educatior: at Graduate level			Relaxation is given in eligibility criterion for admission to courses for higher education
		Engineering/Medical Colleges	2%	31%	
		Polytechnics/ITIs	4%	33%	

1	2	3	4	5	6
14.	Mizoram	No reservation being predominently inhabited by STs.			
15.	Nagaland	No reservation being predominently inhabited by STs.			
16.	Meghalaya	No need for separate reservation being predominantly inhabited by STs.			
		For professional education out of seats alloted by the G/I	5%	80%	
17.	Orissa	School level	10% for SC/ST		
		Ashram schools run by Harijan & Tribal Welfare Department	10%	90%	in ST concentrated areas
			90%	10%	in SC concentrated areas
		Colleges for general education	10% for SC/ST		
		MBBS	8%	12%	
		Engineering & Other professional courses	15%	5%	
		ITIs	16%	24%	
		Polytechnics	15%	25%	
18.	Punjab	No reservation at school level.			Relaxation of 5% marks in the eligibility criterion for admission
		In institutions providing higher education, general, professional and technical education	25%		
19.	Rajasthan	Colleges for general education	16%	12%	Relaxation of 3% marks in eligibility criterion for admission
		Engineering	15%	7½%	Relaxed criterion for admission
		MBBS	8%	6%	-do-
		Other professional courses	16%	12%	-do-

1	2	3	4	5	6
20.	Sikkim	No reservation but priority is given in admission			
21.	Tamil Nadu	All recognised educational institutions	14%	4%	Concession of 10% or more for admission in different courses.
22.	Tripura	At all levels including school level	15%	29%	Relaxation of 10% marks for admission to Engineering/Technical Institutions.
23.	Uttar Pradesh	All recognised educational institutions 18%	2%		Concession in marks for admission to higher education
24.	West Bengal	Educational Institutions at all levels	15%	5%*	Relaxation of 25% marks in eligibility criterion for admission to various courses. No restriction on minimum marks for admission to 1st year pass courses.
25.	A & N Islands	No reservation at school and college level for general education			
		BED	-	16%	Relaxation of 5% marks.
		JBI	-	16%	Minimum qualification of a pass in class XII is relaxed to a pass in class X for ST students.
		Polytechnics		16%	
26.	Chandigarh	No reservation at school level			
		At pre-primary level		10%	-
		Higher education, general & professional		15%	5% Relaxation of 5% marks is given in the eligibility 5% 71/2% criterion to these courses.

1	2	3	4	5	6
		ITI	12½%		5%
		Polytechnics			
27.	Dadra & N. Haveli	No reservation being predominantly inhabited by STs			
28.	Delhi	General, professional & technical education	15%	7 ½%	Concession of 5% marks in the eligibility criterion for admission to these courses. For MBBS courses concession is 10% marks.
29.	Goa, Daman & Diu	No reservation at school and college level for general education			
		Medical, Dental and Pharmacy	15%	2%	Concession of 10% marks for admission to MBBS/Dental courses
		Engineering	15%	7%	Concession of 5% marks for admission to Engineering courses.
30.	Lakshadweep	No reservation being predominantly inhabited by STs.			
31.	Pondicherry	Higher secondary, Undergraduate and postgraduate courses in general education, professional colleges and ITIs	16%	-	

Source : pp. 12-66 of Educational Facilities to SCs/STs, Ministry of Education, Government of India, 1985, since raised to 22% for SC and 6% for ST.

ANNEXURE TABLE XI
RATES OF STIPENDS TO SC DAYSCHOLARS

Sl. No.	*State/UT*	*Incentive scholarships in classes* — *Classes*	*Stipend*	*Remarks*
1	2	3		4
1.	Andhra Pradesh	classes I to II	Rs. 30 p.a.	Income ceiling Rs. 12,000 p.a.
		classes III to VIII	Rs. 45 p.a.	
		classes IX to X	Rs. 85 p.a.	
2.	Assam	classes I to VII	Rs. 5 p.m.	
		classes VIII to X	Rs. 7.50 p.m.	
3.	Bihar	classes I to IV	Rs. 6 p.m. for 10 months	income test
		classes V to VI	Rs. 12 p.m. for 10 months–	non-tax payer
		classes VII to X	Rs. 24 p.m. for 10 months	
4.	Gujarat			
	Government/ Semi-Govt. Schools	classes V to VII	Rs. 40 p.a	income ceiling
		classes VIII to X	Rs. 75 p.a.	Rs. 7200 p.a.
		special rates for students scoring 60% marks and above		
		classes V to VII	Rs. 55 p.a.	income ceiling Rs 7200 p.a.
		classes VIII to X --	Rs. 100 p.a.	
	Non-govt schools run by Voluntary Agencies	class V	Rs. 60 p.a.	no income ceiling
		class VI	Rs. 75 p.a.	
		class VII	Rs. 90 p.a.	
		special rates for those securing 60% marks and above		
		class V	Rs. 80 p.a.	income ceiling Rs. 7200 p.a.
		class VI	Rs. 100 p.a.	
		class VII	Rs. 120 p.a.	
		classes I-VII	Rs. 250 p.a. for boys (Rs. 140 special scholarship and Rs. 110 for foodgrain) Rs. 300 p.a. for girls (Rs. 190 special scholarship and Rs. 110 for foodgrain) belonging to Bhangi, Handi, Serva and Nadia communities of SCs only.	
		classes VIII-X	Rs. 200 p.a. for boys (Rs. 130 special scholarship, Rs. 40 for dress and Rs. 30 for books)	

1	2	3	4	
			Rs. 240 p.a. for girls (Rs. 160 special scholarship, Rs. 50 for dress and Rs. 30 for books) belonging to very backward communities among the SC/ST.	
5.	Haryana	classes IX-XI	Rs. 20 p.m.	income ceiling Rs. 10000 p.a.
		classes I-V	Rs. 10 p.m. for SC girls	
6.	Himachal Pradesh	Primary	Rs. 8 p.m. income ceiling Rs. 7500 p.a.	
			Middle Rs. 12 p.m. -do-	
			High/Higher Secondary --Rs. 15 p.m. -do-	
		classes VI to XI	Rs. 30 p.m. and a lump-sum grant of Rs. 100 to meet expenses on the purchase of uniform/books/ stationery etc.	only SC girls whose parental income does not exceed Rs. 6000 p.a.
		classes I-V	Rs. 20 p.a. for SC girls	for attendance
		classes VI to VIII	Rs. 50 p.a. for SC girls	for attendance
7.	Jammu and Kashmir	classes IV-V	Rs. 10 p.m.	income ceiling Rs. 300 p.m.
		classes VI-VIII	Rs. 15 p.m.	-do-
		classes IX -X	Rs. 20 p.m.	-do-
8.	Karnataka	classes V-VII	Rs. 75 p.a.	
		classes VIII-X	Rs. 100 p.a.	
9.	Kerala	pre-primary	Rs. 10 lump sum annual grant	
		classes I-III	Rs. 30 lump sum annual grant and Rs. 13 p.m.	
		classes IV	Rs. 35 lump sun annual grant and Rs. 13 p.m.	
		classes V	Rs. 65 lump sum annual grant	
		classes VI-VII	Rs. 75 lump sum annual grant	
		classes VIII-X	Rs. 105 lump sum annual grant	
10.	Madhya Pradesh	classes VI-VIII	Rs. 150 p.a. for boys Rs. 225 p.a. for girls	
		classes IX-X	Rs 225 p.a. for boys Rs. 300 p.a. for girls	
11.	Maharashtra	classes I-VII	Rs. 15 p.a.	
		classes VIII-IX	Rs. 5 p.m.	
		class X	Rs. 10 p.m.	
12.	Manipur	classes III-IV	Rs. 5 p.m.	

1	2	3		4
		class V	Rs. 7 p.m.	
		class VI	Rs. 10 p.m.	
		classes VII-VIII	Rs. 15 p.m.	
		classes IX-X	Rs. 20 p.m.	
14.	Mizoram	classes VI-VIII	Rs. 12 p.m. - Rs. 15 p.m.	income ceiling Rs. 9000 p.a.
		classes IX-X	Rs. 15 p.m. - Rs. 25 p.m.	
15.	Nagaland	only for STs		
16.	Orissa	classes VI-VII	Rs. 55 p.a.	Parents paying Income Tax/ Agricultural Tax not entitled
		classes VIII-X	Rs. 75 p.a.	
17.	Punjab	classes VI-VIII	Rs 5 p.m.	income ceiling Rs. 9000 p.a.
		classes IX-XI	Rs. 25 p.m. for students holding first division Rs. 22 p.m. for second divisioners Rs 19 p.m. for the rest (girl students and students belonging to Balmiki community are paid an additional amount of Re. 1 p.m.)	
		classes I-V	Rs. 2.p.m. only for Vimukta Jatis	
18.	Rajasthan	classes VI-VIII	Rs. 15 p.m. for boys Rs 30 p.m. for girls	
		classes IX-XI	Rs 30 p.m. for boys Rs 40 p.m. for girls	
		classes I-II	Rs 5 p.m. for 10 months in a year to 2 girls in schools situated in tribal areas with a minimum attendance of 60%	
		classes III-V	Rs 10 p.m. for 10 months in a year to all girls studying in schools situated in tribal areas having a minimum attendance of 70%	
19.	Sikkim	classes I-X	Rs 850 p.a.	income ceiling Rs. 500 p.m.
20.	Tripura	classes IX-X	Rs 30 p.m.	

1	2	3	4
21. Uttar Pradesh	classes I-VIII	Rs 5 p.m.	
	classes I-V	Rs 3 p.m. for SC boys Rs 15 p.m. for SC girls	income ceiling less than Rs 750 p.m.
22. West Bengal	classes V-X	Rs 25 p.m.	income ceiling Rs. 6000 p.a.
23. A & N Islands		only for STs	
24. Chandigarh	classes I-VIII	Rs 10 p.m.	income ceiling Rs 8000 p.a.
25. Dadra & Nagar Haveli	classes V-VII	Rs 20 p.a.	if attendance is more than 90%
	classes VIII-XII	Rs 500 p.a.	for boys getting 55% marks and above and for girls getting 50% marks and above
26. Delhi	classes V-VI	Rs 30 p.a.	income celling Rs. 6000 p.a.
	classes VII-VIII	Rs 40 p.a.	-do-
	classes IX-X	Rs 50 p.a.	-do-
27. Goa, Daman and Diu	classes V-VIII	Rs 40 p.a.	income ceiling Rs 3600 p.a.
	classes IX-X	Rs 60 p.a.	
	class IX	Rs 20 p.m. for girls obtaining 55% marks and above	
	class X	Rs 25 p.m. for girls obtaining 55% marks and above	
28. Pondicherry	classes VI-VIII	Rs 150 p.a.	income ceiling Rs 9000 p.a.
	classes IX-X	-- Rs 200 p.a.	-do-
	classes I-V	-- Rs 150 p.a. for SC girls	
29. Lakshadweep	Only for STs		

Source : Educational Facilities to Scheduled Castes/Scheduled Tribes, Ministry of Education, 1985, pp. 12-66.

ANNEXURE TABLE XII
FREE SHIPS

Sl. No.	Name of States/UTs	Education Free Up to	Examination Fee Exempted Up to
1	2	3	4
1.	Andhra Pradesh	Intermediate level	-
2.	Arunachal Pradesh	Class XII	Board Examination
3.	Assam	Class X At college level tuition fee is paid by State Govt, if no scholarship is received.	-
4.	Bihar	all levels	all levels
5.	Gujarat	class XII	class XII
6.	Ha.yana	all levels	public examinations
7.	Himachal Pradesh	class XII	all levels
8.	Jammu and Kashmir	postgraduate	Board Examination if parental income is lower than Rs 3,600 p.a.
9.	Karnataka	all levels	all levels
10.	Kerala	all levels	all levels
11.	Madhya Pradesh	all levels	Higher Secondary
12.	Maharashtra	not charged	-
13.	Manipur		
14.	Meghalaya	Class X	-
15.	Mizoram		
16.	Nagaland	Class X	-
17.	Orissa	Matriculation	Matriculation

1	2	3	4
18. Punjab		Class VIII. Free in Classes IX to XI if parental income is less than Rs 9000 p.a.	all levels
19. Rajasthan		all levels	-
20. Sikkim		Class XII	Class XII
21. Tamil Nadu		Class XII	Class XII
22. Tripura		all levels	all levels
23. Uttar Pradesh		Class X if parental income is less than Rs 750 p.m. For higher classes the income limit is Rs 1,000 p.m.	-
24. West Bengal		Class XII	Class XII
25. A & N Islands,		Senior Secondary Stage	Senior Secondary Stage
26. Chandigarh		Class VIII	Class X
27.Dadra and N.Haveli		Class XII	Board Examination
28. Delhi		Class XII	Board Examination
29. Goa, Daman & Diu		Class X	class X
30. Lakshadweep		all levels	all levels
31. Pondicherry		Degree level	—

Source : Educational Facilities to Scheduled Castes/Scheduled Tribes, Ministry of Education, 1986. pp. 12-66.

ANNEXURE TABLE XIII
NUMBER OF SC/ST/BACKWARD HOSTELS, 1985

Sl. No.	States/Union Territories		No. of Hostels SC	ST	Total
1	2		3	4	5
1.	Andhra Pradesh	school level	1930	451	2381
		college level			68 for SC/ST
2.	Bihar	school level	286	272	558
		college level	48	22	70
3.	Gujarat	school level	249	482	731
		college level	16	20	36
4.	Himachal Pradesh	primary level	-	1	1
		middle/secondary level	2	13	15
5.	Karnataka	school level			616 for SC/ST
		college level			63 for SC/ST
6.	Kerala	school level	87	102	189
		college level	19	-	19
7.	Madhya Pradesh	school level	432	1487	1919
		college level	53	73	126
8.	Maharashtra				1600 backward classes
9.	Manipur	secondary level	-	10	10 (6 for boys and 4 for girls)
10.	Meghalaya	school level	-	128	128
		college level	-	9	9
11.	Mizoram	school level	-	62	62
		college level	-	5	5
12.	Nagaland	school level	-	44	44
		college level	-	6	6
13	Orissa	primary level			125 for SC/ST
		middle level			388 for SC/ST
		secondary level			499 for SC/ST
		college level			75 for SC/ST

1	2		3	4	
14.	Punjab		3	-	3 for girls
15.	Rajasthan	school level	186	196	382
16.	Sikkim		2	-	2 for girls
17.	Tamil Nadu	school level		658	for SC/ST
		college level		55	for SC/ST
18	Tripura	school level		66	for SC/ST
19.	Uttar Pradesh		36	8	44
20.	West Bengal	school/college		836	for SC/ST
21.	Dadra & N. Haveli			9	for SC/ST
22.	Lakshadweep	college level	-	22	for boys and 2 for girls)
23.	Pondicherry	school level		18	for SC/ST
		college level		2	for SC/ST

Source : Education Facilities to SC/ST, Ministry of Education, 1985, pp. 12-65

ANNEXURE TABLE XIV
RATES OF STIPENDS IN WELFARE HOSTELS

Sl. No.	*States/UT*	*Rates of Stipends and Other Facilities*
1	2	3
1.	Andhra Pradesh	The difference between the actual mess bill and the rate of post-matric scholarship is reimbursed. Besides, the following facilities are provided to the hostellers : (i) two pairs of dresses @ Rs 100 per boarder (ii) vocational guidance provided by experts in Educational Psychology; (iii) study tours and excursions; and (iv) all ST students are further provided with free textbooks and stationery.
2.	Gujarat	Free boarding and lodging facilities.
3.	Himachal Pradesh	Stipends @ Rs 15 p.m. for classes I-VIII and Rs 25 p.m. in classes IX-XI and Rs 80 p.a. as aid for writing materials/books.
4.	Karnataka	Rs 100 p.m. for boarding charges, Rs 120 p.a. for dresses, Rs 65 p.a. for books and stationery, Rs 5 p.a. for miscellaneous expenses and Rs. 100 for bedding once in 3 years.
5.	Kerala	Free boarding, lodging and dresses in welfare hostels and free boarding and a pocket money of Rs 20–Rs 35 p.m. in general hostels.
6.	Madhya Pradesh	Free residential facilities, electricity, water and services of contingent employees. Besides this, hostellers are also provided stipends @ Rs 80 p.m. for boys and Rs 90 p.m. for girls for hostels located at Divisional/District level and Rs. 70 p.m. for boys and Rs 85 p.m. for girls for hostels located at Tehsil level.
7.	Maharashtra	Free boarding, lodging, equipments and stationery.
8.	Meghalaya	Stipends @ Rs 250 p.a. in classes IV to VI and Rs. 400 p.a. in classes VII to X.
9.	Mizoram	Stipends @ Rs 40 p.m. for 10 months provided parental income does not exceed Rs. 500 p.m.
10.	Orissa	Stipends @ Rs 35 p.m. for 10 months for classes VI-VII and Rs 43 p.m. for 10 months in a year in classes VIII to X provided parents are not income tax/agricultural tax payers.
11.	Tamil Nadu	Stipends at the following rates are given : classes VI to VIII Boys Rs 250 p.m., Girls Rs. 275 p.m. classes IX to X Boys Rs 300 p.m., Girls Rs 350 p.m.

1	2	3
		Higher Secondary and College level: In Madras Rs 70 p.m. Other places Rs 55 p.m.
		Professional Courses: In Madras Rs 75 p.m. Other places Rs 70 p.m.
		Polytechnics and ITIs: In Madras Rs 60 p.m. Other places Rs 50 p.m.
		Also two sets of dresses are provided to hostellers in welfare hostels in classes VI to X.
12.	Tripura	Stipends @ Rs 5 per day for 302 days in a year.
13.	West Bengal	Stipends @ Rs 150 p.m. for 10 months in a year. No income ceiling for STs but in case of SCs parental income ceiling is Rs 3600 p.m. In Ashram hostels for Primary and Junior High School level, SC/ST students are given a stipend of Rs 220 p.m. in addition to Rs 40 p.a. for garments per student.
14.	A & N Islands	Tribal students get a stipend of Rs. 95 p.m.
15.	Dadra & N. Haveli	Free lodging and boarding.
16.	Lakshadweep	Free meals and pocket money of Rs. 15 p.m.
17.	Arunachal Pradesh	Stipends @ Rs 90 p.m. in classes I to X and Rs 100 p.m. in classes XI & XII for 10 ½ months in a year. Parental income ceiling is Rs. 700 p.m.

Source : pp. 12-65 of Educational Facities to SCs/STs, Ministry of Education, Government of India, 1985.

ANNEXURE TABLE XV
PERCENTAGES OF THE DIFFERENT SCHEDULED CASTES IN THE SCHOOL AND COLLEGES SAMPLES TAKEN IN EARLY 70s AND THEIR PERCENTAGES IN THE TOTAL SCHEDULED CASTE POPULATION IN 14 ACCORDING TO THE 1971 CENSUS.

Sl. No.	*Name of Scheduled Castes*	*Percentages in* Scheduled Caste population	School sample	College sample
1	2	3	4	5
	1. Andhra Pradesh			
1.	Adi Andhra	10.67	20	NA
2.	Adi Dravida	0.68	2	NA
3.	Mala	36.60	57	NA
4.	Madiga	43.55	11	NA
	2. Assam			
1.	Bhuimali or Mali	2.4	17	4
2.	Brittial Bania	3.08	2	7
3.	Dhupi or Dhubi	2.27	5	2
4.	Hira	3.57	6	6
5.	Jalkeot	0.28	3	8
6.	Kaibartta or Jalia	32.30	24	51
7.	Muchi or Rishi	4,47	0.4	1
8.	Namasudra	32.97	20	16
9.	Patni	9.4	13	2
10.	Sutradhar	3.58	3	1
	3. Bihar			
1.	Bauri	1.20	-	1
2.	Chamar	29.97	34	38
3.	Dhobi	5.45	14	13
4.	Dom	2.08	1	0.4
5.	Dusadh	26.48	26	36
6.	Ghasi	0.93	1	-
7.	Methar	1.45	1	1
8.	Musahar	14.69	1	0.4
9.	Pan	0.35	3	-
10.	Pasi	4.20	18	8
11.	Rajwar	2.44	1	1

1	2	3	4	5
		4. Gujarat		
1.	Bawa	0.28	2	1
2.	Bhambi, Chamar, Rohit, Khalpa	22.75	21	20
3.	Bhangi	12.76	6	5
4.	Garoda, Garo	2.51	6	4
5.	Mahar	0.26	2	1
6.	Mahyavanshi, Dhed, Vankar	41.09	52	66
7.	Shenva, Sedma	2.62	1	-
8.	Tirgar	0.23	1	-
9.	Turi	0.65	1	1
		5. Haryana		
1.	Balmiki (Sweeper)	19.78	5	7
2.	Chamar	52.98	49	69
3.	Dhanak	14.23	10	11
4.	Kabirpanthi	0.95	-	2
5.	Khatik	1.23	4	2
6.	Kori	1.28	-	1
		6. Karnataka		
1.	Adi Andhra	0.79	1	-
2.	Adi Dravida	11.16	20	30
3.	Adi Karnataka	36.49	27	28
4.	Beda	0.36	1	0.3
5.	Bhovi	7.70	4	5
6.	Chambhar, Chamar	7.72	3	-
7.	Chena Dasar	0.20	-	1
8.	Dhor	0.50	2	1
9.	Holeya, Holar, Halvar	9.72	17	-
10.	Madiga, Mochi, Samagar	5.24	4	2
11.	Mahar	1.39	6	0.3
12.	Mang	0.57	2	-
		7. Kerala		
1.	Ayyanavar	0.42	2	1
2.	Bharathar	0.19	1	-
3.	Kakkalan	0.21	0.4	0.4
4.	Kanakkan	5.93	0.4	0.4
5.	Kavara	0.12	-	0.4
6.	Kudan	0.09	0.4	-
7.	Kurava	10.05	3	5
8.	Panan	1.80	2	1
9.	Paravan	1.16	3	-

1	2	3	4	5
10.	Pathiyan	0.43	0.4	1
11.	Perumannan	0.31	-	5
12.	Pulayan, Cheraman	33.12	55	28
13.	Sambavar, Paraya	8.62	8	16
14.	Thandan	5.39	13	3
15.	Ulladan	0.40	0.4	-
16.	Vannan	0.71	2	1
17.	Velan	2.38	3	-
18.	Vettuvan	2.29	2	-
	8. Madhya Pradesh			
1.	Balai or Balahi	10.46	6	NA
2.	Chamar group of castes	56.62	53	NA
3.	Chadar	0.40	5	NA
4.	Dhobi	0.27	1	NA
5.	Ganda or Gandi	3.17	2	NA
6.	Katia	0.69	3	NA
7.	Khangar	0.18	1	NA
8.	Khatik	1.09	2	NA
9.	Koli or Kori	3.84	7	NA
10.	Mahar or Mehra	6.46	17	NA
11.	Mang	0.27	0.4	NA
12.	Mehtar or Bhangi	3.35	3	NA
	9. Maharashtra			
1.	Bedar	0.03	1	0.4
2.	Bhangi	2.79	1	0.4
3.	Chalvadi	0.03	-	1
4.	Chambhar	3.17	12	18
5.	Dhor	1.68	2	-
6.	Kaikadi	0.09	-	0.4
7.	Mahar	35.40	72	66
8.	Mahyavanshi, Vankar	0.30	-	5
9.	Mang, Matang	29.92	10	5
10.	Meghval	0.55	-	1
	10. Orissa			
1.	Bauri	9.17	8	4
2.	Chamar	2.46	3	4
3.	Dandasi	1.42	-	0.4
4.	Dewar	0.10	-	9
5.	Dhoba	9.73	17	23
6.	Ganda	9.82	-	5
7.	Ghasi	1.70	2	-

1	2	3	4	5
8.	Gokha	2.48	-	11
9.	Kandara	7.50	8	15
10.	Kela	0.04	0.4	-
11.	Khadala	0.92	0.4	1
12.	Kummari	0.06	-	0.4
13.	Laheri	0.11	-	0.4
14.	Namasudra	1.50	15	-
15.	Pano	20.32	25	11
16.	Pantanti	1.30	0.4	1
17.	Panika	0.24	-	0.4
18.	Patratanit	0.70	2	3
19.	Siyal	0.42	2	2
20.	Tamudia	0.07	2	1
21.	Tiar	0.41	-	1
22.	Ujia	0.44	2	1
	11. Punjab			
1.	Ad-Dharmi	13.13	39	55
2.	Balmiki	12.00	11	6
3.	Batwal	0.18	0.3	-
4.	Chamar, Ramdasi	29.31	31	21
5.	Kabirpanthi, Julaha	1.12	2	2
6.	Mazhabi	28.75	7	2
7.	Megh	1.57	6	5
8.	Od	0.04	-	0.4
	12. Rajasthan			
1.	Bairwa	3.43	6	10
2.	Balai	8.31	4	12
3.	Bhangi, Mehtar	4.77	1	1
4.	Chamar, Bhambi, Jatava, Mochi, Raigar	39.32	39	38
5.	Chandal	0.01	1	-
6.	Dhanak	0.05	2	-
7.	Dhankia	1.11	1	-
8.	Dhobi	0.13	3	-
9.	Gavaria	0.23	-	2
10.	Jingar	0.04	-	2
11.	Khatik	3.74	4	7
12.	Koli	4.69	6	9
13.	Meghwal	14.90	18.	10
14.	Mehar	0.68	2	-
15.	Sargara	1.33	1	0.4

1	2	3	4	5
		13. Tamil Nadu		
1.	Adi Dravida	34.82	51	39
2.	Arunthathiyar	3.51	-	1
3.	Chakkiliyan	11.82	1	2
4.	Dambara	0.06	-	1
5.	Kudumban	1.56	0.4	-
6.	Kuravan	1.05	1	1
7.	Pallan	18.14	15	36
8.	Paraiyan	20.96	16	19
9.	Puthirai Vannan	0.14	0.4	-
10.	Samban	2.00	7	-
11.	Valluvan	0.89	3	1
		14. Uttar Pradesh		
1.	Bahalia	0.22	0.2	0.2
2.	Balai	0.01	-	0.3
3.	Balmiki	3.94	2	2
4.	Beldar	0.43	1	0.4
5.	Chamar, Jatav	54.57	78	68
6.	Dabgar	0.02	-	0.3
7.	Dhangar	0.13	-	0.4
8.	Dhobi	6.23	4	6.5
9.	Dhanuk	1.47	0.2	0.5
10.	Dusadh	0.59	1.5	-
11.	Kanjar	0.23	0.2	0.4
12.	Khatik	2.10	2	2.5
13.	Kori	4.90	0.4	4
14.	Nat	0.42	0.2	0.2
15.	Pasi	13.87	8	5.5
16.	Shipkar	2.77	0.5	4
		a	b	b

Source : a - 1971 Census Reports.
b - Chitnis, Suma, *A Long Way to Go*, Allied Publishers, 1981, Appendix I, pp. 319-26.

ANNEXURE TABLE XVI

POSITION OF THE 141 SCHEDULED CASTES CONSIDERED 'UNTOUCHABLES' IN 1911/1917 IN THE SCHOOL AND COLLEGE SAMPLES DRAWN IN 1972-73.

Sl. No.	Name of Scheduled Caste	Percentage of Population in 1971 Census	Percentage in School Sample	Percentage in College Sample
1	2	3	4	5
	1. Andhra Pradesh			
1.	Bavuri	0.01		
2.	Dandasi	0.10		
3.	Holeya	0.01		
4.	Madiga	43.55	11	NA
5.	Mala	36.60	57	NA
6.	Panchama	0.39		
	2. Assam			
1.	Dhubi	2.27	5	2
2.	Muchi	4.47	0.4	1
	3. Bihar			
1.	Bauri	1.20	-	1
2.	Bhuiya	5.51		
3.	Chamar	29.97	34	38
4.	Dhobi	5.45	14	13
5.	Dom	2.08	1.	0.4
6.	Dusadh	26.48	26	36
7.	Ghasi	0.93	1	-
8.	Halalkhor	0.07		
9.	Hari	1.45		
10.	Bhangi			
11.	Mehtar		1	1
12.	Musahar	14.69	1	0.4
13.	Pan	0.35	3	-
14.	Pasi	4.20	18	8
15.	Turi	1.67		
	4. Gujarat			
1.	Bhangi	12.76	6	5
2.	Chamar	22.75	21	20
3.	Madig			

1	2	3	4	5
4.	Dhed	41.09	52	66
5.	Dhor	0.02		
6.	Mahar	0.26	2	1
7.	Mang	0.07		
8.	Mochi	0.004		
9.	Turi	0.65	1	1
	5. Haryana			
1.	Barar	0.03		
2.	Batwal	0.02		
3.	Bawaria	1.26		
4.	Bhanjra	0.40		
5.	Chamar	52.98	49	69
6.	Chanal	0.001		
7.	Dagi	0.001		
8.	Dhanak	14.23	10	11
9.	Dumna	0.39		
10.	Gagra	0.005		
11.	Gandhila	0.01		
12.	Khatik	1.23	4	2
13.	Koli	1.28		
14.	Kori		-	1
15.	Megh	0.44		
16.	Mazhabi	2.93		
17.	Pasi	0.18	-	0.4
18.	Sansi	0.07		
19.	Sapela	0.19		
20.	Sarera	0.007		
	6. Madhya Pradesh			
1.	Balahi	10.46	6	NA
2.	Basor	2.83		
3.	Chamar	56.62	53	NA
4.	Dhobi	0.27	1	NA
5.	Ganda	3.17	2	NA
6.	Ghasia	1.16		
7.	Katia	0.69	3	NA
8.	Kori	3.84	7	NA
9.	Kumhar	2.05		
10.	Mahar	6.46	17	NA
11.	Mehar			
12.	Mang	0.27	0.4	NA
13.	Mehtar	3.35	3	NA

1	2	3	4	5
		7. Maharashtra		
1.	Bhangi	2.79	1	0.4
2.	Chamar	21.68		
3.	Madig			
4.	Mochi			
5.	Dhed	0.30	-	5
6.	Dhor	1.68	2	-
7.	Holeya	0.26		
8.	Mahar	35.40	72	66
9.	Mang	29.92	10	5
10.	Turi	0.004		
		8. Orissa		
1.	Bauri	9.17	8	4
2.	Chamar	2.46	3	4
3.	Muchi			
4.	Dhoba	9.73	17	23
5.	Dom	11.18		
6.	Dosadha	0.003		
7.	Ganda	9.82	-	5
8.	Ghasi	1.70	2	-
9.	Ghusuria	0.14		
10.	Gokha	2.48	-	11
11.	Hari	3.06		
12.	Kandara	7.50	8	15
13.	Kela	0.44	0.4	-
14.	Mahuria	0.10		
15.	Mehtar	0.22		
16.	Bhangi			
17.	Musahar	0.0005		
18.	Pan	20.32	25	11
19.	Pasi	0.003		
20.	Siyal	0.42	2	2
21.	Tior	0.41	-	1
22.	Turi	0.14		
		9. Punjab		
1.	Barar	0.06		
2.	Batwal	0.18	0.3	-
3.	Bawaria	1.27		
4.	Bhanjra	0.06		
5.	Chamar	29.31	31	21
6.	Chanal	0.001		
7.	Dagi	0.001		

1	2	3	4	5
8.	Dhanak	0.83		
9.	Dumna	2.74		
10.	Gagra	0.002		
11.	Gandhila	0.03		
12.	Khatik	0.18		
13.	Koli	0.06		
14.	Kori			
15.	Megh	1.57	6	5
16.	Mazhabi	28.75	7	2
17.	Pasi	0.05		
18.	Sansi	1.17		
19.	Sapela	0.02		
20.	Sarera	0.18		
		10. Tamil Nadu		
1.	Chakkiliyan	11.82	1	2
2.	Cheruman	0.01		
3.	Holeya	0.01		
4.	Madari	1.34		
5.	Madiga	0.10		
6.	Mala	0.23		
7.	Nayadi	0.004		
8.	Pallan	18.14	15	36
9.	Panchama	0.01		
10.	Valluvan	0.89	3	1
		11. U.P.		
1.	Bahelia	0.22	0.2	0.2
2.	Bajgi	0.04		
3.	Balahar	0.06		
4.	Balai	0.01	-	0.2
5.	Bangali	0.14		
6.	Bansphor	0.10		
7.	Chamar	54.57	78	68
8.	Dhanak	1.47	0.2	0.5
9.	Dhobi	6.23	4.0	6.5
10.	Domar	0.08		
11.	Gharami	0.0001		
12.	Khatik	2.10	2.0	2.5
13.	Kori	4.90	0.4	4
14.	Tarmali	13.87	8	5.5
	Source	a	b	b

Source : a —1971 Census Reports Chitnis, Suma, *A Long Way to Go*, Allied Publishers, 1981,
Appendix I, pp. 319-26.

MAIN TABLE
LITERACY RATE OF EACH SCHEDULED *CASTE COMMUNITY* REGISTERED IN THE CENSUSES 1961-81.

P indicates Person; M indicates Male; F indicates Female;

Sl. No.	*All Scheduled Castes*	*1961* P	M	F	*1971* P	M	F	*1981* P	M	F
1	2	3	4	5	6	7	8	9	10	11
	Andhra Pradesh									
	All Scheduled Castes	8.47	13.4	3.4	10.7	15.9	5.3	17.6	24.8	10.3
1.	Adi Andhra	14.8	21.5	8.0	19.8	26.5	13.0	27.5	34.4	20.6
2.	Adi Dravida	7.5	12.6	2.4	11.3	17.8	4.7	20.6	30.0	11.0
3.	Anamuk	0.8	1.5	0.13	1.9	2.6	1.3	37.6	35.0	40.0
4.	Aray Mala	22.6	32.7	13.2	16.9	30.5	7.3	31.9	44.8	18.6
5.	Arundhatiya	8.7	13.0	4.2	14.1	19.1	8.8	14.8	20.2	9.4
6.	Arwa Mala	47.1	58.4	35.4	45.4	56.3	33.9	36.8	44.5	29.1
7.	Bariki	7.6	13.6	1.7	7.9	13.7	2.0	18.7	29.4	16.0
8.	Bavuri	3.6	8.0	--	9.3	18.0	0.6	11.2	18.3	4.4
9.	Beda Jangam, Budga Jangam	7.7	13.4	0.6	8.3	15.2	5.1	18.5	29.0	7.6
10.	Bindla	12.09	22.85	0.88	13.6	24.7	1.8	16.9	29.7	4.0
11.	Byagara	3.2	6.0	0.5	3.7	6.7	0.8	7.6	12.9	2.2
12.	Chachati	9.0	13.3	4.9	10.0	16.0	4.2	8.1	12.9	3.1
13.	Chalavadi	8.6	16.1	1.0	14.4	23.6	5.0	19.0	28.8	8.7
14.	Chamar, Mochi, Muchi	22.6	35.0	9.3	19.1	28.9	9.3	34.2	47.1	20.6
15.	Chambhar	8.2	13.6	2.0	10.6	16.7	4.0	20.0	28.7	9.6
16.	Chandala	2.9	0.0	6.2	7.8	22.5	0.0	19.5	29.2	8.2
17.	Dakkal, Dokkalwar	9.3	17.4	0.3	12.6	21.0	1.1	10.9	20.1	1.2
18.	Dandasi	7.3	13.7	1.7	5.2	9.2	1.8	10.6	17.9	4.0
19.	Dhor	17.7	27.8	7.2	23.7	33.3	13.2	37.6	52.4	22.3
20.	Dom, Dombara, Paidi, Pano	6.7	11.9	2.2	7.5	12.4	2.8	13.8	21.4	6.2
21.	Ellamalawar, Yellammalawandlu	7.5	11.3	2.6	1.8	3.8	0.0	20.1	27.2	14.9
22.	Ghasi, Haddi, Relli Chachandi	10.8	19.6	3.1	12.0	22.7	3.1	8.1	13.7	2.8
23.	Godagali	5.7	10.8	0.8	7.8	12.3	2.1	10.9	17.9	3.4
24.	Godari	20.6	28.0	11.4	27.5	39.3	16.4	18.5	26.4	11.0
25.	Gosangi	6.25	11.4	0.0	18.1	22.2	13.3	8.3	14.5	2.1
26.	Holeya	5.3	6.5	3.7	3.2	5.0	1.9	20.4	28.1	11.6
27.	Holeya Dasari	35.7	65.0	1.4	19.9	31.8	0.0	19.6	35.8	2.6
28.	Jaggali	3.5	6.8	0.3	3.9	6.8	1.1	9.2	14.1	4.2

1	2	3	4	5	6	7	8	9	10	11
29.	Jambuvulu	8.3	13.0	3.4	11.3	17.2	4.8	17.4	25.0	9.7
30.	Kolupulvandlu	8.8	14.1	3.1	17.9	26.6	9.4	21.6	34.2	8.9
31.	Madasi Kuruva, Madari Kuruva	10.8	18.9	1.0	12.0	21.7	3.2	32.4	44.9	19.1
32.	Madiga	5.0	8.3	1.6	6.2	9.9	2.4	11.3	15.9	6.5
33.	Madiga Dasu, Mashteen	20.7	33.9	9.3	22.2	32.6	12.3	26.8	38.4	21.8
34.	Mahar	4.7	8.6	0.96	10.0	16.7	2.9	18.8	31.2	5.6
35.	Mala	10.1	16.3	3.9	12.6	18.9	6.2	21.2	29.7	12.5
36.	Mala Dasari	15.9	28.3	2.8	20.6	36.8	4.5	31.6	47.9	15.4
37.	Mala Dasu	25.9	41.4	10.9	26.9	40.8	14.0	63.8	81.7	25.2
38.	Mala Hannai	2.9	5.35	0.0	16.0	14.2	17.1	20.0	28.9	9.4
39.	Malajangam	20.0	36.1	3.5	19.0	36.4	4.6	27.3	44.1	10.6
40.	Mala Masti	9.4	16.0	1.8	11.9	24.4	0.0	10.9	18.7	3.0
41.	Mala Sale, Netkani	2.9	5.4	0.3	3.8	6.5	0.9	19.1	35.8	1.6
42.	Mala Sanyasi	9.6	15.1	0.0	42.3	51.7	0.0	21.6	36.3	7.7
43.	Mang	2.4	4.4	0.56	4.5	8.2	0.58	7.7	13.5	1.7
44.	Mang Garodi	0.0	0.0	0.0	8.3	6.0	13.3	8.6	8.2	9.1
45	Manne	4.2	7.3	0.9	5.1	9.0	1.3	10.5	16.5	4.2
46.	Mashti	11.0	19.0	1.8	9.6	16.3	2.6	14.2	21.3	6.4
47.	Matangi	9.2	14.0	0.01	10.0	20.0	4.4	13.7	23.1	4.3
48.	Mehtar	19.7	30.4	7.4	17.3	26.3	6.6	28.4	38.8	16.5
49.	Mitha Ayyalvar	27.7	51.2	1.9	31.2	50.2	6.3	37.6	66.7	8.9
50.	Mundala	0.6	1.1	0.0	5.0	13.8	2.4	15.8	21.6	9.7
51.	Paky, Moti Thoti	16.7	24.6	9.3	17.8	27.2	9.2	18.9	28.1	9.7
52.	Pambada, Pambanda	14.4	27.7	2.4	16.0	28.1	4.3	23.7	39.1	8.3
53.	Pamidi	6.2	9.5	0.8	7.6	12.6	2.4	12.1	19.2	4.8
54.	Panchama, Pariah	12.4	18.6	6.1	14.5	20.4	8.8	17.4	23.0	11.6
55.	Relli	12.4	21.1	4.2	15.4	24.1	6.8	24.2	33.6	14.9
56.	Samagara	17.4	22.9	11.6	25.6	34.1	17.5	37.1	47.7	26.2
57.	Samban	0.0	0.0	0.0	18.7	31.3	11.4	16.8	25.5	8.33
58.	Sapru	3.6	6.5	0.5	6.4	8.9	3.7	21.4	29.1	12.8
59.	Sindhollu Chindollu	24.4	43.5	4.3	26.5	49.0	2.2	26.3	48.5	4.4
	Unspecifed	13.1	20.4	5.6	29.1	36.9	19.4	47.3	84.7	10.1
	2. Arunachal Pradesh									
	All Scheduled Castes				36.3	52.8	18.0	37.1	45.8	22.3
1.	Bansphor				0.0	0.0	0.0	20.4	26.2	13.8
2.	Bhuinmali, Mali				0.0	0.0	0.0	33.3	47.3	17.6
3.	Brittial Bania, Bania				75.0	66.6	33.3	58.8	75.7	21.8
4.	Dhupi, Dhobi				0.0	0.0	0.0	29.4	37.8	10.3

1	2	3	4	5	6	7	8	9	10	11
5.	Dugla, Dholi				100.0	100.0	0.0	14.3	16.6	0.0
6.	Hira				100.0	100.0	0.0	55.5	50.0	66.6
7.	Jalkeot				0.0	0.0	0.0	14.7	8.0	33.3
8.	Jhalo, Malo, Jhalo-Malo				0.0	0.0	0.0	44.0	49.1	27.7
9.	Kaibartta, Jaliya				34.6	50.8	17.6	44.5	58.3	26.5
10.	Lalbegi				0.0	0.0	0.0	33.3	41.6	0.0
11.	Mahara				0.0	0.0	0.0	53.8	63.6	0.0
12.	Mehtar, Bhangi				0.0	0.0	0.0	24.8	37.4	9.5
13.	Muchi, Rishi				100.0	100.0	0.0	29.2	34.4	16.6
14.	Namasudra				50.0	66.6	0.0	39.0	44.1	29.8
15.	Patni				0.0	0.0	0.0	63.6	80.0	50.0
16.	Sutradhar				0.0	0.0	0,0	48.0	59.0	26.4
	Unspecified				0.0	0.0	0.0	39.2	46.0	29.0
	3. Assam									
	All Scheduled Castes	24.4		31.6	16.1	25.7	35.0		15.7	
1.	Bansphor	15.7		21.6	8.6	15.16	23.1		4.7	
2.	Bhuinmali, Mali	26.9		35.7	16.5	26.5	35.7		16.2	
3.	Brittial Bania, Bania	28.1		40.5	13.5	38.9	50.4		25.7	
4.	Dhupi, Dhobi	22.9		28.4	15.7	30.1	37.3		21.2	
5.	Dugla, Dholi	17.2		24.6	8.9	14.7	22.0		7.0	
6.	Hira	24.7		37.3	11.7	27.4	38.7		15.3	
7.	Jalkeot	18.4		24.0	10.4	26.3	35.2		14.4	
8.	Jhalo, Malo, Jhalo-Malo	13.7		19.8	6.9	15.2	23.3		5.8	
9.	Kaibartta, Jaliya	27.6		36.5	18.1	30.3	39.9		20.3	
10.	Lalbegi	37.1		53.0	22.2	33.3	40.7		22.2	
11.	Mahara	5.6		8.8	1.2	13.6	19.6		6.5	
12.	Mehtar, Bhangi	8.6		10.1	0.1	14.5	21.8		5.2	
13.	Muchi, Rishi	18.4		23.2	12.2	12.7	18.7		5.4	
14.	Namasudra	19.5		25.4	12.6	21.3	30.6		11.2	
15.	Patni	36.9		44.5	29.0	31.8	41.1		22.2	
16.	Sutradhar	21.9		31.2	11.3	26.3	37.5		13.7	
	4. Bihar									
	All Scheduled Castes	5.9	11.1	0.9	6.5	11.9	1.0	10.4	18.0	2.5
1.	Bantar	12.4	16.4	8.8	3.6	6.9	0.3	5.2	9.6	0.6
2.	Bauri	5.8	10.8	0.6	5.8	10.2	0.8	11.1	19.1	2.6
3.	Bhogta	4.1	7.7	0.5	3.6	6.5	0.5	6.4	11.6	1.2
4.	Bhuiya	1.3	2.5	0.1	1.5	2.9	0.1	4.3	7.7	0.8
5.	Bhumij	6.5	11.1	0.8	3.5	6.8	0.2	7.3	13.4	2.0
6.	Chamar, Mochi	6.3	12.3	0.8	7.0	13.1	1.0	11.5	20.5	2.3
7.	Chaupal	7.5	15.5	0.5	7.7	14.4	0.8	8.8	15.9	1.4
8.	Dabgar	15.2	26.6	4.3	15.5	28.8	1.8	22.2	37.2	6.6

1 2	3	4	5	6	7	8	9	10	11
9. Dhobi	10.0	18.3	1.7	11.9	21.3	2.4	18.56	30.7	5.9
10.Dom, Dhangad	4.8	8.7	0.8	5.0	9.8	0.8	7.9	13.4	2.1
11. Dusadh, Dhari, Dharhi	7.0	13.4	0.8	7.9	14.5	1.1	12.4	21.4	2.9
12. Ghasi	9.1	14.4	3.6	8.2	14.7	2.0	14.6	23.4	5.5
13. Halalkhor	11.0	21.4	2.6	10.3	20.1	1.8	19.3	31.7	6.9
14. Hari, Mehtar, Bhangi	10.5	18.8	2.3	10.1	17.3	2.5	16.4	26.5	5.7
15. Kanjar	8.9	14.5	2.4	4.5	12.6	0.8	11.2	17.7	4.6
16. Kurariar	5.4	11.0'	0.0	7.5	13.7	1.0	10.4	17.3	3.2
17. Lalbegi	11.3	17.8	0.7	14.2	24.6	3.4	18.2	30.0	5.1
18. Musahar	2.1	3.6	0.5	1.3	2.4	0.1	2.1	4.0	0.3
19. Nat	5.4	8.1	2.3	6.5	8.3	2.6	8.5	13.1	3.8
20. Pan, Sawasi	12.3	22.1	1.9	15.2	26.9	3.3	27.0	42.4	11.3
21. Pasi	10.00	17.9	1.6	11.7	20.5	2.2	17.5	28.7	5.6
22. Rajwar	4.8	9.3	0.3	5.3	10.1	0.5	9.1	16.5	1.4
23. Turi	4.6	8.8	0.5	4.9	9.0	0.7	8.1	14.3	1.7
Unspecified	6.3	12.3	1.4	10.2	18.4	3.2	18.4	28.3	7.2
5. Goa									
All Scheduled Castes				23.6	32.4	14.2	36.1	46.5	25.3
1. Bhangi, Hadi				40.2	50.0	26.3	44.7	52.6	35.5
2. Chambar				38.5	46.9	29.4	58.0	66.7	48.9
3. Mahar				14.3	22.8	5.4	25.5	37.1	13.5
4. Mahyavanshi, Vankar				24.3	40.0	9.5	38.6	50.0	24.5
5. Mang				11.3	19.7	40.0	32.7	43.0	22.5
Unspecified				24.9	36.4	11.5	21.7	29.0	13.7
6. Gujarat									
All Scheduled Castes	22.4	33.8	10.7	27.7	39.8	14.9	39.7	53.1	25.6
1. Ager	57.8	44.4	70.0	0.0	0.0	0.0	47.6	57.3	36.2
2. Bakad, Bant	7.0	12.2	0.0	9.3	8.5	11.1	27.3	38.8	18.4
3. Bawa-Dedh, Dedh-Sadhu	24.9	41.6	7.0	23.6	40.1	7.1	34.8	48.4	20.4
4. Bhambi, Bhambhi, Asadaru, Asodi, Chamadia, Chamar, Chambhar, Chamgar, Haralayya, Harali, Khalpa, Machigar, Mochigar, Madar, Madig, Mochi, Nalia, Telugu Mochi, Kamati Mochi, Ranigar, Rohidas, Rohit, Samgar	21.4	33.2	9.2	26.2	38.6	13.2	39.8	53.0	25.7

1	2	3	4	5	6	7	8	9	10	11
5.	Bhangi, Mehtar, Olgana, Rukhi, Malkana, Halalkhor, Lalbegi, Balmiki, Korar, Zadmalli	17.7	28.3	6.7	21.1	32.6	8.9	34.9	47.9	21.2
6.	Chalvadi, Channayya	18.7	12.5	25.0	9.5	3.6	20.6	43.1	53.8	34.3
7.	Chenna Dasar, Holaya Dasar							45.3	62.1	26.1
8.	Dangashia	12.3	24.2	0.1	20.6	38.5	3.5	27.7	43.8	10.1
9.	Dhor, Kakkayya, Kankayya	14.7	23.2	6.7	7.0	9.3	4.0	30.7	40.0	20.4
10.	Garmatang	14.7	27.6	0.5	16.7	26.4	4.1	32.1	52.6	10.0
11.	Garoda, Garo	40.4	59.9	20.7	46.7	64.3	28.3	56.9	73.4	39.3
12.	Halleer	0.0	0.0	0.0	38.4	83.3	0.0	28.5	46.6	7.6
13.	Halsar, haslar, Hulasvar, Halasvar	0.0	0.0	0.0	0.0	0.0	0.0	46.7	55.5	36.9
14.	Holar Valhar	17.6	15.3	25.0	63.6	83.3	40.0	37.0	46.5	33.1
15.	Holaya, Holer	0.0	0.0	0.0	11.7	44.4	0.0	51.0	61.7	40.0
16.	Lingader	37.5	60.0	0.0	66.6	71.4	50.0	57.4	65.4	46.1
17.	Mahar, Taral, Dhegu Megu	22.6	36.3	9.2	29.0	41.7	16.5	34.6	47.5	20.7
18.	Mahyavanshi, Dhed, Dhedh, Vankar, Maru Vankar, Antyaj	27.6	39.9	15.0	33.3	45.9	20.0	44.2	57.7	29.8
19.	Mang, Matang, Minimadig	11.2	17.9	4.9	17.2	23.5	11.2	27.2	41.3	11.9
20.	Mang-Garudi	6.5	12.9	0.0	16.1	25.0	9.8	10.9	16.4	5.2
21.	Meghval, Meghwal, Menghvar	9.1	16.4	1.8	12.5	21.5	3.2	20.9	33.3	8.0
22.	Mukri	0.0	0.0	0.0	50.0	50.0	0.0	34.6	61.5	7.6
23.	Nadia, Hadi	16.3	26.1	6.0	20.4	31.6	8.4	30.5	43.1	17.0
24.	Pasi	16.0	19.0	0.0	31.5	37.9	10.7	31.1	39.9	15.3
25.	Senva, Shenva, Chenva, Sedma, Rawat	14.5	22.3	6.6	17.9	28.3	7.2	28.5	41.6	14.5
26.	Shemalia	0.0	0.0	0.0	0.0	0.0	0.0	28.7	38.3	18.1
27.	Thori	0.0	0.0	0.0	11.3	20.4	0.0	12.2	19.6	4.4
28.	Tirgar, Tirbanda	17.8	28.5	6.8	23.6	37.0	9.4	38.7	56.2	19.7
29.	Turi	30.9	48.7	13.5	34.4	50.3	17.3	46.6	64.0	28.3
30.	Turi Barot, Dedh Barot	20.4	36.9	3.5	24.3	43.7	4.5	39.2	58.4	18.8
	Unspecified	18.2	27.4	9.1	27.5	39.1	15.0	35.4	47.8	22.2

1	2	3	4	5	6	7	8	9	10	11
	7. Haryana									
	All Scheduled Castes				12.5	20.8	3.0	20.1	31.4	5.5
1.	Ad-Dharmi				10.71	19.2	4.1	31.78	38.4	23.5
2.	Balmiki, Chura, Bhangi				9.3	15.4	2.6	14.3	22.3	5.3
3.	Bangali				12.3	13.2	11.5	29.2	36.8	18.6
4.	Burar, Burar, Berar				12.8	22.11	2.1	21.2	33.2	6.5
5.	Batwal				8.1	12.2	3.0	19.7	31.3	8.8
6.	Bauria, Bawaria				7.7	14.1	1.0	12.0	20.5	2.6
7.	Bazigar				4.9	8.9	0.6	10.1	17.4	2.3
8.	Bhanjra				9.2	16.3	1.2	19.4	30.9	6.3
9.	Chamar, Jatia Chamar, Rehgar, Raigar, Ramdasi, Ravidasi				14.1	24.0	3.3	23.6	36.7	8.0
10.	Chanal				14.3	16.7	0.0	22.5	38.9	5.6
11.	Dagi				16.0	19.0	0.0	18.0	25.0	8.5
12.	Darain				0.0	0.0	0.0	20.0	28.6	5.0
13.	Deha, Dhaya, Dhea				2.6	4.9	0.0	2.3	3.4	1.2
14.	Dhanak				11.1	18.7	1.9	17.1	28.1	4.7
15.	Dhogri, Dhangri, Siggi				1.2	1.4	0.9	6.4	11.6	1.4
16.	Dumna, Mahasha, Doom				10.2	17.7	1.7	17.6	27.9	5.6
17.	Gagra				12.5	12.2	12.7	17.2	27.6	6.8
18.	Gandhila, Gandil Gondola				4.1	7.1	0.0	13.3	20.3	5.2
19.	Kabirpanthi, Julaha				20.1	29.5	8.8	31.6	15.6	45.1
20.	Khatik				21.4	38.6	5.7	32.6	47.4	16.0
21.	Kori, Koli				17.5	26.3	5.7	26.5	40.4	9.3
22.	Marija, Marecha				24.3	30.0	0.0	13.8	20.3	7.0
23.	Mazhabi				8.1	11.2	4.5	11.6	15.7	7.0
24.	Megh				15.9	24.7	6.5	28.4	36.4	19.2
25.	Nat				10.9	20.9	0.9	16.8	28.9	3.0
26.	Od				10.8	18.6	2.1	16.6	27.5	5.0
27.	Pasi				26.7	30.9	19.6	33.4	41.1	22.8
28.	Perna				2.4	2.5	2.3	3.3	5.7	0.8
29.	Pherera					0.0	0.0	0.0	20.8	38.5
30.	Sanhai				9.1	17.8	2.8	27.1	37.8	9.1
31.	Sanhal				21.6	40.0	0.0	25.7	31.6	18.7
32.	Sansi, Bhedkut, Manesh				10.3	16.8	3.3	16.2	26.0	5.5
33.	Sansoi				26.0	41.9	0.0	5.9	5.9	5.9
34.	Sapela				1.7	2.9	0.1	3.6	5.9	0.5
35.	Sarera				7.3	12.1	2.8	19.6	21.7	5.6
36.	Sikligar				5.3	9.3	1.0	9.5	13.8	5.1
37.	Sirkiband				3.0	5.0	0.8	8.9	14.8	2.6
	Unspecified				22.9	35.4	66.1	24.1	35.5	10.1
	8. Himachal Pradesh									
	All Scheduled Castes				18.8	27.4	9.7	31.5	41.9	20.6
1.	Ad Dharmi				23.78	33.7	13.1	39.5	50.7	26.9
2.	Badhi, Nagalu				17.4	26.6	6.8	23.2	34.7	11.4
3.	Balmiki, Bhangi, Chuhra, Chura, Chuhre				34.4	41.9	25.3	45.9	53.6	37.0

1	2	3	4	5	6	7	8	9	10	11
4.	Bandhela			27.8	35.6	17.6	33.3		31.2	35.7
5.	Bangali			10.9	12.0	10.0	18.6		23.3	27.6
6.	Banjara			16.9	26.9	4.7	28.2		39.1	15.9
7.	Bansi			14.8	23.6	6.1	22.7		35.5	9.7
8.	Barad			7.6	12.3	1.9	15.1		23.1	6.3
9.	Barar, Burar, Berar			9.8	18.2	4.3	14.4		19.2	8.8
10.	Batwal			23.3	34.2	12.8	34.9		45.7	23.4
11.	Bauria, Bawaria			100.0	100.0	0.0	13.8		13.3	14.3
12.	Bazigar			11.8	19.7	3.6	24.1		36.3	10.0
13.	Bhanjra, Bhanjre			18.2	25.4	10.7	30.8		43.0	17.9
14.	Chamar, Jatia Chamar, Rehgar, Raigar, Ramdasi, Ravidasi, Ramdasia, Mochi			20.6	30.2	10.4	34.2		44.9	23.0
15.	Chanal			12.3	19.8	4.3	21.3		31.5	10.7
16.	Chhimbe, Dhobi			39.1	49.7	26.8	52.2		61.6	42.9
17.	Dagi			7.8	13.8	1.7	15.7		26.9	4.6
18.	Darain			17.2	27.4	7.6	29.3		41.3	17.0
19.	Darai, Daryai			19.2	26.7	12.2	35.3		49.1	22.2
20.	Daule, Daole			15.4	22.8	8.2	27.8		40.8	13.9
21.	Dhaki, Toori			18.6	27.4	9.0	25.3		33.6	16.2
22.	Dhanak			12.9	19.2	8.3	35.3		30.8	50.00
23.	Dhaogri, Dhuai			5.4	9.4	1.0	26.3		39.5	13.0
24.	Dhogri, Dhangri, Siggi			13.1	18.2	7.8	16.1		25.8	5.6
25.	Doom, Doomna, Dumna, Dumne, Mahasha			18.0	25.1	10.7	31.1		40.5	21.1
26.	Gagra			-	-	-	50.0		60.0	0.0
27.	Gandhila, Gandil Gondola			-	-	-	100.0		100.0	100.0
28.	Hali			11.3	16.9	4.7	16.3		26.0	5.9
29.	Hesi			19.6	29.3	9.6	30.7		41.6	19.4
30.	Jogi			21.2	29.3	12.5	35.9		46.0	25.7
31.	Julaha, Julahe, Kabirpanthi, Keer			24.5	34.7	14.6	39.3		49.4	29.5
32.	Kamoh, Dagoli			40.6	46.8	34.1	61.9		68.4	54.4
33.	Karoack			0.0	0.0	0.0	34.0		34.8	33.3
34.	Khatik			39.4	47.9	23.3	49.9		55.1	40.8
35.	Kori, Koli			14.6	22.4	6.4	24.1		35.2	12.5
36.	Lohar			19.0	27.3	10.0	38.2		47.8	28.2
37.	Marija, Marecha			-	-	-	41.7		60.0	28.6
38.	Mazhabi			21.2	25.3	11.4	34.4		39.2	25.6
39.	Megh			15.3	19.6	11.2	30.3		39.3	20.2
40.	Nat			7.9	9.1	6.8	21.1		33.6	8.0
41.	Od			23.1	25.0	20.4	31.9		45.4	18.6
42.	Pasi			18.3	19.6	8.3	38.0		38.3	37.6
43.	Perna			-	-	-	33.3		40.0	27.3
44.	Phrera, Pherera			41.4	55.1	29.4	54.2		60.9	47.5
45.	Rehar, Rehara			19.3	21.0	17.3	28.3		37.5	18.1
46.	Sanhai			23.7	29.0	17.7	42.5		50.3	35.6
47.	Sanhal			0.0	0.0	0.0	83.3		100.0	66.7

1 2	3	4	5	6	7	8	9	10	11
48. Sansi, Bhedkut, Manesh			21.5	29.5	11.8	25.2		34.3	16.0
49. Sansoi			19.8	26.6	13.2	37.4		47.8	25.7
50. Sapela			0.0	0.0	-	30.4		25.0	42.9
51. Sarde, Sarera, Sarare, Siryare, Sarehde			27.7	36.4	17.9	41.6		51.6	30.9
52. Sikligar			20.5	30.4	8.7	22.5		26.5	17.7
53. Sipi			8.2	14.3	1.5	16.8		27.7	5.3
54. Sirkiband			20.0	25.0	0.0	0.0		0.0	0.0
55. Teli			24.2	40.1	7.2	33.0		46.0	19.2
56. Thathiar, Thathera			27.6	35.2	20.1	43.3		56.0	30.8
Unspecified			19.8	28.8	11.0	35.2		45.7	22.2
9. Jammu and Kashmir									
All Scheduled Castes	4.7	7.9	1.1	12.0	19.1	4.2	22.4	32.3	11.7
1. Barwala	2.7	4.7	0.3	9.2	15.6	2.6	19.4	30.2	8.0
2. Basith	3.1	5.6	0.6	11.7	19.4	3.4	29.1	43.1	14.5
3. Batwal	4.6	7.5	1.4	10.9	18.1	3.4	22.4	33.5	10.4
4. Chamar or Ramdasia	5.0	8.6	1.0	14.4	22.4	6.0	27.9	38.0	17.1
5. Chura	3.0	4.6	1.2	9.1	12.2	5.2	12.7	19.1	5.4
6. Dhyar	2.3	4.2	0.3	5.2	9.4	0.9	11.6	20.1	2.1
7. Doom or Mahasha	3.3	5.6	0.7	8.5	13.9	2.5	15.5	23.4	6.8
8. Gardi	2.6	4.7	0.0	6.4	12.8	1.2	22.1	30.9	12.5
9. Jolaha	9.4	19.0	0.0	18.9	30.9	2.5	26.7	37.3	11.3
10. Megh or Kabirpanthi	5.5	9.2	1.4	12.5	19.9	4.3	23.3	33.8	11.8
11.Ratal	1.9	3.3	0.2	5.4	10.2	1.6	12.3	19.7	4.4
12. Saryara	5.5	9.8	1.2	8.4	13.8	3.0	15.4	23.9	6.5
13. Watal	3.2	6.2	0.0	5.7	6.8	0.8	5.7	9.1	2.3
Unspecified	-	-	-	89.0	94.0	1.4	33.3	47.1	13.2
10. Karnataka									
All Scheduled Castes	9.1	14.9	3.0	13.9	20.7	6.7	20.6	29.4	11.6
1. Adi Andhra	13.6	20.8	5.9	22.7	31.6	12.9	36.7	46.4	26.5
2. Adi Dravida	16.0	24.3	7.4	23.8	31.5	15.7	36.7	45.3	27.9
3. Adi Karnataka	7.7	12.9	2.3	12.7	19.1	6.0	19.8	28.4	10.8
4. Adiya	11.8	14.8	7.8	8.2	13.0	2.9	9.0	12.6	5.5
5. Ager	15.0	24.8	5.1	28.9	43.8	13.7	33.3	44.3	21.4
6. Ajila	6.2	11.4	1.4	13.7	21.9	5.7	26.1	32.9	18.2
7. Anamak	-	-	-	4.7	7.1	2.0	68.3	77.8	54.2
8. Aray Mala	6.7	25.0	0.0	0.0	0.0	0.0	34.4	43.9	24.2
9. Arunthatniyar	-	-	-	50.0	50.0	-	25.4	35.3	14.7
10. Arwa Mala	26.1	66.7	11.9	-	-	-	16.4	24.2	7.5
11. Baira	7.6	13.5	3.4	19.3	25.2	13.1	27.4	35.4	18.9
12. Bakad	26.0	41.3	12.0	32.9	44.9	20.1	26.6	37.5	16.4
13. Bant included in Bakad included in Bakad							62.0	71.5	51.0
14. Bakuda	16.2	21.7	11.0	25.0	33.8	16.3	39.5	49.6	28.2
15. Balagai	11.9	18.0	5.9	19.2	27.5	10.3	20.4	28.4	12.1
16. Bandi	10.0	20.0	0.0	40.0	33.3	50.0	64.1	70.7	57.5

1	2	3	4	5	6	7	8	9	10	11
17.	Banjara, Lambani	6.6	11.5	1.4	11.2	18.1	3.9	13.5	21.5	5.0
18.	Bathada	5.3	14.3	0.3	21.3	25.7	17.2	26.1	39.5	13.8
19.	Beda Jangam, Budga Jangam	6.9	14.1	0.6	8.0	13.8	2.4	27.6	37.2	17.5
20.	Bellara	8.0	19.7	0.9	12.6	18.7	7.4	25.7	32.7	18.7
21.	Bhangi, Mehtar, Olgana, Rukki, Malkana, Halalkhor, Lalbegi, Balmiki, Korar, Zadmalli	20.0	33.3	5.9	21.0	32.9	8.2	19.6	28.8	10.0
22.	Bhambi, Bhambhi, Asadaru, Asodi, Chamadia, Chamar, Chambhar, Chamgar, Muchi, Haralayya, Harali, Khalpa, Machigar, Mochigar, Madar, Madig, Mochi, Telegu Mochi, Kamati Mochi, Ranigar, Rohidas, Rohit, Samgar	11.1	18.2	3.9	14.0	21.6	6.4	18.2	26.8	9.6
23.	Bhovi	7.6	13.1	1.7	12.8	19.7	5.5	17.9	26.9	8.5
24.	Bindla	26.7	44.4	0.0	1.8	3.3	0.0	17.0	30.1	4.9
25.	Byagara	3.3	6.4	0.6	6.4	11.2	1.6	9.2	15.1	3.5
26.	Chakkiliyan	0.0	0.0	0.0	15.3	23.5	6.4	12.0	18.9	5.0
27.	Chalavadi, Chalvadi, Channayya	14.4	23.9	4.9	17.7	27.5	7.6	22.4	33.0	11.8
28.	Chandala	4.0	3.6	4.8	15.3	18.9	11.5	13.7	24.7	
29.	Channa Dasar, Holaya Dasar	20.1	34.3	6.0	18.2	28.8	6.4	26.0	40.2	11.9
30.	Dakkal, Dokkalwar	0.0	0.0	0.0	11.5	18.7	0.0	12.8	18.8	6.9
31.	Dakkaliga	26.7	39.5	10.7	18.7	25.4	11.5	18.4	25.5	11.3
32.	Dhor, Kakkayya, Kankayya	20.4	32.3	8.3	24.0	34.5	13.0	37.7	50.3	24.8
33.	Dom, Dombara, Paidi, Pano	9.1	16.7	0.0	0.0	0.0	0.0	19.6	28.0	11.5
34.	Ellamalwar, Yellammalawandlu	6.2	14.1	0.0	3.0	5.9	0.0	53.4	65.4	39.6
35.	Ganti Chores	6.0	9.8	1.3	12.5	17.3	7.0	29.7	39.0	20.1

1	2	3	4	5	6	7	8	9	10	11
36.	Garoda, Garo	0.0	0.0	0.0	23.6	39.6	0.0	29.5	44.6	14.1
37.	Godd	8.9	14.7	2.1	20.0	26.9	13.5	29.3	35.0	23.0
38.	Gosangi	-	-	-	0.0	0.0	0.0	9.1	12.0	6.0
39.	Halleer	11.2	20.3	5.3	14.6	23.5	5.5	22.5	32.2	12.0
40.	Halsar, Haslar, Hulasvar, Halasvar	15.5	23.3	6.9	18.1	24.4	11.0	28.7	38.4	18.8
41.	Handi Jogis	4.3	7.7	0.6	11.1	16.6	5.2	10.8	16.4	5.1
42.	Hasla	4.4	6.1	2.6	12.6	17.9	7.7	14.9	19.3	10.00
43.	Holar, Valhar	9.1	10.0	0.0	30.8	40.9	21.4	18.4	24.1	12.6
44.	Holaya, Holer, Holeya	7.1	12.0	2.3	10.9	17.7	4.0	19.1	29.2	8.8
45.	Holeya Dasari	9.5	16.6	0.9	12.4	21.7	0.3	23.3	35.4	11.8
46.	Jaggali	20.0	0.0	33.3	33.3	50.0	20.0	12.2	22.4	1.847
47.	Jambuvulu	18.9	25.0	11.8	2.0	3.4	0.6	11.7	16.7	6.5
48.	Kadaiyan	100.0	100.0	-	0.0	0.0	0.0	13.9	17.4	10.5
49.	Kalladi	6.1	12.1	0.0	0.0	0.0	0.0	7.2	9.3	4.7
50.	Kepmaris	19.0	40.0	9.3	8.6	12.3	4.3	10.5	16.4	5.0
51.	Kolupulvandlu	-	-	-	100.0	100.0	-	22.4	29.1	15.4
52.	Koosa	10.1	17.6	3.9	16.0	24.5	8.3	19.8	27.9	12.0
53.	Koracha	7.7	13.6	1.6	12.8	20.0	5.1	18.1	28.4	8.6
54.	Korama	13.9	23.2	4.3	16.0	25.1	8.4	24.7	35.7	13.4
55.	Kotegar, Metri	16.5	24.1	9.6	18.1	27.9	7.4	50.0	60.9	39.5
56.	Kudumban	2.1	1.8	2.5	14.5	19.1	9.6	41.5	54.4	30.4
57.	Kuravan	9.1	24.0	3.2	18.1	27.9	8.6	22.5	32.5	11.8
58.	Lingader	20.8	34.4	7.6	34.4	36.4	32.1	33.8	39.5	27.0
59.	Machala	11.9	24.7	3.6	10.0	14.5	4.8	34.3	54.9	12.5
60.	Madari	0.8	2.0	0.0	11.4	12.2	10.5	16.4	24.6	7.7
61.	Madiga	3.2	5.8	0.7	5.5	9.3	1.6	12.1	19.0	5.3
62.	Mahar, Taral Dhegu Megu	12.3	20.0	4.1	19.3	30.3	8.0	32.0	46.0	17.7
63.	Mahyavanshi, Dhed, Vankar Maru, Vankar	9.7	19.4	0.0	33.3	50.0	0.0	38.4	52.9	24.8
64.	Maila	1.6	2.6	0.8	6.0	9.1	3.0	13.5	18.5	8.4
65.	Mala	7.8	14.6	1.4	14.3	21.1	7.6	31.1	42.2	19.6
66.	Mala Dasari	18.8	35.0	5.5	15.6	26.0	4.3	29.7	46.0	13.8
67.	Mala Hannai	-	-	-	-	-	-	22.5	30.0	15.0
68.	Mala Jangam	3.8	33.3	0.0	8.4	14.3	1.3	25.4	39.3	12.6
69.	Mala Masti	-	-	-	-	-	-	17.6	16.7	19.7
70.	Mala Sale, Netkani	-	-	-	-	-	-	18.0	27.3	10.0
71.	Mala Sanyasi	-	-	-	-	-	-	6.4	11.0	1.8
72.	Mang, Matang, Minimadig	5.0	8.3	1.6	8.9	14.7	2.8	14.4	22.5	6.0
73.	Mang Garudi, Mang Garodi	25.1	41.0	12.5	17.9	24.2	10.9	14.7	23.2	6.5
74.	Manne	0.0	0.0	0.0	-	-	-	21.3	31.4	11.4
75.	Masthi	0.0	0.0	0.0	-	-	-	32.5	43.9	20.5

1	2	3	4	5	6	7	8	9	10	11
76.	Mavilan	-	-	-	0.0	0.0	0.0	11.8	17.2	4.5
77.	Meghval, Menghvar	35.0	40.0	30.0	48.3	48.5	48.1	31.8	50.0	0.0
78.	Moger	5.5	7.3	3.3	10.0	15.0	5.0	23.1	31.4	14.4
79.	Mukri	7.3	13.3	1.2	12.0	18.1	5.7	22.1	30.7	13.2
80.	Mundala	21.2	29.0	13.3	29.3	36.5	22.3	43.4	52.1	34.6
81.	Nadia, Hadi	0.0	0.0	0.0	66.7	100.0	40.0	32.2	41.9	21.4
82.	Nalkadaya	12.0	14.5	7.3	12.7	17.9	7.9	23.0	30.8	14.3
83.	Nalakeyava	8.0	11.4	4.4	13.7	19.4	7.6	24.5	31.9	16.7
84.	Nayadi				20.0	28.6	10.0	28.1	34.4	21.0
85.	Pale	6.4	9.2	2.9	9.7	13.9	5.1	14.7	20.0	8.8
86.	Pallan	0.0	0.0	-	57.1	57.1	57.1	43.3	53.5	31.6
87.	Pambada	15.3	22.7	9.4	25.5	31.6	19.2	50.2	58.4	43.5
88.	Panchama	12.6	13.3	11.8	21.0	29.2	12.8	30.1	46.3	11.9
89.	Panniandi	0.0	0.0	0.0	0.0	0.0	0.0	8.2	13.2	2.3
90.	Paraiyan, Paraya	12.4	22.2	0.0	11.0	13.2	8.6	23.1	31.0	14.1
91.	Paravan	5.5	2.8	2.5	12.6	18.9	6.5	20.7	28.3	12.8
92.	Raneyar	15.6	22.6	9.3	14.9	18.8	9.7	29.8	39.3	20.8
93.	Samagara	14.4	22.0	6.9	20.0	29.0	10.6	33.4	45.0	21.5
94.	Samban	0.0	0.0	0.0	0.0	0.0	0.0	50.7	71.9	33.3
95.	Sapari	0.0	0.0	0.0	0.0	0.0	0.0	4.8	11.1	0.0
96.	Sillekyathas,	9.2	16.0	2.6	12.6	19.5	5.0	15.2	24.8	5.3
97.	Sindhollu, Chindollu	70.3	98.5	0.0	-	-	-	31.7	47.6	15.0
98	Sudugadu Sidda	8.4	15.2	1.0	12.3	17.5	6.6	16.7	26.4	6.4
99.	Thoti	16.9	21.1	10.0	30.4	37.1	23.8	18.9	27.4	9.7
100.	Tirgar, Tirbanda	48.4	57.1	30.0	-	-	-	42.8	50.0	34.2
101.	Valluvan	-	-	-	13.1	20.0	6.1	57.2	68.3	46.0
	Unspecified	8.7	24.1	2.7	10.7	15.9	5.0	17.1	25.3	8.6
	11. Kerala									
	All Scheduled Castes	24.5	31.6	17.4	40.2	47.1	33.4	56.0	62.3	49.2
1.	Adi Andhra	23.6	25.0	22.3	23.6	34.0	15.4	40.9	49.3	32.6
2.	Adi Dravida	27.2	36.2	15.8	43.5	52.4	33.7	46.3	57.7	34.2
3.	Adi Karnataka	13.5	22.2	3.4	10.2	16.1	4.5	28.3	35.3	22.0
4.	Ajila	12.5	15.0	9.4	16.9	27.8	5.7	29.7	36.0	21.7
5.	Arunthathiyar	30.0	37.2	22.1	48.7	54.5	42.9	62.5	70.4	54.9
6.	Ayyanvar	42.4	47.9	36.8	56.5	59.9	53.1	68.6	71.5	65.8
7.	Baira	6.0	9.1	2.7	10.9	15.3	6.0	28.1	38.3	16.1
8.	Bakuda	17.5	25.6	8.5	28.8	39.4	18.1	43.1	53.7	32.4
9.	Bandi	-	-	-	100.0	-	100.0	66.7	69.2	63.6
10.	Bathada	24.0	33.0	17.3	-	-	-	43.5	42.9	44.0
11.	Bellara	-	-	-	33.3	40.0	25.0	42.2	46.1	36.8
12.	Bharatar	57.8	67.6	47.8	69.4	75.1	63.8	79.8	81.9	77.5
13.	Boyan	9.9	15.2	4.0	22.9	31.9	13.6	40.2	47.2	32.9
14.	Chakkiliyan	13.4	19.8	6.8	22.2	28.8	15.3	34.7	42.5	26.7
15.	Chamar, Muchi	5.6	10.0	0.0	38.3	61.5	29.4	66.4	76.5	54.4

1	2	3	4	5	6	7	8	9	10	11
16.	Chandala	2.5	5.3	0.0	18.4	38.1	3.6	62.2	70.2	53.5
17.	Cheruman	11.1	15.8	6.5	23.2	29.6	16.9	38.9	46.2	31.9
18.	Domban	2.2	4.5	0.0	5.8	9.8	0.0	16.9	21.0	12.2
19.	Gavara	10.8	15.9	4.6	9.4	15.8	3.1	33.1	40.9	25.0
20.	Godagali	-	-	-	0.0	0.0	0.0	35.1	46.7	27.3
21.	Godda	11.1	16.7	0.0	65.4	82.3	33.3	46.8	58.8	33.7
22.	Gosangi	0.0	0.0	0.0	19.4	15.4	21.7	65.5	68.6	62.5
23.	Hasla	12.5	13.5	11.1	22.8	36.0	12.5	50.0	40.0	100.0
24.	Holeya	10.0	15.3	4.6	12.4	18.4	6.1	18.8	25.0	12.6
25.	Kadaiyan	29.5	33.3	25.8	30.5	40.7	18.8	46.1	57.0	36.1
26.	Kakkalan	48.1	59.1	37.7	60.5	66.8	54.2	69.8	74.2	65.4
27.	Kalladi	12.5	17.0	8.2	25.2	31.3	19.3	41.7	48.1	35.5
28.	Kanakkan, Padanna	19.0	25.4	12.8	33.2	40.3	26.5	50.2	57.0	43.7
29.	Karimpalan	11.9	16.4	7.3	22.7	28.4	16.8	41.7	47.8	35.4
30.	Kavara	4.2	6.1	2.0	10.7	14.3	7.1	18.4	25.2	11.6
31.	Koosa	-	-	-	0.0	-	0.0	41.8	48.9	33.9
32.	Kootan, Koodan	5.7	8.5	3.2	15.7	19.8	11.7	33.2	38.5	28.2
33.	Kudumban	45.1	59.2	30.6	38.5	48.4	28.5	56.2	63.9	48.4
34.	Kuravan, Sidhanar	17.2	23.5	11.1	34.4	40.9	28.2	49.5	56.2	43.1
35.	Maila	1.8	3.3	0.4	5.8	9.2	2.6	17.2	22.8	11.7
36.	Malayan	32.0	33.4	30.5	43.7	45.1	42.3	58.6	60.1	57.1
37.	Mannan	44.2	53.8	34.6	61.6	68.3	55.2	67.7	74.4	61.2
38.	Mavilan	5.4	8.1	2.6	11.7	15.9	7.4	24.8	30.3	19.2
39.	Moger	20.7	27.5	14.0	27.2	35.6	18.4	38.0	46.6	29.1
40.	Mundala	27.6	33.7	22.7	44.7	55.6	35.1	57.0	70.5	44.7
41.	Naladeyava	7.3	11.4	1.7	22.2	32.2	9.7	45.3	51.0	38.9
42.	Nalkadaya	16.7	24.0	7.7	23.8	31.1	13.4	36.2	46.5	23.7
43.	Nayadi	16.5	20.5	12.6	26.6	31.7	21.6	42.9	49.8	36.0
44.	Padannan	39.7	46.2	33.3	54.3	61.6	47.4	67.4	73.3	61.9
45.	Pallan	18.6	28.8	7.9	29.2	40.4	17.6	43.7	54.2	33.1
46.	Palluvan	32.2	41.0	23.4	39.0	48.2	29.4	54.1	60.4	48.0
47.	Pambada	6.9	9.1	5.6	25.5	37.0	10.0	59.0	67.2	48.9
48.	Panan	29.8	37.8	22.1	43.3	52.2	34.7	56.0	63.7	48.7
49.	Panchama	30.5	39.8	20.2	60.0	75.0	0.0	44.0	52.9	34.4
50.	Paraiyan, Paryan, Sambavar	26.5	35.2	17.7	42.9	50.8	35.0	57.6	64.9	50.3
51.	Paravan	46.4	55.9	37.1	62.0	69.2	54.8	73.1	78.4	67.9
52.	Pathiyan	50.2	55.8	44.4	67.3	70.5	64.2	74.3	78.4	70.3
53.	Perumannan	51.9	65.7	39.0	63.6	72.6	55.1	72.6	79.4	66.2
54.	Pulayan, Cheramar	28.3	36.0	20.7	46.1	52.9	39.4	61.5	67.4	55.7
55.	Pulaya Vettuvan	27.6	34.2	24.2	41.2	46.7	35.9	58.3	64.4	52.1
56.	Puthirai Vannan	54.1	67.3	40.3	57.8	69.3	48.0	67.5	76.7	56.9
57.	Raneyar	-	-	-	0.0	-	0.0	73.0	84.6	60.0
58.	Samagara	46.7	57.3	34.2	51.6	55.4	47.2	51.4	64.5	38.9
59.	Samban	29.2	35.0	0.0	46.3	54.2	40.0	61.8	67.5	56.0
60.	Semman	37.5	25.0	50.0	73.7	72.2	100.0	72.4	7.4	66.2
61.	Thandan	35.6	44.0	27.2	54.5	61.4	47.7	63.9	69.7	58.4
62.	Thoti	15.2	22.8	6.6	35.2	46.8	22.2	33.8	43.5	23.1
63.	Vallon	31.5	36.5	26.1	30.9	39.5	23.8	52.0	61.1	43.5

1 2	3	4	5	6	7	8	9	10	11
64. Valluvan	21.0	30.0	12.2	38.4	47.7	29.3	57.1	65.7	48.7
65. Vannan	46.4	54.7	38.0	63.2	69.6	56.9	71.6	77.6	65.8
66. Velan	49.6	60.4	38.9	64.7	72.6	57.4	76.9	82.3	71.5
67. Vetan	10.9	14.4	7.5	24.2	28.0	20.4	37.5	42.3	32.9
68. Vettuvan	25.2	31.5	18.8	44.2	49.7	38.5	57.9	62.6	53.4
Unspecified	100.0	100.0	-	46.0	56.2	35.0	39.3	45.9	32.2
12. Madhya Pradesh									
All Scheduled Castes	7.9	14.3	1.3	12.5	20.6	3.9	19.0	30.3	6.9
1. Audhelia	12.9	23.7	1.5	16.1	28.7	3.1	22.4	38.8	6.1
2. Bagri, Badgi	3.7	6.8	0.3	4.2	7.9	0.4	10.9	18.4	0.4
3. Bahna, Bahana	12.6	23.5	1.9	22.0	33.2	6.6	24.4	37.2	9.9
4. Balahi, Balai	7.3	13.9	0.6	11.5	19.9	2.5	16.9	29.3	3.6
5. Banchada	4.1	7.6	0.6	7.1	12.1	2.1	8.3	15.00	1.6
6. Barahar, Basod	5.6	10.0	0.8	10.5	17.4	2.7	18.0	28.3	6.8
7. Bargunda	5.4	10.0	0.7	8.7	16.6	1.0	10.2	18.3	1.8
8. Basor, Burad, Bansor, Bansodi, Bansphor, Basar	5.6	10.1	0.9	9.0	14.8	2.8	13.2	21.1	4.8
9. Bedia	8.9	13.4	4.8	11.8	16.4	6.7	16.7	25.3	7.8
10. Beldar, Sunkar	6.5	11.8	1.3	7.3	12.3	1.4	20.1	30.2	9.3
11. Banghi, Mehtar, Balmik, Lalbegi, Dharkar	13.1	21.7	3.8	17.9	26.5	8.4	24.9	35.7	13.3
12. Bhanumati	3.5	6.0	1.1	5.4	8.4	2.1	17.2	24.6	9.5
13. Chadar	12.4	21.3	2.4	18.8	31.7	5.0	24.3	37.3	9.8
14. Chamar, Chamari, Bairwa, Bhambi, Jatav, Mochi, Regar, Nona, Rohidas, Ramnami, Satnami, Surjyabanshi, Ahirwar, Chamar Mangan, Raidas	6.6	12.2	0.9	10.8	18.5	2.5	16.6	27.6	4.6
15. Chidar	6.3	11.4	0.8	10.3	17.1	2.5	18.6	29.2	6.6
16. Chikwa, Chikvi included in Khatik							18.7	31.0	6.4
17. Chitar	5.2	9.4	0.0	7.5	13.8	0.4	22.7	35.3	9.2
18. Dahait, Dahayat, Dahat	12.9	22.7	2.0	14.2	23.4	3.9	23.2	36.6	9.0
19. Dewar	5.8	10.5	1.7	7.6	13.1	2.3	9.6	15.9	3.6
20. Dhanuk	6.3	11.0	1.4	9.6	15.5	3.2	14.4	22.1	6.1
21. Dhed, Dher	7.7	11.2	4.5	15.3	27.5	0.0	14.3	20.8	7.6
22. Dhobi	7.1	12.8	1.0	12.0	18.9	3.6	20.8	31.4	9.0

1 2	3	4	5	6	7	8	9	10	11
23. Dohor	-	-	-	50.0	50.0	-	11.2	19.1	2.5
24. Dom, Dumar, Dome, Domar, Doris	14.0	23.6	3.9	13.9	20.8	6.2	33.1	46.3	18.9
25. Ganda, Gandi	10.2	19.4	1.6	14.1	25.4	3.3	19.9	33.7	6.6
26. Ghasi, Ghasia	7.7	14.4	1.3	10.3	18.1	2.6	14.5	24.1	5.0
27. Holiya	11.0	19.3	2.3	27.4	28.3	26.6	19.0	32.2	6.1
28. Kanjar	5.0	9.2	0.7	7.7	13.9	1.5	22.0	30.0	13.6
29. Katia, Patharia	13.3	22.8	3.8	19.0	27.7	9.6	29.5	42.6	15.9
30 Khatik,	14.7	25.3	3.7	21.7	32.9	9.8	34.8	47.8	20.5
31. Koli, Kori	14.2	24.0	33.1	20.5	31.6	8.0	26.3	38.6	12.5
32. Kotwal	2.5	4.0	0.8	6.0	10.5	0.7	3.8	6.7	0.8
33. Khangar, Kanera Mirdha	17.0	29.6	4.4	23.4	37.4	8.5	20.2	32.0	6.8
34. Kuchabandhia	5.7	10.0	0.6	4.4	7.6	1.4	15.1	24.1	5.7
35. Kumhar	3.3	6.2	0.3	4.6	8.0	0.7	9.4	16.9	1.2
36. Mahar, Mehra, Mehar	15.0	25.9	4.2	25.3	36.0	14.3	31.7	45.3	17.6
37. Mang, Mang Garodi, Mang Garudi, Dankhni Mang, Mang Mahasi, Madari, Garudi, Radhe Mang	13.9	24.8	3.0	15.6	23.1	7.6	27.6	39.3	15.3
38. Meghwal	7.6	14.7	0.5	15.2	26.8	2.3	18.3	32.0	3.7
39. Moghia	20.7	29.5	8.1	7.1	13.4	0.0	22.0	40.9	2.1
40. Muskhan	2.2	4.1	0.0	7.7	12.8	2.6	6.9	11.0	2.2
41. Nat, Kalbelia, Sapera, Navdigar, Kubutar	2.2	3.9	0.3	5.1	8.4	1.2	6.7	11.6	1.3
42. Pardhi	3.1	5.4	0.6	3.3	6.0	0.7	8.8	14.0	3.2
43. Pasi	22.0	31.7	7.9	24.4	34.4	11.8	42.7	54.5	29.0
44. Rujjhar	1.9	3.8	0.0	5.5	10.8	0.6	6.2	9.6	2.6
45. Sansi, Sansia	11.2	18.8	3.5	9.9	14.9	3.3	18.8	29.0	7.6
46. Silawat	8.1	14.0	1.6	11.5	19.8	2.7	22.1	33.6	9.3
47. Zamral	4.2	7.3	1.1	7.7	14.4	1.8	8.2	12.4	4.1
Unspecified	15.5	24.9	4.3	14.7	23.1	5.7	18.5	25.7	10.7
13. Maharashtra									
All Scheduled Castes	15.8	25.5	5.7	25.3	37.0	12.8	35.5	48.8	21.5
1. Ager	24.4	36.5	9.3	46.9	61.0	30.2	46.6	57.4	34.9
2. Anamuk	0.0	-	0.0	-	-	-	44.0	67.8	19.3
3. Aray Mala	30.8	29.0	33.3	42.9	-	42.86	51.3	62.6	36.6
4. Arwa Mala	-	-	-	-	-	-	58.1	65.9	48.6
5. Bhna, Bahana	0.0	0.0	0.0	-	-	-	50.5	60.0	39.1
6. Bakad, Bant	29.2	37.6	11.2	54.6	54.2	55.6	60.2	64.9	50.2
7. Balahi, Balai	13.2	22.8	2.9	17.9	32.0	5.0	35.3	49.8	20.4
8. Basor, Burud,									

1	2	3	4	5	6	7	8	9	10	11
	Basar, Bansodi	21.7	35.5	7.0	31.0	45.1	16.7	45.7	59.1	31.9
9.	Beda Jangam, Budga Jangam	43.7	63.6	0.0	21.1	36.3	4.6	59.4	74.4	43.8
10.	Bedar	9.7	13.7	4.7	16.0	28.3	4.4	19.1	29.3	8.1
11.	Bhambi, Bhambhi, Asadaru, Chamari, Chambhar, Chamar, Asodi, Chamadia, Chamgar, Haralayya Harali, Khalpa, Machigar, Mochigar Madar, Madig, Mochi, Ranigar, Telegu Mochi, Kamati Mochi, Rohidas, Nona, Ramnami, Rohit, Samgar, Samagara, Satnami, Surjyabanshi, Surjyaramnami	21.2	32.9	9.0	31.7	44.2	18.5	41.7	54.8	27.8
12.	Bhangi, Mehtar, Olgana, Rukhi, lalbegi, Balmiki, Korar, Zadmalli	26.8	40.2	11.2	34.0	46.2	19.7	41.3	53.7	27.3
13.	Bindla	100.0	100.0	100.0	4.5	4.5	-	44.5	53.4	26.3
14.	Byagara	0.0	0.0	-	14.3	-	14.3	20.5	30.7	10.0
15.	Chalvadi, Channayya	16.9	29.4	6.3	21.0	35.7	9.0	33.6	44.7	22.5
16.	Chenna, Dasar, Holaya Dasar, Holeya Dasari	22.9	31.8	2.1	14.8	17.0	13.2	37.7	48.2	25.6
17.	Dakkal, Dokkalwar	6.5	10.9	1.9	7.5	13.6	3.2	24.8	24.8	47.4
18.	Dhor, Kakkayya, Kankayya, Dohor	26.0	38.3	12.7	36.8	50.1	23.0	48.5	61.0	35.2
19.	Dom, Dumar	29.4	47.2	11.2	39.4	53.5	24.7	43.9	56.2	31.2
20.	Ellamalvar, Yellammala-wandlu	17.3	28.5	4.6	24.0	38.0	9.4	44.5	57.7	30.7
21.	Ganda, Gandi	22.5	32.7	9.2	20.7	38.5	10.5	40.8	55.2	24.6
22.	Garoda, Garo	19.6	28.0	8.8	23.7	38.7	5.8	36.9	46.8	23.5
23.	Ghasi, Ghasia	18.4	32.3	3.3	33.4	48.4	16.9	47.1	61.6	32.2
24.	Halleer	18.9	16.1	42.9	-	-	-	31.9	45.2	17.9
25.	Halsar, Haslar, Hulsvar, Halasvar	11.8	22.9	-	8.1	12.1	4.9	50.4	63.5	30.6
26.	Holar, Valhar	11.0	19.6	2.2	16.1	26.7	5.0	24.6	38.3	10.1
27.	Holaya, Holer, Holeya, Holiya	7.3	12.5	2.0	11.0	18.0	4.0	16.5	26.7	6.3

1 2	3	4	5	6	7	8	9	10	11
28. Kaikadi	13.9	21.7	6.4	23.4	31.5	16.1	30.1	42.6	16.6
29. Katia, Patharia	15.2	25.0	5.5	30.0	37.8	17.4	38.7	50.1	26.2
30. Khangar, Kanera Mirdha	0.0	0.0	-	0.0	0.0	0.0	41.8	62.2	18.3
31. Khatik, Chikwa, Chikvi	27.7	42.9	12.1	38.2	50.7	25.4	54.9	66.0	43.1
32. Kolupulvandlu	1.8	2.7	0.9	8.4	24.0	0.0	41.2	52.5	29.8
33. Kori	22.8	37.7	7.1	27.3	40.8	15.8	39.6	53.5	22.6
34. Lingader	25.3	28.8	17.2	46.5	50.0	40.0	50.5	65.4	34.7
35. Madgi	6.7	12.3	0.8	13.0	20.3	5.4	16.3	25.6	6.9
36. Madiga	5.6	10.4	0.8	9.8	17.6	2.3	27.8	40.1	15.2
37. Mahar, Mehra, Taral, Dhegu Megu	15.7	25.8	5.3	26.8	39.1	13.2	38.4	52.6	23.5
38. Mahyavanshi, Dhed,Vankar, Maru Vankar	47.8	62.0	31.00	54.4	65.5	42.0	69.8	78.5	59.9
39. Mala	27.3	37.2	15.2	41.7	47.7	32.7	51.5	61.9	39.3
40. Mala Dasari	0.0	0.0	0.0	12.7	37.5	2.6	27.8	40.8	13.8
41. Mala Hannai	-	-	-	-	-	-	44.3	59.0	25.8
42. Mala Jangam	20.4	30.1	7.4	41.8	56.2	24.1	55.7	72.2	37.9
43. Mala Masti	-	-	-	3.7	-	3.7	46.7	62.1	32.3
44. Mala Sale, Netkani	0.0	0.0	-	50.0	50.0	-	25.2	37.8	12.7
45. Mala Sanyasi	75.0	100.0	25.0	43.2	65.0	25.0	34.2	45.9	20.7
46. Mang, Matang, Minimadig, Dankhani Mang, Mang Mahashi, Madari, Garudi, Radhe Mang	9.9	17.1	2.5	16.9	26.9	6.6	23.7	36.5	10.5
47. Mang Garodi, Mang Garudi	8.9	14.6	3.5	13.1	21.3	4.8	16.2	25.8	6.3
48. Manne	7.4	14.1	0.0	12.8	35.0	5.2	37.2	47.2	26.4
49. Mashti	0.0	0.0	-	25.0	38.7	4.8	46.4	48.3	44.2
50. Meghval, Menghvar	38.9	55.8	21.8	50.1	62.3	37.3	59.1	70.6	47.4
51. Mitha Ayyalvar	-	-	-	0.0	0.0	0.0	58.4	67.4	50.5
52. Mukri	23.9	24.0	21.4	21.9	26.1	11.1	18.9	22.9	15.4
53. Nadia, Hadi	64.7	50.8	76.4	11.4	15.5	6.3	44.6	54.4	30.4
54. Pasi	33.7	40.2	10.3	36.7	43.0	11.0	45.8	55.9	25.7
55. Sansi	0.0	0.0	0.0	35.5	48.6	18.5	36.2	49.2	23.2
56. Shenva, Chenva, Sedma, Ravat	27.4	85.4	7.5	19.2	19.6	16.7	15.6	23.1	7.5
57. Sindhollu, Chindollu	-	-	-	0.0	-	0.0	29.8	34.8	24.7
58. Tirgar, Tirbanda	29.5	28.9	31.2	14.3	20.0	0.0	48.4	58.7	37.2
59. Turi	19.4	29.9	13.4	49.6	51.0	45.4	58.2	68.6	47.4
Unspecified	22.8	34.4	9.4	30.0	41.7	15.2	32.1	43.3	19.5

1 2	3	4	5	6	7	8	9	10	11
14. Manipur									
All Scheduled Castes	22.4	32.0	12.2	26.4	36.0	15.9	33.6	41.9	24.9
1. Dhupi, Dhobi	32.3	43.2	9.5	41.2	47.8	26.8	58.1	64.7	46.3
2. Doi	21.1	29.6	12.5	23.2	32.0	13.4	30.8	19.3	23.1
3. Muchi, Ravidas	35.7	59.0	0.1	40.5	46.9	16.9	47.1	56.6	31.0
4. Namasudra	18.2	24.3	10.3	39.9	50.7	28.8	39.7	48.9	28.8
5. Patni	41.3	60.6	26.9	29.4	38.5	17.3	40.7	49.5	31.6
6. Sutradhar	-	-	-	32.1	33.3	30.8	27.3	40.0	16.7
7. Yaithibi	21.9	41.2	0.0	21.8	32.5	8.9	21.2	29.3	13.5
Unspecified	-	-	-	100.0	100.0	-	40.3	50.0	24.0
15. Meghalaya									
All Scheduled Castes	14.0	20.1	6.4	20.4	28.0	11.9	25.8	33.3	16.3
1. Bansphor	41.4	57.9	10.0	16.5	23.1	8.0	7.1	11.4	1.1
2. Bhuinmali, Mali	42.8	100.0	20.0	20.4	20.3	20.6	43.3	49.2	34.6
3. Brittial Bania, Bania	26.4	44.7	3.3	33.9	43.1	23.6	55.6	71.0	37.7
4. Dhupi, Dhobi	25.0	32.3	7.1	31.5	43.0	16.7	39.6	44.0	31.1
5. Dugla, Dholi	-	-	-	-	-	-	9.1	10.0	8.3
6. Hira	9.5	22.2	0.0	-	-	-	66.7	80.9	55.5
7. Jalkeot	-	-	-	-	-	-	12.5	20.0	0.0
8. Jhalo,Malo, Jhalo-Malo	15.0	28.6	7.7	20.3	33.0	9.0	28.8	39.1	17.7
9. Kaibartta, Jaliya	62.5	80.0	33.3	24.1	25.2	22.6	59.2	64.2	52.4
10. Lalbegi	-	-	-	-	-	-	50.0	46.7	53.3
11. Mahara	3.8	5.0	0.0	5.7	4.2	9.1	-	-	-
12.Mehtar, Bhangi	9.8	17.1	1.6	13.4	14.7	11.9	13.7	18.7	7.1
13. Muchi, Rishi	16.9	18.8	12.2	13.7	26.8	2.3	13.4	20.1	4.7
14. Namasudra	6.3	8.3	4.3	19.7	30.8	8.2	23.6	31.7	14.2
15. Patni	-	-	-	11.9	13.5	9.9	46.3	50.0	40.9
16. Sutradhar	34.8	35.3	33.3	44.4	50.0	33.3	41.8	52.4	24.5
Unspecified	-	-	-	21.6	29.1	13.3	35.9	36.0	35.7
16. Mizoram									
All Schduled Castes	0.0	0.0	-	25.6	26.6	0.0	84.4	88.3	63.3
1. Banspnor	-	-	-	-	-	-	50.0	57.1	0.0
2. Bhuinmali, Mali	-	-	-	-	-	-	66.7	100.0	0.0
3. Brittial Bania, Bania	-	-	-	-	-	-	100.0	100.0	
4. Dhupi, Dhobi	0.0	0.0	-	18.2	19.0	0.0	84.8	88.9	66.7
5. Dugla, Dholi	-	-	-	100.0	100.0	0.0	75.0	75.0	
6. Hira	-	-	-	0.0	0.0	-	100.0	100.0	-
7. Jalkeot	-	-	-	-	-	-	50.0	50.0	
8. Jhalo, Malo, Jhalo-Malo	-	-	-	-	-	-	100.0	100.0	-
9. Kaibartta, Jaliya	-	-	-	-	-	-	100.0	100.0	-
10. Lalbegi	-	-	-	-	-	-	33.3	33.3	-

1 2	3	4	5	6	7	8	9	10	11
11. Mahara	-	-	-	66.7	66.7	-	100.0	100.0	-
12. Mehtar, Bhangi	0.0	0.0	-	-	-	-	100.0	100.0	-
13. Muchi, Rishi	0.0	0.0	-	50.0	50.0	-	93.3	92.3	100.0
14. Namasudra	-	-	-	100.0	100.0	-	83.3	100.0	0.0
15. Patni	-	-	-	-	-	-	75.0	75.0	-
16. Sutradhar	-	-	-	-	-	-	-	-	-
Unspecified	-	-	-	-	-	-	86.7	92.3	50.0
17. Orissa									
All Schduled Castes	11.6	19.8	3.4	16.6	26.0	6.2	22.4	35.3	9.4
1. Adi Andhra	12.2	20.7	2.3	13.2	21.0	5.5	22.8	33.00	13.0
2. Amant, Amat	9.0	16.0	1.9	8.9	15.8	1.8	11.2	19.1	2.9
3. Audhelia	-	-	-	50.0	44.4	66.7	20.0	28.6	12.5
4. Badaik	6.4	10.8	1.4	17.7	24.8	9.9	17.0	6.4	27.8
5. Bagheti, Baghuti	8.5	12.1	4.3	8.7	12.1	3.1	14.5	23.5	5.0
6. Bajikar	11.1	23.5	0.0	11.8	17.1	4.8	19.2	22.7	15.0
7. Bari	2.2	4.0	0.0	29.6	51.7	7.0	32.6	44.8	14.0
8. Bariki	19.3	31.7	6.5	26.1	38.3	13.8	31.2	46.1	16.3
9. Basor, Burud	2.9	5.1	0.0	26.5	31.6	20.0	17.4	24.5	7.9
10. Bauri	11.2	19.8	3.0	13.5	23.4	3.6	19.5	33.6	5.2
11. Bauti	9.4	13.5	5.0	8.2	9.7	6.0	47.2	84.7	11.5
12. Bavuri	25.0	100.0	0.0	50.0	100.0	0.0	24.0	28.6	18.2
13. Bedia, Bejia	5.0	6.8	3.1	7.1	12.4	1.8	22.0	33.7	9.5
14. Beldar	19.6	34.7	3.0	20.2	34.1	6.3	23.0	38.4	8.1
15. Bhata	15.4	28.9	3.2	29.0	48.1	10.3	36.8	52.2	21.0
16. Bhoi	12.8	20.1	5.2	13.6	22.6	4.0	20.4	33.3	7.2
17. Chachati	-	-	-	26.7	50.0	-	15.8	22.4	8.7
18. Chakali	21.0	36.0	4.6	12.7	25.3	0.0	23.7	33.6	14.4
19. Chamar, Mochi, Muchi, Satnami	13.4	22.0	4.4	17.3	27.8	6.4	23.7	35.1	12.0
20. Chandala	8.5	15.8	1.3	13.5	25.3	1.8	23.5	37.3	9.5
21. Chandhai Maru	18.7	28.8	10.0	-	-	-	25.0	25.0	25.0
22. Cherua, Chelia	4.8	10.2	0.0	16.9	29.0	6.2	25.6	37.2	13.6
23. Dandasi	10.9	19.7	2.8	12.3	22.7	2.9	16.4	28.7	4.9
24. Dewar	13.3	22.2	4.8	18.9	35.2	3.1	37.2	50.7	22.7
25. Dhanwar	2.1	3.9	0.3	1.3	2.4	0.2	6.2	9.2	3.4
26. Dhoba, Dhobi	15.7	26.7	4.8	22.4	35.4	9.4	31.3	46.5	16.0
27. Dom, Dombo, Duria Dom	6.4	11.2	1.6	7.8	13.8	1.8	13.2	22.4	4.1
28. Dosadha	4.5	8.2	1.2	25.7	40.7	4.8	37.8	49.4	22.2
29. Ganda	9.9	17.8	2.1	12.8	22.9	3.1	20.1	33.0	7.0
30. Ghantarghada, Ghantra	10.7	18.3	2.5	12.7	23.1	2.7	14.8	25.3	3.9
31. Ghasi, Ghasia	9.4	17.0	2.3	13.2	22.2	4.3	19.1	31.0	7.4
32. Ghogia	16.6	23.8	5.6	22.7	39.4	5.8	28.5	47.0	8.8
33. Ghusuria	10.0	14.8	5.1	12.8	20.0	4.5	17.1	27.8	6.4

1 2	3	4	5	6	7	8	9	10	11
34. Godagali	4.2	5.9	0.0	0.0	0.0	0.0	29.2	33.3	25.0
35. Godari	-	-	-	26.4	37.2	10.3	16.4	24.8	9.2
36. Godra	7.8	14.3	1.3	8.7	15.5	1.7	13.5	22.5	3.3
37. Gokha	15.2	21.9	8.4	19.9	35.2	4.2	25.0	39.7	9.6
38. Gorait, Korait	21.4	25.0	16.7	9.1	18.2	0.0	13.4	24..1	3.0
39. Haddi, Hadi, Hari	10.9	18.2	3.8	15.1	23.6	6.5	23.0	35.3	11.0
40. Irika	14.1	27.3	2.9	38.6	53.3	25.3	40.0	53.0	27.2
41. Jaggali	6.5	10.7	2.1	8.9	13.8	4.4	9.9	15.7	4.6
42. Kandra, Kandara	12.5	21.3	3.8	20.6	33.7	7.5	27.6	41.0	13.7
43. Karua	7.2	12.1	1.7	10.7	18.1	3.2	18.5	27.7	9.4
44. Katia	13.3	24.4	2.1	18.5	32.3	3.5	30.7	49.4	10.8
45. Kela	14.4	22.8	5.4	10.5	16.7	4.4	22.4	34.6	10.00
46. Khadala	11.1	20.5	2.6	12.4	23.0	2.6	22.7	37.7	8.5
47. Kodalo, Khodalo	10.3	17.8	4.0	27.5	36.1	17.2	23.9	36.4	11.5
48. Kori	21.4	24.4	17.8	18.8	25.5	12.1	26.6	37.1	13.4
49. Kummari	12.9	25.7	0.3	14.1	23.1	56.4	16.3	26.4	5.5
50. Kurunga	12.4	16.2	8.6	15.1	22.8	7.2	22.9	34.6	10.4
51. Laban	5.2	9.3	1.9	6.1	11.5	1.4	11.8	20.2	3.7
52. Laheri	12.2	20.8	2.9	6.9	12.2	1.8	8.9	14.5	3.2
53. Madari	7.1	11.6	3.2	15.1	30.3	2.1	15.9	27.0	4.7
54. Madiga	5.6	8.3	2.5	20.4	29.8	11.2	19.1	28.3	10.0
55. Mahuria	12.9	18.3	7.6	17.6	26.3	0.3	24.4	35.8	12.9
56. Mala, Jhala, Malo, Zala	11.4	18.5	6.0	16.7	27.9	6.6	26.0	36.5	15.6
57. Mang	3.8	5.6	1.5	0.0	0.0	-	5.1	6.6	3.3
58. Mangan	10.1	22.3	2.1	4.6	7.9	1.0	13.9	22.5	5.3
59. Mehra, Mahar	12.4	21.8	3.1	12.9	22.2	3.7	16.7	28.8	5.0
60. Mehtar, Bhangi	16.8	29.5	5.3	17.5	26.3	8.8	29.2	43.1	15.9
61. Mewar	15.2	27.5	0.9	13.8	23.5	3.5	17.2	28.07	5.3
62. Mungapotta	6.6	12.0	1.5	0.8	1.6	0.0	3.9	6.2	1.7
63. Musahar	7.5	13.5	2.3	31.6	41.7	19.3	58.6	61.1	54.5
64. Nagarchi	8.9	14.4	3.5	5.6	8.7	0.0	32.9	45.3	19.4
65. Namasudra	14.3	18.4	9.9	21.0	30.9	10.2	30.1	41.7	17.9
66. Paidi	4.4	7.1	2.0	-	-	-	23.9	40.4	9.3
67. Painda	6.2	9.4	1.0	11.3	19.5	5.6	20.7	27.8	13.6
68. Pamidi	4.8	3.0	6.8	3.8	6.2	0.0	10.9	12.8	9.1
69. Pan, Pano	12.0	20.7	3.5	16.7	26.9	4.3	22.8	36.5	8.9
70. Panchama	5.4	10.3	0.5	,7.6	16.7	1.3	16.7	27.0	4.1
71. Panika	9.2	16.0	2.0	12.5	21.7	3.1	18.1	31.7	4.8
72. Panka	86.7	77.8	100.0	-	-	-	8.8	16.4	1.8
73. Pantanti	14.2	22.8	6.4	18.3	30.5	5.8	26.7	41.6	11.7
74. Pap	13.3	25.1	2.7	13.2	23.9	2.9	17.2	29.4	5.5
75. Pasi	10.7	20.4	2.3	39.4	44.6	20.0	37.4	51.2	20.9
76. Patial, Patikar, Patratanti, Patua	14.4	24.5	9.2	19.2	32.1	6.4	27.6	43.4	11.8
77. Rajna	20.9	35.2	1.8	46.1	100.0	22.0	9.4	13.0	5.2
78. Relli	13.0	20.1	6.2	16.5	26.5	6.6	16.3	25.8	7.1

1	2	3	4	5	6	7	8	9	10	11
79.	Sabakhai	4.3	7.5	0.8	11.6	19.4	4.5	17.5	27.9	5.6
80.	Samasi	12.5	17.8	8.2	15.4	26.3	5.0	25.4	40.1	9.6
81.	Sanei	8.4	14.7	2.3	13.1	24.8	1.7	25.3	42.0	9.6
82.	Sapari	31.0	27.3	37.0	4.9	5.0	4.8	23.3	30.7	13.0
83.	Sauntia, Santia	11.0	20.0	1.7	10.6	19.5	2.0	16.3	29.4	3.5
84.	Sidhria	26.9	36.8	16.6	5.9	10.9	0.8	10.5	18.5	3.0
85.	Sinduria	0.4	0.5	0.3	12.8	15.0	10.5	34.5	44.0	24.4
86.	Siyal	18.7	31.4	6.0	23.8	37.4	10.0	36.1	53.0	18.7
87.	Tamadia	9.1	15.7	2.4	17.6	29.7	5.0	21.0	34.3	10.5
88.	Tamudia	7.6	14.7	1.4	14.5	20.2	8.2	20.3	33.3	7.4
89.	Tanla	11.3	20.3	2.6	13.3	23.6	3.3	18.7	31.0	6.2
90.	Tiar, Tior	18.8	29.6	7.8	24.7	38.7	10.5	30.6	46.9	13.9
91.	Turi	12.0	23.0	1.2	9.3	16.6	1.7	13.8	23.9	3.5
92.	Ujia	7.5	13.1	1.6	11.0	16.0	6.0	11.1	18.5	3.4
93.	Valamiki, Valmiki	14.5	28.0	3.9	14.3	27.5	2.0	22.9	37.9	8.5
	Unspecified	15.7	22.4	9.7	18.6	28.5	8.3	24.0	29.9	18.5

18. Punjab

1	2	3	4	5	6	7	8	9	10	11
	All Scheduled Castes				16.1	22.9	8.1	23.9	31.0	15.7
1.	Ad Dharmi				27.3	38.2	14.7	40.4	29.3	13.8
2.	Balmiki, Chura, Bhangi				13.8	20.0	6.8	22.1	28.9	14.3
3.	Bangali				8.0	10.5	5.2	14.0	18.2	10.8
4.	Barar, Burar, Berar				14.4	21.6	4.7	23.2	30.1	15.1
5.	Batwal				16.8	25.1	7.4	26.9	34.8	17.9
6.	Bauria, Bawaria				6.0	10.3	1.2	8.3	13.2	1.7
7.	Bazigar				6.6	11.1	1.7	12.4	19.1	5.2
8.	Bhanjra				30.7	39.4	18.8	34.7	42.2	26.4
9.	Chamar, Jatia Chamar, Rehgar Raigar, Ramdasi, Ravidasi				19.8	28.0	10.1	28.7	37.0	19.0
10.	Chanal				54.0	60.6	41.6	36.0	42.8	29.0
11.	Dagi				41.4	47.0	33.3	61.1	75.0	40.9
12.	Darain				19.1	33.3	1.4	28.2	36.1	19.2
13.	Deha, Dhaya, Dhea				1.5	2.7	0.1	2.5	4.0	1.0
14.	Dhanak				11.0	17.6	2.8	12.4	18.7	5.1
15.	Dhogri, Dhangri, Siggi				50.0	52.0	47.6	12.4	13.7	10.9
16.	Dumna, Mahasha, Doom				17.5	25.9	7.7	28.4	37.5	18.1
17.	Gagra				16.4	22.8	5.0	21.5	26.6	14.2
18.	Gandhila, Gandil/Gondola				2.8	4.8	0.5	6.2	10.2	1.6
19.	Kabirpanthi, Julaha				29.6	38.6	19.6	39.3	47.4	30.0
20.	Khatik				25.8	40.5	9.1	23.0	33.9	11.3
21.	Kori, Koli				18.1	23.1	7.2	25.0	29.2	17.7
22.	Marija, Marecha				20.2	26.1	9.2	16.6	19.3	13.8
23.	Mazhabi				8.3	12.2	3.8	12.9	17.8	7.4
24.	Megh				23.5	31.2	14.6	30.9	38.3	22.4
25.	Nat				34.9	50.0	0.0	13.9	17.5	9.9
26.	Od				5.3	9.9	0.3	9.0	15.0	2.7

1 2	3	4	5	6	7	8	9	10	11
27. Pasi				20.4	25.0	12.0	25.0	30.3	16.1
28. Perna				25.0	25.0	-	18.7	22.2	15.4
29. Pherera				45.8	48.0	40.9	28.0	34.0	20.6
30. Sanhai				6.7	12.1	0.0	16.4	17.9	14.7
31. Sanhal				26.4	37.6	5.6	35.9	48.9	23.5
32. Sansi, Bhedkut, Manesh				11.0	17.1	4.2	14.8	21.6	7.4
33. Sansoi				6.5	6.8	6.0	31.2	39.4	18.9
34. Sapela				1.6	2.5	0.5	3.7	5.0	2.2
35. Sarera				28.6	38.9	16.4	41.4	50.0	32.1
36. Sikligar				4.6	7.3	1.2	12.1	16.1	7.6
37. Sirkiband				12.8	19.0	6.1	16.9	23.2	10.1
Unspecified				17.7	23.9	10.0	27.2	34.0	18.9
19. Rajasthan									
All Scheduled Castes	6.4	11.6	0.8	9.1	16.3	1.2	14.0	24.4	2.7
1. Adi Dharmi	15.3	22.2	3.3	18.2	25.3	9.2	35.3	46.7	19.1
2. Aheri	9.2	16.2	1.2	13.3	22.4	1.2	15.7	24.8	4.9
3. Badi	8.5	13.7	1.6	3.3	5.0	1.4	7.2	13.1	1.1
4. Bagri, Bagdi	2.5	4.4	0.5	3.7	7.0	0.3	5.2	9.3	0.7
5. Bairwa, Berwa	6.9	14.5	0.6	10.8	19.0	1.7	15.1	26.4	2.7
6. Bajgar	3.3	5.7	0.8	3.7	6.7	0.4	6.9	12.3	0.9
7. Balai	5.6	10.2	0.6	8.7	15.9	0.9	14.5	25.9	2.2
8. Bansphor, Banshod	10.0	18.8	2.0	5.8	10.7	1.0	9.4	16.7	1.6
9. Baori	6.3	11.0	1.5	9.9	18.1	0.3	5.5	10.2	5.5
10. Bargi, Vargi, Birgi	4.4	5.6	2.6	24.2	37.5	8.5	31.3	43.5	18.2
11. Bawaria	3.2	5.8	0.3	4.7	8.5	0.5	6.6	11.8	1.0
12. Bedia, Beria	6.5	10.9	1.7	19.8	31.4	10.1	19.6	31.9	8.3
13. Bhand	10.3	19.4	1.3	13.0	23.7	1.8	19.2	33.4	4.4
14. Bhangi, Chura, Mehtar, Olgana, Rukhi, Malkana, Halalkhor, Lalbegi, Balmiki, Valmiki, Korar, Zadmalli	7.6	13.5	1.5	10.4	18.2	2.0	15.3	25.8	3.9
15. Bidakia	16.8	30.9	0.8	0.5	0.9	0.0	8.2	15.4	0.8
16. Bola	3.7	6.9	0.2	6.2	11.9	0.4	9.9	18.2	0.7
17. Chamar, Bhambhi, Bambhi, Bhambi, Jatia, Jatava, Mochi, Raidas, Rohidas, Regar, Raigar, Ramdasia, Asadaru, Asodi, Chamadia, Jatav, Chambhar, Chamgar, Haralayya, Harali, Khalpa, Machigar,, Mochigar, Madar, Madig, Telegu Mochi, Kamati Mochi, Ranigar, Rahit, Samgar	6.2	11.4	0.6	9.2	16.7	1.0	15.3	27.0	2.4
18. Chandal	13.3	23.9	1.0	15.5	28.1	2.4	28.4	43.1	12.2
19. Dabgar	9.7	17.2	0.7	24.5	41.3	3.4	33.1	53.5	11.7
20. Dhanak, Dhanuk	31.2	49.0	9.9	38.9	53.1	21.7	15.4	26.1	4.0
21. Dhankia	7.5	13.6	0.6	11.4	20.1	1.8	25.5	40.6	9.0

1	2	3	4	5	6	7	8	9	10	11
22.	Dhobi	15.7	24.5	6.4	5.9	20.4	33.3	7.2	19.2	30.9
23.	Dholi	22.9	38.4	4.4	22.0	38.8	3.9	20.5	36.1	4.3
24.	Dome, Dom	11.5	21.9	0.9	10.1	18.6	0.8	16.5	27.5	3.8
25.	Gandia	3.0	7.5	1.5	1.7	3.0	0.0	23.9	32.1	7.5
26.	Garanch, Gancha	10.0	19.9	0.4	13.5	24.4	1.9	20.8	36.1	6.3
27.	Garo, Garura, Gurda, Garoda	14.5	25.5	1.6	17.9	32.7	1.5	21.5	38.6	3.0
28.	Gavaria	4.2	7.6	0.5	4.5	8.3	0.3	13.2	23.8	1.2
29.	Godhi	13.4	19.6	0.0	5.1	8.8	0.8	12.9	18.9	5.8
30.	Jingar	20.0	35.1	2.5	24.4	40.1	8.0	37.9	57.3	16.6
31.	Kalbelia, Sapera	1.4	2.5	0.03	2.0	3.6	0.2	2.5	4.4	0.4
32.	Kamad, Kamadia	10.3	18.7	1.3	11.5	21.8	1.3	19.2	35.1	2.8
33.	Kanjar, Kunjar	4.2	7.8	0.3	4.8	8.4	0.9	6.0	10.7	1.0
34.	Kapadia, Sansi	3.4	6.2	0.8	10.8	19.5	2.0	8.8	14.7	2.4
35.	Khangar	24.4	42.2	3.3	15.3	27.6	2.3	21.2	36.1	4.7
36.	Khatik	11.0	19.7	1.1	15.4	28.1	1.7	23.8	41.6	5.1
37.	Koli, Kori	9.3	16.6	1.5	14.9	24.8	3.9	22.0	35.0	7.6
38.	Kooch Band, Kuchband	2.6	3.6	1.3	16.0	30.9	1.6	6.61	1.2	1.4
39.	Koria	6.3	10.3	0.0	10.3	18.2	1.4	19.2	31.3	4.8
40.	Madari, Bazigar	6.8	10.3	0.0	3.3	5.8	0.2	60.3	11.1	1.1
41.	Mahar, Taral, Dhegu Megu	-	-	-	31.4	36.4	23.1	27.1	40.6	10.2
42.	Mahyavanshi, Dhed, Dheda, Vankar, Maru Vandar	11.0	16.9	2.7	6.1	10.5	1.8	11.2	18.0	3.6
43.	Mahabi	8.0	13.3	0.6	4.5	7.7	0.7	7.5	12.2	2.0
44.	Mang, Maang, Minimadig	-	-	-	-	-	-	25.7	34.0	12.8
45.	Mang Garodi, Mang Garudi	100.0	100.0	-	-	-	-	15.8	26.2	1.3
46.	Megh, Meghval, Meghwal, Menghvar	4.2	7.7	0.5	5.7	10.6	0.5	9.1	16.5	1.0
47.	Mehar	9.9	18.0	1.2	15.7	26.1	3.7	22.5	37.0	6.4
48.	Nat, Nut	4.4	8.2	0.4	5.6	10.2	0.7	8.1	14.9	1.3
49.	Pasi	17.2	22.0	5.6	21.6	26.8	11.3	33.9	44.0	19.1
50.	Rawal	5.7	10.6	0.5	16.4	29.7	2.7	20.5	36.7	4.3
51.	Salvi	15.2	27.4	2.4	16.1	28.0	3.7	25.1	39.9	9.4
52.	Sansi	5.1	8.7	1.2	5.0	9.0	0.9	6.5	11.6	1.2
53.	Santia, Satia	1.3	3.1	0.5	2.1	3.9	0.1	2.5	4.8	0.2
54.	Sarbhangi	1.3	2.5	0.4	21.8	38.3	1.4	16.5	30.5	1.7
55.	Sargara	5.9	10.8	0.6	7.9	14.6	0.8	14.3	25.0	3.0
56.	Singiwala	10.6	17.2	0.0	5.0	8.4	1.2	6.0	10.2	1.3
57.	Thori, Nayak	4.6	8.4	0.5	5.1	9.1	0.7	7.7	13.6	1.3
58.	Tirgar, Tirbanda	6.8	15.9	0.4	3.6	7.2	0.1	8.3	16.0	0.4
59.	Turi	-	-	-	20.7	54.5	0.0	14.1	27.4	0.4
	Unspecified	7.7	13.6	1.4	12.5	21.4	2.7	13.4	22.0	4.1

1	2	3	4	5	6	7	8	9	10	11
	20. Sikkim									
	All Scheduled Castes				17.4	24.0	9.6	28.1	35.7	19.9
1.	Damai (Nepali)				14.8	14.9	14.8	31.0	39.3	21.7
2.	Kami (Nepali), Lohar (Nepali)				10.9	13.0	8.6	27.2	34.65	19.3
3.	Majhi (Nepali)				-	-	-	23.6	30.1	15.4
4.	Sarki (Nepali)				22.7	27.6	4.8	16.6	24.0	6.8
	Unspcified				20.1	29.7	9.3	38.5	62.5	0.0
	21. Tamil Nadu									
	All Scheduled Castes	14.7	23.6	5.7	21.8	32.2	11.3	29.2	40.0	18.2
1.	Adi Andhra	18.8	27.7	9.2	28.3	37.1	18.5	35.5	45.8	24.6
2.	Adi Dravida	16.7	25.7	7.5	24.7	34.9	14.1	32.1	43.0	20.8
3.	Adi Karnataka	13.7	22.3	4.8	21.8	31.8	11.3	29.9	40.8	18.7
4.	Ajila	-	-	-	46.1	57.1	33.3	57.1	59.3	50.0
5.	Arunthathiyar	13.1	21.3	4.6	15.6	23.3	7.7	21.8	31 3	12.1
6.	Ayyanavar	46.5	52.2	40.1	56.0	62.5	50.0	64.8	70.0	59.8
7.	Baira	10.7	14.3	3.8	21.8	31.1	12.7	23.0	33.5	10.6
8.	Bakuda	6.0	10.3	0.0	8.8	14.9	4.5	31.8	27.9	34.8
9.	Bandi	32.4	43.5	14.3	41.4	51.3	30.3	38.3	38.9	49.4
10.	Bellara	-	-	-	36.4	33.3	37.5	29.5	41.7	15.0
11.	Bharatar	45.8	54.1	39.1	52.1	58.1	44.8	65.5	72.9	57.7
12.	Chakkiliyan	6.1	10.0	2.1	10.6	16.4	4.6	46.4	23.9	8.7
13.	Chalavadi	0.0	-	0.0	27.9	35.7	15.4	44.3	61.8	31.6
14.	Chamr, Muchi	57.1	80.0	0.0	14.7	24.1	5.1	74.5	81.6	60.7
15.	Chandala	50.0	100.0	0.0	18.1	26.0	10.9	73.5	81.6	60.7
16.	Cheruman	20.6	27.7	12.9	29.2	34.0	24.0	48.9	56.3	41.6
17.	Devendara-kulathan	20.3	34.9	7.9	35.5	47.2	23.6	46.7	58.2	36.0
18.	Dom, Dombara, Paidi, Pano	9.7	15.2	4.4	10.1	15.1	4.6	15.5	22.2	8.2
19.	Domban	0.0	0.0	0.0	22.6	38.9	0.0	18.3	26.6	9.7
20.	Godagali	-	-	-	3.2	5.3	0.0	58.3	73.3	33.3
21.	Godda	25.0	50.0	0.0	11.9	22.0	4.4	69.8	75.4	64.4
22.	Gosangi	5.9	13.9	0.0	14.3	25.0	0.0	29.3	46.2	11.7
23.	Holeya	7.9	13.2	18.6	28.6	36.6	19.8	22.6	28.8	16.1
24.	Jaggali	0.0	0.0	0.0	14.5	19.6	6.9	26.0	46.0	5.4
25.	Jambuvulu	10.0	12.5	0.0	83.3	0.00	100.0	6.9	10.0	4.2
26.	Kadaiyan	22.9	38.1	8.5	21.5	35.4	7.8	28.2	40.7	12.8
27.	Kakkalan	65.4	78.6	50.0	60.3	69.6	54.3	66.7	71.0	62.9
28.	Kalladi	31.6	42.7	11.9	17.8	27.4	8.3	18.8	26.9	12.0
29.	Kanakkan, Padanna	8.3	0.0	13.8	33.1	36.4	27.9	43.7	44.8	42.5
30.	Karimplan	-	-	-	25.0	-	25.0	55.6	50.0	60.0
31.	Kavara	59.9	65.0	56.4	54.2	63.3	43.9	63.7	70.6	56.5
32.	Koliyan	24.9	42.6	8.4	31.0	48.0	14.9	42.5	58.2	26.9

1	2	3	4	5	6	7	8	9	10	11
33.	Koosa	-	-	-	20.0	33.3	0.0	21.9	23.5	20.8
34.	Kootan, Koodan	0.0	0.0	0.0	45.3	59.3	35.1	40.8	54.7	26.4
35.	Kudumban	14.5	24.8	4.4	20.7	32.0	9.5	24.7	35.5	13.8
36.	Kuravan, Sidhanar	13.2	21.2	5.1	20.2	29.7	10.4	27.8	38.6	16.8
37.	Madari	6.9	10.9	2.9	9.3	14.6	4.0	12.5	18.5	6.3
38.	Madiga	7.1	12.0	2.0	6.9	10.6	3.0	9.5	14.8	3.9
39.	Maila	100.0	100.0	-	0.0	0.0	0.0	48.9	57.6	37.4
40.	Mala	5.2	9.0	1.4	8.6	13.9	3.0	12.7	19.4	5.7
41.	Manna	0.0	0.0	0.0	81.1	66.7	57.2	59.8	61.1	58.8
42.	Mavilan	9.2	13.0	0.1	25.0	50.0	0.0	12.45	21.0	0.0
43.	Moger	-	-	10.2	14.3	4.0	20.2	27.2	27.1	12.2
44.	Mundala	75.0	-	75.0	43.5	37.5	57.1	50.0	68.7	20.0
45.	Nalakeyava	0.0	-	0.0	0.0	-	0.0	28.6	40.0	0.0
46.	Neyadi	12.1	26.7	1.6	25.5	17.8	29.9	28.3	33.5	23.4
47.	Padannan	-	-	-	100.0	100.0	-	-	-	-
48.	Pagadai	8.9	15.2	2.7	16.4	25.4	7.4	16.8	26.9	8.3
49.	Pallan	16.1	26.9	5.4	24.2	36.7	11.7	30.3	42.7	17.8
50.	Palluvan	100.0	-	100.0	31.3	43.2	9.8	31.8	40.5	23.4
51.	Pambada	8.3	16.7	0.0	22.3	34.1	11.1	40.2	59.6	19.3
52.	Panan	58.2	70.4	46.8	63.0	74.7	51.5	77.9	86.6	68.0
53.	Panchama	29.5	48.1	18.0	23.6	33.3	13.7	27.6	29.3	25.7
54.	Pannadi	19.4	30.4	8.3	25.5	38.0	12.7	27.3	38.6	15.7
55.	Panniandi	10.4	18.3	1.3	15.4	22.6	7.1	18.2	25.8	10.5
56.	Paraiyan, Parayan, Sambavar	15.0	24.7	5.3	22.0	33.4	10.6	30.9	43.2	18.4
57.	Paravan	39.0	61.6	25.1	54.0	64.8	43.1	61.9	71.0	52.3
58.	Pathiyan	46.7	55.6	33.3	-	-	-	60.9	61.5	60.0
59.	Pulayan, Cheramar	33.0	38.6	27.6	51.3	57.9	45.2	30.4	37.3	23.1
60.	Puthirai Vannan	19.1	26.6	11.5	25.2	35.4	14.9	36.1	48.5	23.7
61.	Raneyar	-	-	-	0.0	0.0	0.0	25.0	33.3	0.0
62.	Samagara	15.8	33.3	0.0	25.0	100.0	0.0	18.9	18.2	20.0
63.	Samban	11.9	20.5	3.2	19.7	30.9	8.4	27.0	39.0	14.8
64.	Sapari	-	-	-	15.6	26.1	4.5	21.0	27.3	12.5
65.	Semman	32.4	34.2	31.0	52.2	65.3	31.8	58.9	67.3	50.2
66.	Thandan	33.3	42.2	25.0	46.2	53.2	39.0	49.0	54.0	44.0
67.	Thoti	8.8	14.5	3.0	19.2	27.9	10.9	24.9	34.6	15.1
68.	Tiruvalluvar	33.8	59.0	11.5	40.3	64.0	19.0	50.4	68.1	32.0
69.	Vallon	-	-	-	0.0	-	0.0	54.8	60.0	47.7
70.	Valluvan	34.2	55.6	12.6	42.8	64.7	21.1	52.7	70.9	34.2
71.	Vannan	38.0	47.5	28.9	49.5	59.0	40.7	64.5	70.1	58.7
72.	Vathiriyan	-	-	-	-	-	-	51.0	57.0	44.5
73.	Velan	25.0	-	25.0	39.0	50.1	26.6	41.8	44.0	39.3
74.	Vetan	59.6	70.2	48.2	68.4	78.2	57.1	67.8	74.3	60.8
75.	Vattiyan	9.1	16.4	1.8	18.4	28.9	7.8	27.5	40.0	13.9
76.	Vattuvan	51.1	65.6	40.0	21.9	28.8	16.8	74.8	86.3	62.9
	Unspecified	18.3	27.4	9.0	29.9	42.4	15.2	29.8	41.2	17.4

1 2	3	4	5	6	7	8	9	10	11
22. Tripura									
All Scheduled Castes	13.4	22.1	4.1	20.5	30.3	10.1	33.9	43.9	23.2
1. Bagdi	6.8	13.2	0.0	12.1	24.0	3.0	15.9	25.2	5.4
2. Bhuimali	11.9	17.9	0.7	20.0	28.8	7.7	36.3	46.3	26.0
3. Bhunar	0.0	0.0	0.0	26.5	40.0	13.9	23.3	32.1	10.8
4. Chamr, Muchi	7.9	12.8	1.9	10.4	16.0	4.3	21.4	30.6	11.6
5. Dandasi	30.0	0.0	60.0	-	-	-	24.6	36.7	11.1
6. Dhenuar	11.1	25.0	0.0	100.0	100.0	0.0	46.1	62.5	20.0
7. Dhoba	18.9	30.6	6.3	24.5	35.2	13.2	39.5	49.8	28.5
8. Dum	4.5	7.6	1.3	9.1	14.4	0.0	22.6	30.1	13.4
9. Ghasi	7.3	15.0	0.6	19.4	35.0	0.0	25.3	40.7	9.2
10. Gour	7.6	14.2	0.6	9.4	14.4	1.9	16.4	26.1	5.9
11. Gur	3.9	8.5	0.7	7.1	18.2	0.5	10.1	16.7	3.3
12. Jalia Kaibarta	14.0	23.3	4.2	21.0	32.1	9.3	36.2	46.7	25.2
13. Kahar	12.8	22.8	4.4	13.8	23.3	5.3	39.5	47.1	30.4
14. Kalindi	10.0	11.5	7.1	0.0	0.0	0.0	20.6	31.6	6.7
15. Kan	60.0	60.0	-	8.7	16.7	0.0	37.5	66.7	20.0
16. Kanda	8.5	15.4	0.4	12.5	21.9	2.6	15.7	25.5	5.8
17. Kanagh	-	-	-	26.7	28.6	25.0	51.8	63.6	37.8
18. Keot	11.3	17.7	1.8	11.6	28.0	1.0	21.8	34.4	10.2
19. Khadit	0.0	0.0	0.0	-	-	-	-	-	-
20. Kharia	4.5	7.9	6.4	4.7	6.0	3.3	16.7	23.7	8.6
21. Koch	12.8	22.5	3.3	12.1	21.6	3.0	28.7	42.3	15.3
22. Koir	16.9	26.1	5.7	5.0	11.6	0.0	31.7	38.6	20.8
23. Kol	11.0	19.9	1.4	10.0	18.2	0.8	17.0	25.9	8.0
24. Kotla	0.0	0.0	0.0	0.0	0.0	0.0	85.7	85.7	85.7
25. Kora	17.6	23.5	6.9	-	-	-	18.6	31.8	4.8
26. Mahisyadas	18.2	28.3	7.3	25.3	36.0	13.4	42.0	52.4	30.9
27. Mali	15.1	24.4	5.1	22.9	32.7	12.9	36.4	45.7	26.4
28. Mehtor	10.5	15.7	2.3	21.6	27.5	14.6	33.4	42.2	23.0
29. Musahar	1.9	3.1	0.0	14.3	100.0	0.0	4.2	5.4	2.2
30. Namasudra	11.8	19.9	3.3	18.9	28.3	8.8	29.4	39.3	18.9
31. Patni	19.3	23.1	4.1	16.2	24..6	8.2	36.0	45.9	25.6
32. Sabar	5.3	10.0	0.3	8.3	13.3	2.9	13.2	21.1	4.3
Unspecified	-	-	-	100.0	100.0	0.0	88.8	94.0	16.7
23. Uttar Pradesh									
All Scheduled Castes	7.1	12.8	1.1	10.2	17.1	2.5	15.0	24.8	3.9
1. Agariya	5.8	10.5	0.8	7.5	12.4	2.0	11.9	17.9	5.3
2. Badhk	5.3	9.5	0.6	9.3	13.8	3.6	13.6	22.5	3.9
3. Badi	10.1	13.2	6.8	11.9	18.3	4.1	11.2	18.3	3.6
4. Baheliya	8.0	13.5	1.9	10.0	15.8	3.0	11.8	19.2	3.1
5. Baiga	1.2	3.0	0.0	1.7	2.9	0.4	4.3	7.4	0.9
6. Baiswar	7.7	16.0	1.1	18.7	28.4	8.9	28.3	41.1	13.7
7. Bajaniya	2.7	4.3	0.7	4.1	6.4	1.7	11.6	19.0	3.8

1	2	3	4	5	6	7	8	9	10	11
8.	Bajgi	4.9	10.4	0.8	10.7	17.1	3.4	14.8	26.3	3.0
9.	Balahar	6.7	11.0	0.8	8.6	13.5	2.7	11.0	17.6	2.8
10.	Balai	16.4	25.0	4.3	16.1	22.4	7.8	15.4	24.0	3.4
11.	Balmiki	8.1	13.1	2.5	12.2	19.1	4.4	14.3	21.6	6.0
12.	Bangali	8.1	13.2	0.7	14.2	20.2	7.1	12.9	19.5	5.8
13.	Banmanus	2.0	4.1	0.1	2.6	3.8	1.4	3.7	6.7	0.5
14.	Bansphor	4.2	7.5	0.7	7.7	11.1	3.8	9.3	15.5	2.2
15.	Barwar	11.1	20.4	1.7	12.3	19.8	3.8	19.6	31.5	6.0
16.	Basor	6.0	10.5	1.2	7.7	18.8	1.3	12.5	21.1	2.5
17.	Bawariya	10.3	16.5	2.3	7.8	13.3	1.0	13.7	21.1	5.1
18.	Beldar	4.7	8.8	0.4	6.5	11.4	1.4	9.9	18.5	1.2
19.	Beriya	12.5	17.4	7.4	16.0	21.9	9.6	23.3	32.5	13.5
20.	Bhantu	8.9	14.5	3.5	16.6	26.2	5.3	48.8	59.0	36.8
21.	Bhuiya	3.1	5.7	0.3	3.5	6.4	0.2	8.5	14.3	2.4
22.	Bhuyiar	3.7	7.2	0.4	5.6	9.1	1.5	20.2	32.9	5.3
23.	Boria	2.2	3.3	0.9	10.5	16.6	4.1	21.0	29.9	11.6
24.	Chamar, Dhusia, Jhusia, Jatava	7.4	13.5	0.9	10.5	17.8	2.3	16.0	26.6	3.9
25.	Chero	4.0	8.2	0.1	4.4	7.5	1.5	3.8	7.0	0.5
26.	Dabgar	16.9	28.0	5.2	15.0	24.3	5.0	23.1	36.6	8.6
27.	Dhangar	7.3	11.9	1.5	11.6	18.2	3.8	20.5	33.2	5.9
28.	Dhanak	8.2	13.7	2.1	11.7	18.3	3.9	15.8	23.7	6.2
29.	Dharkar	6.5	11.4	1.1	8.7	13.8	2.7	11.7	19.9	2.8
30.	Dhobi	7.2	12.6	1.4	10.9	18.2	2.7	15.8	26.2	4.1
31.	Dom	5.4	9.6	0.9	8.7	14.5	2.3	10.4	17.2	2.9
32.	Domar	5.7	8.0	3.1	9.3	15.2	2.9	8.8	15.3	1.7
33.	Dusadh	7.1	13.5	0.8	10.1	17.5	2.2	13.8	24.8	2.6
34.	Gharami	0.0	6.0	-	47.6	70.0	27.3	26.2	38.5	9.5
35.	Ghasiya	4.7	6.0	3.5	12.1	20.3	3.1	31.9	39.7	21.8
36.	Gond	5.1	9.7	0.8	4.5	8.1	0.8	15.0	25.8	3.7
37.	Gual	9.5	20.4	0.6	12.4	20.9	2.6	16.6	27.2	4.2
38.	Habura	5.7	7.9	3.4	11.2	15.3	6.9	16.1	23.4	7.2
39.	Hari	13.2	25.4	1.4	9.6	16.3	2.3	11.9	18.7	3.8
40.	Hela	10.1	16.2	4.1	14.2	21.9	5.2	24.5	36.4	11.6
41.	Kalabaz	6.6	12.1	2.3	5.4	7.4	3.1	10.4	15.9	3.7
42.	Kanjar	5.8	9.7	1.6	8.7	12.9	3.5	7.0	11.8	1.5
43.	Kapariya	6.2	9.2	2.2	8.4	11.5	4.5	10.3	17.9	2.5
44.	Karwal	5.7	10.1	0.9	8.4	14.7	1.4	15.2	25.0	3.5
45.	Khairaha	2.4	3.4	0.3	13.8	19.7	6.6	17.5	26.7	6.1
46.	Kharwar	3.6	7.4	0.2	5.1	9.1	0.2	13.8	21.9	5.0
47.	Khatik	9.5	15.7	2.7	12.6	20.1	3.8	17.9	28.0	6.5
48.	Khorot	3.6	7.1	0.0	5.2	8.2	2.0	11.0	18.4	2.5
49.	Kol	2.2	4.1	0.2	4.2	7.4	0.6	14.6	27.3	0.7
50.	Kori	6.5	11.4	1.5	9.9	16.8	2.5	15.2	24.7	4.5
51.	Korwa	10.3	17.8	2.1	11.2	17.7	3.1	15.5	25.0	4.6
52.	Lalbegi	11.2	18.1	3.5	11.2	16.6	4.4	12.4	18.4	6.0
53.	Majhwar	7.6	13.5	1.4	9.9	17.4	2.1	17.3	27.4	6.7

1 2	3	4	5	6	7	8	9	10	11
54. Mazhabi	18.0	35.9	5.9	13.9	18.2	7.9	23.7	34.8	6.8
55. Musahar	2.2	3.6	0.9	4.9	8.5	0.9	2.1	3.9	0.3
56. Nat	6.7	10.6	2.0	6.7	10.4	2.6	9.5	15.8	2.5
57. Pankha	5.0	10.3	0.2	5.0	9.7	0.4	7.6	13.1	1.6
58. Parahiya	1.2	2.8	0.0	1.9	3.9	0.1	11.7	20.8	3.1
59. Pasi, Tarmali	5.2	9.5	0.8	7.2	12.6	1.5	10.2	18.0	1.7
60. Patari	10.7	18.6	0.2	9.6	16.1	0.7	16.0	23.9	7.7
61. Rawat	2.1	3.5	0.5	9.9	15.2	3.8	15.4	22.6	7.4
62. Saharya	1.2	2.3	0.03	4.0	6.6	1.2	3.0	5.5	0.3
63. Sanaurhiya	12.5	27.8	0.0	11.1	13.7	8.3	30.1	39.1	18.9
64. Sansiya	10.4	17.3	1.4	8.9	14.1	3.1	27.5	44.3	9.5
65. Silpkar	11.6	21.0	1.7	16.1	26.9	5.0	25.9	41.2	10.1
66. Turaiha	2.4	5.8	0.2	11.9	19.5	4.1	14.3	23.1	4.9
Unspecified	7.3	12.4	2.0	13.1	20.0	3.9	12.8	20.4	4.5
24. West Bengal									
All Scheduled Castes	13.6	21.8	4.6	17.8	25.8	9.2	24.4	34.3	13.7
1. Bagdi, Duley	8.7	15.2	2.1	10.8	17.2	4.2	14.0	21.7	5.9
2. Bahelia	11.6	19.2	3.7	14.4	17.5	10.1	22.5	30.8	13.3
3. Baiti	12.7	19.2	4.4	18.0	22.7	12.6	32.9	41.2	23.9
4. Bantar	15.4	19.9	4.6	18.0	29.1	6.7	17.8	26.8	8.3
5. Bauri	5.5	9.5	1.0	10.1	15.5	4.6	9.4	15.9	2.6
6. Beldar	9.6	11.6	4.5	20.2	21.2	18.3	18.7	25.5	8.6
7. Bhogta	3.1	5.0	1.2	33.3	58.8	6.7	16.2	26.2	5.5
8. Bhuimali	11.3	18.6	2.8	17.4	21.0	13.5	21.2	28.3	13.5
9. Bhuiya	7.1	12.2	2.2	9.9	14.9	4.0	14.2	22.4	4.6
10. Bind	6.6	12.3	0.7	10.9	17.0	3.1	12.7	20.8	3.9
11. Chamar, Charmakar, Mochi, Muchi, Rabidas, Ruidas, Rishi	8.3	13.3	2.2	12.0	17.1	6.0	14.4	21.9	5.5
12. Chaupal	3.2	20.4	1.3	16.3	13.6	19.1	20.8	31.3	9.1
13. Dabgar	29.2	48.9	0.0	20.4	17.5	25.0	22.4	30.2	13.5
14. Damai (Nepali)	21.1	28.3	14.2	37.2	55.5	17.4	37.5	48.1	26.7
15. Dhoba, Dhobi	18.9	28.3	8.7	24.3	33.8	13.7	38.8	50.4	25.9
16. Doai	6.2	10.8	1.7	17.3	28.3	4.5	22.5	33.0	11.6
17. Dom, Dhangad	7.1	11.5	2.1	9.9	15.2	4.2	12.6	19.8	4.8
18. Dosadh, Dusadh, Dhari, Dhari	12.9	18.4	5.0	16.7	24.3	8.5	23.7	33.8	10.0
19. Ghasi	5.8	11.3	0.5	10.2	16.1	5.4	9.0	14.9	2.8
20. Gonrhi	5.6	10.2	0.9	18.6	24.6	12.7	25.2	34.7	14.6
21. Halalkhor	24.5	27.9	0.0	10.4	17.9	2.2	29.9	41.7	16.7
22. Hari, Mehtar, Mehtor, Bhangi	9.4	14.8	3.6	13.8	19.7	7.0	15.3	23.3	6.6

1	2	3	4	5	6	7	8	9	10	11
23.	Jalia Kaibarta	17.9	25.7	9.7	20.5	28.5	11.4	30.2	40.1	19.6
24.	Jhalo Malo, Malo	14.4	22.0	6.4	19.2	25.6	11.6	25.5	33.5	16.8
25.	Kadar	12.2	19.1	4.7	22.8	33.8	9.7	25.5	36.7	13.1
26.	Kami(Nepali)	18.0	26.8	9.2	27.9	36.1	18.3	34.7	45.7	23.6
27.	Kandra	15.1	24.2	4.3	24.0	36.2	10.3	31.5	46.4	15.8
28.	Kanjar	16.2	29.0	1.4	8.4	6.9	9.4	16.0	25.2	5.9
29.	Kaora	9.6	16.7	2.3	17.3	24.5	9.3	17.8	26.8	8.0
30.	Karenga, Koranga	9.5	17.5	1.5	12.3	18.9	5.5	18.4	28.4	7.9
31.	Kaur	12.3	17.9	2.0	14.5	19.3	7.4	16.5	25.8	6.1
32.	Keot, Keyot	13.8	20.7	3.4	16.6	24.9	5.6	23.2	34.6	10.0
33.	Khaira	5.3	9.9	0.7	9.2	14.2	4.0	11.0	18.5	3.2
34.	Khatik	25.3	33.4	8.0	18.0	28.8	6.0	30.0	40.8	17.5
35.	Koch	8.6	14.3	1.2	16.1	24.6	5.9	15.2	23.0	6.8
36.	Konai	7.4	13.2	1.4	9.1	15.1	2.6	15.9	23.9	7.3
37.	Konwar	15.7	23.6	3.2	24.5	28.8	16.1	45.7	53.9	34.9
38.	Kotal	12.5	19.1	4.5	14.4	20.8	7.6	21.7	31.1	11.9
39.	Kurariar	5.4	30.0	1.0	21.9	32.3	7.3	25.1	34.8	13.6
40.	Lalbegi	18.1	27.1	8.5	21.5	28.5	15.5	25.9	35.7	13.9
41.	Lohar	8.3	14.0	2.2	12.4	17.7	6.6	15.1	23.7	6.0
42.	Mahar	11.8	18.6	4.5	13.3	19.0	6.9	19.8	27.9	11.2
43.	Mal	5.9	10.3	1.5	9.6	15.5	3.4	12.2	18.5	5.5
44.	Mallah	14.1	21.0	5.3	15.4	23.2	6.9	23.8	33.9	12.0
45.	Musahar	3.2	5.5	0.6	8.3	13.0	2.8	5.3	8.2	2.1
46.	Namasudra	21.0	31.6	9.4	26.9	36.2	16.2	35.9	45.7	25.1
47.	Nat	4.4	5.4	0.0	39.2	50.0	31.8	31.2	41.7	19.7
48.	Nuniya	11.0	17.2	2.1	15.8	23.0	7.4	20.7	30.5	8.2
49.	Paliya	11.7	20.6	1.8	20.9	30.4	10.7	18.5	29.4	6.9
50.	Pan, Sawasi	16.9	24.4	3.5	16.4	25.3	5.9	27.2	38.3	15.0
51.	Pasi	15.6	19.2	8.7	17.9	24.1	9.9	26.8	35.8	13.4
52.	Patni	16.2	22.6	7.2	18.9	28.1	9.4	25.4	35.2	15.1
53.	Pod, Poundra	21.7	35.3	6.9	27.3	40.0	13.8	36.5	50.0	21.8
54.	Rajbanshi	14.7	24.2	4.3	17.6	26.0	8.7	24.6	35.9	12.6
55.	Rajwar	9.2	13.7	2.8	11.4	17.7	3.1	16.6	26.8	4.8
56.	Sarki(Nepali)	14.3	21.0	6.7	26.0	29.7	22.3	27.3	37.9	16.8
57.	Sunri (excluding Saha)	28.6	42.6	13.8	22.4	31.6	13.1	54.9	70.1	38.7
58.	Tiyar	8.1	14.5	1.8	20.4	26.9	13.8	25.3	36.1	13.6
59.	Turi	7.3	12.9	1.2	12.9	18.4	6.4	14.2	21.6	6.2
	Unspecified	15.0	23.1	6.6	20.2	28.6	11.1	28.6	38.6	14.2

25. Chandigarh

1	2	3	4	5	6	7	8	9	10	11
	All Scheduled Castes				24.4	33.4	12.1	37.1	46.0	25.3
1.	Ad Dharmi				51.9	65.2	33.2	65.4	73.0	54.9
2.	Bangali				14.1	9.0	100.0	63.3	72.4	50.0
3.	Barar, Burar, Berar				22.8	27.3	0.0	34.5	41.5	26.6
4.	Batwal				-	-	-	53.7	50.0	60.0

1	2	3	4	5	6	7	8	9	10	11
5.	Bauria, Bawaria				12.2	12.8	11.4	29.5	41.8	14.7
6.	Bazigar				8.0	13.0	2.1	11.3	18.3	4.0
7.	Bhangi, Chura, Balmiki				18.5	27.5	7.3	32.0	42.1	19.7
8.	Bhanjra				25.0	31.8	10.0	57.0	62.6	51.0
9.	Chamar, Jatia Chamar, Rehgar, Raigarl, Ramdasi, Ravidasi				33.2	43.5	18.9	45.2	53.3	33.8
10.	Chanal				-	-	-	32.2	42.9	7.4
11.	Dagi				-	-	-	0.0	0.0	0.0
12.	Darain				-	-	-	30.4	37.5	14.3
13.	Dhanak				21.7	30.4	10.9	21.3	28.3	12.8
14.	Dhogri, Dhangri, Siggi				-	-	-	71.4	83.9	55.6
15.	Dumna, Mahasha, Doom				29.4	28.6	30.8	54.5	63.6	34.3
16.	Gagra				-	-	-	40.5	45.4	33.3
17.	Gandhila, Gandil, Gondola				100.0	100.0	-	27.3	35.3	0.0
18.	Kabirpanthi, Julaha				31.9	44.7	17.9	44.0	52.9	33.2
19.	Khatik				16.2	26.6	6.8	41.2	48.2	33.2
20.	Kori, Koli				15.8	20.4	3.9	32.3	40.5	16.2
21.	Marija, Marecha				65.0	74.2	33.3	55.3	69.6	33.3
22.	Mazhabi				36.6	47.5	23.8	56.8	64.8	46.9
23.	Megh				41.2	63.6	0.0	34.0	37.7	29.2
24.	Nat				-	-	-	0.0	0.0	0.0
25.	Od				-	-	-	37.1	52.6	18.7
26.	Pasi				18.4	21.2	8.4	27.9	30.6	21.4
27.	Perna				0.0	0.0	-	83.3	77.8	88.9
28.	Pherera				-	-	-	75.0	85.7	60.0
29.	Sanhai				-	-	-	68.5	75.5	60.0
30.	Sanhal				-	-	-	47.3	66.7	30.0
31.	Sansi, Bhedkut, Manesh				6.4	11.5	1.0	11.8	17.7	5.5
32.	Sansoi				-	-	-	14.0	18.5	9.4
33.	Sapela				-	-	-	0.0	0.0	0.0
34.	Sarera				45.7	54.9	34.9	61.4	72.3	47.9
35.	Sikligar				3.4	6.4	0.0	8.6	12.3	4.7
36.	Sirkiband				-	-	-	0.6	1.1	0.0
	Unspecified				36.3	42.1	23.5	43.6	53.2	28.7

26. Dadra & Nagar Haveli

1	2	3	4	5	6	7	8	9	10	11
	All Scheduled Castes	26.6	35.9	20.1	33.2	44.4	24.4	51.2	58.5	44.7
1.	Bhangi	44.4	50.0	42.9	40.6	46.7	35.3	45.4	40.7	52.9
2.	Chamar	10.2	18.0	1.6	23.7	36.3	9.9	40.4	50.2	32.3
3.	Mahar	33.3	33.3	-	-	-	-	50.6	66.7	31.6
4.	Mahyavanshi, Dhed	37.0	53.8	28.5	42.5	56.6	34.8	61.1	69.3	55.4
	Unspecified	-	-	-	-	-	-	61.8	76.9	41.4

1	2	3	4	5	6	7	8	9	10	11
	27. Daman & Diu									
	All Scheduled Castes				41.5	52.4	33.6	54.4	67.5	44.0
1.	Bhangi, Hadi				33.1	50.8	15.7	43.9	63.4	24.3
2.	Chambhar				100.0	100.0	100.0	18.2	22.2	15.4
3.	Mahar				-	-	-	83.3	66.7	100.0
4.	Mahyavanshi, Vankar				45.9	53.4	41.2	60.9	71.5	53.6
5.	Mang				100.0	-	100.0	18.7	25.0	12.5
	Unspecified				-	-	-	53.3	68.0	35.0
	28. Delhi									
	All Scheduled Castes	20.9	32.1	6.8	28.1	39.3	14.3	39.3	50.2	25.9
1.	Adi Dharmi	48.5	65.3	23.4	62.2	75.2	46.1	62.2	75.2	46.1
2.	Agria	11.9	24.9	1.3	29.1	38.7	16.3	41.9	56.3	25.5
3.	Aheria	24.5	29.3	10.0	21.4	34.3	6.3	29.8	38.8	17.6
4.	Balai	12.7	20.8	2.6	20.4	30.6	7.6	33.1	45.3	18.6
5.	Banjara	15.0	27.5	1.7	22.0	35.1	6.7	30.5	43.8	15.0
6.	Bawaria	15.8	27.3	2.5	15.8	24.3	3.5	23.9	34.0	12.1
7.	Bazigar	12.2	18.5	4.8	12.6	21.7	4.3	28.7	34.0	22.6
8.	Bhangi	16.6	28.6	4.0	21.7	33.3	7.9	31.9	43.5	17.9
9.	Bhil	7.1	11.1	2.7	10.1	17.3	1.1	20.5	30.8	8.8
10.	Chamar, Chanwar, Chamar, Jatav or Jatav Chamar, Mochi, Ramdasia, Ravidasi, Raidasi Rehgarh or Raigar	22.4	34.7	7.7	31.4	43.5	16.5	43.3	53.9	30.1
11.	Chohra (Sweeper)	16.3	23.6	4.2	26.0	32.0	13.3	40.6	52.4	26.5
12.	Chuhra (Balmiki)	22.3	34.7	5.7	26.1	38.5	10.9	35.9	48.1	21.5
13.	Dhanak or Dhanuk	18.3	28.0	5.7	24.2	33.8	12.0	37.3	47.2	25.3
14.	Dhobi	20.3	29.1	8.6	34.3	41.9	24.8	43.6	52.5	32.5
15.	Dom	19.4	45.2	3.0	23.7	34.8	9.5	36.6	50.1	19.5
16.	Gharrami	5.4	14.3	2.0	27.6	37.3	8.8	41.1	47.9	31.0
17.	Julaha (Weaver)	22.5	33.7	8.5	31.6	43.3	17.2	45.4	57.6	30.6
18.	Kabirpanthi	22.2	38.4	5.0	32.7	43.8	18.2	42.7	52.6	29.1
19.	Kachchandha	15.7	19.3	0.0	22.5	29.0	13.3	38.2	48.0	24.6
20.	Kanjar or Giarah	17.1	28.9	1.7	14.7	24.0	6.9	28.4	37.8	18.4
21.	Khatik	19.7	30.8	6.4	26.1	37.2	13.0	37.9	49.7	13.0
22.	Koli	20.3	31.0	6.6	26.6	36.7	13.2	36.5	47.4	23.0
23.	Lalbegi	39.3	73.3	0.0	36.1	42.9	31.8	47.0	63.5	26.7
24.	Madari	58.3	50.0	67.7	12.5	19.2	0.0	22.2	26.1	17.9
25.	Mallah	31.3	41.4	15.5	35.6	41.5	25.5	43.7	49.9	34.9
26.	Mazhabi	42.1	55.7	23.9	50.0	59.8	40.2	59.6	70.0	46.6
27.	Meghwal	4.6	2.9	8.8	22.4	33.7	7.1	27.7	38.8	13.3
28.	Naribut	5.1	9.6	0.5	2.9	5.2	0.0	8.6	15.4	1.0
29.	Nat (Rana)	12.8	13.7	11.4	7.8	12.8	1.9	15.9	24.9	5.7

1 2	3	4	5	6	7	8	9	10	11
30. Pasi	19.9	22.0	13.7	26.9	30.3	18.5	33.4	39.1	22.6
31. Perna	-	-	-	8.5	12.9	2.1	40.2	50.7	26.8
32. Sansi or Bhedkut	34.0	45.1	20.9	34.0	46.8	19.2	40.1	52.9	25.6
33. Sapera	23.5	4.1	0.0	6.6	8.5	3.1	11.3	17.7	3.2
34. Sikligar	10.7	16.0	4.9	9.4	14.2	4.4	20.9	26.3	15.1
35. Singiwala or Kalbelia	-	-	-	6.5	5.7	7.5	3.1	3.8	2.3
36. Sirkiband	10.3	7.6	11.4	10.3	16.8	0.8	20.9	27.5	14.0
Unspecified	23.0	33.6	9.2	30.1	39.9	17.4	36.8	45.2	25.0
29. Pondicherry									
All Scheduled Castes	11.1	17.7	4.4	17.3	27.5	9.6	32.4	43.1	21.2
1. Adi Andhra	26.4	32.6	20.4	30.6	36.6	24.6	41.1	47.7	34.3
2. Adi Dravida	10.7	16.8	4.5	15.9	23.8	7.6	32.1	42.5	21.3
3. Chakkiliyan	8.3	15.9	0.5	15.0	22.2	7.6	35.9	48.2	23.7
4. Jambuvulu	7.1	11.1	0.0	0.0	0.0	0.0	29.1	42.7	15.8
5. Kuravan	7.5	12.8	2.1	9.7	12.2	6.7	19.6	28.7	10.2
6. Madiga	9.9	14.8	6.0	26.3	28.6	24.1	61.5	70.8	46.7
7. Mala, Mala Masti	0.0	0.0	0.0	0.0	-	0.0	0.0	0.0	0.0
8. Paky	0.0	0.0	0.0	12.5	23.8	0.0	28.6	38.1	19.6
9. Pallan	14.4	23.6	5.9	14.0	24.1	6.0	26.2	37.1	15.8
10. Paryan, Sambavar	9.6	15.9	3.3	18.5	27.8	9.1	31.4	42.8	19.4
11. Samban	2.5	4.4	0.0	2.7	4.1	0.0	25.0	33.3	14.3
12. Thoti	5.3	6.7	4.3	5.9	9.4	2.4	31.0	38.0	21.6
13. Valuvan	34.5	57.9	10.7	37.5	57.8	16.7	49.3	64.6	33.0
14. Vetan	2.9	5.7	0.0	5.0	8.4	1.8	3.9	4.3	3.5
15. Vettiyan	4.0	8.6	0.0	13.9	19.8	7.4	27.1	43.1	10.7
Unspecified	-	-	-	38.2	49.3	26.2	28.2	31.0	25.4

Source : Calculated on the basis of data in *Census of India, 1981,* Series 2 to 32, Part IX (1) (2) *Census of India, 1971,* Series 1, Paper 1 of 1975, Appendix to Table C-VIII Part A; and (3) *Census of India,* 1961, Vol. I India, Part V-A (1), SCT II, part A.

Index